The Institutional Order

Economy, Kinship, Religion,
Polity, Law, and Education
in Evolutionary
and Comparative Perspective

Jonathan H. Turner
University of California, Riverside

 LONGMAN

An imprint of Addison Wesley Longman, Inc.

New York • Reading, Massachusetts • Menlo Park, California • Harlow, England
Don Mills, Ontario • Sydney • Mexico City • Madrid • Amsterdam

Acquisitions Editor: Alan McClare
Project Coordination and Text Design: York Production Services
Cover Designer: Rubina Yeh
Production Manager: Valerie Zaborski
Manufacturing Manager: Helene G. Landers
Electronic Page Makeup: York Production Services
Printer and Binder: R. R. Donnelley & Sons Company
Cover Printer: Phoenix Color Corp.

Library of Congress Cataloging-in-Publication Data

Turner, Jonathan H.
   The institutional order: economy, kinship, religion, polity, law, and education in evolutionary and comparative perspective/Jonathan H. Turner.
       p. cm.
   Includes bibliographical references (p.   ) and index.
   ISBN 0-673-98125-8
   1. Social institutions.   I. Title.
HM131.T86   1997   96-32441
301--dc20   CIP

Copyright © 1997 by Addision-Wesley Educational Publishers Inc.

ISBN 0673981258

1234567890—DOC—99989796

To Louis Bozzetti, M.D.

Thank you

Contents

Chapter 7
RELIGION IN INSTITUTIONAL
CONTEXT   127

Chapter 8
POLITY   142

Preface

In 1972, I published *Patterns of Social Organization: A Survey of Social Institutions*. The present book builds on this 1972 effort and remains true to its goals: to explore the structure and operation of institutions and their effects on one another in long-term historical and evolutionary perspective. Though it may be difficult to recognize on the surface, my analysis has been inspired by Talcott Parsons and Neil J. Smelser's *Economy and Society*. I do not adopt the details of their functional analytical scheme, but I embrace their broad intent: to explain the dynamic connections among an institutional system—in their case, the economy—and its functional environment. My vocabulary is different from theirs, devoid of the complicated systems building of Parsonian action theory, but I seek for all institutions what they sought for the economy: to understand the structure and operation of institutions not only in terms of their internal forces but also in terms of their dynamic relations to other institutions. Parsons and Smelser saw these connections with great analytical insight; I borrow, extend, and elaborate on their seminal analysis.

Each core institution—economy, kinship, religion, polity, law, and education—is examined in a roughly similar manner. In an opening chapter, the basic and defining elements of an institution are discussed, followed by a review of the long-term evolutionary and historical transformations in an institution; then, in a second chapter on an institution, the effects of other institutions on these transformations are systematically reviewed. In my view, this kind of analysis is not undertaken as often as it should be. For, at the most macro level of analysis, human populations are organized into societies by an interconnected complex of institutional subsystems. These institutional subsystems are built from, but at the same time provide, the overarching structure for micro- and meso-level social units, such as encounters, groups, organizations, social classes and strata, communities, and social categories like gender, age, and ethnicity. Yet, these micro- and meso-level social formations cannot explain the dynamic interconnections of the more-inclusive institutional systems in which they are lodged. The complex of institutional subsystems constitutes, in my view, an *institutional order* whose dynamic interconnections constitute a distinctive and important level of analysis. It is time, therefore, for sociology to resurrect an interest in a more purely institutional-level mode of inquiry. I hope to demonstrate in these pages the utility of this line of sociological inquiry.

Jonathan H. Turner

xiii

Chapter
1

The Institutional Structure of Society

THE EMERGENCE OF SOCIAL INSTITUTIONS

The human ancestral line emerged between five and eight million years ago. This first ancestor looked like an ape, because it *was* a kind of ape who sought to survive in the predator-ridden African savanna. Somehow this animal and its kind had to find food, fend off predators, and reproduce themselves in an environment that was not hospitable, or safe, especially for a primate whose ancestors had evolved in the arboreal habitat of now dwindling trees. Natural selection first worked on the body of this animal, making it upright by five million years ago. Thus it could see above the grasses where danger lay, run from and after prey, and use its dexterous hands to carry food, throw objects at predators, and perhaps even make crude tools. Natural selection also worked on social organization, creating the bonds, attachments, and solidarities that would enable groupings of this vulnerable-looking ape to stand together in the face of danger and, equally important, to organize the quest for food and the reproduction of their kind (Maryanski and Turner 1992). Organization was thus to be the key to this ape like animal's success; and the more these hominids (i.e., primates on the human line) could organize their activities, the greater their chances of survival.

Survival for each of the successive species of hominids would be a momentous achievement, since apes were in decline five million years ago, and as we now know, only four species of apes—gibbons, orangutans, chimpanzees, and gorillas—are still with the human descendants of these first hominids. If we count humans as an evolved ape, then only five species have survived the last eight million years—five out of many hundreds of species. Apes are thus one of the great failures in the evolutionary record.

Yet, hominids beat the odds, probably because they organized. At some point, natural selection favored ever more intelligent hominids who could organize in even more sophisticated or flexible ways and who could use their intelligence and organization to enhance their fitness in a difficult environment. But even as the brain got larger, patterns of social organization remained simple—consisting at most of bands of a few dozen males, females, and offspring. Perhaps they had families, but at first, only the mother and her offspring could be seen as "family." Later, males became more attached to mothers and their offspring; and even as this occurred, the structure of the band was still very simple: clusters of families wandering in search of food to gather or kill. Apparently, this simple structure, coupled with the intelligence of its incumbents who could use fire and make tools, was sufficient for hominids to prosper. By two million years ago, descendants of the first hominid—*Homo habilis* and, then, *Homo erectus*—had been able to migrate out of Africa and populate much of the globe.

And so it remained for the rest of hominid evolution. At some point, perhaps as long as 250,000 years ago with Neandertal or with another ancestor, the human line emerged. By 100,000 years ago or even earlier, *Homo sapiens sapiens*, or modern humans, could be found in Africa and the Middle East. Even with this threshold of full humanness having been crossed, gathering and hunting bands were still the basis of survival. However, by fits and starts, humans began to settle down and to cultivate their food in simple horticulture. In the process, populations began to grow and, out of necessity, to elaborate social structures and the symbol systems. No longer were kindred and band sufficient to sustain the growing populations. Many of these populations could not make the adjustment and elaborate social structure and culture; and as a result, these societies collapsed and disintegrated. Selection forces were ruthless, and if a population could not create new sociocultural arrangements—whether by luck, chance, creative innovation, or borrowing—then its survival became problematic.

Natural selection thus works on more than body (and the underlying genetic coding) of an animal; it also shapes its organizational patterns. In the case of humans, natural selection increased the intelligence of the species in ways that enabled its members to use symbols, or culture, rather than biological codes to form simple bands of several families who would gather and hunt food. This rudimentary structure was all that was necessary, but it was based on cultural more than genetic codes and, hence, could be elaborated in creative new ways—given the necessity.

Once populations settled down and their numbers grew, this necessity was at hand, and new selection pressures for more complex patterns of social organization emerged. Some populations used their intelligence or got lucky in coping with new problems of organizing the larger social mass, and they were able to make the adjustment to this new environment of their own making. Other populations could not, and they disintegrated into wandering individuals in search of a way to survive.

The analysis of human social institutions begins with the recognition that social structures and systems of cultural symbols have been used to sustain humans in an environment. This environment consists not only of the biophysical sphere but also of the social sphere that humans have built around themselves. As a species that must now survive inside sociocultural cages it has made, humans find many of the problems of survival in their environment inside these cages. Ironically, as humans' organizational capacity to support biologically larger numbers of people has increased, the very social structures created to do so can, themselves, become humans' biggest problem of survival. Indeed, our social constructions can even get in the way of meeting more fundamental biological needs—for example, when political institutions mobilize people for mass warfare, when crushing stratification starves portions of the population, and when kinship encourages birth rates beyond the capacity to support the newborn. The development of new social institutions or changes in older ones is, therefore, often a response to survival problems inhering in the institutions themselves or other social structures that are spawned by institutions (Spencer [1874–96] 1898; Turner 1995).

Humans, as the culmination of the line of hominids that began millions of years ago, no longer must fear the predators of the African savanna as much as the monsters contained in complex institutional orders. War, disease, pestilence, and famine were Thomas Malthus's ([1798] 1926) "four horsemen" who rode once population growth outstripped the ability to organize in ways that could support the population. But these and other destructive horsemen now come even without overpopulation. Built into the very institutional structures that have been created to resolve some survival problems emerge ever new challenges to human survival.

THE INSTITUTIONAL ORDER

For the vast majority of our time on earth, then, the history of humans was carried out in very simple societies with a correspondingly simple institutional order. Most institutional activity—economic, political, religious, legal, and educational—was conducted within one institution, kinship or the family. The institutional order was thus relatively undifferentiated, being folded into kinship and bands. This simple institutional order worked well; indeed, it is what enabled our ancestors—both hominid and human—to survive. But this history began to change somewhere between twelve to fifteen thousand years ago; and by ten thousand years ago, hunting and gathering systems were being rapidly replaced by more complex societies. And with this change, a more elaborate and differentiated institutional order began to emerge. The history of humans since this time has been—with periodic reversals and collapses as Malthusian pressures overwhelmed populations—one of increasing societal complexity and a corresponding differentiation among, and considerable elaboration of, social institutions. As horticulture or gardening using only human power became a distinctive form of economic activity, kinship was elaborated as the basic organizing principle of the population. Within more complex kinship systems the beginnings of polity (leaders and governments), religion (shamans and magicians), and law (rules, councils of leaders, mediators) could be clearly observed. With agrarianism or farming using nonhuman power, the economy became more complex, kinship scaled down as new organizing principles in expanding governmental, legal, and religious institutional systems came to organize ever more human activity, and new institutional complexes such as education became more distinctive and took their place alongside the expanding political, legal, and religious systems. Furthermore, still-emerging institutional complexes like science and medicine made their first explicit appearance about this time, some five thousand years ago. With industrialism and post-industrialism, kinship completes its journey back to the simple nuclear family of hunting-gathering societies, while other institutional systems—economy, polity, law, religion, and education—become highly differentiated and developed; and science and medicine continue their movement toward becoming distinct institutional complexes.

As the subsystems of the institutional order have differentiated and, in most cases, grown, the connections among institutions have also become more complex and varied. For example, the economy influences, and is influenced by, activities in all other institutional subsystems—polity, law, kinship, religion, and education. Because of these mutual influences, the economy or any other institution cannot be studied in isolation from other institutions. Human institutions constitute a network of interrelations among the organizational units and the cultural symbols making up each institution.

These interrelations take many forms: People move from one institutional position to another, as when they leave the family to go to work or to school. Material resources travel from one institution to another, as when government changes tax laws or interest rates in ways that affect the amount of capital available to the economy or to family households. Symbolic resources move across institutions, as when values of a religious movement begin to influence economic and political activities, or vice versa. Institutional structures often overlap even in highly differentiated systems, as when families own businesses, scientific research is conducted at universities, and political bodies enact laws. Institutions thus constitute an order of interconnections among, and embeddedness in, one another. Even with differentiation of distinctive institutions, the structure and operation of one institution are constrained by a complex of other institutions.

DEFINING SOCIAL INSTITUTIONS

Ultimately, a social institution is defined in terms of its consequences—often termed "functions"[1]—for maintaining, reproducing, and organizing a population so that it remains viable in an environment (Hawley 1986; Aberle et al. 1950; Wells 1970; Turner 1972). Institutions exist because they are important for human survival. While institutions can become so elaborated and complex that they seem remote from such considerations, Malthus's four horsemen and other sources of disintegration are never but a few hoofbeats away, nor are social chaos and disintegration ever obviated by the complexity of social institutions. Indeed, institutions often aggravate the potential for disintegration, as when coercive political leaders hang on to power at all costs, when the political-economy systematically generates conflict-producing inequalities,

---

[1] The term "function" is, in reality, a short-hand way to make a "selectionist" argument: In the evolutionary past of a population, a particular structure was discovered to resolve basic problems of survival. And since it enabled a population to survive and reproduce itself, it was retained (and usually elaborated upon) in the sociocultural repertoire of that population. See Jonathan Turner (1995) for a review of selectionist arguments. See also Michael Faia (1986) for an application of functional and selectionist theory.

when the political system is paralyzed by an incapacity to make decisions, when a family system generates a high proportion of illegitimate births, when an educational system cannot adequately train citizens, or when an economy collapses as a result of overheated market speculation (Turner 1995). Hence, while institutions are defined by their functions for sustaining people and the structures organizing them in viable ways, they can also operate to decrease this viability. And ultimately all institutions fail, setting off chain reactions that lead to societal disintegration from within or conquest from without.

Social institutions are relatively stable, and when they are transformed, a considerable amount of social dislocation occurs as people and organizational units reevaluate the moral premises inhering in old institutional forms and as they seek niches in a new institutional order. For most of human history—that is, for humans' 100,000 to 250,000 years as hunter-gatherers—the institutional order hardly changed at all. But once population growth[2] forced people to become more sedentary and engage in horticulture, this new institutional order was, successively, to be replaced by those revolving around agriculture, industrialism, and post-industrialism at ever accelerating rates. Thus, the stability of institutions is of relatively short duration for highly advanced industrial populations lasting a generation or two at best. That is not to say, of course, that institutions are completely remade: A business corporation in a capitalist economy has looked roughly the same in basic structure and operation over the last one hundred years, as has the fundamental structure of the nuclear family even as rates of illegitimacy, divorce, single-parenthood, and dual-income households have transformed relations within this unit. Thus, even when change is rapid, it often takes time for alterations in specific structures to accumulate to the point where a fundamental transformation in the very nature of an institutional system can be said to exist. Institutions are, therefore, a conservative force in human organization, even as their constituent structures undergo transformation.

Institutions are conservative because the positions, roles, and norms, as well as the organizational units into which these elements of structure are molded, embrace values or general standards of good/bad, appropriate/inappropriate, worthy/unworthy, and other evaluative criteria. Institutions thus have a moral character in which people's roles as mothers, fathers, workers, politicians, teachers, or lawyers are subject to evaluations and emotional arousal. Similarly, the organizational units in which these roles are played—family, factory, legislature, university, or legal system—are also subject to moral evaluations. This is so because institutional structures are organized to reflect—indeed, to implement—widely held values guiding a population (Parsons [1935] 1990, 1951).

Institutions are inclusive and cut across diverse types of structures, ranging from groups and organizations to communities, social classes, and social cat-

---

[2] There is, of course, some debate over whether or not population growth was the key factor forcing humans to take up gardening as an alternative or, at first, as a supplement to hunting-gathering. See Maryanski and Turner (1992) for a review. But once this step was taken, social institutions became ever more-clearly demarcated and complex.

egories. Thus, a worker in a business corporation is part of an economy embracing other workers and corporations; a professor in a university is an element of a broader system of education; a mayor of a community is also a player in a larger societywide institution of polity; or a mother, father, or child in a family is a part of a broader system of kinship organization. The positions, roles, norms, values, and organizational units of institutions are thus inclusive systems that embrace other kinds of structures and, in so doing, provide a broad framework for patterning distinctive classes of human activity—economic, political, familial, religious, legal, educational, and other arenas of human endeavor.

With the above considerations in mind, a social institution can be defined as *a complex of positions, roles, norms, and values lodged in particular types of social structures and organizing relatively stable patterns of human activity with respect to fundamental problems in producing life-sustaining resources, in reproducing individuals, and in sustaining viable societal structures within a given environment.*

PROBLEMS IN INSTITUTIONAL ANALYSIS

The analysis of social institutions poses a number of problems and invites criticism. One problem is that the definition of a social institution initially may appear vague, but as specific social institutions are examined, the definition of each institution will become more precise. The essential point to be made in an opening definition of institutions is this: Humans are a species that, in order to survive and reproduce itself, must create social structures and systems of symbols; the more positions, roles, norms, organizational units, and symbols are directly engaged in survival and reproduction of the species, the more institutional they are.

A second problem is that the notion of institutions is often seen as a reification—as a mere name that is made into a thing. Many would argue, for example, that the institution of the economy is not a real thing; rather, the actual actors such as workers, owners, and businesses in capitalist systems are what is real. They can be seen and touched, whereas the notion of an institution cannot; it is only a label. But, by ignoring the *interconnections* among the actors and structural units organizing them, we miss an important level of reality, and obtain incomplete analyses. If, for example, we only examine corporations, labor unions, markets, or any specific feature involved in a capitalist economy, we can miss the larger picture of how these are all *connected to one another* and to other social institutions. These interconnections are not just labels; they can be seen, measured, and analyzed.

A third issue in institutional analysis is that it eventually resurrects a mode of analysis (discredited in the minds of most sociologists) called "functionalism" and all of the problems imputed to this theoretical approach.[3] Since institutions are defined in terms of their consequences for survival of a

---

[3] See Turner (1991, 71–73) and Turner and Maryanski (1979) for more-detailed review of these problems as well as citations to the key literatures.

population in its biotic and social environments, some argue that institutional analysis must soon begin to posit lists of needs or requisites necessary for the survival of a society and then to analyze structures and symbols only in terms of how they meet these needs (e.g., Aberle et al. 1950). In turn, once this step is taken, a host of unfortunate consequences follow:

1. Analysis becomes ideological and conservative, implicitly stressing that the existing institutional order is more essential rather than potential alternatives for human survival and well-being.
2. Analysis becomes tautological as structures and symbols are viewed as meeting survival needs, with these needs being defined in terms of the structures and symbols that meet them (e.g., Radcliffe-Brown 1935).
3. Analysis becomes illegitimately teleological because the goal of an institution (i.e., meeting a survival need) is seen to create the institution, thereby making the outcome the cause of itself without specifying how and through what processes the end state brought itself about.

These are all old, and essentially correct, criticisms of functionalism, but institutional analysis need not fall into these functionalist traps. We can avoid ideological conservatism with the simple recognition that any existing institution will ultimately fail and, moreover, that it reveals contradictions (within itself, or in relation to other institutions) which should be topics of inquiry—indeed, perhaps the *major* topics to be pursued. Tautologies and illegitimate teleologies can be avoided by recognizing that, although institutions are the products of "selection" in the face of problems of survival, they represent only temporary and imperfect "solutions," whose discovery is only a starting point for more detailed analyses seeking to determine why an institution emerged and why it reveals a particular profile.

THE IMPORTANCE OF INSTITUTIONAL ANALYSIS

To understand the social universe, it is important to see "the big picture," in two senses: (1) the picture provided by looking at long-term, historical, and evolutionary transformations of human organization; and (2) the picture offered by looking at the nature of, and interrelations among, the largest structures comprising a society. Big institutional pictures offer a broad temporal and organizational perspective; they provide a sense for the context in which other, less inclusive sociocultural processes operate; and they allow us to remember that the structures of a society are "survival machines" for the species which, despite our often unfounded sense of ascendancy and dominance, is never very far from Malthus's four horsemen and other disintegrative forces.

Big pictures do not, of course, capture the fine-grained detail, and so institutional analysis is always incomplete in terms of generating understanding of sociocultural processes. More meso-level analysis of organizations, social categories (e.g., class, ethnicity, gender, age), and communities is also essential to sociological analysis. More micro-level analysis of groups and patterns of face-to-face interactions is equally important. Thus, institutional analysis is but *one way* to look at the social universe, but nonetheless an important and often neglected way to understand human societies.

THE CORE INSTITUTIONAL SYSTEMS

Our goal in the following pages is to understand how the core institutional complexes of human society (i.e., economy, kinship, religion, polity, law, and education) first emerged. Then, we will focus on how these complexes operate, how they have developed over time, and how they influence one another. We will not separately examine other complexes still emerging from these core institutions, such as science and medicine, because they are not as fully autonomous as the group of institutions that will occupy our attention. One could, no doubt, make a case that science and medicine are also core institutions, but in this review, they are seen as being still in the process of differentiating as distinct and relatively autonomous institutional systems.

Each of these core institutional systems (economy, kinship, religion, polity, law, and education) has distinctive elements that have been selected—whether by chance, forethought and innovation, or borrowing and diffusion—in order to deal with problems confronting a population. Humans have had to cope with ever more complicated problems as the size of populations and the scale of society have grown. And in coping, they have created new institutional systems that were only implicit in the older institutional forms. This master process of institutional differentiation has created an increased number of institutional systems whose relations with one another inevitably pose additional problems which lead to more institutional differentiation.

At first, there were the band and family or kinship, from which economic activity differentiated; then, religion became more distinct; it was followed successively by polity, law, and education. In the first bands of nuclear families, elements of all of these institutions existed in incipient form; and the evolution of human societies has involved the creation of more-differentiated structures and systems of symbols for what was once buried in kinship and band. Our goal in the pages that follow is to review the emergence, development, and dynamics of these institutional systems over the long course of humans' evolutionary history as well as to understand the mutual effects these institutions have had on one another as they become distinctive systems.

Thus, two chapters address each institution. The first examines the basic nature of the institution, its dynamic properties, and its transformations over humans' evolutionary history—from the simple bands of hunter-gatherers to the colossal institutional complexes of post-industrial society. The second chapter examines how the other core institutions have influenced the emergence, dynamics, and transformations of the focal institution. And, as we work our way through all the second chapters on each institution, we will have examined the reciprocal or mutual effects of institutions on one another. This interconnectedness comprises the *institutional order* which, ultimately, is the backbone of all human societies. It is for this reason that institutional analysis is so essential in understanding patterns of human social organization.

Chapter
2

Economy

All life forms must secure resources from their environment, convert them, if necessary, into usable substances, and then distribute these substances to their vital life-sustaining parts. When life forms must be organized to survive, these processes can be carried to a higher level whereby the activities of group members are coordinated in the pursuit of resources. Ultimately, of course, it is the individual organism that must receive life-sustaining inputs; but some animals make this process more group-oriented by organizing their gathering, conversion, and distribution of resources in ways that enhance their collective fitness in an environment.

Gathering, conversion, and distribution of resources are thus fundamental to the survival of a species. In the case of humans, these processes reveal a structure—that is, the organization of distinctive types of status positions, normative expectations, enacted roles, and embellishments from cultural value premises. This structure is the economy, and it is the institutional system that organizes members in a population for the purpose of gathering resources from the environment, converting them into usable commodities through production, and distributing these usable commodities of production.

Although all other institutional activities and forms are guided by the economy, we do not want to go so far as to assert that the economy determines the profile of all other institutions, because other institutional systems have important effects on the economy. But we can say this much: If we know how economic activity is organized, we can make fairly accurate predictions about the structure and operation of other institutions. To know a population's economy is to comprehend much more about how that population is organized. Therefore, we begin the analysis of the institutional order with the economy.

ELEMENTS OF ECONOMY

For economies to operate, they must reveal certain basic elements (Turner 1995, 1972):

9

a. *Technology*, or knowledge about how to control and manipulate the natural and social environments.

b. *Physical capital*, or implements used to gather, produce, and distribute as well as the liquid resources like money that can buy such implements.

c. *Human capital*, or the number as well as the distribution of characteristics (knowledge, skill, motivations) among those who occupy positions and play roles in the economy.

d. *Property*, or the socially constructed right to own, possess, and use physical and symbolic objects of value.

e. *Entrepreneurship*, or the way in which a, b, c, and d are *organized* for gathering, producing, and distributing (Parsons and Smelser 1956).

Economies thus can be characterized by their technologies, physical and human capital, entrepreneurial structures, and property systems as these operate on gathering, producing, and distributing.

BASIC TYPES OF ECONOMIES

In the history of humans, a number of distinctive types of economies have existed—ignoring, of course, the many variants of these types: hunting-gathering, simple and advanced horticulture, simple and advanced agrarian, industrial, and post-industrial.

Hunting and Gathering[1]

Hunting and gathering societies were typically small, usually consisting of a band of fifty to eighty people. Bands tended to be autonomous, although each remained in contact with others sharing the same language and region. The largest single grouping of hunters and gatherers ever discovered in the archeological record was a settlement numbering about four to six hundred people in a highly fertile area of France. A band of hunters and gatherers wandered a region or territory, often in a somewhat circular pattern. The band would settle for a time—perhaps several weeks—in one area, extract

---

[1] This composite description is drawn from numerous sources, including Turner (1984, 1972), Lenski (1966), Maryanski and Turner (1992), Lenski, Nolan, and Lenski (1995), Roth (1890), Hose and McDougall (1912), Radcliffe-Brown (1930, 1914), Spencer and Gillen (1927), Linton, (1936), Steward (1930), Holmberg (1950), Childe, (1951), Clark (1952), Elkin (1954), Goldschmidt (1959), Davis and Reeves (1990), Goodhale (1959), Turnbull (1961), Washburn (1961), Service (1966, 1962), Clark and Piggott (1965), Lee and DeVore (1976, 1968) Sahlins (1972, 1968a, 1968b), Coon (1971), Bicchieri (1972), Earle and Ericson (1977), Rick (1978), Tonkinson (1978), Lee (1979), Winterhalder and Smith (1981), Hayden (1981), Hultkrantz and Vorren (1982), Riches (1982), Schrire (1984), Johnson and Earle (1987), Hart, Pilling, and Goodhale (1988), Howell (1988).

the available resources, and then move on to exploit a new location. Eventually, when resources replenished themselves, the band might return to its starting point and initiate a new round of movement to and from favored locations. Band members appeared to have a sense of their own and others' home range; and as a result, they tended to wander within a delimited area, respecting the home ranges of others. If resources were scarce, the band may have dispersed for a time (and even permanently), with some members seeking a new area to exploit. This demographic and spatial profile required low population densities, so that the environment would not be overtaxed. The bands themselves sought to maintain their population size at an optimal level through a combination of infanticide, abortion, and birth control (which included women nursing children for prolonged periods and maintaining a low level of body fat and weight; see Kolata 1974).

Hunter-gatherers revealed only minimal levels for each of the basic elements organizing their economic activity (Maryanski and Turner 1992, 83; Turner 1972). Technologically, they possessed limited, albeit highly useful, knowledge about how to exploit the environment. This knowledge concerned such practical matters as how to gather various food sources at different times of the year; how to hunt with spears and, for some, bows and arrows; and how to search for hidden water sources in times of drought.

Physical capital formation in the economy was extremely limited, consisting of the equipment for hunting (e.g., spears, bows and arrows), and gathering (e.g., digging sticks and baskets), as well as a few utensils for preparing food. Human capital was strictly divided between men and women, with men performing almost all the hunting and women doing virtually all the gathering, which normally involved picking or digging for food, as well as carrying it back to camp for processing. Many hunters and gatherers did not appear to work hard in order to meet their nutritional requirements, even under extreme environmental conditions (Sahlins 1972, 1–32; Lee and DeVore 1968; Woodburn 1968). Yet, their work could be tedious and probably varied greatly in its difficulty and arduousness. In general, the men's labor normally provided far less food than the women's primarily because hunting was not always successful. When successful, however, a short-term (and perishable) economic surplus might emerge. Women and their offspring were much more likely than men to secure the necessary food among hunter-gatherers. However, the number of hours needed to gather fruits, nuts, berries, roots, and other edible foods generally varied considerably. Some have argued that hunters and gatherers usually lived a "leisure-intensive" lifestyle (Eibl-Eibesfeldt, 1991, 55), although these populations could be subject to environmental variations that might put them on the brink of starvation.

Entrepreneurship, or the organization of other economic elements, was performed by the band and nuclear kinship units. The nuclear family unit, consisting of mother, father, and children, was organized for two explicit ends: the procurement of food and the procreation/socialization of the young. The band as a whole might also be seen as an entrepreneurial unit, since it sought to organize nuclear families in ways that facilitated movement to available resources. But unlike the corporate units of more complex societies, the bands were typically not elaborate, hierarchical, or highly constraining. They were simply places where individuals had considerable freedom to choose when and how they would pursue their various lines of activity.

Finally, property as an element of economic organization was minimal. The physical capital—spears, bowls, bows and arrows, digging sticks—was usually defined by hunter-gatherers as private property; and at times, the home range or territory of the band as a whole was defined as their collective property. Understandings about how to distribute a hunting kill evoked a sense of property (for example, the person who actually made the kill would get the most valued parts).

In this kind of simple economy, all institutional structures folded into, or were fused with, the nuclear family units and the band. Just as the economy was embedded in kinship and band, so other institutional systems—such as religion, law, and education—were coextensive with kin and band. Indeed, the history of human societies has been one of differentiating new institutional systems as populations have grown and as the economy has expanded. But we should remember that for most of our history as a species, humans' biological nature was conditioned by hunting-gathering economies. We are, at our evolutionary heart and soul, hunter-gatherers who have created complex social structures and systems of culture over the last fifteen thousand years. The first step along this developmental path was the adoption of horticulture.

Horticulture[2]

Population growth probably forced humans to settle down and adopt horticulture, or simple farming and gardening without the benefit of the plow or nonhuman sources of energy. Humans only slowly eased into horticulture, because it involves considerably more human capital than a hunting-gathering system (in terms of time and energy spent). Horticultural systems varied enormously in size, from 100 to 150 people in simple systems to many thousands in complex systems. Horticulturalists often had to resettle as they depleted the soil or as overpopulation forced them to seek new resources.

In terms of the elements of economy,[3] horticulturalists differed considerably from hunting and gathering populations. Although it is difficult

---

[2] This general description of horticultural populations, or variants such as pastorialism (Evans-Pritchard 1940), is drawn from Maryanski and Turner (1992), Lenski (1966), Lenski, Nolan, and Lenski (1995), Gordon (1914), Malinowski (1922), Landtman (1927), Childe (1964, 1960, 1952, 1930), Herskovits (1938), Goldschmidt (1959), Leach (1954), Schapera (1956), Sahlins (1958), Sanders (1972), Murdock (1965, 1959, 1953), von Hagen (1961), Mair (1962), Chang (1963), Mac-Neish (1964), Hawkes (1965), Flannery (1973), Gibbs (1965), Earle (1984), Mann (1986), Johnson and Earle (1987), Bates and Plog (1991).

[3] For descriptions of horticultural economies, see: Sahlins (1968a), Boserup (1965), Turner (1972, 25–27).

Table 2.1 HUNTING-GATHERING ECONOMIES

Technology	Practical knowledge of: indigenous plant resources, including at times seeding and harvesting; animal resources and hunting; seasonal effects on availability of plant and animal resources. Knowledge of how to make tools—spears, digging sticks, hatchets, bow and arrow, baskets, and at times pottery.
Physical Capital	Hunting equipment; digging implements; cooking utensils
Labor	Clear sexual division of labor: males hunt and females gather
Entrepreneurship	Band and nuclear family units organize economic activity.
Property	Personal possessions. At times, collective territory. No material inequality, although rules about how to distribute a hunting kill can be seen as early definitions of property.

to determine if horticulturalists had theoretical or intellectual understanding of certain technologies, they nonetheless had practical knowledge of (a) farming (planting, harvesting, storing, and grinding grains, and cooking; and in more complex systems, breeding, fertilizing, and crop rotation); (b) tool making (initially with stones and later, in more complex systems, with metal); (c) masonry; and (d) pottery making (with kilns), which later led to metallurgy (annealing, smelting, casting, and eventually alloying).

Physical capital included tools, pottery, storage facilities, and city walls; and, slowly, negotiable capital—at first with barter of hard goods, but eventually with money. Human capital revealed a clear division of labor, with females doing most of the gardening and males increasingly involved in specialized trades and occupations (weapon-making, pottery, house and boat building, bartering and commerce, metal-working, leather-making, masonry). However, women also pursued some trades, such as weaving. The level of skill and energy output of human capital thus increased significantly with horticulture.

Entrepreneurial structures also changed—and dramatically so. In simple systems, more complex kinship structures linking nuclear families together into larger kinship units (as is explored in Chapter 4) organized much of the economy; and even in more advanced horticultural populations, these large and more complex kinship systems still organized activity.[4] Villages and eventually larger cities also ordered the economy in terms of distributing gardening plots, trade specialization, barter, and eventually com-

---

[4] For analyses of these kinship systems, see: Keesing (1975), Schneider and Gough (1961), Fox (1967), Pasternak (1976), Ember and Ember (1971), Ember, Ember, and Pasternak (1974), Graburn (1971).

mercial systems using money. Markets where goods and services were bought and sold (either through barter or money) also began to appear as a prominent way to structure distribution and, consequently, gathering and production as well. True political leaders could now be found, and these leaders dictated the distribution of land and economic roles of kin members.[5] For some populations, a "Big Man" political system emerged, in which an individual and usually his fellow kinsmen accumulated foodstuffs and then redistributed this surplus through elaborate feasts. In this manner the Big Man gained prestige and, at times, power (Johnson and Earle 1987). Although such systems were more typical of hunter-gatherers like those "Indians" in the Pacific Northwest who were in the process of settling down, they could also be found among simple horticultural populations, such as those in Polynesia (Sahlins 1963).

Property became more clearly defined with horticulture. In simple systems the headman or chief could theoretically own everything and received most productive output, but this leader was also required to redistribute what was given to him. Similarly, in Big Man systems, the leader usually had to give away most of what he and his kinsmen had accumulated in order to maintain his standing. In larger and more complex horticultural systems, political and religious elites as well as those engaged in market activity could claim private property, as could individuals with respect to their personal possessions. As claims to private property were allowed, inequality and stratification became prominent features of human society (Turner 1984; Lenski 1966). Rights to land, physical capital, human capital (whether as slaves, apprentices, or wage workers) and occupations increasingly became the basis for stratifying the members of the population (usually leaving a large mass with little property). Such inequality was aggravated by the widespread, though highly variable, practice of slavery among horticulturalists.

Institutional differentiation began to accelerate with horticulture. Even as kinship expanded and became the basic organizing principle of the population—especially in simple horticultural systems—the beginnings of separate economic, political, religious, legal, and educational activity could be seen. Once differentiation was initiated, it operated to encourage population growth, forcing expanded efforts at gathering, producing, and distributing, which, in turn, furthered the process of institutional differentiation and development.

---

[5] For descriptions of the emerging political system, see: Schapera (1956), Mair (1962), Sahlins (1963), Fried (1967), Lenski (1966), Parsons (1966), Carneiro (1970), Cohen and Service (1977), Claessen and Skalnick (1978), Murra (1980), Haas (1982), Kirch (1984), Mann (1986), Lenski, Nolan, and Lenski (1995, 151–209), Johnson and Earle (1987), and Sanderson (1995, 106, 269–287).

Table 2.2 HORTICULTURAL ECONOMIES

	Simple	Advanced
Technology	Practical knowledge of herding, farming (planting, harvesting, storing, grinding, and cooking of grains), tool making (initially with stone, then with metals); pottery making (with kilns, which later led to annealing, smelting, casting, and eventually, alloying).	Practical knowledge of herding, breeding, farming, fertilizing, and crop rotation, tool making with metals (with exceptions, such as ancient China), pottery making, metallurgy, and masonry.
Physical Capital	Tools pottery, housing-storage sheds, negotiable items used (in most cases) in barter; unstable economic surplus; little ability to horde perishable commodities.	Tools, pottery, housing-storage sheds, walled cities, and the beginnings of liquid capital or money; stable economic surplus, which could be used in exchange and horded.
Human Capital	Clear division of labor between males and females (with females doing most of the tending of gardens); specialized occupational "trades" in weapon making, pottery, house building, boat building, and bartering; some use of protoslaves captured in war.	Clear division of labor between males and females; increased level of specialization in trades and occupations, especially in masonry, metal working, weaving, leather-making, pottery ceramics, boat and housebuilding, and commerce; frequent use of slaves captured in war
Entrepreneurship	Community/village structure; kinship units in villages are principal organizing structure, though village leaders/headman often allocate gardening plots and other resources, extracting some of the product to redistribute to village members; at times, a few trade specialists.	Community structure; kinship and headman are principal organizing structure at village level, with leaders and headman involved in resource allocation and redistribution; increased number of trade specialists; in larger core cities, merchants and markets become major entrepreneurial mechanisms.
Property	Emerging system of property; moderate inequality in distribution of property. Headmen, religious specialists, heads of kin units, some craft specialists and paramount chiefs receive surplus material goods (food, lodging, weapons, land), though redistribution requirements on political leaders mitigate degree of material inequality. Some stratification in terms of material property, but not developed into homogeneous ranks or social class; clear differentiation of headman and religious elites from others. If there is a dominant kin group (lineage or clan), then some differentiation among kin grouping; also, at times, village differentiation, with one village dominating others. Vast majority population forms a single class, with distinctions by kin group, sex, age, and at times, craft specialization being salient but not producing distinctive social classes. Slavery could also create a distinct class.	Hardening system of private property, with high inequality. Headmen, religious elites paramount chiefs, military elites, successful craft specialists, and especially king and his court receive surplus material goods. Accumulation of wealth becomes possible as more material surplus becomes durable and redistribution requirements begin to recede. Several homogeneous subpopulations in a hierarchy of ranks and beginnings of class system. Political leaders and their kin constitute distinctive grouping, as do religious specialists; military elites and economic specialists can become distinctive subgroupings. Slaves, where found, constitute a distinctive class. Vast majority of population forms a single class, with distinctions by kin group, sex, and age being salient but not producing distinctive social classes. However, craft specialties and other Economic positions can produce identifiable classes, and ethnic distinctions can also create a new basis of class formation. Slavery creates a distinct class.

Agriculture

Agrarian systems began[6] the process of harnessing nonhuman power, especially animal power, to new forms of physical capital, most notably the plow. Because of the increased gathering and production made possible by this harnessing of nonhuman power to physical capital, agrarian societies were generally much larger than horticultural societies. Settlements were bigger and more permanent, with some migration to market towns and cities as well as the core capital city (Sjoberg 1960; Hammond 1972; Eisenstadt and Shachar 1987). Although simple agrarian systems could remain quite small, with perhaps only a few thousand people, they often had populations numbering into the millions. More advanced systems usually ranged from a few million people to many millions. Cities could have up to one hundred thousand inhabitants in simple systems, or as many as one million in advanced ones. Advanced systems also had a larger number of cities with as many as one hundred thousand inhabitants. Yet even with these larger urban centers, the vast majority of the population (usually over 90 percent) lived in rural areas, working land owned and controlled by elites. Agrarian systems tended to have a period of rapid growth, followed by a leveling off as the denser population succumbed to disease, war, and poverty. The population could even decline after particularly violent wars or virulent diseases—and dramatically so in Europe during the successive waves of "the plague."

Most of the population in agrarian systems was arrayed in small villages and towns connected by extensive road networks to regional market cities and to a core capital city. Moreover, agrarianism used considerably more land than horticultural systems in order to increase the production of food so necessary to support the larger population and the growing privilege of elites. Indeed, resources tended to flow from rural villages to regional centers and market towns, and then, ultimately to the capital city as the state and its elites extracted ever-greater amounts of surplus from peasants and the local nobility (Lenski, Nolan, and Lenski 1995, 196–97). Agrarian societies also occupied considerably more territory than typical horticultural systems—not just because of increased population and production but also because of war, conquest, and empire-building (Mann 1986; Skocpol 1979; Giddens 1985; Turner 1995).

This increase in the size, scale, and scope of activity was made possible by higher levels for each of the basic elements of the economy, as is summa-

---

[6] This description of agrarian populations is drawn from Maryanski and Turner (1992), Lenski (1966), Lenski, Nolan, and Lenski (1995), Childe (1953), Kramer (1959), Mellaart (1965), Eberhard (1960), Sjoberg (1960), Clough and Cole (1941), Blum (1961), Curwen and Hatt (1961), Wolf (1982), Bloch (1962), McNeill (1963), Cambridge (1963), Wolley (1965), Moore (1966), Bender (1975), Hammond (1972), Postan (1972), Anderson (1974), Moseley and Wallerstein (1978), Tilly (1975), Johnson and Earle (1987).

rized in Table 2.3 for both simple and advanced agrarian populations. In broad strokes, new technologies, heightened levels of physical capital formation, more complex divisions of labor or human capital, new entrepreneurial mechanisms, and increased access to resources greatly expanded gathering and production, with the surplus being usurped as property for the privilege and power of elites (Lenski 1966). As production increased, new entrepreneurial mechanisms (markets, law, territorial specialization, guilds) and the ever-expanding and restrictive hierarchy of state power (local and regional elites connected to a monarch) replaced kinship as the organizational basis of the economy. Family structures—mostly nuclear but at times extended and/or patrimonial (family-owned business with slaves, workers, or apprentices)—still organized many portions of the labor force, such as peasants, artisans, and merchants. However, complex structures of kinship receded as an important societywide integrative mechanism (Weber [1916–17] 1958; Laslett and Wall 1972; Collins 1986: 267–321).

Replacing family structures was the expanding state, with a hereditary monarch at its apex and a variety of military and administrative positions in an ever-growing administrative and coercive bureaucracy. In centralized polities, most typical of advanced agrarian populations, the monarch used the state bureaucracy and coercive capacity of a professional army (and local enforcement capacities as well) to control territories, other elites, peasants, artisans, and merchants. The burden of financing the state, the army, and the privileges of the monarchy and nobility fell mainly on the peasantry, whose surplus was extracted by the state (usually directly from lands owned and controlled by the monarch, or indirectly through taxes on other land-holding nobility), although the monarch often turned to artisans and merchants for additional revenue to finance military adventures and large-scale undertakings such as public works or infrastructural development (Goldstone 1990). In such a system, property became an important force not only for economic activity but also for sustaining inequality and stratification (Turner 1984; Lenski 1966).

Because of the inequality and the constant usurpation of surplus as property for elites, incentives for technological innovation and investment in physical capital could decline (unless the monarch financed "public works" projects), especially as human capital saw little incentive for working hard; and the system could stagnate and, in the end, disintegrate (Maryanski and Turner 1992, 118; Lenski, Nolan, and Lenski 1995, 187, 222). But as we will see shortly, the combination of markets as a major distributive mechanism[7] and nonkin entrepreneurial structures possessed highly dynamic qualities. At times, this dynamism has overcome the tendency of agrarian societies to

---

[7] For descriptions of markets in such systems, see: Silver (1985), Oates (1978), Kohl (1989), Braudel (1982).

Table 2.3 Agrarian Economies

	Simple	Advanced
Technology	Knowledge of herding, farming with animal-drawn plow, irrigation, fertilization, sailing, wheel and its use on vehicles, orchards, husbandry, ceramics, metallurgy, writing, mathematical notations, and solar calendar. Rate of innovation high, but tending to decline as political-economy begins to circumscribe activity in more-advanced systems.	In addition to technology of simple systems, knowledge of smelting and hardening iron mark a significant advance. Other innovations include improved harnesses for horses, wood-turning lathe, auger, screws, printing, clocks, spinning and weaving, windmill and watermill technology.
Physical Capital	Plow, work animals, wood, ceramic, and sometimes iron tools; large facilities for storage and milling of grains; roads and often large-scale irrigation projects; and most significantly, increased use of money.	In addition to capital of simpler systems, widespread use of metal tools marks a significant increase in capital formation; also, larger facilities for storage, transportation, and milling; more elaborate and extensive roads and irrigation projects; light "industry," made possible by new sources of power (water, wind); and most importantly, money becomes fully integrated into the economy.
Human Capital	Dramatically increased division of labor as occupational trades expand; continued clear division of labor by age and sex; more merchants and other "trade specialties"; development of "free labor" and artisans who "sell" services in labor markets.	Continuing increase in division of labor; peasantry increasingly constrained by slavery and serfdom, but also a growing pool of "free" or unattached laborers (as a result of losing their land or tenancy rights) available for hire, leading to sale of free labor in urban labor markets. The most prominent axes of differentiation are among merchants/traders and artisans, now typically pursuing 100–200 different occupational specialties.
Entrepreneurship	Kinship and village structures decline as major entrepreneurial mechanisms and are supplemented by new political and economic forms of entrepreneurship. Political consolidation of territories creates hierarchies of authority and resource flow. Market expansion generates new methods of stimulating production and distributing labor, goods, and services; and merchants, beginnings of banking and insuring, and early craft guilds become evident. But	Kinship and village as entrepreneurial mechanisms replaced in rural areas by servitude obligations to ruling elites. Polity thus becomes a major entrepreneurial structure assuring the flow of resources from poor to rich, and from rural areas to urban centers. Dramatic expansion of markets, along with money as a medium of exchange; increasing volume and velocity of goods and services exchanged across ever-larger territories (in fact, large networks of ties among merchants *Continued*

Table 2.3 *Continued*

	Simple	Advanced
Entrepreneurship	for a given individual, the first entrepreneurial structure is the family, increasingly less connected to larger kinship structures and dramatically more circumscribed by the state, but nonetheless a crucial unit organizing economic activity.	often develop across an empire, and certainly within a society or region of an empire). Artisans and merchants increasingly organized into guilds that coordinate their activity and assure their privileges. Law begins to regulate contracts and the enforcement of obligations
Property	Clear system of private property, leading to very high levels of inequality. Almost all material resources owned by nobility and church. Some material accumulation possible by merchants, bankers/financiers, and craft specialists, but for vast majority (i.e., the peasantry) all surplus usurped by the state and religious elites. Produces system of stratification with very clear class cleavages, each with its own subculture. Ruling class (including religious and military elites) clearly distinguished from rest of the population, which has virtually no say in political decisions (except during periodic revolts). Urban minority vastly different from large rural majority, and there is a growing split between literate few and illiterate masses. Additionally, there are highly salient class distinctions for various occupational specialists, especially for artisans, craft specialists, merchants/traders, and perhaps slaves.	Clear system of private property, leading to very high levels of inequality, similar to that in simple systems, but altered somewhat by monarch's increased power to extract surplus and expansion of new trading/merchant occupations permitting accumulation of wealth. Produces system of stratification with very clear class cleavages, similar to those in simple systems, with several modifications: The increased number of occupations allows for expansion of classes between the elites and peasants (and slaves, if still evident); there is increased capacity for some artisans, merchants, and even peasants to acquire wealth exceeding that possessed by some sectors of nobility; and the growing number of state bureaucrats, military personnel, and retainers for the nobility create additional classes, whose members can acquire wealth, power (or at least influence), and some prestige.

stagnate or fall apart as a result of the tension and conflict over inequalities in property. The culmination of these more dynamic forces was for industrialization to emerge in western Europe in the late eighteenth and early nineteenth centuries—setting into motion a mode of economic organization that would transform all agrarian populations as well as the last remnants of horticulture and hunting-gathering.

Industrial and Post-Industrial Systems

The key technological breakthrough of industrial economies was the harnessing of inanimate sources of power (most notably fossil fuels) to physical capital, and with highly advanced industrialism or what is often termed "post-industrialization," the use of information systems made possible by the computer to control escalated processes of gathering, production, and distribution.[8] The level of physical-capital formation in machines, factories, bureaucracies, infrastructures, and money (and instruments like stocks and bonds, made possible by money for buying physical capital) is thus very high in industrial and post-industrial economies. Moreover—through market forces, state initiatives, or both—the rate of physical capital formation accelerates rapidly. Correspondingly human capital becomes highly differentiated, and with post-industrialization, nonmanual skills are increasingly required as mechanization of physical capital and its regulation by information systems shift human effort toward the service sector away from gathering and manufacturing, thereby making the production of services and the distribution of goods and services dominant over gathering and production of hard goods and commodities. Entrepreneurial activity becomes more complex and dynamic, being performed by combinations of nonkin corporate units (both private and governmental), state initiatives, legal-system processes; and, most importantly, markets for distributing goods, services, labor, or money (and the financial instruments that money enables). Property and property rights become critical forces in the economy, as technologies, physical capital, contracts with labor, and entrepreneurial systems are all seen as property. Indeed, virtually all aspects of the economy (e.g., patent rights to technology, stocks in corporations, money in money markets, contracts for labor, and machines) become "commodified" and are defined as property to be possessed as well as bought and sold in highly differentiated markets. Yet, despite the great increase in what is seen as property, inequality in property declines somewhat over that evident in agrarian systems

---

[8] This discussion on industrialization draws on Turner (1972, 30–42), Heilbroner (1985), Hilton (1976), Davis and Scase (1985), Chirot (1986), Beaud (1983), Kumar (1992), Smelser (1959), Turner (1990). The notion of "post-industrialization" is perhaps vague, but it is intended only as a rough distinction between early industrial and currently industrializing societies, on the one hand, and those where more than 50 percent of the work force is employed in services, gross domestic product is very high, per-capita incomes are high, and per-capita use of energy is very high, on the other.

(Lenski 1966; Lenski, Nolan, and Lenski 1995; Turner 1984, 1972). As production makes ever more goods available for purchase and as the polity is pressured to pursue some redistribution of wealth from elites to nonelites, inequality is reduced.

We are now in a position to revise slightly the provisional definition of the economy offered earlier. As is evident, the development of economies involves an ever-increasing production and distribution of services—banking, insuring, engineering, brokering, selling, advertising, and the like—which facilitate the operation of the economy. Moreover, services are produced for more general consumption—media, medical care, and entertainment, for example—by the population at large. Thus, we can redefine economies as *those structures (of positions, norms, roles, networks, and organizational units) and those cultural symbols (norms, values, beliefs, and ideology) that are implicated in entrepreneurial activities organizing technology, physical and human capital, and systems of property for the gathering of resources and for the production and distribution of goods and services.* With this definition in hand, we can now turn to the dynamics involved in the movement of economies toward industrial and post-industrial forms.

DEVELOPMENTAL DYNAMICS OF ECONOMIES

Slowly Accumulating Technology

Over the long course of human history, the level of technology, the amount of physical capital, the diversity and skill levels of human capital, the dynamism of entrepreneurial mechanisms, and the complexity of property systems have changed only slowly. For 100,000 to 250,000 years, humans and their ancestors were hunter-gatherers; and as late as 10,000 years ago, only pockets of horticulture existed. Large-scale agrarian societies (such as early Egypt) emerged around 5,000 years ago, and industrialization occurred only 200 years ago (Singer 1954–56).

This developmental sequence was hardly uniform, for horticulturalists often reverted back to hunting and gathering; agrarian systems got trapped in cycles of destructive inequalities which wasted surplus resources on elite consumption and political adventurism while creating disincentives for technological innovations, capital investments, and expenditures of human energy. War and conquest—and even more significantly, disease and pestilence—provided further Malthusian corrections to agrarian populations, seemingly locking them into cycles of population growth and decline, as well as episodes of political consolidation and internal collapse or external conquest.

The technological, capital, and entrepreneurial base of large-scale agrarian systems had in fact been produced by advanced horticultural and small-scale agrarian populations—harnessing of animal power, artificial irrigation, the simple plow, fermentation, sail power, production of copper, firing of

Table 2.4 Industrial and Post-Industrial Economies

	Industrial	Post-Industrial
Technology	Harnessing of inanimate sources of energy to machines creates search for more efficient fuels (resulting in heavy reliance on fossil fuels, supplemented by water-generated electricity, nuclear power, and for limited application, solar energy). Leads to mechanization of all productive sectors and generates both new social technologies—the factory system, assembly line, and corporation—and new productive technologies, especially with respect to new materials (metals and synthetics), new machines (machine tools, robotics), new modes of transportation (trains, ships, cars, airplanes), and new capacities to store, process, and send information. Technological innovation becomes institutionalized in the educational system, scientific establishment, secularized values and beliefs, economic/political competition, research and development by corporations and government, and laws (i.e., patents).	Same as industrial societies, except for increasing emphasis on developing ways to make new materials (especially synthetic products), to use information in the production process (robotics, computers, communication networks), and to reduce time and cost of transportation. Institutionalization of innovation proceeds, increasingly driven by world-level economic competition.
Physical Capital	Capital formation and accumulation increase dramatically, with money used to buy and construct tools, machines, factories, and large-scale infrastructural projects (revolving around transportation, energy, and communication). Capital may be heavily concentrated in either the private sector or the state. New mechanisms—bond, stock, and money markets—are used to concentrate capital coming from increasingly diverse sources: taxes, pension funds, mutual funds, individuals, and corporations.	Same as industrial societies, except that capital formation and accumulation increase and become more and more a global process involving multinational corporations, foreign governments, and private investing consortiums.
Human Capital	Division of labor becoming dramatically more differentiated and complex, while revolving less around primary industries (farming, mining, and other basic producer sectors) and more around secondary industries (mills, factories, construction) and tertiary industries (services, such as retailing, banking, insuring, education health care, police, social welfare, government, and managing). Women increase their nonhousehold economic roles; self-employment decreases as a proportion of work force; labor increasingly allocated to economic positions by a labor market guided by expertise as determined by educational credentials.	Division of labor increases in complexity, along with marked shift from secondary to tertiary industries as machines coupled with information-processing computers increasingly perform many routine activities in the secondary sector. Women continue to increase as proportion of nonhousehold work force, and self-employment continues to decline. Educational credentials and labor markets increase as criteria for allocating workers to economic positions.

Continued

Table 2.4 *Continued*

	Industrial	Post-Industrial
Entrepreneurship	Household and family lose virtually all their integrative functions, except for the relatively few remaining family-run businesses. Markets, corporations, law, and state become principal entrepreneurial structures, with law and state predominating in some systems and private corporations in others.	Same as industrial societies, except that there are more-differentiated and varied markets (labor, money, commodities, bonds, precious metals, etc.), larger corporations, more-extensive bodies of law, and increased state regulation of markets and corporations. Increasing use of markets, combined with state regulation, evident in all post-industrial systems. World-level economic integration by global markets, world-level banking, international economic alliances (partnerships, joint ventures, stock purchases, and government-to-government/cooperative agreements) become increasingly evident.
Property	Most material things and labor activities defined as property and assessed in terms of monetary value. Decreased inequality compared with agrarian systems as result of governmental tax-redistributive policies, increased productivity (making distribution less of a zero-sum game), and episodes of political-economic-social conflict between privileged and nonprivileged sectors, but still considerable material inequality. Nobility as a class virtually disappears, although continuing in some systems as symbols and in some cases as holders of considerable wealth. Very clear modal differences in behavior, culture, and income, and sources of power and prestige among elites, high education/salaried professionals, small business entrepreneurs, white collar workers, blue collar workers, and the poor; but considerable income overlap among members of different classes. Higher rates (compared with agrarian systems) of mobility (both individual and structural) also work against maintenance of hard class barriers. The few continuing cultural differences between rural and urban mitigated by smallness of rural population, with ethnic and urban-suburban differences becoming more salient than rural-urban distinctions.	Virtually all material things, labor activities, and cultural symbols defined as property or as property rights and assessed in terms of monetary value. Material inequality about the same as in industrial systems, except for widening gap between unskilled, and skilled, especially information-literate. Same as industrial societies, except that cultural capital (in the form of educational credentials as property to be sold) becomes more salient for making class distinctions.

23

bricks, use of mortar, glazing, calendars, writing, numerical notation, and bronze. Indeed, add to these knowledge of how to construct capital infrastructures (roads, ports, canals, walls, buildings), and the feats of the larger agrarian systems seem less fundamentally new and less spectacular. The knowledge of how to organize nonkin specialization of labor in trades and crafts similarly existed before the big agrarian societies and empires. Moreover, knowledge of how to develop entrepreneurial systems (e.g., markets, the beginnings of nonkin corporate units, systems of law, and consolidation of power) was also part of earlier horticultural and smaller agrarian systems. Yet, large agrarian populations expanded the scale and scope of these technologies and added several key breakthroughs, including the knowledge of how to smelt iron on a large scale, how to construct a true alphabet for creating and storing information, how to use decimal notation for more accurate counting, and how to construct aqueducts for supplying water in support of larger cities (Childe 1964; Lenski, Nolan, and Lenski 1995, 186).

For industrialization to emerge, one additional step was required: a source of energy beyond animal, wind, and water power, along with the capacity to harness that power to physical capital (machines) and coordinate energy and machines with human capital (labor). With this breakthrough came the Industrial Revolution and the potential capacity to gather, produce, and distribute on a monumental scale.

Slowly Expanding Entrepreneurial Systems

Technology alone does not drive an economy, although it is perhaps its most important element because it provides the knowledge base for other elements of the economy. For technology *to be used*, however, organizational forms or entrepreneurial mechanisms must exist that connect technology to physical and human capital. Several are crucial: (1) the development of market systems, (2) the existence of nonkin corporate structures, (3) the consolidation of power and administrative systems, and perhaps (4) the nature of organized religion.

Market Development Gathering and production are greatly influenced by the capacity to distribute what is produced. The greater this capacity, the more of a stimulus it provides for expanded gathering and production (Smith [1776] 1937). These reciprocal dynamics will be reviewed shortly, but for the moment, it is important to stress that industrialization could not have occurred without market development in agrarian systems. Indeed, markets in agrarian societies were often quite well developed (Ekholm and Friedman 1982; Sanderson 1995:119–20). Some have gone so far as to argue that "market dynamics are the engine of historical change" (Collins 1990), but one must acknowledge at least that a commercial revolution occurred before industrialism and was, no doubt, a key force leading to its emergence in the West (Swedberg 1994, 273–75; Gills and Frank 1992).

Fernand Braudel ([1979] 1985, 1977) has visualized the markets of agrarian systems in terms "'lower" and "upper" levels. At the lower level are found (1) person-to-person barter in terms of commodities, (2) person-to-person exchanges using money, (3) peddlers who make goods and sell them for money and who extend credit, and (4) shopkeepers who sell goods that they do not make for money and on credit. The vast majority of transactions in agrarian systems occurred in these lower markets, and the limitations of such markets in terms of volume and velocity of transactions that they could handle placed restrictions on the level of gathering and production.

Yet, two critical features of the third and fourth levels represented important breakthroughs: the use of money, and the extension of credit. Without these breakthroughs, markets could not become more complex; nor could they generate the physical capital necessary for industrialization. As early sociologists like Georg Simmel ([1907] 1978, 1903) and Max Weber ([1922] 1978) recognized, the use of money dramatically alters exchanges, because it is a neutral medium that can be used to express a wider range of preferences and, hence, demand in markets. As such, money can encourage the production of increasing varieties of commodities to meet more-individualized tastes, needs, and preferences which now can be expressed by the expenditure of money in markets. Credit was also crucial to early market exchanges because it enabled buyers and sellers to conduct transactions without full payment, thereby accelerating exchanges as the buyer need not delay in making purchases for lack of immediate funds. Moreover, the charging of interest for credit became yet another way to accumulate physical capital which could be used to expand production or to finance further extension of credit so as to accelerate distribution.

Money and credit also transformed the economy as a whole (Turner 1995). First, the widespread use of money and credit created pressures for their regulation, since if money inflates (and loses value) and if credit obligations are not honored, markets collapse. Such pressures have brought governmental power into distribution processes—especially with respect to maintaining the stability of money as, increasingly, the legitimacy of political authority has rested on its capacity to sustain the value of money and the corresponding security of those who use it. Second, money and credit became the basis for expanding government, because it is easier to collect taxes in money than hard goods, because payment of administrative staff in money enables government to grow beyond kin-based nepotistic and elite-based patronage systems of recruitment, and because it becomes possible for government to borrow the means to sustain itself (often to excess, creating fiscal crises) and to support larger-scale projects (and, of course, elite privilege). As government grew, it became an important entrepreneurial mechanism as well as a source of technology and capital—topics to be examined in the next chapter. Third, the use of credit and money initiated the production of services in banking, insuring, mortgaging, and other activities which money and credit stimulate. And fourth, the existence of money as a neutral and generalized marker of value that is not tied to a specific good or commodity enabled value to be potentially bestowed on all objects, behaviors, symbols, and organizations, thereby increasing the capacity to denote and differentiate new forms of property (Marx [1867] 1967; Harvey 1989, 100–102).

Thus, contained in lower-market activities of agrarian societies were the beginnings of important dynamics which became the mainstay of upper markets and, eventually, prime movers of industrialization and post-industrialization. These upper markets in Braudel's analysis of agrarian systems were of varying types: (1) fairs or relatively stable geographical locations where higher volumes and varieties of goods were exchanged in terms of money and credit (Verlinden 1963); (2) permanent trade centers where brokers sold goods and services, including credit and other financial instruments; and (3) private markets where merchants engaged in high-risk and high-profit speculations involving long chains of exchange between producers and buyers. For Braudel and others (Verlinden 1963; Moore 1966; J. Hall 1985; Mann 1986; Wallerstein 1974), the existence of the last two kinds of markets became critical for industrialization in the West, although such markets existed in many parts of the world where industrialism did not spontaneously emerge (Abu-Lughod 1989). The coexistence of a relatively nonintrusive state—along with a system of brokers, a stable currency, and an efficient set of credit mechanisms—enabled parts of Europe to engage in long-distance buying and selling. This eventually would become the basis for commercial capitalism, which initiated the Industrial Revolution. Without markets that could extend across territories, use stable currencies, employ credit mechanisms, and evidence brokerage, banking, insuring, and other servicing activities, industrialization could not occur, nor could it ever reveal the dynamic qualities that led to post-industrialism (White 1988; 1981).

Nonkin Corporate Units   As we will see in Chapter 3, the kin-based organization of horticultural economies broke down in agrarian systems, forcing the development of alternative corporate structures (Laslett and Wall 1972). The manorial estate—with a mass of tenant peasants, with overseers such as the squire, and with the "lord" of the manor—was the basic economic unit organizing most gathering processes in advanced agrarian systems. In urban areas as well nonkin structures emerged—guilds of craftsmen, "patrimonial" families (of kin and nonkin apprentices running a business or performing a craft), bankers and brokers, government officials (as part of emerging governmental bureaucracies), warehousing organizations, cartels of businesses, and chartered (by government) companies. All of these nonkin structures—including even the patrimonial household, which was only partly kin-based—provided a structural base from which industrialization could emerge and on which it could build.

As long as kinship and, hence, restrictive norms and traditions were the sole entrepreneurial structures organizing economic activity, change was difficult (although small kin-based "cottage industries," such as weaving, were important in the beginning of the Industrial Revolution in England [Smelser 1959]). Moreover, once kinship no longer dominated entrepreneurship, it became possible for money, markets, and government growth to stimulate alternative entrepreneurial structures which were increasingly freed from constraining networks of kindred.

The State   Agrarian societies (and advanced horticultural ones as well) all revealed a state, usually comprising a monarch and land-owning nobility organized in a feudal pattern (Tilly 1990). Hereditary descent lines or violent takeovers by other kin leaders controlled the succession of elites at the top of the state bureaucracy, but the day-to-day administration often was organized in a quasi-bureaucratic form, where incumbents were paid a salary and recruited for their competence as much as their kin affiliation or other ascriptive criteria. The existence of this structural form, even when revealing kin-ascription or nepotism and patronage to members of elite families, provided a model or template for organizing economic activity for a larger, more productive economy. Furthermore, the state had some interest in economic growth to support its privileges and projects—often leading it to subsidize economic units, such as chartered companies or franchises to particular organizations.

The Church   Religion was often a source of resistance to change, since it is the keeper of traditional values and beliefs. In the West, the Roman Catholic Church became a wealthy bureaucratic structure, thereby providing another template for bureaucratization. More significantly, the church was a land-owning and productive unit, organizing agricultural activity in a more bureaucratic pattern, especially when compared to the feudal manor. And once again, it could serve as a model for the accumulation of physical capital and organization of nonkin human capital (Hall 1985).

Additionally, as we will examine in more detail in the next chapter, the Protestant Reformation altered the religious belief system in ways encouraging accumulation of physical capital and its use to expand productive activity (Weber [1904–5] 1958). While the Catholic Church clearly evidenced the capacity for capital accumulation and large-scale production, the Protestant Reformation shifted the Christian belief system toward an emphasis on secular and productive economic activity by individuals outside of the church. Whether this shift ultimately caused the Industrial Revolution or simply removed a potential barrier is debated, but there can be little doubt that Protestant beliefs (and perhaps Catholic ones as well) facilitated the kinds of economic activity—individual accumulation of physical capital and hard work to that end—which were to foster capitalism.

Slowly Developing Systems of Property

In feudal agrarian systems, the nobility controlled property, and the great mass of the population had none. The widespread use of money and credit in markets began to change not only the distribution of property but also how it was defined. Great wealth could be accumulated by merchants, brokers, and bankers in markets. This wealth was more than purely monetary; it was also attached to an ever-increasing variety of objects (e.g., ships, warehouses and other buildings, rights to paid labor, roads, shops, houses, ports and the like) and to financial instruments (e.g., mortgages, bonds, and insurance premiums), which contained rights to property and income from property.

What Karl Marx ([1867] 1967) was to call "commodification"—indeed, a "fetishism of commodities" for industrial societies—was well under way in agrarian systems with upper market activity. This development was crucial to capitalism because without the capacity to possess property and to enjoy its rewards, there was no incentive for developing technologies and new forms of gathering and producing. As long as most property was controlled by elites and used for their privilege, the diversity of property and its distribution to those who could develop new technologies and modes of gathering, producing, and distribution were constrained. Without increases in the diversity and distribution of property, then, capitalism could not flourish.

INDUSTRIALIZATION

The slowly accumulating technologies, the changing system of religious beliefs, the new entrepreneurial systems, and the widening diversity and distribution of property set the stage for the rise of capitalism, or the production of goods and services for sale in comparatively free and open markets. The market mechanisms were, at least incipiently, in place; but without a new source of energy, the inherent dynamism in these markets could not be fully realized. Although a precise date is impossible to pinpoint, the application of steam to gathering and producing processes initiated the Industrial Revolution in Europe about two hundred years ago. While practical knowledge about steam had existed for hundreds of years, the additional knowledge or technology necessary for its widespread application as well as interest in such application emerged only recently in the history of human societies.

The Dynamics of Machines and Technology

The historical consequences of steam technology for generating a physical capital base that could expand gathering and producing processes were immense. Steam eliminated the exclusive reliance on not only human and animal power but on wind power as well (Cottrell 1955). Steam enabled the construction of powerful pumps and drilling shafts in mines, thereby generating ready access to resources such as coal and iron ore. Steam power also enabled the development and operation of blast furnaces, automatic hammers, and rollers for converting iron ore into more-refined metals.

With these advances in conversion of resources, new and more-efficient machines for expanding resource extraction and conversion could be built. A machine capital base not only produces goods at a rapid rate but also generates new knowledge or technology about how to make more extensive and efficient machinery—thereby further expanding the processes of gathering and conversion. For example, the original blast furnaces provided for the large-scale conversion of iron ore into metal, but they also generated a legacy of knowledge and experience which could improve production—hence the Bessemer converter and open-hearth process. Similarly, through trial and error, other sources of power such as oil, electricity, uranium, and hydrolysis were discovered and applied to the revolution ushered in by the application of steam and resulting mechanization of gathering and producing.

Some of the commodity outputs of an industrializing economy are machines that come back into the economy via markets for factory equipment. This marketing of machine capital increases access to natural resources and the capacity of converting these resources into more goods and commodities. And once well-developed and specialized markets exist for new types of machines, incentives for their production and distribution accelerate the accumulation of a machine capital base. The same is true of knowledge. Experience in machine producing and gathering can generate new knowledge about how to expand these processes which, if a market exists, can be sold, thereby creating incentives to expand the technological storehouse.

Without markets for distributing machine capital and technology, these elements can accumulate only slowly. New machines, or refinements of existing ones, stay in the local area where they are created; and new ideas similarly only diffuse gradually. With markets, there is a mechanism for the broader distribution of capital and technology. Moreover, if the market is profit-oriented, there is incentive for such distribution. Thus, once markets for capital and technology exist, they provide the means for the spread of capital and technology to ever-wider circles of potential users at ever-accelerating rates.

The level of technology available to an industrial and post-industrial economy has also been dependent on the organization of science, or the systematic search for knowledge. The organization of science has varied in different societies. In the United States, for example, the research-oriented university, coupled with publicly-funded laboratories and with private research in market-oriented firms, became the pattern, with the greatest proportion of pure research being conducted by graduate faculties and students of research universities. In other societies (primarily those of the old Soviet bloc in Eastern Europe as well as those in the now-defunct Soviet Union), national academies of science operating as politically sponsored organizations were, and still are, the predominant locus of scientific research. Other societies, such as Japan and China, reveal a pattern between the Soviet Union and the United States.

What emerges is "Big Science" or a set of organizations, funded primarily by governments and, to a lesser extent, by private capital in market-driven economies, to generate technology (Price 1982, 1963). In some societies, much of this technology is military and, as a consequence, can distort production toward military ends. Even with the end of the Cold War and corresponding downsizing of many military programs, the United States still devotes a considerably higher proportion of its science organizations and productive capacities to "defense."

When this occurs, as was dramatically evident in the Soviet Union, technology loses much of its stimulus effect on gathering, producing, and distribution. Such technology must be kept secret and, hence, remains unavailable as a source of innovations for the domestic economy. Even when made available, as today in the post-Cold War era, it is often either unusable or difficult to translate from military to domestic applications. The rise of Japan and Germany as serious economic competitors to the United States was partly the result of the greater proportion of investment of American technology (and capital), especially of the high-technology end, to military ends. In the case of the Soviet Union, which had a far less-productive economy than the United States, the technological and capital drain were so great as to stagnate the economy by the end of the 1960s.

Thus, modern Big Science is very much a result of needs for military technologies, and these needs affect the nature of science and the total technology available to the domestic economy (Price 1963). But Big Science is also stimulated by economic forces, especially the need for innovations by corporate units and their government sponsors in an increasingly competitive world system. In the post-Cold War era, science will be tied increasingly to the demand for economic innovations. We could expect, then, that research in Academies of Science and graduate programs in research universities will rise to meet this demand; and to the extent that they do, gathering, producing, and distributing will increase.

The Dynamics of the Factory System

The initial expansion of gathering and producing processes with the application of new technologies and new forms of physical capital has usually resulted in centralization of the domestic economy, especially its physical-capital base of machines and money. Machines and other capital resources increasingly become located near sources of fuel, resources, transportation, and commerce. And as capital becomes centralized, so must the labor force. Moreover, workers must now schedule, pace, and standardize their work in specialized ways to the requirements of machines. Work that must be highly coordinated tends to become hierarchically organized, with work at one level being supervised and coordinated by work at higher levels, resulting in the proliferation of supervisory and managerial roles in the factory system.

The factory system allows for the organization of larger numbers of employees around networks of machines. Once this system is established, it facilitates the concentration of more human capital around even bigger machines, resulting in expansion of the factory system. This continues at least to the point that the very size of the factory creates inefficiencies and increases costs. But, in general, larger machines are usually cheaper to run while increasing productivity and profits. (There are, however, limits to this process as large factory systems can become inefficient because supervising functions begin to drain resources from manufacturing and create rigidities that reduce innovation and flexibility.) Still, enlarging the factory also has advantages in obtaining resources and other materials, thereby stimulating greater industrial productivity. In so doing the factory system generates positive feedback which often encourages its own expansion up to the point where it becomes so large as to be less-efficient than smaller, niche-oriented manufacturers.

Larger factories are most typical of early industrialization—especially state-managed patterns but more market-driven forms as well. Larger factories are, however, only part of a system of factories, some of which are rather small and oriented to the manufacture of specialized products. A tension always exists in free market systems between large-scale factories and smaller, niche-oriented factories. This tension runs along several fault lines. First, smaller factories often supply parts and materials to larger ones, becoming dependent on them and always fearing cost-cutting competition from other suppliers. Second, smaller and larger factories can also be in direct competition. This is the case with U.S. steel production, in which large factories' economics of scale must compete with the flexibility, quality control, and lower administrative overhead of smaller "mini-mills." Increasingly, with the clear exception of capital-intensive mass-market goods (automobiles, chemicals, airplanes, and the like), it appears that large factories in the most economically advanced societies are losing ground to smaller centers of manufacturing operating in specialized niches, although this trend may be only an oscillation in the competition between larger and smaller factories.

Smaller factories also allow for the deconcentration of physical and human capital, thereby encouraging movement of labor to new areas and away from the early large industrial cities. Yet, equally often, smaller factories are clustered together in industrial zones in or near older cities, thereby having less impact on geographical dispersion.

The factory system helps create a labor market of wage employees. The availability of a mobile and semiskilled pool of workers, unencumbered by kinship and traditional trades or farming, encourages the development of the factory system. In early state-managed industrial economies, such as those in the former Soviet Union and post-Revolution China, the labor market was regulated by the state, resulting in wages being set by political policies rather than by supply and demand for various skills. In contrast, early industrialism in free markets tends to create exploitive tendencies by capital, which seeks to maximize profits by paying workers as little as possible, especially when the supply of labor can be manipulated to remain in excess of demand for this labor (Braverman 1974). In so doing, capital encourages labor to organize (into unions and other collective-bargaining bodies) and exert political pressure both on the state and on corporate managers to give labor more-favorable wages and benefits. In the more-mature industrial nations, after a period of conflict and turmoil, this negotiation is well institutionalized, although the importation of lower-priced labor and the exportation of physical capital (and hence jobs) to other countries have created new points of tension as capital seeks to bargain down the price of domestic labor by threatening to import workers or export jobs.

The Dynamics of Bureaucracy

Accompanying the factory system is bureaucracy—whether as the administrative component of the factory or as separate structures producing services, such as banking, insuring, advertising, marketing, engineering, accounting, and many other service functions required by an industrial economy. Although bureaucracies are often portrayed as inefficient and rife with "red tape," especially as they become large, they are essential to large scale administrative activity. They facilitate coordination of specialists by organizing them into offices, which in turn are arranged into hierarchies of offices; and in so doing, they focus activity on specific goals. As long as the economy is small, with low productivity, limited market facilities, and few servicing requirements, large bureaucracies are unnecessary. But when the economy becomes large and complex, the scale of activity eventually stimulates bureaucratization.

Once large-scale bureaucratization occurs, it feeds back and allows for the further expansion of the factory system, markets, and service organizations. In this way, bureaucratization actually provides the structural base for growth and development in an economy. However, if bureaucratization is "undisciplined" by market competition—as in state-owned corporations or market-controlling oligopolies and monopolies—it can stagnate the economy by increasing the proportion of administrative roles and hierarchies of authority to the point where the efficiencies of the bureaucratic system are undermined by rules, regulations, administrative infighting, and pursuit of short-term interests of bureaucrats rather than the preferences of consumers. Still, without bureaucratization, there is an inadequate structural base for economic development.

The degree of bureaucratization can vary enormously in different sectors of the economy. The more professional and skilled the tasks, the less rigid is the bureaucratic system. Moreover, the full effects of the current information revolution—from computers to the worldwide internet—are difficult to forecast on the future of bureaucratization. No doubt there will be considerable leveling of authority systems in bureaucracies, as well as a horizontal stretch in the space of economic activity as information networks allow some workers to work at remote distances—even in their homes. Only the most elite workers today, or those providing highly skilled contracted services to bureaucratic organizations, exhibit this horizontal dimension in work patterns. Indeed, some analysts have predicted the end of traditional bureaucracies with the information revolution. But thus far, computers have simply changed how human capital sits at its desk and how it performs its administrative functions. For the present, the obituary proclaiming the demise of bureaucracy is perhaps premature.

Like the factory system, bureaucracies generate a new labor market and, moreover, a differentiation of this market in terms of skill and training requirements for human capital. The existence of such a market facilitates the development of new bureaucratic systems in more and more economic arenas (and other institutional arenas organized bureaucratically, such as the state and the educational system). Indeed, despite incessant public criticisms of bureaucracies by industrial and post-industrial populations, alternatives will have to prove more efficient than bureaucracies—a transformation which has yet to occur even in the most advanced post-industrial society.

The Dynamics of Markets

Markets pervade all aspects of industrialization. Internal to the economy, they determine the distribution of technology, capital, and labor. Externally, they distribute goods, services, resources, and materials to the population as a whole. Without the expansion and differentiation of markets, industrialization is not dynamic. For this dynamism to be sustained in terms of developing new technologies, new forms of capital, higher wages and living standards, and new products and services, markets must have the capacity to stimulate *new kinds of productive outputs* of both goods and services. Many of the problems of state socialism before the Soviet collapse and Chinese reforms inhere in the nature of their markets, which were guided by state edicts and production quotas rather than consumer needs, tastes, and interests. Such state-controlled production and markets worked well (ignoring, of course, the human costs of the corresponding political repression) in jump-starting industrial development. Nonetheless, all of these economies were stagnant by the mid-1960s, because without incentives for private profit among producers and without a well-cultivated freedom among consumers for expressing their preferences in market demand, markets cannot grow, proliferate, and develop in ways that encourage new kinds of production.[9] They simply become dreary state-run distribution depots. In contrast, when property and profits can be owned, there are incentives for developing new technologies, new concentrations of physical capital, new skills and types of human capital, and new entrepreneurial systems so that profits can be realized as preferences are expressed.

The problem with such dynamic markets in capitalism is that they are inherently unstable, along several fronts. First, these markets tend to pyramid into hierarchies of metamarkets where the terms and instruments of exchange in a lower market become themselves objects of highly speculative trade in a higher-order market (Collins 1990). This trend has been facilitated by globalization of markets for capital. For example, instruments facilitating exchange in one level of market—such as money, credit contracts, mortgages, stocks, bonds, and futures on commodities—become themselves the objects exchanged in a higher-order market; and such exchanges are often highly speculative and leveraged (i.e., bought and sold on credit). The recent advent of "derivatives" and their marketing takes this speculation to yet another level whereby financial instruments from different metamarkets are commingled in ever-further speculation, as when bonds are purchased by borrowing in money markets or stocks traded for futures on commodities. All these processes eventually cause reversals which reverberate across metamarkets and down to lower-level markets, in which the instruments of exchange in a metamarket (say, credit and money) become less available to

---

[9] For a review of the literature on this issue—a more sympathetic one than presented here—see Szelenyi, Beckett, and King (1994). See also Nee (1989).

facilitate exchange, thereby sending the lower market into instability or at least retraction.

A second problem with these more dynamic markets of capitalism is that, short of collapse through overspeculation, they oscillate between periods of high demand, production, and employment and episodes of lower demand, decreased production, and layoffs of human capital which further dampen demand (since workers have lost income and, hence, purchasing power). Indeed, left to themselves, free markets produce periodic depressions and corresponding social chaos—especially when oscillations are stimulated or accelerated by speculation and collapse in higher-order metamarkets.

A third tendency of free markets is to produce oligopolies, hidden networks, and monopolies of corporate control within a sector of production and marketing, As a result, competition is reduced or eliminated, enabling corporations to charge prices that no longer correspond to demand. Prices, as a consequence, are fixed in much the same way as a state-run enterprise fixes prices, except that private corporations will tend to fix artificially high prices whereas those in state-run markets tend to charge artificially low prices.

A fourth problem occurs when markets remain truly competitive and avoid oligopoly and monopoly control. Under these conditions, cut-throat competition tends to generate a decline in the rate of profit as producers constantly cut prices to gather market share from competitors (Marx [1867] 1967; Applebaum 1978). If this process continues unabated, profits cease to exist, thereby forcing the liquidation of physical capital and causing the unemployment of human capital.

A fifth problem, noted earlier, is that production for open and free markets also creates a labor market for human capital in which conflict between owners and managers of capital, on the one side, and the wage employees, on the other side, escalates as owners and managers of capital seek to keep wages low while human capital seeks to do the reverse. Such conflict can often turn violent unless a system of labor-management negotiation can be institutionalized.

A sixth problem is that unregulated markets invite fraud, corruption, abuse of occupational and environmental hazards, and other ills, as drives for profits at any cost and in any way create incentives for doing social harm. Thus, the dynamism of capitalist markets is not without its problems. As we will see in the next chapter, these problems pull centers of power into the gathering, producing, and distributing process while forcing the development of new kinds of entrepreneurial activity to mitigate against these difficulties.

Industrial capitalism is built on the constant expansion and differentiation of markets.[10] Without the capacity to expand existing markets or create new ones, incentives for capital investment are dampened, because, in the

---

[10] For a review of the sociology of markets, see: Swedberg (1994). Also see Swedberg (1994, 272–74), an interesting typology on the social structure of markets. Another interesting typology on modes of exchange can be found in Sanderson (1995, 120). See also White (1988, 1981).

end, it is the drive for higher profits that sustains capitalism. As Marx ([1867] 1967) recognized, there are only a limited number of ways to increase profits: Eliminate competitors and fix prices; pay labor as little as possible; develop new technologies that provide more efficient machines; and expand/differentiate markets.

The need of capital to expand markets makes capitalism global, always reaching out beyond nation-state boundaries. In the early phases of capitalism during the nineteenth century, a kind of coercive laissez-faire was practiced (first by Britain and later by other European powers), whereby raw materials were extracted (often under coercive threats or control) from less developed countries, shipped home for conversion into manufactured goods, and then distributed on both domestic and international markets (Gereffi 1994, 207–8). The coercive side of this internationalism led to the partitioning of the nonindustrial world into colonies or spheres of influence by dominant powers. Between the world wars in the twentieth century, this system was disrupted by the Depression and the wars themselves. In the aftermath of World War II, a "monopoly capitalism" (Baran and Sweezy 1966) phase emerged as transnational corporations invested capital and technology abroad (at first, disproportionately by the United States, but increasingly by all other industrial nations). More recently, a new phase of "global capitalism" is arising. In this phase, the organization of capital and technology within the boundaries of, or at least under the guidance of, states is giving way to more-fluid patterns, where capital (money and machines) and technology move easily across state boundaries and increasingly out of state control (Gereffi 1994, 208).

Markets are now truly global, as are the corporate actors in them. Over the last thirty years, very rapid development of the nonindustrial world has ensued as technology and capital from foreign corporations—often in partnerships with domestic governments or private companies—have been invested in order to secure indigenous natural resources or to take advantage of lower priced labor (Gereffi and Wyman, 1990). Thus, when a country possesses natural resources (e.g., oil, minerals, or agricultural lands) that can be extracted and marketed to other nations and when it is inhabited by lower-priced human capital than in developed nations, incentives exist for manufacturers to relocate their manufacturing operations. As markets have become global, this process enabling all elements of economic activity to be bought and sold across state boundaries has accelerated. Development of this kind, however, is always uneven, with some sectors of physical and human capital changing while others remain undeveloped (Frank 1980, 1975, 1969; Amin [1973] 1976, [1970] 1974). Development that is dependent on foreign capital and technology is often exploitive, as resources and productive outputs are sold overseas for profits that do not come back to the producing nation.

Still, the incentives to the global markets for generating profits have worked to transform capital flows throughout the world (Mizruchi and Stearns 1994). Liquid physical capital, or money and other financial instruments, moves very rapidly through international metamarkets—especially as deregulation of national money and financial markets has occurred (Mizruchi and Stearns 1994, 333). Much of this money is simply shifted from one short-term speculative financial instrument to another, but much is also invested in technology and manufacturing physical capital in foreign countries—a situation that accelerates economic development and, in more advanced economies, increases the interconnections among corporations and governments.

POST-INDUSTRIALIZATION

As those involved in services surpass those in manual labor connected to gathering and producing, post-industrialism supplants industrialism (Bell 1973; Block 1990; Harvey 1989; Lash 1990). As is evident in the advanced economies of the world today, primarily in North America, western Europe, and Japan, nonmanual service positions far outnumber those in agriculture and factory system production; and consumption levels of goods, services, and energy are very high because per-capita income is high relative to industrial societies.

This shift is due to the increasing automation of gathering and production, as machines and information systems made possible by the computer organize and perform many of the routine gathering and production processes formerly conducted by less-sophisticated machines and labor. This process of reducing the manual work force can be accelerated with the export by advanced economies of manual-machine labor to less developed economies where labor costs are low—or if labor costs are not lower, where markets are closer.

This shift in the relative proportions of manual and nonmanual work reflects other economic forces beyond mechanization or export of manual work. Accompanying mechanization and the information systems that make automation possible are changes in: (1) the way production is organized, (2) the kinds of productive outputs that such organization generates, and (3) the manner in which outputs are distributed. Each of these alterations is examined in the sections that follow.

The Reorganization of Production

The corporate units in which production occurs undergo important transformations. First, as noted earlier, smaller manufacturing units, involved in flexible production of specialized goods, become as prominent as the large-scale factory. Second, in both large and small factories, many changes are occurring in their operation, including: new systems of managing inventories (e.g., "just-in-time" stocking, which eliminates the need for large inventories); new procedures for quality control (at the point of error rather than after the product is finished); new systems of contracting and subcontracting (increasingly, parts supply, accounting, maintenance, sales, and other functions are turned over to subcontractors); new planning procedures (whereby longer-term assessment of markets occurs); new procedures for ownership and regulation by the state (with states increasingly deregulating private corporations and privatizing state-owned corporations); new patterns of planning and subsidy by the state (increasing reliance on indirect subsidies through government purchases and taxing policies rather than direct state subsidies); new levels of competition among smaller, niche-oriented companies; and renewed emphasis on technological innovation as the means to maintain or increase market share. Third, a greater proportion of production is export-oriented, seeking markets in other nations, while attempting to deal with competition from imports. Fourth, as noted earlier, the global orientation of the large multinational company, and many more moderate-sized companies, makes them truly multinational and increasingly involved in production outside national boundaries.

The Production of Services

All of these changes increase reliance on service production for sustaining flexibility, for planning, for innovation, for marketing, for maintaining information systems, for managing subcontracting, and for providing the administrative and fiscal infrastructure—accounting, banking, computing, selling of financial instruments (stocks, bonds, futures), advertising, marketing, insuring, capitalizing, managing, and so forth—on which manufacturing depends. Separate companies that produce these and many other services are now as numerous as those that manufacture hard goods and products. Many of these companies, especially at the high-technology and high-skill end, have begun to adopt less-bureaucratized work settings, offering flexible working hours, horizontal dispersion (even to one's home) via information nets, less rigid authority, and more-collegial teamwork.

The Expansion of Markets

Distribution processes reflect and, at the same time, cause these transformations in production. As markets expand, differentiate, and globalize, demand drives production more than the reverse. When market demands for goods and services dictate what is produced, the diversity and volume of production escalate. This is because of the infinitely variable needs of consumers to create ever more market niches that serve as incentives for producers. Conversely, once well-developed markets exist, they can be used to create new needs in consumers that determine what will be produced. For example, most advertising is directed at consumers to generate a need, often one that consumers did not know they had. Moreover, once needs are widespread, such as a desire for video games or high-technology skateboards, consumers and manufacturers begin to seek variants of these products, like home computer games and in-line skates. Thus, as consumers become conditioned to being stimulated by marketing ploys, their desires and needs for new products are constantly escalating, stimulating increasingly diverse market demand. And, as manufacturers become dependent on shifts in needs and consumer preferences, they assume the risks in producing new outputs.

As markets become the driving force of the economy in post-industrial systems, the production of services for facilitating the constant reformation of capital for new market niches and for conducting transactions in ever more differentiated and global markets increases. This production of services is also market driven, and it tends to create metamarkets in which financial instruments (stocks, bonds, money, mortgages, insurance premiums, pools of debt and capital) are themselves marketed in increasingly complex ways. This complexity furthers demand for services—from computer systems, sales brokers, and highly trained analysts to clerks and secretaries. Thus, as physical capital—whether in both its more liquid forms or in actual productive implements—moves about the domestic and world economic systems, markets for servicing this flow expand and differentiate in ways providing even more demand for services. Just how far this process can go is uncertain, but it is clear that the servicing revolution is not over.

The net result of these forces is for some pools of human capital to find themselves in a more vulnerable market position. High-skill service positions are less vulnerable, although efforts of corporations to "downsize" and become more efficient in world-level economic competition can make even this sector of the labor market vulnerable. Semiskilled clerical labor becomes even more vulnerable with such downsizing, increasingly pushed into a reserve labor pool of "temporary" workers who work for subcontractors. The semiskilled worker in manual manufacturing is the most vulnerable, as automation and/or export of their jobs shrink demand relative to supply in this portion of the labor market. Labor markets thus are driven by changes in productive forces in several directions: (1) the loss of lower- or semiskilled manufacturing jobs, even as the factory system differentiates; (2) the gain in high-technology, high-skilled service positions, (e.g., research and engineering, brokering, accounting, computer science, research, education, banking, finance, insuring, etc.), which require advanced educational credentials and which cannot be exported; and (3) manual and nonmanual service positions (e.g., secretaries, fast-food employment, maintenance, caretaking, retail sales, repair, upkeep, etc.), which are necessary to keep the domestic economy operating. The dilemma facing such systems is twofold: (1) can the low- and semiskilled pool of human capital be fully employed?; (2) can corporate units increasingly involved in world-level gathering, manufacturing, and distribution be controlled by national-level political, social, and economic forces?

POST-MODERNIZATION?

Post-industrialization can be seen as inherent in industrialization, per se. In the eyes of many, however, the processes of industrialization and post-industrialization have created a fundamentally new kind of society—indeed, a new phase in societal evolution. If new technologies attaching inanimate sources of energy to machines and labor in factory systems, new nonkin organizational forms like corporate bureaucracies, new systems of private property, new and differentiated markets, and new service-oriented production were all the marks of modernization driven by industrialization and post-industrialization, then these forces have reached such high levels that a new "postmodern" stage in human development has begun (see e.g., Crook, Pakulski, and Waters 1992; Harvey 1989; Lash 1990; Lash and Urry 1987; Seidman and Wagner 1992; Touraine 1988). There is no clear consensus on just what distinguishes modernization from post-modernization, but certain trends in economy are viewed as particularly important driving forces in reorganizing human societies.

Commodification

Once open markets become highly differentiated and dynamic, virtually all domains of the social world can be viewed as a commodity that has a "price" and that can be bought and sold. Even arenas of social life previously immune to such market forces, such as personal feelings, life-styles, values, and traditions, can now be invaded and "colonized" (Habermas [1973] 1976). When virtually all things, persons, relationships, behaviors, activities, symbols, thoughts, and ideas can be bought and sold, the social order is fundamentally changed—at least, according to those who see a new post-modern phase to have evolved.

Commodification is not only the result of free, open, and profit-driven markets, it is also the result of media processes that give individuals access to the symbols, life-styles, behaviors, traditions, tastes, and preferences of others. Advertising is built on these media processes, and its effectiveness depends on stimulating consumers to want new products and services. But advertising must constantly create "newness" to exert its effects on market demand—sometimes by repackaging and recycling the old; at other times by actually making something innovative and original, and frequently by usurping the symbols, tastes, life-styles, and traditions of other nations, communities, ethnicities, and classes. In this escalating process, little is sacred or off-limits, and all can be used to make advertising pitches or to make products. Such commodification, it is argued, makes traditions, ethnicity, community, tastes, life-styles, behaviors, dress, symbols, and ideas less real, less powerful, and less attached to the social structures in which they once were embedded. These new commodities, which previously marked important social activities and structures, can now be purchased and used as life-style props or as expressions of taste in ways that dilute their original meaning and significance. These commodities become symbols that float free from their origins, thereby losing their significance and making social life an incessant consumption of superficial markers of once-important realities.

Hyperdifferentiation and Dedifferentiation

For some, differentiation of activities, symbol systems, organizations, and other activities reaches such high levels that a kind of *de*differentiation occurs (Crook, Pakulski, and Waters 1992). The idea here is that as culture and social structure become hyperdifferentiated—incessantly splitting into ever more distinct types of symbols, categories, and economic specialties—the boundaries among these hyperdifferentiated dimensions of social life are weakened, becoming open to all and easily penetrated. The result is that any person or group can usurp the symbols, dress, mannerisms, and organizational forms of other persons and groups, especially in an economy that makes everything available for purchase and that produces media access to virtually any aspect of culture, activity, or organization. As partitions break down, cultural symbols marking these boundaries have been disconnected from the structures that generated them. As a result, these symbols become free-floating and easily adopted by others. Social life becomes a collage of symbols with little capacity to inspire and even less capacity to denote and mark points of difference and differentiation. And as hyperdifferentiation, coupled with commodification, produces this outcome, social life loses texture, substance, and meaning.

Hyperrationalization

Rational calculation of costs and benefits comes to dominate a society as profit-oriented markets extend to virtually all spheres of life. Increased levels of impersonality, formality, technical specialization, and cost calculations all become essential features of social relations as bureaucratization prevails in economic and other arenas of social organization. As these processes continue, they generate a hyperrationality—a concern with efficiency, speed, and profit—which, ironically, can generate less efficiency, speed, or profit (Ritzer 1993). For example, "fast-food" restaurants are often not very fast, because they attract too many customers at peak times and force them to line up and wait; bureaucracies can become big, bloated, inflexible, and inefficient; computer trading in stocks, using programmed "rationality," can cause markets to collapse when all programs simultaneously seek to "sell."

Hyperrationality also invites countermovements in art, alternative lifestyles, and religious fundamentalism, which seek to overcome or even to attack the impersonality of cost-benefit calculations. Rationality thus invites its opposite—social movements against rationality—and these movements can often seek to destroy what is rational.

More significantly, the recognition of the imperfections of rationality leads some corporate units to reduce hierarchy; to extend boundaries via information hookups; to require flexible and generalized skills of human capital; and to construct more flexible, fluid, and informal work networks—all of which discourage precise cost-benefit analysis, speed at all costs, and impersonality in favor of less calculable informal and personal work relations. Or because economic activities often can be performed more efficiently and cheaply outside a corporate structure, subcontracting to small-scale specialists increases, creating cadres of self-employed providers of services (from computer consulting, engineering, payroll, and finance to maintenance and transportation) that are less bureaucratically organized, especially if they remain small. Thus, some argue that the "irrationality of hyperrationality" creates fundamentally new forms of economic organization, revolving around teamwork, flexibility, reduced authority, temporary employment, and contracting services to outside providers (Kanter 1989).

CONCLUSION

Just whether these transformations represent a "new type" of society—as distinguishable from the industrial as the industrial was from the agrarian—is difficult to tell. There can be little doubt that certain trends will change the organization of human economies (Block 1990). However, with less hyperbole than post-modernist, we can conclude by listing some of these changes:

1. Increased production of services as a proportion of economic output, and increased reliance on computer-driven machines or less expensive human capital outside an economy's borders.
2. Mass and differentiated marketing, with niche markets for an increasing variety and volume of goods, services, symbols, or virtually anything.
3. Globalization of all economic activity so that gathering, producing, and distributing of all goods and services will involve the economies of other states.
4. Bifurcation of human capital into an elite, highly skilled and high-wage labor pool on one side, and a vulnerable less-skilled and lower-wage labor pool on the other side.
5. Restructuring of gathering, producing, and distributing corporate units toward less hierarchy, more extension of boundaries across space (through information technologies), more flexible and changeable teamwork activity, and more reliance on outside service providers.[11]
6. Ever greater reliance on new technologies for gathering, producing, and distribution, especially as world-level competition among corporations and their state sponsors intensifies.

It cannot be known whether these trends will go on forever, or whether they mark the beginnings of a new post-modern society. Whatever the merits of these changes in creating a new phase in societal evolution, these transformative forces are not solely generated by the economy alone. Rather, the economy is dramatically influenced by its institutional environment, the topic of the next chapter.

---

[11] For a review of the various views of organizational structure, especially "post-bureaucratic" forms, see: Nohria and Gulati (1994).

Chapter
3

Economy in Institutional Context

Much of what occurs in an institution inheres in the internal dynamism of its elements, but no institution is isolated from its environment. The dynamic interplay among the basic elements of an economy—technology, physical capital, human capital, entrepreneurship, and property—are thus influenced by other institutional systems, such as kinship, religion, polity, law, and education (Granovetter 1985). Conversely, as we will explore in successive chapters on other institutional systems, the economy shapes how each of these other systems is structured and operates. Indeed, the economy is perhaps the single most important institutional environment for other institutional systems, and for this reason we have opened with a long chapter on the economy. For the present, however, our concern is with how the economy *is influenced by* its institutional environment—particularly kinship, education, religion, polity, and law.

KINSHIP AND ECONOMY

The system of kinship, or the organization of relations among individuals by blood and marital ties, will exert varying effects depending on the type of economy—whether hunter-gatherer, horticultural, agrarian, industrial, or post-industrial. This variation becomes evident when assessing the consequences of kinship on each of the basic elements of the economy.

Kinship and Technology

Kinship was the principal source of technology in more-traditional societies, from hunting and gathering to more advanced agrarianism. In highly traditional societies without a written language or with very high levels of illiteracy, technology was stored in people's minds; and while in some advanced agrarian systems written language and schools began to store technology, the technology needed for most economic tasks was cerebral (Parsons 1966). Such technology was thus made available to the economy through family socialization of the young by older kinsmen. Just as the family imparted other cultural components such as values, beliefs, religious dogmas, and traditions, so it passed on to children basic knowledge about the environment. By the time the young were ready to become full-fledged participants in the economy, much of the knowledge about manipulation of the environment, or technology, had been implanted in their minds and was therefore available to the economy.

In more-advanced traditional economies, some children were partially socialized in school structures where knowledge was disseminated by reading books and other manuscripts, but much knowledge acquired in this way in agrarian societies tended to be religious or connected to a profession such as law rather than technological. For only in industrial and post-industrial economies do these new structures and methods of knowledge retrieval come to revolve primarily around technology.

Technological expansion was limited when it had to be stored in people's minds and transmitted through family socialization. Kinship norms specified what knowledge was to be transmitted by whom and how; therefore, innovation became difficult since norms did not encourage people to discover new ways to manipulate the environment. Rather, emphasis was on the transmission of existing knowledge. Aside from inhibiting technological innovation, kinship systems could also discourage the acceptance—at least initially—of knowledge from other populations, because it could threaten traditional kinship practices. Thus while kinship was a major source of technology for horticultural and agrarian activity, it often could inhibit the expansion and discovery of new technologies.

This inhibitory effect of kinship was greatest in horticultural systems where kinship systems were more elaborate and revolved around linked nuclear families (of parents and their offspring) in ever-larger social units. Typically, extended families composed of linked nuclear families were joined to form lineages; lineages, in turn, were grouped to form clans; and clans could be linked to form moieties. Here, because virtually all activity in the society was organized by kinship, the norms tended to be conservative, vested in tradition, and less open to what could be perceived as potentially disruptive changes in knowledge.

In hunting and gathering systems, where kinship was very simple—being comprised of nuclear families loosely grouped into bands—the kinship was also a conservative force, because it was one of the organizing principles of the society. And if new technologies were introduced, the entire society would change—as has occurred again and again over the last ten thousand years as hunting-gathering populations have virtually disappeared when exposed to, and forced to compete with, horticultural and agrarian populations.

When kinship began to differentiate from the economy, technological innovation became more likely since it would not directly threaten the organization of the family and its key functions of procreation, socialization, and social support. Such innovative potential escalated as alternative structures within the economy itself or outside the economy in other institutions, such as education, were successively differentiated. Only with advanced agrarianism and dramatically with industrialization, however, did a full separation between economy and kinship occur, isolating kinship from important technological effects on the economy.

Kinship and Human Capital

In all societies, kinship is the ultimate source of the labor pool, since without kinship to regulate reproduction, procreation, and socialization, human capital would not exist, nor could it possess the necessary motives, orientations, and skills to play roles in the economy. For hunting-gathering, horticultural, and even advanced agrarian economies, kinship was sufficient as a source of human capital. But beginning with some advanced agrarian systems and accelerating with industrialization and post-industrialization, kinship became inadequate for imparting at least some of the crucial attributes of human capital. These attributes include (1) new kinds of *trade skills*, (2) new *interpersonal styles*, and (3) new forms of highly *specialized knowledge*.

Trade Skills   Skills in all economic positions are both mental and manual. In developed post-industrial economies, extensive manual skills, such as those required of machine operatives, mechanics, and repair personnel, still must be utilized. But increasingly mental skills and the ability to gather, sort, and evaluate information and make decisions are necessary. Instead of physical dexterity, mental dexterity is crucial because the economic processes of gathering and producing become relatively unproblematic in industrial and post-industrial economies and are better handled by technology and its byproduct, the machine. Furthermore, occupations involved in the processes of distributing and servicing are distinctly mental in character, requiring expanded mental skills in the work force.

Interpersonal Styles   Economic positions, whether the factory assembly line or administrative bureaucracy, rely on a host of interpersonal skills, or styles, which usually cannot be acquired within kinship. Such interpersonal styles include (Parsons 1951): (a) neutrality and (b) specificity.

Norms in modern economic structures require labor to interact comparatively neutrally, controlling somewhat the expression of emotion. A factory or bureaucracy is a complex web of specialized positions, and if employees could freely vent frustrations, depressions, hates, loves, and jealousies, the efficiency of the organization would decline as the capacity to pace, schedule, time, or standardize work became increasingly disrupted by emotional strains. Under these conditions, norms will tend to emphasize some degree of neutrality, and workers must become capable of interacting in such neutral situations.

Interaction on the job in a factory or bureaucracy tends to be highly compartmentalized, as most others are treated as specialized functionaries to whom only delimited and job-related obligations are owed. This situation forces employees in economic organizations to display at least some capacity to interact only segmentally—or with what is sometimes termed "specificity"—with their coworkers.

And even as the organization of work becomes less hierarchical, more informal, team-oriented, and spread across space via information networks, some degree of neutrality and specificity must be retained. Indeed, the interpersonal skills become even more complex, requiring interpersonal "fronts" of informality even as neutrality, specificity, and goal-directness prevail (Goffman 1967).

Specialized Knowledge Norms in modern economies frequently require workers to have specialized knowledge, with each displaying expertise in only a delimited area. Acquiring such narrow expertise often involves a period of technical and specialized training and instruction. And as more-generalized but still highly technical skills are increasingly required in many positions of post-industrial systems, the inadequacy of kin socialization to provide these skills becomes even more evident.

Yet kinship is not irrelevant to acquiring trade skills, interpersonal skills, and knowledge. Family apprenticeships and family-run businesses are still very prominent features of even post-industrial economies, and obviously in these cases family can be both the organizing and socializing units of workers. Still, in both family-run and nonkin businesses, kinship's influence on acquiring the motivations, skills, and knowledge necessary for participation in economic positions is indirect, operating through its effects on other socializing agents, most notably the educational system. The motivations to perform well in the school system, which will bestow those credentials that give access to jobs, are acquired primarily in the family. Similarly, many of the interpersonal skills necessary for success in schools, such as classroom demeanor and attentiveness to teachers, as well as background knowledge acquired through preschool training and parental instruction, are imparted to children in the home. A family's resource levels are also crucial in terms of the finances and time that can be devoted to helping students do well in the classroom and in assisting them to move up through the educational hierarchy (especially the financing of university education, but also in preparing students for standardized tests which are so important in most educational systems of the world for determining which high school and college students can attend). Thus, with industrialization and post-industrialization, the most important effects of family increasingly become indirect, influencing school performance as it certifies human capital for insertion into varying positions within the economy or other institutional systems where they will earn a living.

EDUCATION AND ECONOMY

In advanced horticultural and agrarian systems, education began to emerge from kinship as a distinct set of structures. Yet education tended to be confined to elites, who, for the most part, acquired knowledge and skills that confirmed their membership in a privileged status group rather than knowledge or skills relevant to their participation in the economy. Moreover, to the extent that emerging higher-educational systems during the agrarian era imparted skills and knowledge beyond those confirming elite status, they emphasized training for professions, such as the clergy, law, and medicine, rather than skills and knowledge directly involved in the economy (Ben-David 1971). Some organizations of higher learning in the Arabic world and, later, in Europe and China did train students in what was to become science, although the connection between science and economic technology was not strong (Huff 1993). More typically, some nonelites began to be recruited to the emerging educational system so that they could acquire skills that would enable them to perform administrative duties in the state and elsewhere in the society. As this process of nonelite recruitment was extended, education historically became an increasingly visible institutional system. Still, the vast majority of the population in agrarian systems remained illiterate, acquiring knowledge and skills within kinship structures.

With industrialization, the educational system expands and begins to perform many of the socialization and social placement functions that were formerly the exclusive domain of kinship. It is not clear whether it is the economy and its need for reskilled labor that initiates this process (Meyer 1977) or the polity and its need to create a nation-state and civic culture bestowing legitimacy on the state (Boli 1989) as well as its need to break down traditional patterns of ascription toward a merit system (Fuller 1991). In either or both cases, a set of cultural beliefs that expansion of education is the key to economic development and state building have emerged in the industrial societies of the world. As a result, the polity has worked to extend the lower educational system of primary and secondary schools to the masses of the population and, at the same time, to increase selective access to higher education based on merit and achievement (Rubinson and Browne 1994, 591–92). Indeed, this set cultural beliefs has become so pervasive that the leaders and the population of late-industrializing societies all view the extension of education at all levels as a way to jump-start the economic growth and to cultivate political stability (Meyer 1992). These leaders of developing societies are also encouraged by the World Bank to develop their educational systems. Yet, the expansion of education and the upgrading of the skills posed by human capital tend to increase economic growth only when polity is able to avoid war, restrain its tendency to impose despotic control on citizens, develop coherent economic policies, and construct trade alliances. Thus, expansion of education is a contingent factor (Brint 1996); by itself, it does not cause economic growth in industrializing societies. Only in combination with the effective use of power does education "kick in" and stimulate economic growth.

Indeed, the economies of China, India, Korea, Singapore, and Taiwan, and other emerging economic powers of east Asia only began to grow with liberalization of governmental policies, but the existence of a well-educated pool of human capital has made this growth spectacular.

The effects of differentiation and expansion of the educational system on the economy are complicated by additional considerations. First, expansion of the educational system is only partly the result of demands for reskilled workers; and thus the new skills—both trade and interpersonal—of the human capital can be acquired without needs for them within the economy. Rather, the political system may want resocialized citizens for its political agenda; or as we will see, educational credentials often become more a way to certify membership in status groups than a response to needs in the economy for a highly skilled labor force. Second, the effects of education on the economy can be indirect. For example, if the extension of education produces "new citizens" loyal to the state, then it may be in the resulting political stability produced by political socialization and the state's capacity to direct physical capital to the economy (and away from social control) that education exerts its influence on the economy. Thus, in assessing the effects of education on the economy, we must remain attuned to the difficulty in making this assessment (Sanders 1992).

Education and Human Capital

In general terms, as noted above, education of human capital can encourage economic growth when governmental policies have entrepreneurial consequences for encouraging physical-capital investment, for infusing technology, and for redefining property in ways that stimulate investments of physical capital and technology in production. With investments in physical capital and technology, the capacity of education to generate both the interpersonal and trade skills of incumbents in the economy can then augment these investments.

With respect to interpersonal skills, schools are formal bureaucracies, requiring performance and evaluation in terms of objective standards. As a consequence, they impart capacities for interpersonal neutrality and specificity, as well as willingness to learn bodies of knowledge and to be judged in accordance with established standards. This organization of education approximates the bureaucratic organization of the modern economy and serves not only as a building ground but also as an arena for rehearsal of some of the fundamental attributes necessary in a modern labor force. Schools have thus represented a "halfway house" between the family and economy, imparting what the family cannot and, in so doing, becoming the principal institutional source of labor in modern societies.

In regard to trade skills, a review of the relevant studies suggests that education affects economic growth in a conditional manner (Rubinson and Browne 1994; Brint 1996). The impact of education on economic growth is greatest when there is a high degree of correspondence between the trade skills required in the economy and the skills actually imparted in the schools. This correspondence is difficult to maintain, for several reasons. First, because national educational systems are often created for political and ideological reasons (such as indoctrination into a political culture), the curricula can come to reflect these political priorities for social control more than the demands of the labor market for workers with particular skills. Under these conditions, the needs of the economy are not so readily translated into the school curricula, thus reducing the influence of educational socialization on economic growth. Second, the effects of education on the economy vary for different levels of the educational system. In general, those positions of the educational system that respond more directly to demands in the labor market for skilled technical workers will exert the most influence on economic growth; and typically, this responsiveness is (a) greatest in the vocational portions of the secondary (high) school systems that service the broad middle classes of a society and (b) least in secondary schools servicing the lower classes and in the universities that socialize elites, who are often as much interested in acquiring cultural capital as labor skills (Garnier and Hage 1990).

Socialization in schools is connected to their allocative and social placement functions, which, ironically, further distort the effects of education on the economy. Schools become the principle allocative mechanism in industrial and post-industrial societies, but only part of this social placement process is directly connected to the actual needs of the economy. Much of the pressure for expansion of higher education comes from status competition, as individuals seek to acquire credentials that give them prestige and honor. Similarly, the push for educational credentials often comes from those portions of the labor market, such as the bureaucracies of the state or the educational system itself, that are not economic. Thus, the educational system often responds to labor markets not directly involved in placing individuals in organizations involved in gathering resources, producing goods, and distributing goods and services (Fuller and Rubinson 1992).

These forces can potentially initiate "credential inflation," where ever-escalating levels of educational certification (with higher and higher degrees) become essential for success in the labor market. Such is particularly likely in market-driven economies where demand in the labor market is driven by noneconomic organizations, where sectors of human capital must compete intensely for positions in both the economic and noneconomic sectors of employment, and where employers look for easy and standardized ways to evaluate skill and knowledge. Such inflation of educational credentials often occurs *before* there is need in the economy for a highly educated labor force. Even in post-industrial economies like the United States, many college-educated persons (and even those with graduate degrees) must work in lower-level service occupations requiring (in terms of actual skill levels) only a high school diploma. The United States is the most extreme case, sending half of its secondary school graduates on to college and assuring that there will be intense competition in the labor market, thereby driving labor to seek even higher educational credentials in search of a competitive advantage (Collins 1979).

As a consequence of such inflation, relatively low-level positions, such as clerks, receptionists, and secretaries, begin not only to absorb but demand highly educated incumbents. These incumbents will be overeducated for their jobs, but as they become more of a fixture in these positions, the demeanor, "cultural capital," and interpersonal styles required of incumbents in these positions will change toward those of the middle classes, thereby placing non-college graduates at yet another competitive disadvantage in the labor market. As the "cultural capital" (knowledge, tastes, demeanor, speech styles, life-styles) associated with overeducated and underemployed human capital escalates, those without this cultural capital become increasingly excluded from positions that they formerly held, dividing the society further—not only in terms of educational credentials and income, but associated cultural symbols and other aspects of cultural capital (Bourdieu 1984).

Education and Technology

The technology of modern economies is complex and extensive, and no one person can store much of this technology in the mind. Because of these limitations in human intellect, complex networks of storehouses for technology emerge in modern societies—for instance, schools, libraries, research organizations, patent offices, government files, and offices within various economic organizations.

These elaborate storage facilities generate severe problems of retrieval concerning how to make the technology in this vast cultural storehouse available to the economy. The institution of the family is inadequate to the task, for the combined knowledge of all family members is very small in comparison to the vastness of technology in post-industrial systems. As a consequence of this limitation, educational structures in post-industrial societies are not only a cultural storehouse of libraries, computer files, and research facilities, but also a principal source of retrieving technology and making it available to the economy. Just how this transformation of education from a training ground for religious and political elites or for narrow professions like law and medicine to a principal source of technology occurs varies greatly from society to society. Sometimes political elites, such as those in Russia and China, have deliberately initiated technical schools and institutes to store and retrieve technology. In other instances, as in the United States and England, the process has occurred mostly by trial and error as school curricula and facilities slowly and sporadically adjusted under pressures from the economy or polity. Whatever the exact historical process, educational structures in modern societies eventually develop close connections with the economy and come to store and provide its technology.

Universities are particularly crucial in this interchange between the economy and education. By viewing the graduates of undergraduate, graduate, and professional schools of all the colleges and universities in a modern society in the aggregate as a "knowledge mass" to be inserted into the economy, it is easy to picture one way in which socialization processes within the institution of education have retrieval consequences for the economy. No one graduate may possess large amounts or a wide scope of technological knowledge, but the total knowledge of the millions of graduates injected each year into the economy is enormous.

The level of technology is constantly increasing in industrial and post-industrial societies, primarily because of the interconnections among economy, education, and science. Within the economy many roles concern the expansion and application of new knowledge—usually termed "research and development"—to basic economic processes, but these are still related to education and science. The still-emerging institutional complex of science is concerned with the acquisition and systemization of knowledge about the world. As the profession of scientists becomes increasingly widespread and interrelated in modern societies, so do the general value premises and idealized norms guiding conduct in these positions (Merton 1957, 574–606): universalism, communism, disinterestedness, and organized skepticism. "Universalism" refers to the normative ideal emphasizing that data about the world are to be judged by preestablished, agreed upon, and objective criteria; "communism" in Merton's sense concerns the scientist's obligation to communicate findings and discoveries to other scientists; "disinterestedness" holds that scientists are concerned most with truth rather than glory and personal gain; and "organized skepticism" stipulates that no idea or finding is sacred and above reexamination and formulation. Only in advanced industrial and post-industrial systems do these norms and the status position of scientists become widespread, being lodged in a variety of core institutional systems.

Of course, these norms represent cultural ideals and are often violated in actual practice. In fact, only within higher education do they exercise their full effect; for within private industry and government, norms of communism are compromised as scientists engage in secret and applied research. Even within research universities, where governmental and military research is often performed, norms of secretiveness can prevail and displace those of communism. In fact, it might be safe to hypothesize that as scientists become more widely distributed within various institutional spheres in modern societies and as they increasingly become engaged in applied research, many of the cultural ideals of pure science begin to break down (Bloch 1973; Cotgrove and Box 1970). This projection rings true for education in the United States and other countries with long traditions of higher education.

However disruptive applied research within educational structures may be to the norms of science, one fact is inescapable: The amount of technology flowing from educational structures to the economy and other institutional spheres is increasing. Despite the clear dangers to pure (as opposed to applied) scientific research, educational structures will continue to be a major institutional source of technology for the economy. For example, much of the basic knowledge for genetic engineering, for lasers used in surgery and weapons, for new imaging techniques, for computers, and in virtually all areas of advanced technology has come from university research and from the labor skills of knowledge acquired in universities.

RELIGION AND ECONOMY

Religion is organized around beliefs and rituals directed at asupernatural realm of forces, powers, and deities. Religion deals with many of the nonempirical and cosmic parameters of social life. Nonetheless, this fact does not mean that religious beliefs and rituals cannot have profound impact on everyday activities within the economy—especially in advanced hunting-gathering and horticultural systems, where religious beliefs and rituals have far-reaching entrepreneurial consequences for the economy. In such economies, religion mobilizes actors to perform crucial economic roles and reinforces economic norms guiding role behavior.

Religious beliefs can, for example, mobilize actors to engage in economic roles by reducing the anxiety often associated with economic behavior. By providing people with a recourse to rituals designed to invoke the benevolence (or at least suspend the malevolence) of supernatural beings and/or forces, individuals become willing to engage in uncertain and hazardous economic activity. One of the best illustrations of this comes from Bronislaw Malinowski's ([1925] 1955) account of the Trobriand Islanders' use of extensive magic rites before participating in dangerous deep-sea fishing expeditions. Such rituals alleviated anxiety and thus mobilized individuals to engage in this difficult economic activity.

Religious beliefs and rituals can also have entrepreneurial consequences for the economy by reinforcing crucial economic norms, as is illustrated by Firth's (1936) account of Tikopian fishing rituals. One of the more elaborate rituals among the Tikopians revolved around preparation of fishing equipment—especially canoes—for expeditions into the open sea. Such preparation was an obvious economic necessity, but it was considered particularly necessary because it was a religious ritual having significance for the supernatural. Hence overhauling and preparing canoes for fishing was just one part of an elaborate ritual concerning the Tikopians' obligations to secure food offerings for the gods. Under these conditions, economic tasks were performed more rapidly, efficiently, and with greater harmony.

In a very real sense, then, religious rituals in "sacredizing" crucial economic norms increase normative conformity. This religious reinforcement of norms, coupled with the mobilizing consequence of religious rituals, represents a major institutional source of entrepreneurship in traditional societies since religion secures the involvement of labor in key economic activities and makes this activity more efficient and harmonious.

Perhaps one of the most dramatic statements on the entrepreneurial effects of religion on the economy is Max Weber's ([1904–5] 1958) essay on the impact of the Protestant Reformation on the emergence of modern industrial capitalism. Weber hypothesized that the worldly ascetic elements of Protestant beliefs and the forms of behavior that they condoned (e.g., individualism, acquisitiveness, thrift, and good works) accelerated the accumulation and organization of basic economic elements into an early industrial economy. Weber's thesis was not a one-sided assertion that these religious beliefs and the behavior that they initiated were the sole cause of economic development in Europe. On the contrary, Weber emphasized that given a certain level of capital, labor, technology, and private property, Protestantism encouraged the pursuit of profit which, in the end, led to the organization of technology, physical, human capital, and property in ways causing the Industrial Revolution. Weber was thus pointing to Protestantism as a major institutional source of entrepreneurship during early industrialization. However, many critics argue that the causal arrow should be reversed: Expanding market activity and commercialism changed religious beliefs to a pattern more compatible with emerging capitalism (Swanson 1967; Wuthnow 1980, 64; 1989). In either scenario, however, the transformation of religion, once in place, would have facilitated the dynamism of capitalism.

Yet, because religion is often a conservative force, embodying traditional values, it can work to retard and arrest economic development—as Weber argued was the case for China ([1915] 1951), India ([1916–17] 1958), and ancient Judea ([1917–20] 1952) which, in the agrarian era, were as technologically advanced as Europe but which did not make the breakthrough to industrialism. It is this conservatism inhering in religion that eventually has led to the differentiation and segregation of religion and economy with industrialism and post-industrialism. The dynamic and change-generating processes in market-driven economies often become incompatible with traditional religious beliefs, causing some degree of separation between the economy and religion in order for gathering, producing, and distribution to be freed from religious traditionalism.

Even if religion becomes structurally differentiated from the economy, however, it still subtly and perhaps indirectly influences economic processes (Wuthnow 1994). First, religion is, itself, a large-scale enterprise which creates (a) demand in the labor market for those who sustain the organizational base of this enterprise, and more importantly, (b) flows of capital from economic investment to support the operation of organized religion. As such, religion influences the distribution of human and physical capital in the economy.

Second, and probably more important, the actions of individuals and corporate units in an economy—even a relentlessly market- and profit-driven economy—are influenced, to varying degrees, by religious values and beliefs. This influence takes a number of potential paths. One is that human capital is guided by religious beliefs and value premises. The extreme case is Karl Marx's view that religion is the "opiate" of masses who, because of their religious beliefs, cannot see their true class interests. Or as E. P. Thompson (1966) later argued, nineteenth-century Protestantism disciplined the working classes, keeping them from being too unruly and walking off their jobs, restraining them from alcohol use and the resulting disorderly conduct, and, in general, turning them into responsive and comparatively docile appendages to machines. A less-extreme scenario sees religion as influencing human capital to maintain religious values (e.g., hard work, honesty, charity) in the workplace in ways that further productivity. Religious values also influence the economy comes via corporate actors who perform "good works" and "charity" in the name of religiously sanctioned values. Here, the corporation as a whole mobilizes to realize noneconomic goals—as, for example, when corporations collect money from employees for charities (often through systematic payroll deductions) or as when employees are organized for community service.

Third, and perhaps most significant, there is always a tension between the rational-instrumental goals and requirements of capitalism, on the one side, and the value-laden goals of religion, on the other (Wuthnow 1994, 630–34). For even as religion works compatibly with economic action—as when workers perform diligently in the name of the gods, or when corporations perform charitable works—there is a potential tension, sometimes subtle and hardly noticeable but at other times clearly manifest. This tension can exist at the individual level, as when workers question the meaning, ends, and reasons for their labor in terms of religiously-inspired value premises. Or, it can operate at a more macro level, as is the case when corporate (self-) interests for profits clash with religious (value) interests. Even as these points of tension play themselves out, religion is rarely the dominant force in industrial and post-industrial societies. Its effect is often difficult to measure because of the overpowering force of market-driven economies and their sponsorship by state power.

At times, however, religion is more dominant, as when religious rather than business elites gained control of the revolution in Iran, setting up a conservative theocracy and restricting the activities of merchants and markets (Arjomand 1988). This system has proven to be at least minimally viable because of the export nature of oil production, which can be implemented without generating internal pressures for change. However, Islamic fundamentalism can inhibit the internal dynamism of markets and, in turn, gathering and producing; and we can expect that without oil exports, the Islamic societies economically stagnate would, resisting secular technological innovations, concentrations of secularly-directed physical and human capital, and profit-oriented and secular entrepreneurial organizations.

Religion is, therefore, increasingly likely to become segregated from economy with industrialization, freeing the economy from the constraints of tradition and releasing the potential for internal dynamism (Bellah 1964). Some of this dynamism will come from the economy itself, but much will still depend on other institutions, particularly law and polity.

LAW AND ECONOMY

For societies to become more complex, they must develop a legal system, consisting of laws regulating relationships and defining deviance, agents to enforce laws, mediating procedures for resolving disputes, and legislative procedures for developing new laws (Vago 1994, 1–47; Evan 1980; Hoebel 1954).

In hunting-gathering, horticultural, and even some agrarian systems, law was a recessive institution, being fused with kinship, religion, and polity. A connection to polity has always remained as a distinct legal system has become differentiated; but except in religious theocracies like Iran, the system reveals considerable autonomy from other institutions, including the polity where only the legislative functions of the legal system remain embedded.

In simple horticultural economies, kinship and religion were major sources of entrepreneurship, as kinship norms and religious rituals guided, coordinated, and directed economic activity as well as mobilized commitment and willingness of actors to play economic roles. Such entrepreneurial mechanisms were adequate in economies with low levels of all economic elements (technology, physical and human capital, and property) and very simple gathering, producing, distributing, and servicing processes. As the economy expanded and became more clearly separated from kinship and religion, however, these entrepreneurial mechanisms increasingly proved inadequate. Through political edict and/or a long process of trial and error as conflicts in the economy intensified, law began to exert an influence on the organization of economic activity (Turner 1980).

Probably the initial economic sphere in which law exerted a visible influence was in the emerging marketplace. As soon as economies could generate a surplus, exchange of goods and commodities occurred, with such exchanges eventually becoming regularized through laws and their enforcement. For example, if a Trobriand Islander in the Pacific failed to meet exchange obligations, laws prescribed that others in the community should refuse to engage in further exchanges with the offending party, resulting in the defaulter becoming isolated and economically vulnerable. In economies with more-developed markets, laws tended to expand their consequences for regulating exchange. This process was not always deliberate or intended, but rather occurred sporadically as individuals and organizations attempted to deal with conflicts, default, bad faith, and dishonesty in exchange transactions, as illustrated by the legal systems of feudal, preindustrial Europe. In the societies and territories comprising this area, laws tended to be tied to local urban centers and were established by common-law precedents as local court judges attempted to deal with emerging disputes. In the marketplace, a series of "merchant laws" also developed as merchants attempted to regularize market exchange. But even though these laws were binding and enforced, they often remained outside the formal legal system until long after they had become established among traders and merchants.

As economic activity became clearly differentiated from kinship with advanced agrarianism and industrialization, entrepreneurial problems expanded beyond those evident in the marketplace. For once kinship and religion ceased being the primary sources for the organization of gathering, producing, and servicing, nonkinship principles of entrepreneurship began to coordinate technology, capital, and labor. Hence, definitions of property and property relations became too complex for existing institutional systems. Just as when distributive or market processes moved outside the exclusive purview of kinship and were assumed by new principles of organization, so gathering, producing, and servicing had to be gradually organized in new ways. Two of these new forms of economic organization were the factory system and corporate administrative bureaucracies of industrial economies. While these structures have had far-reaching entrepreneurial consequences for the economy, they never can completely resolve problems concerning the organization of land, labor, capital, technology, and property rights.

And so, by various routes, with varying degrees of success, and under different historical conditions, selection processes have worked to create in most modern societies a legal system capable of having entrepreneurial consequences for these remaining problems. The legal system is also capable of dealing with a whole cluster of new problems created by the emergence of factories and bureaucracies (Block 1994). As is explored below, the history of economic development in the United States provides a useful illustration of how law has increased its entrepreneurial functions over the last 150 years.

Law and Physical Capital Accumulation

One of the contradictions inherent in a free-enterprise or capitalist system is that some corporations tend to gain a market advantage and then attempt to restrict and limit competition or enterprise. The end result of this process is that monopolies and oligopolies are likely to be formed, creating a situation where a few companies possess or control disproportionate amounts of the capital resources in a particular economic sphere. Monopoly and oligopoly are endemic tendencies in competitive market economies. During early industrialization, physical capital—money, machines, and other resources—became increasingly owned by a few companies in key productive areas, particularly steel, oil, lumber, and sugar. Once this concentration of capital had occurred, competition in the market decreased because a few corporations could fix prices, control distribution, and force suppliers of raw materials to sell exclusively to them. Beginning in 1890 in the United States, a series of antimonopoly laws—the Sherman Antitrust Act of 1890 and later the Clayton Act of 1917—began to regulate the degree of monopolization possible in the economy. Since then this trend has been buttressed by many additional laws—Robinson-Putnam Act, McGuire Act, Public Utility Holding Company Act, Miller-Tydings Act, Federal Reserve Act, and a host of others—restricting and regulating the formation of capital by a single corporation.

Even in more state-managed systems outside the United States, where government monopolies are common (though there is a recent trend toward "privatization" of government monopolies), laws must be developed to define the purview of these monopolies and their relationship to privately held capital. Thus, law becomes the major mechanism by which the distribution of physical capital is regulated. And in societies like Russia which have privatized rapidly, the selling of physical capital has been both chaotic and corrupt, since development of an adequate system of law for property and property rights—especially for property previously "owned" by the state—has lagged behind the selloff of government assets. Indeed, without adequate laws and their enforcement, a "Russian Mafia" has emerged to control much capital accumulation, increasing the corruption and violence associated with formation of physical capital.

Law and Human Capital

Violence has punctuated labor movement in the United States, and elsewhere as well. The issues of debate—child labor, minimum wages, eight-hour working days, overtime pay, retirement benefits, workers' compensation, and collective bargaining—often have moved toward open confrontation and violence. As the U.S. economy went from an agrarian to industrial basis of organization, the traditional ways of securing, organizing, and maintaining a labor force became increasingly inadequate; and though some laws pertaining to labor-management conflicts existed as early as 1915 (for example, the Adamson Act provided for an eight-hour day in some jobs), a concerted legal-system response to the problem occurred only in the 1930s with the passage of a series of laws specifying some of the conditions of labor's participation in the economy. The titles of these early laws best describe their entrepreneurial consequences: National Labor Relations Act, Labor-Management Reporting and Disclosure Act, Federal Mediation and Conciliation Service Act, Fair Labor Standards Act, and the Social Security Act. Less-descriptively named labor-management laws (e.g., the La Guardia Act and Taft-Hartley Act) also began to regulate the processes of securing and maintaining a labor force in the economy. Even more recent acts to rebalance labor-management relations (usually toward management's favor) are entrepreneurial in character.

Thus, as labor increasingly is inserted into economy via market processes—indeed, it is commodified and certified by educational credentials—the problems of integrating human and physical capital intensify to the point that they must be regulated. Law provides for this regulation, and without it, entrepreneurial processes in the economy will be problematic.

Law and Technology

Since the beginnings of the United States as a nation-state, law has encouraged technological expansion. Even the Constitution specifies that inventors should be protected; and George Washington noted in his inaugural address of 1789 the importance of "giving effective encouragement as well as the introduction of new and useful inventions." As early as 1790, the first patent law was implemented to protect and regulate the discovery of applied knowledge; and in 1836 this law was revised to outline the legal procedures for verifying inventions. In 1862 the Morrill Act established guidelines for founding and maintaining colleges "where the leading object shall be . . . to teach such branches of learning as are related to agriculture and mechanic arts."

The American legal system, like that in other market-driven industrial economies, has thus traditionally had entrepreneurial consequences for generating and organizing technology for the economy. Once law encourages, tolerates, and specifies procedures for cataloging and storing technology, then knowledge expands and proliferates at a rapid rate, because there exist a set of principles organizing the base upon which knowledge can be further extended.

The critical breakthrough in the relationship between technology and law in the United States and other market systems is the capacity to define and defend knowledge as property. Copyrights and patents are, in essence, legally sanctioned rights to claim ideas as private property which can be bought, sold, and licensed in markets. Once this becomes a realistic possibility, incentives for innovation escalate because profits can be made on the basis of the ideas alone, without having to instantiate them in physical capital. Moreover, when subject to market forces, the laws sanctioning technology as private property bias the development of idea systems toward economic ends, since this is where they are most likely to be supported and sold. As such, property laws facilitate technological innovation.

Law and Property

The Declaration of Independence in America defines "life, liberty, and the pursuit of happiness" as "inalienable rights." The original phrase, borrowed from French philosophy, was "life, liberty, and *property*" as inalienable rights—a point of emphasis that more directly reflects the dynamics not only of the U.S. system but all market systems as well. For until laws give rights to property, and unless a legal system can continually legislate additional laws that constantly define new domains and types of property, severe limits will constrain the development of technology, physical capital, human capital, and entrepreneurial activity.

Like technology, innovations defined as property are developed partly for their profit potential. However, other systems of incentives also exist (such as prestige in science for making important discoveries, and political elites' needs to possess superior military technologies). What is true of technology is true of all basic elements of an economy: Physical capital cannot be creatively assembled and utilized without legal guarantees on rights to enjoy profits from investments; human capital will not work as hard, or be readily organized in noncoercive ways, without legally binding regulations of work for wages; corporate structures, market systems, and other entrepreneurial forces will not be effective without the higher-order entrepreneurial effects of law on defining the nature and boundaries of corporate units and on regularizing contracts and exchange in markets.

The United States developed these legal rights to property at its founding, borrowing much from English common law (dressed up in French-inspired constitutional principles). In the history of many other populations, however, the legal system was insufficiently developed and differentiated from other institutions, with the result that developing legally defined property rights has been more difficult. Indeed, conflicting legal systems, such as those of the church versus those of the state, have presented problems of developing clear and consistent definitions of property. Under these conditions, tradition defines property, or "might makes right"—neither of which leads to dynamic entrepreneurship. Indeed, in the aftermath of a coercive system of state ownership in the former Soviet Union and its bloc of satellites, one of the biggest obstacles to economic development is that existing laws, law-enacting bodies, courts, and enforcement agents are not well suited for defining and adjudicating conflicts over property—especially technology, physical capital, and human capital. The result in Russia is chaos, corruption, conflict, and inefficiency in a society that desperately needs to mobilize these economic elements in a coherent way.

Law and Entrepreneurship

As is evident from these examples of law and economy in the United States and elsewhere in the industrial and post-industrial world, law operates as a higher-order entrepreneurial mechanism organizing physical and human capital, technology, and property. Without a semi-autonomous legal system, kinship, religion, elite privilege, and state coercion interfere with the development of these elements and their organization. As a result, a society will stay arrested and stagnated within a more traditional economic mode, or if industrialism is initiated, it will stumble and stall without the institutionalization of law.

POLITY AND ECONOMY

Polity is the consolidation and concentration of power or the capacity to control and regulate others for the purpose of mobilizing, allocating, and distributing a population and its resources towards ends and goals. Economy and polity are inexorably connected (Block 1994); as economy has expanded and produced a surplus beyond the subsistence needs of a population, the consolidation and use of power has increased (Lenski 1966)—slowly at first and then dramatically with movement to advanced horticulture and agrarianism.

In mobilizing, allocating, and distributing resources, the polity's main effect on economy has been to influence the amount of hard physical capital (gathering and producing implements), liquid capital (like money and other financial instruments), and infrastructures (such as roads, ports, railways) available to economic activity (Parsons and Smelser 1956). In so doing, polity also has influenced indirectly the level of technology, the pool of human capital, property, and entrepreneurship.

Polity and Physical Capital

In a hunting and gathering economy, where little capital exists beyond the bow and arrow, spears, and sticks, polity was comparatively inconspicuous because the economy of these societies could not generate sufficient economic surplus to support a distinctive political subsystem. Nor was one really necessary, because needs for regulation and control of a small, wandering population were easily managed by kinship and band. This lack of a need for polity is clearly illustrated by such geographically dispersed societies as the Inland Eskimos or Inuit and the !Kung-san of Africa. Among the traditional Inuit, leaders arose and receded in terms of how successful they were in basic economic activities (Fried 1967, 86–87). For example, a successful hunter would be followed by others and his advice sought, but he had no power to compel conformity to his wishes. Should he cease being successful, he also ceased being a leader. Among the !Kung-san, leadership was more stable, with an established headman directing certain crucial economic activities and tribal migrations. But this headman had no real power to sanction nonconformity to his wishes and directives (Schapera 1956). These two illustrations document probably the simplest kind of political subsystem, if we can even call it that (Fried 1967, 28–101); and though these leaders had some capacity to regulate how capital such as spears, bows and arrows, and other crude tools were used for hunting and gathering, their ability to regulate capital flows was not great and represented only the rudiments of the political power that was to become so evident in more-developed societies.

In horticultural and agrarian societies of the past, which were capable of generating an economic surplus and hence supporting a semi-autonomous political subsystem, and in which needs for regulating the larger population were escalating—and dramatically so—the polity came to have the power to appropriate economic surplus and then redistribute it. The typical pattern in horticultural systems involved certain kin groups in a society acquiring more territory and power than other kin groupings and utilizing this power to appropriate the economic surplus of other familial-economic units. In advanced horticultural and agrarian systems with an autonomous and clear-cut state army and administrative staff, appropriation became institutionalized into norms allowing the polity to tax economic surplus in accordance with some formula. Much of this surplus simply went to increase the wealth and privilege of an elite ruling class, but some was allocated to system goals—such as war, conquest, and public works—which had been established by the polity.

The dual processes of appropriation and reallocation profoundly affect the level of capital available to the economy because just how much economic surplus is extracted by government determines how much privately held capital is potentially available to expand the economy. In turn, the amount of appropriated capital reallocated to particular economic processes (as opposed to elite privilege and geopolitical adventurism through war) determines the basic profile of the economy. In traditional societies of the contemporary Third World, where a major system goal is economic development, these appropriation-allocation processes influence the rate and sector of industrialization. Frequently to control more precisely the accumulation of capital in the economy, these polities assume ownership or nationalize major concentrations of capital. Nationalization allows the polity to regulate directly the flow of appropriated capital into various economic processes while enabling government to control more directly the ratio of consumer to capital goods, the amount of money capital devoted to technological expansion, the distribution of labor, the kinds and levels of goods to be placed in the market.

In order for extensive appropriation by the polity to occur, it must possess the power to coerce compliance of other system units. More important for the long run, however, is the capacity of government to cultivate legitimacy, or the perception and belief by members of a population in the right of the polity to wield power and establish system goals. With legitimacy, the ability of polity to control the accumulation of capital in the economy is greatly expanded and the values, beliefs, religious dogmas, and customs that the polity may use to legitimate itself can also be employed to manipulate the population into accepting certain forms of appropriation and allocation of capital. Because the polity has control over many communication processes in a society, it can manipulate these symbolic aspects of culture to achieve certain goals. For example, when capital is accumulated for the production of weapons of war, it can be done much more effectively in the name of a "holy crusade," "national integrity and prestige," "to preserve cherished traditions," "in the name of God," "to save face," or to go to war in order to "end all wars" or "defend the world against some evil." By such *symbolic manipulation,* polity can pacify other system units and make endurable the accumulation of capital in areas not to their immediate interests.

In more-traditional societies, the related mechanisms of appropriation and symbolic manipulation increasingly are utilized by the polity to regulate the accumulation and flow of capital in the economy. In more-advanced economies, where clear systems of private property and dynamic markets prevail, these are supplemented by additional mechanisms for regulating capital formation, including tariffs and subsidies. *Tariffs* are limitations or bans imposed by the polity on the importation of certain goods and commodities in order to protect internal gathering and productive processes. Such limitations and bans enable the economy to accumulate capital in areas that would not develop if imports were allowed. By changing and altering such tariff restrictions, the polity can regulate the degree to which capital is accumulated around various productive processes. *Subsidies* are the bestowal of capital on certain economic units and sectors in gathering, producing, and distributing that government wishes to develop. These subsidies can take many forms, including direct purchases (as when government buys military hardware) and tax expenditures where government does not collect taxes on income that would otherwise be owed.

Polity also affects capital accumulation by infrastructural investments in roads, airports, ports, communications, sanitation, utilities, and other concentrations of physical capital that facilitate the operation of economic activities. On the one hand, expenditures on infrastructure pull capital that could be used to subsidize other economic activities. But on the other hand, these expenditures are usually seen as necessary "investments" to achieve societal goals, such as winning wars or spurring economic growth. With respect to the economy, these infrastructural investments facilitate additional capital investments, which in turn initiate the organization of technology, human capital, and property for new types of gathering, producing, and distributing.

Perhaps the most obvious way to influence the level of capital is for the government to print more or less money—thereby influencing how much liquid capital is available for investment. But these are risks in either case: If too much money is printed, inflation increases (money loses its purchasing power); if too little is printed, capital for investment becomes scare and costly to borrow. Less-direct ways of affecting the capital available are to raise or lower interest rates charged by the central bank (or in the United States, the Federal Reserve), to buy or sell the government's currency in domestic and world money markets, to issue governmental bonds so as to pull capital out of immediate circulation, and to impose new restrictions or loosen old ones on metamarket transactions (such as the equity required in credit purchases of stocks).

As world capitalism (involving international markets in goods and services, coupled with metamarkets in financial instruments) is extended to ever more populations, the intricacies of government policies on capital formation escalate (Stearns 1990; Mizruchi and Stearns 1994). Capital less and less is tied to a particular nation-state; it now flows around the world through many paths. These include the open and highly volatile metamarkets for money and other financial instruments; the central banks of states that buy and sell their own and other nations' money; the transnational banks such as the World Bank and International Monetary Fund; the profits and expenditures of multinational corporations that gather, produce, and distribute goods as well as services inside one another's borders; the deployment of military installations in other nations, the giving of gifts as foreign aid to other nations; and many other mechanisms. The result is that one nation's decisions on physical-capital formation affect others', leading to efforts such as the periodically renewed General Agreement on Tariffs and Trade (GATT) among the Western economic powers and Japan, or the system of appeals to the World Trade Organization to resolve trade disputes among nations, or the various agreements creating "trading blocs" in Europe and North America to manage and stabilize the flow of capital.

Polity and Human Capital

As physical capital is manipulated by government, so is the distribution of human capital. As physical capital is concentrated in some activities, whether directly through purchases of goods or services and infrastructural development or indirectly through tax, subsidy, monetary, and other policies, the labor market is affected, even in more state-managed systems. In essence, the government either is *directly* creating labor demand by spending tax revenues on certain types of physical capital or is *indirectly* creating this labor demand by encouraging private corporations in some gathering, producing, and distributing processes more than others.

Because more-developed labor markets require educational credentials, government often works on the supply side of human capital or labor markets by subsidizing certain types of education. For example, in the 1960s at the peak of the Cold War, the U.S. government invested vast amounts of money in science and technical training, as did the Soviet Union. Thus, a large pool of science-oriented human capital was created.

World system forces often create problems in either the supply or demand side of the labor market. Large numbers of immigrants influence the supply and distribution of skills in the labor pool, whereas emigrants leaving a country do likewise. Some of this movement in and out of countries can be controlled; although, at times (as in the current U.S./Latin American situation), it is more difficult to stop or regulate. Often government capital policies influence immigration, as in the 1960s when very high taxes in some northern European societies discouraged economic growth and thereby caused a brief "brain drain" of educated professionals to the United States. More significantly, government capital policies, such as taxes on corporate profits or tariffs on imported goods, can have an enormous effect on whether jobs are exported to societies with cheaper sources of labor or to societies willing to provide subsidies, such as infrastructural development. Indeed, as multinationals move about the globe to avoid tariffs on their goods and services or to seek subsidies, the labor market will be reshuffled; and while some of this movement of physical capital cannot be controlled by government, much of it can. As a result, government decisions in the emerging world economic system over such matters as tariffs, subsidies, capital markets, open trade, immigration, and emigration will alter the supply and demand of varying labor skills in the human capital market of a society.

Polity and Technology

Elites in the polity typically have had an interest in military technologies, whereas interest in economic technologies is more recent, accelerating with industrialization. In a sense, the general lack of subsidy for economic innovations in agrarian systems is surprising because these technological innovations would lead to increased gathering, producing, and servicing, which in turn could generate additional surplus that could be usurped to support elite privilege. But since innovations in the economy can stimulate change in social structures and cultural traditions on which traditional elites depended and which they used to justify their privilege, it is perhaps not surprising that pushes for technological innovations in horticultural and agrarian systems did not come from this sector. In fact, the constant need to extract surplus to support privilege, patronage, and adventurism of leaders in agrarian polities created disincentives for innovation among those who gathered and produced.

Yet despite these disincentives, innovations slowly accumulated, and during the transition from agrarianism to industrialism in western Europe, the greatest innovations occurred in the distributive sector, where the emerging bourgeoisie were engaged in highly profitable commerce in upper markets and metamarkets, as discussed in the last chapter (Braudel 1982). So conservative were many elites that they did not immediately change their tax policies away from land to the liquid and more useful capital held by the bourgeoisie. Perhaps Napoleon was the first to see clearly the wealth of the bourgeoisie for what it was and to tax effectively this wealth in order to subsidize military adventurism (and the ultimate disaster at Waterloo). Indeed, instead of imposing new kinds of taxes that would disrupt traditional systems of privilege based on land holdings, elites in agrarian systems often borrowed money from the bourgeoisie, placing them into debt and periodically creating a fiscal crisis of the state (Goldstone 1990). This commercial revolution, building momentum under the elites' turned-up noses, facilitated industrialism in the West by offering the prospects for new sources of raw materials and extended markets for distributing manufactured goods.

Once polity lost its monarchical and feudal character—thereby becoming less of a status group of consuming elites overly concerned with protecting their culture and privilege—the relationship between polity and economy was transformed. Government began to take an active interest in technologies for reasons not just military, but purely economic: to increase gathering, producing, and servicing in ways that could support the projects of the expanding state. Technology now increasingly is seen as a tool for generating resources necessary for state action, although until the state begins to support research-oriented education, academies of science, and research in the emerging institution of science, much of government's impact on technology is indirect, coming via its subsidy of physical capital.

Yet, at some point, activist governments begin to create "Big Science," and once this occurs, technological innovation takes off (Price 1986). Ironically, modern science in Europe emerged out of elite patronage in the agrarian era, where elites engaged in a kind of status competition over who could support and be patrons to the best scientists. Even after the Industrial Revolution, scientists were drawn disproportionately from the families of old elites and the newly wealthy bourgeoisie. But as the scientific base of knowledge accumulated and began to accelerate, specialization of research activities increased and science became bureaucratized in types of diverse structures, ranging from the research-and-development arm of corporations through the national academies and to top-rung research universities. Such bureaucratization is made possible by government subsidy, coming in many forms: tax credits to private firms for research and development, research grants to universities, funds for laboratory construction, salaries and grants to incumbents in government-sponsored national academies, and direct funding and control of national laboratories or specialized research equipment or facilities. Once this connection between Big Science and government is institutionalized, polity becomes a major source of technological infusion into the economy.

This infusion can be dampened by diversion of subsidies to secret military projects or by the inability to institutionalize the governmental connection to science in ways that encourage independent and creative thinking.

The recent drive by the U.S. Congress, for example, to fund "practical science," which has immediate engineering applications for the economy, represents one way in which the rate of technological innovation can potentially be dampened (as pure and theoretically oriented research programs having long-term consequences for innovations are scrapped in favor of more-immediate economic returns).

Polity and Property

Hunting-gathering economies could not support a polity, save for informal leaders. Therefore, property was mostly personal and, occasionally, collective when claims were made to territories. In most simple horticultural systems, the headman often "owned" all property—gardening plots and their products—but he had to redistribute this property to the members of the society. Thus, as polity began to emerge with simple horticulture, definitions and control of property became more evident. Such definitions and control were crucial to the allocation of gardening plots and the smooth distribution of their outputs to members of the population. While the headman's titular rights to property gave him (and it is nearly always a "he" in horticultural systems) and his close kin some extra privilege, material inequalities in the broader population were mitigated.

But with more-advanced horticulture and agrarianism, political elites used definitions and control of property to generate high levels of inequality. The result was for relatively few to "own" the land and implements, as well as the rights to labor used in gathering and producing. As a consequence, they also owned the rights to most of the goods produced, and hence, the right to distribute the surplus to themselves (although in feudal agrarian systems they had, in turn, to give this surplus to the monarch who, in essence, had given them rights to their estates). Polity thus became the tool of elites for controlling physical and human capital by specifying both as their property. Use of slaves to farm land was the extreme case; more typical was ownership of land and the right to usurp much of what was produced by those who worked the land (usually peasants as tenant farmers). As merchant classes emerged in advanced horticultural and agrarian economies, merchants always experienced considerable anxiety over the ability to retain their profits; but over time, polity began to define what was theirs to keep. In fact, polity often gave merchants property rights to engage in particular kinds of trade in specified places, as was the case with "chartered" (by the monarch) companies.

Historically, the state has always become involved in defining and allocating property, because it has needed the wealth that property can produce to support itself. Thus, as the capacity to generate wealth has increased, the growing state has become even more actively involved in specifying what is property and how it should be taxed. The need to tax property is one of the forces that propels the state to define more and more things and services as property; for when they are seen as property, they can be taxed.

Eventually, the polity initiates an autonomous legal system to facilitate definitions of property, rights to its control, and procedures to resolve conflicts over property. As it does so, polity encourages dramatic increases in the amount and diversity of property that can become implicated in gathering, producing, and distributing. As definitions and rights to the control of property are specified and stabilized, property becomes a dynamic element of the economy, serving as a way to expand gathering as more and more resources (such as mineral rights) beyond the agricultural functions of land are defined and protected; as physical capital is accumulated in ways that give its owners rights to use it and enjoy the profits that ensue; as labor is redefined in terms of mutual rights of work for income, with such income becoming private property to be spent in markets according to preferences; as organizational or entrepreneurial structures are defined as legal entities with rights to operate in certain ways; and as technology becomes protected property that can be used to generate profits.

Polity and Entrepreneurship

To the degree that polity influences the level of technology, the amount of physical capital, the composition and organization of human capital, and property rights, it is acting as a higher-order source of entrepreneurship for the economy. But most of this entrepreneurial activity is ultimately turned over to the legal system as its adjudication and enforcement functions become differentiated from decision making within the polity. Polity does, however, retain more-direct control of physical capital, for the simple reason that this is the ultimate source of the tax revenues on which it depends.

CONCLUSION

As is evident, economy often is embedded in its institutional environment; and even as the economy historically became differentiated from kinship and other institutions in which it was initially instantiated, it has not operated independent of these institutions. What is true of the economy is also true of each of the institutions of human societies. Economy is perhaps the most important driving force in human societies, as we will see in the equivalent of this chapter on the institutional environments of kinship, religion, polity, law, and education, respectively. The structure and operation of these institutions is influenced disproportionately by the economy. Yet as we have seen in this chapter, these institutions exert reverse causal effects on the dynamic elements—technology, physical and human capital, entrepreneurship, and property—that comprise an economy.

Institutions thus constitute a web of reciprocal effects on one another. In these two chapters, we have only begun to spin this web. As we successively examine kinship, religion, polity, law, and education, the fibers of the web will become dense and complex, especially for those modern societies where institutional systems have become differentiated and, yet at the same time, serve as the environments for one another. In both spinning and analytically untangling this web of reciprocal connections we will find the value of a distinct institutional-level analysis.

Chapter
4

Kinship

*I*n the earliest human societies, revolving around hunting and gathering, kinship units within small bands were the organizing principle of social life. All other institutions were fused with kinship, being discernible only by the distinctive types of family members' activities as they sought food (economic), raised their children (education), addressed the supernatural (religion), and resolved disputes (law). Other institutions, such as polity, were hardly visible even in this minimal sense of observable activities among family members. In very global terms, the history of human development over the last fifteen thousand years has revolved around two trends in kinship: (1) the initial elaboration of kinship from its simple form in hunting and gathering societies to accommodate the increased size and complexity of activities among humans as they discovered horticulture, and (2) the differentiation of new institutional systems outside of kinship and, because it was no longer needed to house and organize all institutional activities, a corresponding reduction in the scale of kinship back to its simple form (Blumberg and Winch 1977; Turner 1972).

SELECTION PRESSURES AND KINSHIP SYSTEMS

Systems of kinship emerged and have persisted in human populations for the simple reason that they have facilitated survival. They were selected because they provided a solution—not always the best or most efficient one, but a solution nonetheless—to six basic survival problems facing the species: (1) sex and mating, (2) biological support, (3) social reproduction, (4) social support, (5) social placement, and (6) social coordination. In the beginning, kinship was the only solution to these pressures. As other institutions have emerged in the course of humans' developmental history, alternative nonkin structures can, or could, take over these functions; but even in these cases, kinship remains the easiest and most viable way for revolving most of these survival problems. Let us review each in more detail.

Sex and mating constitute the first survival problem. All species must reproduce themselves, and sex drives are the evolved mechanisms of nature assuring that the appropriate parties get together. Without sex drives, members of a species would not regenerate themselves. But sex among humans is never unregulated; it is always controlled by norms that specify "appropriate" persons, times, places, ways, ages, and circumstances where sex can occur—although the specific content of norms naturally varies from society to society (Davis 1949; Murdock 1949). Although the exact processes leading to this situation are buried in the unwritten history of early social evolution, we can block out at least the generalities of this process: Sex drives can lead to competition among individuals for sex objects, and out of such competition arise jealousies, anger, and perhaps murder. Furthermore, since males tend to be physically stronger than females, sexual dominance and exploitation of females by males can also occur, leading to more anger, frustration, and hostility. Such a situation can create tremendous personal anxieties as well as threaten the survival of the human species, since newborn children depend for a long time on physical and emotional support from parents (or surrogates). Building on the inherited legacy from their ape and hominid ancestors, humans developed implicit "understandings" about how competition for sexual objects was to be mitigated and how enduring physical relations among adults were to be established. Initially these understandings were probably not consciously or deliberately instituted, but over time, because of their success in mitigating sexual conflict and in establishing enduring sexual relations, they persisted. As they persisted, these implicit understandings became translated into binding norms about sex and mating that combined with other norms arising out of similar processes to form a kinship system.

The second survival problem is biological support. The newborn are biologically helpless, for a baby cannot feed, clothe, shelter, or protect itself. For a brief period, the mother is similarly vulnerable, especially if she must care for the infant. Through processes similar to those delineated above, norms originally emerged to assure the protection of biologically helpless members of the species. Although societies have different kinship norms regarding who and how many people are to protect the infant, the biological father and mother, with some exceptions, were designated to be the primary caretakers of infants. However, in many societies the cast of protectors can be much more extensive and include grandparents, aunts, and cousins. The biological-support functions of kinship can, moreover, be encompassing and can include taking care of the incapacitated, aged, and diseased.

Third, social systems regenerate themselves not only through biological reproduction of the species but also through social reproduction, in which the young acquire through socialization those personality traits necessary for participation in the social positions of the society. All known societies have evolved structures having consequences for social reproduction, and the most prominent of these structures was the family. The father and mother are usually intimately involved, but sometimes aunts, uncles, grandparents, and other relatives do as much or more to assure social reproduction.

The fourth survival need is social support. Humans can experience a wide range of potentially disruptive emotions—fear, frustration, uncertainty, anger, and jealousy—which can generate tremendous anxiety and tension while immobilizing individuals and disrupting social relations. Humans require at least some social relations that provide emotional support and affection to mitigate the many sources of fear, anxiety, and uncertainty inherent in social life. The family historically has been the most readily available source of the social and emotional support that humans need to perform social roles effectively.

After years of biological and social support as well as socialization of the young, the issue of how and where to insert the young adult into the wider society appears. This fifth survival issue, social placement, has been one of the most fundamental for all populations, because it involves the transition from child to adult. Such a transition raises questions of where the young adult will go in a society, how this decision will be made, and what criteria will be employed in making it. Through varied historical and evolutionary processes, two basic ways of resolving the problem have developed (Davis 1949; Stephens 1967):

1. Insert the young into the wider society on the basis of *ascription*, where a child's adult status in the society is determined at birth and where children assume the occupational, religious, political, and legal status of their families or their birth order and status of their parents within a larger kinship system. Because social placement is determined at birth, family support and socialization are directed toward preparing youth for this predetermined slot in the wider society.
2. Insert youth into the larger society on the basis of *performance*, where role performance in key activities becomes the criterion by which one is inserted into various statuses. In turn, such performance is a reflection of inherited and socialized personality traits. Because kinship circumscribes both biological inheritance and socialization, it has had far-reaching consequences for social placement in nonascriptive, performance-oriented societies, although performance systems almost always have intermediary structures, like a school system, that become the arbitrators of performance.

The sixth survival problem is social coordination. Historically, the kinship subsystem has had far-reaching consequences for organizing and coordinating much societal activity. Among hunters and gatherers, the respective economic roles of males and females were dictated by the family division of labor. Or, as was evident for the entrepreneurial elements of the economy in horticultural societies, kinship is the principle by which most economic activity is organized. In these systems, what is true of the economy is also true of political, religious, and legal activity. Thus, kinship often has been very much involved in the coordination of activities in human populations.

In sum, then, kinship has represented a solution to a whole series of fundamental issues facing humans—sex and mating, emotional support, biological maintenance, socialization, placement, and social coordination. We therefore can define tentatively the institution of kinship as those marriage and blood ties organized into structures and mediated by cultural symbols that regularize sex and mating, provide biological support, reproduce societal members, offer social support, engage in social placement, and at times, coordinate societal relations.

ELEMENTS OF KINSHIP

Kinship is a set of norms specifying relationships among (a) those who are related by blood (or who share genes) and (b) those who are related by marriage. These norms specify who is to be considered kinfolk as well as who is to marry whom and how; who is to be related to whom and how; who is to live with whom and where; who is to perform what duties and how; who is to have authority over whom; and who is to inherit property, authority, and other resources. Norms that so fundamentally organize people's lives are heavily infused with values, or imperatives—what *should* occur. These value elements give norms a moral quality, increasing the chances that people will abide by them. Populations that could not develop normative agreements and underlying value premises over such matters did not persist and reproduce themselves. Therefore, the basic types of normative systems that have emerged are worth more-detailed review because they have been so essential to human survival.

Norms of Family Size and Composition

If one maps out the genealogy chart of kinsmen on both sides of a couple's respective families, the potential size and composition of the family becomes quite large. And in some societies where just about everyone is related in some way, a few large kinship groupings would be virtually coextensive with the total society. Many Polynesian societies came close to doing just this, because kin ties could be traced for just about everyone in a village, district, or even the total society. As Raymond Firth noted in his description of the Tikopia, virtually everyone could trace kin relationships in a community numbering well over one thousand, so that "the whole land is a single body of kinfolk" (Firth 1936, 234). Kinship ties have often been less extensive, however, because specific norms limit the scope of family and kinship. One set of such norms that has evolved is those regulating the size and composition of family groupings in a society, creating three general structural forms: (1) nuclear, (2) extended, and (3) polygamous.

The *nuclear family* is small and contains only father, mother, and their children. Immediate relatives are excluded from the household or living unit. This nuclear form was the dominant type in both the earliest societies (i.e., hunting and gathering), and it is also the type most prevalent in the complex industrial and post-industrial societies of the West.

The *extended family* family is large and includes several nuclear units, thereby bringing other relatives to a household. In this way, not only parents and their children, but also grandparents, great-grandparents, aunts, cousins, and others potentially can become part of an extended household unit. The degree of extendedness in such families can vary greatly, with family members living within one house or a compound of houses. Yet regardless of how concentrated their residence, the members of the family perceive themselves as a discrete unit that must control and coordinate activities. Their perceptions of themselves as a distinct unit are often bolstered by the fact that extended families own and work property on which their subsistence depends.

A *polygamous family* unit is one in which plural marriage and residence are allowed. The most common form of polygamy is *polygyny*, where norms permit inclusion of several wives (and their children) in a single house or where norms allow each cowife to occupy a dwelling of her own clustered together within a family compound or homestead. Norms allowing women to have multiple husbands are termed *polyandry*. Where polygyny or polyandry have existed, families tended to be large. Even in societies that have permitted polygamous families, monogamous marriages often have been more common, because most males in societies allowing polygamy could not afford multiple wives.

Norms of Residence

Once two people get married, they confront the problem of where to live. There are three logical possibilities: (1) alone and where they wish; (2) with the groom's family or in their community; or (3) with the bride's family or community. Respectively, these three possibilities are labeled *neolocal*, *patrilocal*, and *matrilocal* residence norms.[1] Generally, matrilocal or patrilocal residence rules are most pronounced for extended and polygamous family units. Since these types of families connect multiple adults together, there needs to be a residence rule specifying who is to move into whose household. For example, if a kinship system is composed of extended families and has a patrilocal residence norm, then the married couple lives not only in the groom's community but most likely in his parents' home, compound, or village. The reverse would be the case for a matrilocal residence rule in a kinship system composed of extended families. And in systems with a polygamous family unit, residence norms also tend to be either matrilocal or patrilocal, since multiple spouses will be recruited from different families and villages, typically moving to the household and village of the single spouse.

---

[1] These definitions differ somewhat from those commonly employed by anthropologists. Frequently when a newly married couple does not move into one of their parents' family compounds, but still remains within the same community, this is referred to as a neolocal residence pattern. In the definitions offered here, this would be either a matrilocal or patrilocal pattern. For us, *neolocality* pertains to norms allowing for the free choice of residency by married couples.

There can be other residence rules, such as the *avuncular*, which requires that a married couple move to where the mother's brother (or the uncle of their children) lives. Here, the mother's brother will have considerable authority over the male and his children (Ember and Ember 1983, 249–59; 1971). Thus, while most human populations have had neolocal, patrilocal, or matrilocal residence rules, considerable variation can occur.

Norms of Family Activity

Most kinship systems display clusters of norms concerning family activities. These rules revolve around three major concerns: (1) household tasks, (2) child care, and (3) socialization of the young.

The household-task obligations of males and females within the family are usually spelled out by norms, although the specific norms vary from one society to another. Frequently males are required to engage in economic activity, with females involved in household or domestic tasks. But equally often in the history of human societies, females have engaged in as much or more economic activity than males. Children in most kinship systems assume the status of student apprentice, acquiring the skills of their parents.

There are numerous ways to bring up a child, and rarely is this decision completely left up to the discretion of parents (or other kin). Just how a child is to be fed, clothed, and sheltered is usually specified by kinship rules, which establish minimum standards for child care. Should the adults responsible for this care not meet these standards, child care then becomes the responsibility of designated kin, or—in societies with a developed political system—of the state and its welfare agencies.

In all societies, general norms exist indicating how children are to be socialized. The ways love, affection, discipline, and instruction are administered by adults are greatly circumscribed by kinship norms, although these have displayed great diversity in the course of humans' evolutionary history. Although parents generally socialize their young, in many kinship systems one parent is excluded from socialization. For example, a mother's brother (or child's uncle) in an avuncular system may have more responsibility for a young male's socialization than does the biological father. Other arrangements excluding a parent from socialization have existed in the world's kinship systems.

Norms of Dissolution

Even when there are clear and powerful kinship rules, marriages in all societies become unstable, with the consequence that all societies have provided ways for their dissolution. In general, three types of rules in kinship systems govern dissolution: (1) conditional rules, (2) procedural rules, and (3) rules of dependence.

Conditional rules indicate the conditions under which dissolution is possible. The conditions appropriate for dissolution differ greatly from society to society; among them are lack of female fertility, mutual incompatibility, infidelity, criminal offense, and mental cruelty. Conditional rules can be either broad or narrow and encouraging or discouraging.

Procedural rules indicate how dissolution should occur. They have been simple (moving belongings out of one's spouse's house) or exceedingly complex (going to court, pleading a case, and establishing guilt).

Dissolution usually involves children (and sometimes other dependent members, such as the elderly). Kinship rules tend to insure that these dependents are cared for and/or socialized.

Norms of Descent

At birth, one inherits two separate bloodlines, raising the question of whose bloodline—the male's or the female's—is to be more important. The norms specifying which side of the married couple's family is to be more significant are termed *rules of descent*, and there are three general types: *patrilineal, matrilineal,* and *bilateral.* For example, in a patrilineal descent system, a person belongs at birth to a special group of kin on the father's side of the family. This group includes siblings (brothers and sisters), father, father's siblings, father's father and his siblings, and father's brother's children. In such a system, the mother's kin are not important. To this special group of male kin an individual owes allegiance and loyalty, and it is these kin who will protect and socialize the individual, and eventually place him or her into society. Further, from these kin the succession of authority and inheritance of property and wealth will pass. In a matrilineal system, the mother's instead of the father's kin assume this important place in the life of the young. Bilateral descent systems, which assign influence to both sides of the family, are comparatively rare because working out a division of power and influence between family lines is awkward. Where bilineal descent exists, therefore, it is almost always truncated so that both mother's and father's kin are equally recognized and respected but neither kin group exerts much influence or power over the children.

Unilineal descent rules (that is, patrilineal or matrilineal norms) divide up a particular residential unit, since one member of the family (either spouse) must be an "outsider" (Stephens 1963, 105). For example, in a patrilineal descent system, father and children generally belong to the same descent grouping, with the mother as an outsider. Aside from dividing up a particular family group or household, descent norms also divide societies into segments (Murdock 1949). In a unilineal society one belongs to a patrilineal residential unit and then to other patrilineally reckoned units in the village, community, and perhaps territory. In this way various residential units within some geographical territory are linked together through a patrilineal descent system or the male bloodline. Such linkages, usually referred to as *lineages,* frequently own property and can be considered a kind of "corporation" that can be engaged in wars, feuds, economic competition, and be subject to legal liability. When several lineages are connected by a descent norm, a *clan* can be said to exist. And when clans are linked together by descent norms, a *moiety* is formed, representing the largest kind of unilineal kin grouping. Many historical societies have been divided into moieties, each with its constituent clans, lineages, and residential family units. The extensiveness, clarity, and scope of such descent groupings have varied tremendously in the history of human societies, although these more complex forms reached their zenith in the horticultural era.[2] In these societies the descent rule, as it laced together kindred, was the principal basis of societal organization and integration.

Norms of Authority

Rules of authority exist in all kinship systems. These rules concern who makes the important and ultimate decisions affecting the welfare of a particular family or larger kin group such as a lineage or clan. But even where rules clearly specify authority, others in the family may still exert considerable decision-making powers in other areas. The rules of a kinship system usually endow specific statuses with authority. These rules are of two general types: (1) *patriarchal* and (2) *egalitarian.* In patriarchal kinship systems, the father makes major decisions for his family or residential unit. Eldest and/or ablest males make decisions governing the larger kin grouping embodying all kin wherever they may reside. Egalitarian systems usually feature a division of labor in decision making, with males making major decisions in some areas and females in others.

In addition to patriarchy and egalitarianism, a third type exists, at least theoretically, revolving around matriarchy. However, such systems do not invest women, per se, with ultimate authority. Rather, the woman's male kin historically have been invested with authority because the modest but decisive strength differences between males and females places men in a better position to force conformity. Thus, the authority resides in the female's *side of the family* more than in the female herself. In modern single-parent households, women may have full authority, albeit under difficult circumstances. However, such systems have been comparatively rare.

Norms of Marriage

Almost all societies require a mother to be married. Marriage sets up a series of mutual obligations between husband and wife concerning domestic duties, child rearing, and sex, while at the same time it perpetuates the kin grouping. Aside from the general rule requiring marriage of all mothers, most kinship systems have norms concerning whom one may or may not marry. The three most prominent types of marriage rules have been (1) incest taboos, (2) norms of exogamy, and (3) norms of endogamy.

---

[2] For references on unilineal descent systems, see: Fox (1967), Radcliffe-Brown (1952), Keesing (1975), Ember and Ember (1983), Fried (1957), and Fortes (1953).

Incest taboos are norms prohibiting sex and marriage among close kin. Some of these have been universal or nearly so: Mothers and sons, fathers and daughters, and siblings may not have sex or marry. Usually more-distant kin (aunts, uncles, cousins, nieces, or nephews) are also covered by an incest taboo. The effect of such rules is that they force people out of their immediate residential kin group in search of partners.

Often marriage rules are also *exogamous*—that is, they prohibit marriage to members of one's community or larger kin grouping. This forces marriage with partners from other communities, lineages, regions, clans, or moieties.

At times marriage rules are also *endogamous*, requiring marriage within certain groups—usually a social class, kin group, caste, or village. Coupled with incest (and perhaps exogamy) rules, endogamous norms severely restrict the pool of potential mates. In contrast, some kinship systems, such as that in the United States, have few rules of marriage: Mothers are "encouraged" to be married; incest rules apply only to close blood kin; and no explicit norms of exogamy or endogamy exist.

We are now able to revise our earlier, provisional definition of kinship. Kinship can be viewed as *those normative systems, infused with values, that specify the size and composition, residence patterns, activities, authority relations, and lines of descent within those units organizing blood and marriage ties in ways that have consequences for regularizing sex and mating, socializing the young, providing biological and social support, placing the young into the broader social structure and, at times, coordinating other institutional activities.*

BASIC TYPES OF KINSHIP SYSTEMS

The nature of kinship is very much connected to the type of economy. In hunting and gathering, kinship was very simple[3]: nuclear family units, at times connected together to form an extended family unit; marriage was relatively unconstrained, although rules of incest and, at times, exogamy and endogamy applied; dissolution of marriages was relatively simple; relations were egalitarian, although men and women engaged in very different activities and only men tended to garner high prestige; residence varied and could be neolocal, bilocal (both mother's and father's sides), or patrilocal, but even if there was a clear residence rule, considerable flexibility prevailed; and descent was bilateral and truncated, indicating that family lines were not emphasized.

When human populations began to grow, selection favored new ways to coordinate economic activity in order to support the larger population. As a

---

[3] For general references on hunting and gathering, see: Sahlins (1972, 1968a, 1986b), Lee and DeVore (1968), Schrire (1984), Winterhalder and Smith (1981), Service (1966), Malinowski (1913).

Table 4.1   STRUCTURE OF KINSHIP IN HUNTING AND GATHERING SOCIETIES

Size and Composition	Nuclear units and extended units
Residence	Neolocal, bilocal, and patrilocal
Activity	Clear division of labor: Males hunt, and females gather and do domestic chores
Descent	Usually bilateral, but truncated
Authority	Egalitarian, although considerable variability exists (with some systems giving males more authority over women)
Marriage	Incest prohibited; exogamy and endogamy; considerable freedom of choice; divorce easily effected

result, many populations were forced to give up their nomadic hunter-gatherer life-style[4] and adopt horticulture (Cohen 1977; Binford 1968). But they faced a dilemma: How were they to build these more complex structures? The solution was to increase the salience of the descent norm (specifying whose side of the family was to be more important) and then build the organization of the society around kinship principles. Without the capacity to build bureaucracies and other structures coordinating larger numbers of individuals, kinship was the only and perhaps the easiest solution because it involved elaborating on an existing structure. And so, with the emergence and expansion of horticultural technologies, unilineal descent systems grew as a mechanism to coordinate and regulate physical and human capital (Harner 1970). The result was for the size and composition of family units to grow, being connected into extended units in accordance with a patrilineal descent in the vast majority of cases or, in a lesser number of cases, matrilineal descent. Residence then followed the descent rule, being either patrilocal or matrilocal, although there were exceptions. Authority was male-dominated or patriarchal in both descent systems (since men on average are somewhat stronger than women), although in the matrilineal-matrilocal system, it was the males on the female's side of the family who generally exercised authority. Marriage became much more regulated, not only by incest rules but also by rules of exogamy (having to choose partners outside one's lineage, clan, or moiety) and, frequently, by rules of endogamy (where partners must be chosen outside one's own family but inside a specific lineage, clan, moiety and, at times, social class or village). In these larger kin units, the division of labor between males and females, as well as between generations, became much more explicit and rigid.

---

[4] There appear to be transitional ways to organize larger hunting and gathering populations. For example, hunter-gatherers can settle down if they live in a verdant environment, as where fishing near the ocean or other types of waterways is possible. Under these conditions, more-permanent settlements can emerge, even though the technology of the economy remains hunting (fishing) and gathering (of fruits and other plant life). In these systems, a "Big Man," or political leaders often emerge (Johnson and Earle 1987, 62; Maryanski and Turner 1992), but eventually, some form of unilineal kinship becomes necessary as the population becomes larger and more permanently settled.

Such a system served as a functional equivalent of bureaucracy because it could organize and coordinate large numbers of people in an authority system. This kind of kinship was, however, riddled with tension because it constrained kindred to a high degree, forcing them to manage potentially volatile outbursts. Feuds, external warfare (perhaps displacing internal aggression), and sporadic fighting were very typical of these kinds of kinship structures—as one might expect when kinfolk were forced to live together in large numbers within a rigid system of authority and highly prescribed activities (Maryanski and Turner 1992, 91–112).

With advanced horticulture (see right side of Table 4.2) and then with agrarianism, sufficient economic surplus could be produced to support nonkin organizational structures, manorial estates composed of more nucleated tenant farmers; administrative bureaucracies attached to the state; and new corporate structures such as guilds, cartels, and companies. These alternatives could organize far greater numbers of people, and they allowed people to escape the "cage of kinship" (Maryanski and Turner 1992). Under these changes, kinship began its odyssey back to the simpler system of hunters and gatherers. The descent rule lost much of its salience, except for the inheritance of property and titles, and the construction of lineages and larger structures like clans and moieties became increasingly less viable. Extended family units remained but were not essential and were often converted to patrimonial structures of kin and nonkin workers or apprentices. Residence retained some of the patrilocal bias of horticultural systems, but neolocality

Table 4.2   STRUCTURE OF KINSHIP IN HORTICULTURE SOCIETIES

	Simple	Advanced
Size and Composition	Extended units	Extended units, but some nucleation becomes evident
Residence	Patri- or matrilocal, but mostly patrilocal	Residence rule begins to break down, especially as migration to urban centers occurs; but patrilocal bias continues
Activity	Clear division of labor between males and females in economic, community, political, religious, and domestic tasks	Same as simple system
Descent	Unilineal, generally patrilineal; organized to lineage and clan level and at times, to moiety level	Descent rule begins to break down, but still regulates inheritance of wealth and power in kinship units that remain linked
Authority	Male-dominated	Male-dominated
Marriage	Incest prohibited; considerable exogamy and endogamy; dissolution allowed	Incest prohibited; exogamy declines; endogamy becomes increasingly based on class as much as kinship

became more frequent as people migrated to new lands or emerging urban areas. Authority remained patriarchal, and activities of men and women were strictly divided; but as the extended family began to decline in prevalence and as neolocal residence became possible, intergenerational authority and division of labor were less explicit and restrictive. Incest rules remained for marriage partners, but rules of exogamy and endogamy declined and then disappeared. Dissolution often became more difficult, however, as males made divorce difficult to achieve as a means for controlling women.

Industrialization completed the odyssey back to the basic structure of hunting and gathering, primarily because kinship was no longer needed to organize societal activities. In fact, large kinship systems get in the way of rational and efficient corporate units and market mechanisms for distributing of goods, services, and human capital. As a result, they are increasingly eliminated in favor of small, mobile nuclear families, unencumbered by descent rules which move toward a truncated bilateral pattern and unconstrained by mandatory residence rules which become neolocal. Authority remains some-

Table 4.3   STRUCTURE OF KINSHIP IN AGRARIAN SOCIETIES

	Simple	Advanced
Size and Composition	Extended units still very evident but decline in frequency and embeddedness in larger kin structures; patrimonial family (male-dominated and including others, such as workers, beside kin) appears.	Fewer extended units; extended and patrimonial families frequent among artisans and merchants; extended units still found among peasants, but patterns of political servitude disrupt kinship ties.
Residence	Explicit rules begin to lose power, though offspring usually remain close to parents, or even in their household.	Few explicit rules, but patterns of servitude in rural areas restrict mobility (though roving landless peasants are, at times, evident); in urban areas patrimonial households organize much economic activity.
Activity	Clear division of labor by sex and age in all activities.	Same as simple societies.
Descent	Increasingly bilateral and truncated.	Except for "royal" family, lineage less important, and increasingly bilateral and truncated; only royalty and nobility continue to use descent rules to a high degree.
Authority	Male-dominated, and in patrimonial units, considerable male authoritarianism.	Male-dominated, especially in patrimonial families.
Marriage	Incest prohibited; rules of exogamy and endogamy decline; dissolution allowed but economically difficult and rarely formal.	Incest prohibited, except in a few cases for nobility; rules of exogamy and endogamy decline further; dissolution allowed but difficult and rarely formal.

what patriarchal, although as women enter the labor force, a more egalitarian pattern of authority and family activities begins to emerge. (However, vestiges of patriarchy remain, especially among manual, nonprofessional labor.) Marriage is still guided by incest, but exogamy rules have disappeared, and endogamy is purely informal, being guided more by social class, ethnicity, and other nonkin criteria. Divorce is easier to get, and rates of divorce and non-marital childbearing begin to rise with post-industrialization.

Tables 4.1 to 4.4 summarize these transformations of kinship from hunting and gathering to post-industrialization. The tables illustrate that with

Table 4.4   STRUCTURE OF KINSHIP IN MODERN SOCIETIES

	Industrial	Post-Industrial
Size and Composition	Extended kinship virtually disappears except for various ethnic migrants/businesses and for some portions of agricultural sector; decrease in birth rates reduces family size to nuclear units of parents and two to three offspring.	Same as industrial societies, except modal family size decreases and number of childless families increases.
Residence	Neolocal, with freedom to move in accordance with labor-market opportunities; multiple-family residence typical only of poor underclass, ethnic migrants, and portions of agricultural sector.	Same as industrial societies.
Activity	Increasingly ambiguous division of labor by sex and age as women enter non-household labor force and children become integrated in peer cultures.	Same as industrial societies, with considerable ambiguity over division of labor by sex and age; incipient trend toward increased egalitarianism by sex and, to a lesser extent, by age; also, increased activity by all family members outside family
Descent	Unilateral descent virtually disappears in favor of a truncated, bilateral system.	Same as industrial societies.
Authority	Still male-dominated, but with less clarity and decisiveness.	Still male-dominated, but with considerable ambiguity and with trend toward egalitarian or, at least, sharing of authority between males and females.
Marriage	Incest prohibited; no explicit rules of exogamy or endogamy; dissolution allowed and increasingly easy to secure; rising rates of divorce and dissolution initially but tending to level off.	Same as industrial societies, except divorce rates increase again.

post-industrialization, kinship becomes structurally close to the hunting and gathering form. However, some important differences exist, which in closing, we should examine.

DYNAMIC TRENDS
IN CONTEMPORARY KINSHIP SYSTEMS

Several trends have accompanied the structural transformation of kinship to truncated bilateral descent, isolated nuclear units, and neolocal residence. These revolve around: (1) the changing authority relations within nuclear units, (2) the division of labor for family activities, and (3) the patterns of marriage dissolution. Although there are large differences among post-industrial systems, especially between the eastern and western hemisphere, there is some convergence of these trends in the western post-industrial societies—the United States and western Europe. These converging trends in the western hemisphere are the result of pressures which have yet to exert great influence on Japanese kinship and other eastern industrial societies, although we might speculate that they will become more manifest in the decades ahead.

Changing Authority Relations

As the family unit became more nuclearized beginning with late agrarianism (Flandrin 1979; Laslett and Wall 1972) and increasingly with industrialization and post-industrialization, norms of patriarchy have not gone completely back to a more egalitarian pattern evident among many hunter-gatherer populations. The horticultural-agrarian system of male control persisted, primarily because it was in the male's interest to have such norms and because women were not in an economic position to demand changes, especially as they remained burdened with household-domestic obligations.

Those under authority always resent it. Therefore, as women have begun to participate in the labor force and to command economic resources, they have been able to make claims for egalitarian decision making—much like many hunter-gatherers of the past. If they too are "breadwinners," then there must be a sharing of power. A complete shift to egalitarianism has not occurred, however. Males have resisted, and although there is a trend in the direction of egalitarianism, norms have not completely gone over in this direction (Hochschild 1989; Hertz 1986). Indeed, there is considerable normative ambiguity over authority, especially with respect to who has it in what domestic spheres. This ambiguity will, no doubt, persist well into the twenty-first century, even in the West and certainly in the eastern industrial systems.

Changing Division of Labor

As with authority relations—and in fact, as a partial reflection of authority norms—norms about the division of labor in industrial and post-industrial kinship systems reveal considerable ambiguity. Even as women have entered the labor force, they are more likely than men to feel obligated to perform domestic chores: socialization/nurturance of the young, food preparation and clean-up, housework. Indeed, men actively resist performing these chores, or if avoidance is not possible, they seek to minimize their involvement (Robinson 1988). Such a situation generates considerable tension in families as women resent having to perform a "second shift" of domestic chores (Hochschild 1989). Norms are clearly changing to a more equitable division of labor in the West among families where women work. But change is slow; and in families where women do not work, the older patriarchal pattern prevails. Thus, not only are norms ambiguous, there are multiple normative systems in the division of labor. The existence of the traditional division-of-labor norms for nonworking women often makes it difficult to substitute a more liberal/egalitarian normative profile in families where women work. Indeed, women themselves may feel caught between the two normative systems, moving back and forth between them and trying to create a viable normative system for their families.

Changing Marriage-Dissolution

With post-industrialization, marriage occurs later in life, childbearing often occurs outside of formal marriage, and dissolution rates increase. These last two trends—childbearing out of wedlock and high divorce rates—potentially pose problems.

Child-bearing outside of marriage has increased throughout the West, but particularly in the United States. If there is a father in the household, this trend need not cause problems, especially since the couple usually gets married eventually. It is when fathers never become part of the household or soon leave it that a special burden is placed on the nuclear unit: Earning an income, providing adequate child care, and giving nurturance and guidance all become difficult. And, the younger the mother in this situation, the more problematic are these necessities. As a result, the basic functions that family has always provided in human societies are abrogated, often forcing the bureaucratic structures of the state to intervene in an area where it is ill suited. In American society, especially among some poor minority populations, rates of out-of-wedlock birth are extremely high, causing severe problems for children and the broader society in which these children cannot always participate.

Rates of divorce increase with post-industrialization, although rates of remarriage are also high. But the breakup of families, per se, creates many of the same problems that out-of-wedlock families reveal: inadequate income, child care, and nurturance/guidance. And if children of divorced parents become part of a reconstituted family through remarriage, then problems of integrating step-parent(s) and step-sibling(s) can become acute, placing considerable tension on all family members. There are no well-institutionalized norms for either single-parent or step-families. As a result, families must cope and grope to find solutions, often compromising some of the critical functions of kinship systems in the process.

CONCLUSION

All of these trends are the result of the changing institutional environment of kinship. For as kinship has lost most of its social coordination functions and has become just one subsystem in a complex of differentiated institutional subsystems, the dynamics of these other subsystems exert a growing influence on the organization and operation of kinship. For now, kinship is not the organizational backbone of the entire society, as it was in hunting-gathering and horticultural socieities. Indeed, kinship becomes a reactive institutional system, trying to sustain a viable operation as the dynamic forces of other institutions—especially economy, polity, and education—increasingly dictate how kinship is to be structured and what functions it is to retain in the fast-changing industrial and post-industrial eras. Thus, to understand the trends in kinship requires us to explore its institutional environment, as we shall in the next chapter.

Chapter
5

Kinship in Institutional Context

*I*n the beginning, were the wandering band and the close bond between mother and children. From this primitive mammalian base, fathers increasingly became attached to mothers and children, thereby creating the nuclear kinship unit. Whether this development occurred before hominids crossed over to *Homo sapiens sapiens* can never be known, but this much is certain: Kinship evolved as a response to powerful forces of selection—as a way to regularize sex and mating, to reproduce the species biologically, to socialize the young, to alleviate tensions and provide emotional support, and to guide the placement of new adults. Along with the band, kinship was the first structure to house institutional activity. Yet during the course of long-term evolution many of these functions of kinship would be passed over to new institutions, and as a consequence, both the structure and operation of kinship would change. More than any other institution, then, kinship has responded to the basic institutional pressures placed on it—first, emerging and elaborating to house institutional activity and, later, shrinking to accommodate the rise of new institutional systems.

ECONOMY AND KINSHIP

Economic Selection Pressures and Kinship Formation

The addition of the father to the mother-child bond was, no doubt, selected as a solution to the fundamental economic questions of how to organize gathering, conversion, and distribution of food in ways that promoted reproduction of the species. Once there was a nuclear family unit of mother, father, and offspring, the structure of social life could be more stable and attuned to gathering, producing, and distributing resources. Indeed, the nuclear unit organized technology as well as human and physical capital for gathering and producing, while providing the unit within which distribution was to occur.

Without kinship, where individuals could be free to go their own way and where mother and dependent children would be left to fend for themselves, production and reproduction of the species would be problematic. Thus, the creation of the elementary nuclear unit occurred under economic selection pressures for stabilizing and coordinating the elements needed in gathering, producing, and distributed in ways that enabled the species to survive.

Economic Selection Pressures and the Elaboration of Kinship

As populations grew and settled down, they needed to gather more, produce more, and distribute to more people. To do so, it was necessary to:

a. Utilize horticultural technologies (planting and harvesting gardens).[1]
b. Pool larger amounts of human capital in ways that assured the cultivation of gardens.
c. Amass the physical capital necessary to break the soil, garden, harvest, and prepare food.
d. Define property in ways that reduced conflicts over gardening plots and the distribution of their output.
e. Organize the above into a coherent system.

Each of these problems can be viewed as a selection pressure—as demands on humans to reorganize or die. The simplest path under these pressures was to elaborate new rules about blood and marriage ties in ways that were conducive to increased gathering, producing, and distributing. Thus, norms of extendedness or polygamy resulted in larger family groups which could perform necessary labor. Rules of residence insured that some family members would remain close and that new recruits would be brought by either the daughter or son into the family compound; norms of exogamy forced the incorporation of new members from outside the community into the family labor pool. Unilineal descent rules insured that the labor pool would remain loyal and tied to the familial economic unit, while also insuring that capital and property would be concentrated in a particular kin grouping, whether an extended family, lineage, clan, or moiety. Rules of authority allowed for the coordination and control of the family labor pool and capital, as did unambiguous rules concerning family activity, especially rules concerning the division of household tasks (which often shaded into economic role behaviors). And norms of dissolution kept the labor force intact by spelling out where dependents (future labor) were to reside.

---

[1] This civilization was not a great technological leap, however, because hunter-gatherers had practical knowledge of planting. In fact, contemporary hunter-gatherers often scatter seeds in breaking camp in the hopes that when they cycle back to this area, they can reap what they sowed. But generally, hunter-gatherers consider gardening to be too difficult and not worth the effort. Thus, it is likely that humans were *forced* into horticulture—most likely because of overpopulation or by invasion of their territories by horticulturalists.

By becoming more elaborate, kinship made it possible for the economy to become more complex and, thereby, to gather and produce more, while providing a kin-based system for the distribution of increased productivity to larger numbers of people. This kin-based organization of the economy however, eventually would prove inadequate as populations grew larger, requiring even higher levels of gathering, producing, and distributing. Still, unilineal kinship systems represented an elegant and ingenious solution to very real economic pressures.

Consequences of the Differentiation of Economy from Kinship

With more-advanced horticulture, and accelerating with agrarianism, came alternatives to kinship as the way to organize technology, human and physical capital, and property for gathering, producing, and distributing. Markets using money and credit became a new entrepreneurial mechanism for distributing many goods and services and for encouraging nonkin corporate units to emerge. Manorial estates of tenant farmers became new ways to define property and to pool human and physical capital in gathering and distribution. Corporate units such as guilds, cartels, associations, leagues, and companies began to organize technology, property, labor, and physical capital. State-based political systems also assumed important entrepreneurial functions for organizing technology, physical and human capital, and labor. And law increasingly came to define property rights and to organize exchange transactions. These and other nonkin structures were, however, supplemented by kin-based structures, such as extended families on farms, patrimonial families engaged in craft and commerce, family-owned and managed corporate units, family estates, and kin-based states. Some of these continued into industrialization and post-industrialization and can be found in the world today. But increasingly over the course of humans' evolutionary history, the economy has become structurally differentiated from kinship, with the result that kinship has ceased to be a major locus of economic activity. Such differentiation or separation of kinship and economic roles is both a reflection and a cause of the emergence of new entrepreneurial mechanisms for pooling and organizing labor around capital and technology. These changes in the relationship between economy and kinship inevitably cause alteration in the norms of the kinship subsystem.

As markets, factories, and bureaucracies become the loci of economic activity, the entrepreneurial functions of kinship receded. Kinship no longer needed to be the organizing mechanism for technology, human and physical capital, and definitions of property. As a result, the pressures that originally had generated unilineal descent—and, relatedly, extended families and restrictive residence rules—lessened. Indeed, long before industrialization, agrarianism had done much to break unilineal descent norms, which are the backbone of more-complex kinship systems. Yet, even as entrepreneurial pressures on kinship have receded, change can be slow because traditions die hard, but, more importantly, because extended family units have provided economic security as a source of pooled income—particularly in poor industrializing societies. Eventually, norms of descent, family size and composition, and residence lost their power; in their place, smaller nuclear units moving about in terms of neolocal residence rules and truncated bilateral descent reemerge, taking kinship back to the original hunter/gatherer pattern. Norms of authority and family activity often have lagged behind descent and residence, however, typically burdening women with the legacy of patriarchy. Still, there is pressure for more-egalitarian authority and a more equitable division of family activities in post-industrial societies, especially as women enter the labor market and bring income home.

As work is separated from home and is performed for wages, pressures for nuclearization of the family mount (except in poor societies where low wages have forced nuclear family units to pool income in a single residence). But in more-advanced industrial systems, extra children and other nonwage-earning relatives become liabilities rather than assets; they compromise standards of living rather than contributing to them (Boserup 1981, 1965). Moreover, as women work outside the home for wage incomes, the logistics of large families with many children become more difficult, thereby encouraging not only nuclear families but smaller families as well. However, this trend toward smaller families is often counteracted by cultural traditions and/or (mis)perceptions among the poor that extra children will eventually be an additional source of income.

Separation of work from family, coupled with a wage income, enable families to be more mobile, moving as supply and demand in labor markets change. Descent, nonneolocal residence rules, and extended families all hinder mobility; and if the mobility allowed in agrarian systems has not broken down these norms, industrialism usually does, because labor markets are more diverse and geographically dispersed as gathering and production processes seek new resources or customers.

The effects of geographical mobility on kinship are compounded by career mobility, as children move into different occupations, thereby acquiring training and skills different from their parents'. Such mobility generates cultural and social distance, or at the very least, diverse experiences which make it difficult to sustain extended families, descent, authority, or residence restrictions. Neolocal residence, small nuclear-family units, and free choice in marriage partners are all more compatible with both geographic and occupational mobility.

Vocational mobility reflects structural changes in industrializing and post-industrializing economies. New kinds of economic positions and occupations are constantly being created; and educational credentials for these positions are escalating. Thus, children are forced to "move away" culturally, experientially, occupationally and, often, geographically from the parents' household. Such mobility begins with schooling of children, because children "move out of" the family for significant periods a day. Thus, at an early age and increasingly over a long period of years, children become ever more independent of their families. And eventually, when the time comes to move away from the family (in accordance with neolocal residence rules), the young experience little difficulty, since a lifetime of daily departures has preceded the final move. This is particularly true as youth leave home for extended periods to attend college, often never to return and reside in their parents' residence (although anecdotal accounts suggest that college graduates frequently return home at least until they can become economically independent of parents).

Aside from reinforcing neolocality, participation in school structures has tended to undermine, somewhat, rigid authority relations within nuclear families. With participation in the educational system, a child's level of knowledge and skills becomes sophisticated at a comparatively early age, and by adolescence it may surpass those of his or her parents. Yet adolescents must remain in the household unit under parental supervision—a situation that can become problematic because the young participate in so many nonfamilial activities, such as peer groups and voluntary organizations, for most of their waking hours. Just how parents and other kin are to regulate and control their offspring, who are tied to them financially and emotionally but at the same time independent of them socially, can become a source of tension in the family. One typical family adjustment to this problem has been for parental authoritarianism to give way to more-egalitarian relations between kin generations. As this weakening of authority occurs, other kinship norms also become less salient. For example, rules of endogamy and exogamy become difficult to enforce, as do rules of residence and descent. Thus, economic conditions requiring the young to participate in school structures disrupt traditional kinship norms, although such disruption generates a series of new problems: How much freedom should the young have? How egalitarian should relations be? How should parents and children interact? What socialization practices should parents employ? How is the generation gap to be handled? The isolated, nuclear family has few clear-cut kinship norms guiding its members in these areas. And perhaps it never can, since the ever-changing economy and educational system generate new gaps between each generation of parents and young. Thus, societies with rapidly changing economies requiring prolonged participation of the young in schools will always face ambiguity in kinship norms concerning family activity, especially socialization.

Norms of authority, family activity, and socialization become even more problematic as women work for wages. Once women's work has a precisely defined value (in terms of money), the wife can claim authority and can renegotiate the family division of labor—not only with her spouse but her children as well. As long as women's domestic labor and its resulting contribution to economic survival remained vague and unmeasurable, demands for women's equality were difficult, especially in a patriarchal kinship system or in families with some of the legacy of patriarchy (Chafetz 1990; Blumberg 1984; Berk 1985, 1980). Once women's contribution can be measured precisely in money, there is a strain toward greater equality in the family between men and women; and increasingly women move away from the wife-mother roles to full partner roles, in which spouse and children share in domestic duties and spheres of authority.

Economy, Kinship, and Changing Functions

As the kinship system becomes nucleated and as it loses its entrepreneurial functions for organizing economic elements, dramatic changes in the distribution and importance of its functions ensue. The family releases some socialization functions to schools; and increasingly, the family only places individuals into the broader society indirectly through its effects on children's performance in schools. Kinship retains its functions for regulating sex and mating as well as biological support of the young. But even here, high rates of childbearing outside of marriage and high rates of divorce in western societies produce many single-parent households, underscoring that kinship is less effective in performing key functions than previously.

Kinship, however, has assumed increased social and emotional support burdens for several reasons. First, smaller and mobile nuclear units are more often isolated from other kin who could help parents and children with support. Second, market-driven systems, coupled with the bureaucratic organization of most spheres of activity, demand neutrality and specificity of individuals—with the result that supportive, familiar, and emotionally laden relationships are more difficult to create and sustain outside the family. As a consequence, the family often must shoulder this increased emotional and social support burden. However, the kin unit becomes less able to do so as rates of divorce and remarriage produce tension-filled step-relations, as single- working-parent families increase, as working parents force children into bureaucratized day care, and as generational differences (behavioral, cultural, experiential) grow.

POLITY AND KINSHIP

The Emergence of Kin-Based Polity

Small bands of hunter-gatherers did not need government; people performed traditional economic and familial roles, talking over problem that might come up. If conflict erupted, the band generally split apart, with the antagonistic parties forming new bands. Leaders in these simple systems were informal, noted for their abilities, and followed only if others were so inclined.

But once humans settled down, and populations began to grow, leadership became more imperative. If protagonists could no longer go their own way, how was conflict to be resolved? If land became property, who was to distribute it and the rights to its use? If surplus food was now produced, who decided what was to be done with it? If outside populations invaded territories, who was to coordinate people for war?

One can see beginnings of polity in hunter-gatherers who had settled down, usually near a waterway or ocean that provided food to support a larger, year-round population. Under these conditions, a Big Man often emerged and made decisions for the population as a whole, although once this leader died, there was no clear heir to his position—a situation that often threw villages into conflict (Johnson and Earle 1987, 160–93; Boas 1921). As populations grew and moved into full-fledged horticulture, however, the demands or selection pressures for more-stable leadership intensified. At the very least, there were more people to coordinate, more property to distribute, more economic surplus to allocate, and more enemies to defend against. And hence, much as economic pressures forced the elaboration of kinship, so these pressures for leadership put pressure on members of populations to use blood and marriage ties to create kin-based polity. The descent rule became the key to building a system of leaders, primarily because it could provide instructions about lines of authority and was, therefore, the easiest evolutionary path to take.

As lineages, clans, or moieties were constructed in unilineal descent systems, norms designated certain kin as decision makers for the larger kin grouping—usually the eldest and/or ablest male of a descent grouping in a patrilineal system. These norms delineated and delimited the spheres of influence for various decision makers in a society, and coupled with family-authority norms, descent rules could provide an efficient way to delegate authority or establish a chain of command in a society without a governmental bureaucracy and administrative staff. Such rules could resolve administrative problems by indicating which adults in each family unit would possess ultimate authority. And when combined with descent norms, family-authority norms indicated just who the "chief executive" and his "lieutenants" were. Extended or polygamous family norms also promoted clarity in decision making by specifying the sphere of authority that each decision maker possessed within the larger descent grouping.

In indicating where kin were to live, residence norms enclosed kin within various geographical areas, thereby facilitating coordinated decision making by cutting down on geographical dispersion. Too much dispersion would inhibit decision making, especially when systems of transportation and communication were cumbersome and could not effectively unite large territories. Residence rules also sought to stabilize the boundaries and numbers of those in a political sphere by attempting to regularize and keep in balance immigrants and emigrants. Ideally, but rarely in actual practice (because of varying sex ratios, age distributions, and mortality rates), rules sought to assure that for each daughter who left a territory, a new daughter-in-law would come in (assuming patrilocal residence rules). The reverse was attempted in a matrilocal system.

Marriage rules such as exogamy forced actors outside their kin group or village in search of partners. In gathering partners from other kin groups (or villages), a system of political allegiances and alliances emerged among kin groupings and communities. Exogamy in conjunction with rules of residence forced kin to exchange kindred with other kin groups and/or villages. To be at war or have strained relations with these other groups or communities would make life miserable for transplanted kin. Thus, these cross-cutting kin ties promoted allegiances and some degree of political stability in societies lacking a well-articulated state or military apparatus.

Thus, kinship rules can create a very effective system of authority by establishing a chain of command and a system of political alliances. Yet, as the size and scale of society increased, kinship began to recede as the basis for organizing polity. In its place came the state, because the problems of coordination and control—representing "political selection pressures"—began to exceed the organizational capacities of kinship.

The Emergence of the State and Kinship

One of the structural problems of kin-based polities is that they were rife with tension (Maryanski and Turner 1992). Fights, feuds, and warfare were endemic, primarily because people resented, or were jealous of, control by relatives. Power is always resented by those without it, and when family and power are interwoven, these resentments can take on double force.

In addition to this structural weakness, kin-based systems could only work effectively when the kinship was organizing economic activity. As economy and kinship began to differentiate with agrarianism, alternatives to kin-based government were sought. Indeed, there was often intense selection pressure on a population to find alternatives or face disintegration.

The first states were, no doubt, kin-based—at least at the top where a feudal monarchy or kin-based chiefdom was often organized along the lines of descent rules, with authority, residence, and marriage among elites very much influenced by the norms of the older kinship system. Below the hereditary nobility, however, a less-kin-based bureaucracy began to emerge as warfare, tax collection, public works, policing and managing other nobles, accounting, recording, law making, and other activities were performed. This bureaucracy was, of course, filled with personnel receiving noble favors and with appointments based on elite patronage—thereby making it rather inefficient and filled with corruption. Yet the structural form of elites and their administrative staff was set, and as the scale and complexity of tasks increased, a growing percentage of incumbents in polity came from nonelite families.

As this process unfolded, kinship was no longer needed to organize power, authority, and leadership. Indeed, kin-based authority, such as a clan in a particular region, would be seen by a monarch as a threat to the emerging state and would be pressured to disband or be destroyed in conflict with the state. As unilineal kinship was disbanded, descent and residence rules lost much of their power. People were reassembled in a more feudal pattern on manorial estates as tenant farmers and craftspersons, or they migrated to emerging urban areas to seek new economic opportunities. Agrarianism thus differentiated economy, polity, and kinship from one another, breaking the hold of kinship but imposing the hold of the nobility and state (Maryanski and Turner 1992).

State and Kinship in Industrial Societies

Usually during late agrarianism, but almost always with industrialization and post-industrialization, the state and kinship began to enter a new form of exchange: Welfare to kin units and individuals was exchanged for political support and commitment to the goals established by polity. Exploitation by the agrarian nobility (who it took all they could get) was replaced incrementally by increased responsiveness to the demands of the general populace—although coercion, corruption, and exploitation still prevail in the industrial world.

Smaller, nuclear kinship units are vulnerable economically, since if one loses one's job or one's wages decline, little backup can be expected from kindred (at least, kin are not *required* to provide assistance). Added to this economic vulnerability are other problems associated with nuclear kinship systems: how to support the elderly; how to help children in out-of-wedlock or single-parent households; how to overcome the pathological consequences of poverty on all family members, but especially children; and how to limit family size in an economy that cannot absorb all its people or a family system that cannot support all its members.

These issues have brought government directly into family life, providing support and encouraging family planning. As government has intervened, its interests increasingly revolve around how to cut the costs of such support. Thus, government directly or indirectly pushes members of nuclear units to plan and regulate their size in accordance with their ability to support family members. The polities of western Europe have well-planned systems of welfare, whereas others such as the United States and Japan reveal less-coherent systems of state intervention (Esping-Andersen 1994). Less developed industrial polities often cannot afford welfare, or must cope with traditional beliefs in large, extended family systems, whose poverty only burdens the state further.

Out of intervention, however, have come pressures—sometimes subtle and indirect and, at other times, heavyhanded—to reduce family size (and hence, costs to the state) and, relatedly, to break the last vestiges of extended kinship norms where additional family members are seen as a means of support. Moreover, for whatever assistance is offered, the polity attempts to extract loyalty through its control of the education system.

EDUCATION AND KINSHIP

To encourage economic development or to keep it going in post-industrial societies, governments have supported systems of education that not only train people for the economy but also socialize them into a political culture and, hopefully, into becoming loyal subjects of the state and its goals. Education thus pulls children out of the family—thereby altering the structure and functioning of the family—and gives the state some control over what children learn.

At times, the state intervention into the socialization functions of the family is direct and extensive. In the old Soviet Union, for example, the Soviet "kindergarten" could take children from infancy up to seven years. In these kindergartens, children were fed, provided with medical care, and given instruction for up to twelve hours each day (Bronfenbrenner 1968). Parents would drop children off in the morning and pick them up in the evening. Similarly in the Israeli kibbutz (Spiro 1956), socialization came under the control of the polity, with children from an early age spending the majority of their waking hours in schools. The consequence of such intervention was that it removed from the family almost completely the early socialization, biological-support, and social-placement functions. Perhaps it increased the social-support consequences of the family, although many Soviet kindergartens had professional counselors to provide necessary emotional guidance (Bronfenbrenner 1968, 57–65).

The major effect of such direct state control of socialization has been the transformation of kinship norms. With state socialization, both parents have been able (or required) to work—thus promoting egalitarianism in principle but rarely in actual fact, as old norms of patriarchy persist. And with the abandonment of many socialization functions, one of the major forces promoting the persistence of descent, residence, and marriage rules has been eliminated. Only rarely has the political system directly assumed functions usually performed by the family, however, and only under special pressures has the state intervened. (In the case of Israeli kibbutz, workers in fields as well as defenders of borders were needed; and in the post-Revolution Soviet Union, pursuit of rapid economic development along with the desire to develop a new "Soviet Citizen" were paramount.)

These facts permit a few generalizations about the conditions under which the polity has been most likely to take on the socialization burden:

1. When a major system goal such as economic development requires a new kind of incumbent with traits radically different from those of the previous generation.
2. When human capital shortages exist and all adults must work, and when elders in the traditional kinship system cannot assume the socialization burden.
3. When the polity must create a generation of incumbents loyal to a new political system.
4. When the polity needs to engage in excessive social control and manipulation.

But more often than not, even under these conditions, the polity has refrained from direct involvement in family affairs, because state socialization is expensive and because people strongly resist intrusion into their families.

More typically intervention is indirect, revolving around state-supported public education. The goals of the polity—whether economic development, social equality, eliminating poverty, national defense, or world dominance—generally require citizens to have personality traits that can be acquired only in educational structures. To the extent that the polity cannot achieve major goals, its long-run legitimacy and viability will be undermined. Thus, because of the centrality of education to the state's achievement of goals and to its legitimacy, the polity has often had to promote education in order to persist.

In poor industrializing societies, education has been viewed as the symbol of, and the key to, modernization. Polities, therefore, are likely to encourage the development of educational structures, per se, even though there are few positions—especially economic—to absorb graduates. For example, in India, educational structures have proliferated and expanded beyond the capacity of the economy or other institutions to absorb all of the educated work force, leading to situations where, for example, people with engineering degrees drive taxicabs or buses. Such systems also suffer from a severe "brain drain," since their students studying abroad are reluctant to return to an economy that cannot place them. One major consequence of extensive educational development is that polities divert potential economic capital to education and thereby impede economic development and the emergence of those economic positions where the educated actor could become employed. The solution to this problem may appear easy—to strike a better balance in the allocation of resources between the economy and education. But the populations of developing countries often define education as welfare, as something that polity *must* do for the people to make their lives better. Educational structures are highly visible and offer impoverished people hope that things are getting better; should the polity not invest in education, the population might withdraw its legitimacy and approval from government. In essence, the polity is forced to concentrate on education in developing systems, even if it does not want to or is aware of the long-run consequences. These facts lead to an important conclusion: Economic and political pressures on the emergence of education as an institution are often separate. Polities can accelerate or retard the emergence of education somewhat independently of economic conditions.

In most industrial and post-industrial societies—where the polity supports extensive preschool educational programs as well as primary, secondary, and higher education—the impact of the polity on kinship can be profound, whereas in other societies where only primary and secondary education are heavily financed by the polity, the effect on kinship will be lessened. In the long run, however, the polity's support of education tends to expand; and once the polity supports preschool through graduate education, kinship is usually altered. In these societies, the family releases to the schools many of its social reproduction, social placement, and social support functions. Children at an early age leave home for significant periods of their waking hours and participate in formal education structures. Preschool and kindergarten are less formal, emphasizing social support functions for the student, but as a student progresses in the educational system, social placement and socialization functions come to dominate. Students learn those traits that will largely determine where they become incumbent in the wider society—especially the economy.

As a kinship system loses significant portions of its socialization and placement consequences for a society, the last remnants of traditional kinship norms begin to break down. Norms of parental authority are difficult to enforce as children reach adolescence, since dependents' level of knowledge, mental skills, and interpersonal styles approach or surpass those of their parents. Residence rules become less salient as the child increasingly participates away from home in school structures or in peer groupings and organizations; and in systems where universities are dominant structures and where adolescents must leave the home for long periods of time, traditional residence rules disappear. Marriage rules also change under these conditions, since heterosexual activity can occur in a setting geographically separated from the home. Once residence, authority, and marriage rules break down, extendedness of the family unit is difficult to maintain. For as the young feel no obligation to live near parents, question the authority of elder kin, and choose their own mates, maintaining a large and stable family unit with several generations of kin becomes highly problematic. With all these changes, descent necessarily becomes truncated, especially since social placement is now as much an educational as a familial function.

And so as the extensiveness of the educational subsystem supported by the polity increases, the last vestiges of the descent, size and composition, residence, authority, and marriage rules of traditional kinship systems lose their force. In their place come new norms as kin groupings attempt to cope with the conditions generated by an advanced educational system: Neolocal residence makes less problematic the separation from home in order to participate in educational statuses; egalitarian family norms make the authority (and generation-gap) problems generated by schools less severe; "romantic love" norms are more compatible with mate selection away from home; and truncated descent rules remove the young student from troublesome problems concerning loyalty and involvement with kin. In late agrarianism, much of this change usually has already occurred, but industrialization completes the nuclearization of the family and the hold of descent rules and other traditional restrictions on residence, marriage, and authority.

RELIGION AND KINSHIP

As the purveyor of the supernatural, religion has had the power to bestow special meaning—indeed, a sacredness—on norms and behaviors in society. Thus, if the norms of kinship can be made sacred, as embodying the will and wishes of supernatural forces, they will be given additional salience and will be subject to more intense sanctions. For now, to violate a kinship norm is to invite the wrath or intervention of the supernatural (Wallace 1966; Harris 1971). Ancestor worship among hunter-gatherers was one of the first ways in which religious beliefs gave power to kinship norms (although probably less than 25 percent of hunter-gatherers practiced ancestor worship; see Lenski, Nolan, and Lenski 1995, 150). As kinship systems elaborated during horticulture, ancestor worship became much more prevalent, and new religious beliefs enhanced the sacred quality of kinship norms, thereby increasing the chances that kin members would abide by them. More elaborate rituals were directed toward ancestors, who were seen to inhabit the supernatural realm, and as these rituals were emitted, they reinforced descent rules and strengthened the sense of kin continuity. Kinship was not just for the living; it reached back to include the dead. Moreover, fears of being labeled deviant, particularly by virtue of special powers such as witchcraft, kept people in line and, in so doing, reinforced key kinship norms (Wallace 1966; Swanson 1960; Whiting 1950).

Religious rituals were also critical to *rites de passage* within kinship, marking transitions to new statuses and roles and, in the process, reenforcing the norms of kinship. As children grow, they assume new statuses within their family and larger kin grouping; and the new normative obligations accompanying these statuses require a new set of attitudes, dispositions, and self-identity. Religious rituals surrounding such major status transitions generate particular awareness of these new obligations by bringing to bear supernatural forces and admonishing the young under the threat of supernatural intervention to display the dispositions and behavior appropriate to their newly acquired station in life. The puberty rites of many traditional societies were a conspicuous example of how religious rituals solemnly informed adolescents that they were now close to assuming adult status, marking emphatically the transformed relationship between these new adults and their fellow kinsmen. In this way, internal family reorganization occurred with a minimal amount of internal role strain and conflict among kinsmen. Marriage is another major status transition, for it marks the creation of a new family or the incorporation of new members into an existing extended family. In either case, a reorganization of the kinship system occurs; and by marking such reorganization with religious or sacred significance, the new obligations attendant on both the marrying partners and their kinsmen are made explicit, if not emphatic. The birth of a child confers another cluster of obligations on parents and surrounding kinsmen and has, therefore, become marked by religious rituals. Since birth is the beginning of social reproduction and ultimately a society's persistence, these rituals often have been very elaborate, as among the Zuñi. In delivering her child, a mother called upon a Zuñi priest to enact the appropriate rituals. The child was placed in a bed of hot stones covered with sand and then appropriate prayers were offered for a long life and good health. Four days later, the child and mother were brought to the Sun Father at dawn to be ritually washed and to offer more prayers (Turner 1972, 128).

Probably the most dramatic status transition experienced by members of a kinship system is death. A death profoundly reorganizes family and kinship relations, since a person for whom strong attachments and emotions existed is simply removed from the daily life of the kin group; and when a kinship leader dies, reorganization of the larger kin grouping must ensue. It is therefore not surprising that elaborate religious rituals have surrounded death, since the removal of a kinsman have always generated both intrapersonal anxiety and the need for structural reorganization of the family. Death rituals have thus provided for the alleviation of anxiety and grief, as well as the ritual reintegration of the disrupted kinship group.

Historically, as populations no longer relied on kinship to organize economic and political activity, new forms of social integration have emerged—polity, law, markets, and nonkin corporate units, for instance—and these can displace religion as well as kinship as the principle integrative forces in society. This transformation of religion is clearly evident within the kinship system, where religious rituals have lost much of their significance in marking major status transitions. Birth, marriage, and death are still observed ritually, but these rituals have come to have less importance for maintaining the social organization of kinship. The small size of the family unit and the lack of powerful descent norms in the kinship systems of industrial and post-industrial societies have further diminished the necessity for religious integration. Coordination and control in a small, isolated, and conjugal family may come more from interpersonal adjustment and accommodations of members than from the implied threat of divine intervention and sanction. Furthermore, crucial kinship norms in modern societies increasingly become reinforced by law and the threat of *secular* sanctions. Still, for many families in industrial and post-industrial societies, religion remains salient and gives a sense of sacredness to the bonds of family members, but even in these circumstances, religion is more salient for the well-being of the individual than for the family as a whole.

LAW AND KINSHIP

Law and Kinship in Pre-Industrial Societies

For most of human history, law was embedded in kinship, religion, and polity, becoming structurally autonomous only with advanced horticulture and agrarianism. Indeed, for law to begin differentiating, a population had to have a written language (to write down law) as well as an economic surplus sufficient to support separate courts, legislative bodies, and policing activities. For hunter-gatherers and simple horticulturalists, and often well into agrarianism, the rules of the legal system remained unwritten, bound with tradition, lodged in people's minds, and frequently infused with religious overtones (Turner 1980; Lloyd 1964; Hoebel 1954).

In such societies, laws concerning kinship roles were often fused with kinship norms—a fact that poses an analytical problem of how to discover which kinship norms are also a part of the undifferentiated legal system in a society. One way to get around this problem is to examine those kinship norms which if violated were *enforced* by specific persons and statuses, and around which mediating statuses (or primitive courts) were invoked. Some kinship norms could be violated and not much happened, whereas violation of other norms automatically led to specific types of punishment by designated kin. For example, to desert one's family, in some traditional societies, automatically gave the adult male kin of the deserted party the right to punish the deserter. These kin constituted the counterpart of a police force in a modern society; and though they did not have precinct headquarters or a radio dispatcher, they temporarily occupied the status of police officers. There could be other kin, perhaps elders, who when family desertion occurred, assumed the status of court judges and decided on appropriate punishments. Most of the time they were just elderly kin, but with certain violations of norms, they assumed the legal position of judge, and their behavior was guided by a set of norms evoked specifically for their temporary status. Legal systems function in this way where economic resources and social needs do not allow or justify a separate system of laws, police, and courts (Hoebel 1954).

In general, those kinship norms most relevant to the functions of kinship—regularizing sex and mating, biological and social support, reproduction, and placement—were the likely candidates for legal action. These functions were performed exclusively by kin units in traditional systems, and their neglect would pose serious survival problems for the society, making rules concerning the minimal performance of these activities by kin part of the incipient legal system. Naturally, the content of these laws would be as varied as the profile of kinship in human societies. But over time, as populations coped with the disruptions and conflicts generated by violations of crucial kinship norms, these norms became incorporated into a special body of rules that carried with them specific sanctions by designated members of a society. Because so much human activity in hunting-gathering and simple horticultural societies was organized and carried out within kinship, many of these laws as well as their mediation and enforcement focused on the "correct" performance of kinship roles.

This legal embellishment of crucial kinship rules gave them extra power because individuals knew that violating these rules would bring adjudication and sanctions by specific kindred; and in the face of such well-understood consequences, kin norms were more likely to be obeyed. Thus, although law was not differentiated and highly visible in these simple societies, it was nonetheless operating to facilitate order and societal integration.

Law and Kinship in Industrial and Post-Industrial Societies

With late agrarianism, and rapidly accelerating with industrialization and post-industrialization, law became a clearly differentiated institutional system, revealing distinguishable networks of statutes, police, courts, agencies, and law-enacting bodies. Not only was law clearly differentiated from other institutions such as kinship, but it began to display considerable internal differentiation and specialization. One differentiated area of specialization in industrial and post-industrial societies is "family law," where separate codes, courts, and agencies are concerned with sources of disruption, conflict, and deviance in family relations. While many aspects of family law tend to be anachronistic and/or reflective of the moral biases of legislators and enforcement agencies, some of these specialized family laws can have consequences for managing problems associated with unstable or pathological families. Some of the most important arenas for such intervention are discussed below.

Law and Premarital Sex   Premarital sex relations occur in all populations—even those prohibiting them. In modern societies there is a trend toward removing both legal and informal rules and restrictions against sex. But even with contraceptive techniques widely available, pregnancy out of wedlock occurs; and it is in this area that the rules, courts, and agencies of a modern legal system intervene. Despite enormous variability in laws applying to childbirth out of wedlock, almost all modern legal systems require the father to support his child financially, although they vary enormously in how stringently the law is enforced. In some instances the father must also support the mother, but again, these laws often go unenforced. The intended consequence of such laws is to assure the biological support of children in the absence of other kin; and in so doing, the law encourages and facilitates a nuclear kinship system that does not have to rely on additional kin to support single-parent arrangements.

Law and Marriage   In modern societies marriage becomes a *legal contract.* Even where no official marriage ceremony is performed, common-law marriages are usually considered legally binding after a specified period of time. While marriage is perhaps one of the most frequently violated contracts, it is still both a reflection of, and a stimulus to, nuclearization of kinship. One effect of this situation is that family units created by marriage can be neolocal and hence, less concerned with descent, because laws rather than kindred regulate the general obligations of marriage partners. Thus legal intervention in marriage becomes likely when the breakdown of traditional sources of social control such as kinship, religion, and community begins to occur. At the same time, legal intervention accelerates the dissipation of these traditional sources of social control, and in doing so, it encourages further nuclearization of kin units.

Law and Socialization   Populations cannot persist without reproduction through socialization of new generations to replace the old. In societies where much of this socialization must occur outside the family in schools, compulsory-education laws are likely to be enacted in order to assure the socialization of the young. As outlined earlier, such legal intervention into socialization can have multiple consequences for kinship modernization: Compulsory-education laws remove from the exclusive purview of family one of its traditional functions—socialization. By forcing children to participate in formal structures requiring specificity and neutrality, these laws increase the social support consequences of the family. Forced education away from the family creates a sense of independence and a cosmopolitan outlook in the young, decreasing the salience of norms of residence, extendedness, and a unilineal descent. Socialization in structures outside the family also makes strict authority patterns difficult to maintain for more-cosmopolitan children. Thus, while compulsory-education laws probably are enacted for economic, political, and humanitarian reasons, they have the consequence—usually unanticipated—of reinforcing nuclearization of kinship.

Law and Child Care   The legal system in all modern societies establishes minimal criteria for biological maintenance of infants and the young. These laws usually concern neglect and brutality. In systems with an isolated conjugal family structure where kin are excluded from family life, child-care laws become essential because there are no kindred to control and inhibit neglect of the young. These laws can support the exclusion of kin from the household (as well as other features of a modern kinship system) by removing extended kin from the obligation of overseeing child care and support.

Law and Family Authority   While several economic pressures contribute to this trend toward egalitarianism in the family, there are also supports from the legal system. Women in post-industrial societies have legal rights not typical of women in patriarchal traditional societies, including rights to make contracts, vote, own property, make wills, sue and be sued, as well as rights for equal employment, education, and recreation. Before the law, men and women are usually equal in industrial and post-industrial societies. These general rights are codified in a myriad of laws from civil rights to business contracts, and they give women an equality in the wider society which inevitably spills over into family relations. When the legal system supports the rights of women to engage in economic, legal, and recreational activities outside the home, kinship norms of male authoritarianism no longer receive the institutional support from law evident in agrarian and early industrial systems. Once the legal system undermines this authoritarianism, the remnants of other kinship rules become less viable: Descent rules to the male's side of the family are weakened; family socialization changes; residence becomes a joint decision made by both adults; and extendedness becomes difficult to maintain.

Law and Divorce   Family dissolution represents a problem in all societies because it raises questions of what is to be done with dependents, especially children. In traditional kinship systems, rules of residence, descent, and authority, plus the existence of a large and extended family unit, made these problems less difficult. Children were allocated to the kin deemed appropriate by these kinship rules; thus, even high divorce rates did not seriously threaten the performance of biological support and socialization in traditional societies. But in systems with an isolated nuclear family, truncated descent, neolocal residence, and egalitarian authority norms, a high dissolution rate poses a more serious problem, because kinship rules do not offer guidelines as to how children are to be allocated or cared for. Under these conditions, laws and various family-service agencies attached to courts tend to emerge to cope with these problems (Bohannan and Hickleberry 1967). Extensive bodies of divorce law, specialized courts, and state-managed agencies dealing with family dissolution thus become a prominent feature of modern legal systems.

Yet surprisingly, the legal agencies revolving around family dissolution—especially divorce—do not always facilitate, ease, or regularize family breakup. One reason for this situation is that laws—especially in early stages of industrialization—often reflect moral biases appropriate to preindustrial times and are changed only under strong public pressure. As the susceptibility of the family to breakup increases under economic and other pressures, however, laws inhibiting family dissolution increasingly become self-defeating since they encourage desertions and unregulated separation. Desertions and separations can generate even more-serious problems, because under these circumstances it is unclear how the child is to be cared for and socialized.

Legal systems in post-industrial societies are now in transition. As the inevitability of family breakup in modern societies is recognized, laws, courts, police, and agencies are being restructured to cope with this inevitability. Rather than being prohibitive, legal systems are becoming restructured to either correct the sources of dissolution and/or facilitate it by providing clear procedural guidelines for such dissolution. Increasingly, the conditions for divorce are liberalized, the court proceedings simplified, and the processes for allocating property and dependents clarified. The effect of these changes is to encourage and facilitate further nuclearization of kin units in modern post-industrial societies.

CONCLUSION

Kinship was once the locus of virtually all institutional activity—economic, political, religious, legal, and educational. But as the scale of societies kept increasing over the last ten thousand years, separate institutions differentiated out from kinship. At each step in this process—beginning with advanced horticulture and accelerating successively through the agrarian, industrial, and post-industrial eras—kinship has become increasingly nucleated, losing its earlier majesty and many of its functions to other institutions.

Yet, for most humans life begins in the family, which in broader terms means that survival of the species begins in kinship. Both biological and social reproduction thus remain important, as do the emotional and social support functions of kindred. Though kinship is no longer the dominant organizational principle of society, and even though it must respond and adapt to external institutional forces that make its burden greater, human society is not possible or viable without a kinship system.

Chapter
6

Religion

Neandertals began to populate the earth at least 250,000 years ago. One of their most interesting habits was that they buried their dead, and around these burial sites have been found the remains of ritual and perhaps worship: pollen from bouquets of flowers, skulls placed on sticks, paintings marking entrances to burial caves, and stones arranged in patterns around graves. Just what these artifacts mean never can be known for sure, but they suggest concern about the afterlife and the nonempirical world of beings and forces existing in a special realm. In a word, they suggest religion among hominids whose brain was equal and, in fact, some larger than contemporary humans. (Whether Neandertals are the immediate ancestors of humans or a closely related species is debated.)

Religion was thus one of the earliest human inventions and is nearly universal in all known human societies, which argues for its importance to humans psychologically and for their organization into society. Why, then, did humans create visions of another realm inhabited by special forces and/or beings to whom ritual appeals were owed? The general answer resides in the additional power that is given to activities believed to be sanctioned by the supernatural. Before exploring these functions in more detail, however, let us first see what makes religion a distinctive kind of institutional activity (Turner 1972, 342–46; Wallace 1966; Kurtz 1995, 51–101).

ELEMENTS OF RELIGION

The Sacred and Supernatural

All religions involve a notion of the sacred, or the special qualities imputed to objects and events that have been touched by supernatural forces or that symbolize the supernatural. Because the sacred arouses intense emotions, it gives religion tremendous influence in mobilizing and controlling human action in a society (Durkheim 1912).

Though there are some notable exceptions (Wuthnow 1988, 474), religions usually contain assumptions about the supernatural, or a realm lying outside the everyday world and having the capacity to bestow sacredness on things and events. This other world is conceived as being occupied by forces, beings, spirits, and powers which in some way alter, circumscribe, and influence this world's happenings and occurrences. Sometimes the supernatural is a series of forces—all seeing and all knowing. The "mana" of many traditional societies was such a force which could change, alter, intervene in the world, and bestow sacred power to objects, but which itself was not an object—only a vague and diffuse source of power underlying natural events. But frequently the supernatural is conceived of as a set of personified beings—gods and deities. And sometimes the supernatural is seen as a spirit having the form of animals and other living creatures (Swanson 1960, 8). Whatever its form, societies have viewed the supernatural as underlying and influencing the natural world.

Ritual

Rituals are *stereotyped* ways of behaving with respect to the supernatural (Goode 1951, 38–50). The content of ritual varies tremendously and can involve such forms of behavior as prayer, music, dancing, singing, exhortation, reciting a code, taking drugs, eating, drinking, making sacrifices, and congregating (Wallace 1966, 52–70). Basically there are two types of rituals: *calendrical* and *noncalendrical*. Calendrical rituals are enacted on a regular schedule—day or night, at the waxing or waning of the moon, at the beginning or ending of seasons, at eclipses and positions of planets and stars, or on the birthdays of supernatural beings. In contrast, noncalendrical rituals are performed sporadically, on special occasions, or in times of crises. Some noncalendrical rituals, such as the puberty rites or *rites de passage* of many societies, follow something of a cycle and occur at certain more- or less-determined times in the life of an individual. However, the time, place, and period of such rituals are not precisely set by the calendar. Both calendrical and noncalendrical rituals serve to link the natural and supernatural worlds by activating the emotions of individuals toward the sacredness of the supernatural (Collins 1988; Durkheim [1912] 1965). Much of what is observable about a religion is, therefore, seen in ritual activities of a community of worshipers (Wallace 1966, 71; Goode 1951, 48–52).

Beliefs

Beliefs articulate conceptions of the supernatural and sacred realms, defining the meaning of rituals (Goode 1951) while rationalizing their performance (Wallace 1966). Religious beliefs usually become part of the broader culture of a society and generally consist of two components, (1) a *cosmology* and (2) a *system of values*.

Cosmology   A cosmology is a set of beliefs concerning the nature of a universe, including the natural and supernatural. A cosmology often includes a *pantheon,* or group of supernatural beings and/or forces that in varying degrees affect and alter social processes in the natural world. In many religions, the beings and forces in the pantheon are ranked in a hierarchy of power and influence—from the most powerful god, to lesser gods, to mortals who are godlike. A cosmology also contains a body of myths that describe the historical events leading to the current hierarchical ordering of supernatural beings and that describe the origin, career, and interaction of gods with ordinary or only quasi-sacred mortals. In some societies, these myths are codified into basic texts, such as the Old Testament, the New Testament, and the Koran. Cosmologies typically include *substantive beliefs* about planes of existence lying outside the natural world—heaven, hell, nirvana, and other realms in the supernatural. Yet in many simple religions, the cosmology is not well developed, consisting of a series of entities and forces who reveal no clear hierarchy and who inhabit only a vaguely conceived supernatural realm.

Values   Religious values guiding, justifying, and sanctioning ritual are usually very similar to those more secular values of a society's culture which regulate everyday activity. Values indicate what is right and wrong, proper and improper, and good or bad; and religious values are frequently codified into a religious code, such as the Ten Commandments in Christianity, the Ethics of Confucius in Confucianism, or the Noble Eight-Fold Path in Buddhism. Such values provide a highly general and overarching framework within which many secular values and specific norms in a society operate.

Cult Structures

A cult is the structural unit where those rituals made meaningful and justified by supernatural beliefs are enacted. As such, the cult is the most fundamental unit in the *institution* of religion in any society; and as we will see, the structure of cults can vary from a worldwide system (such as the Catholic Church) with a vast bureaucracy to a small and exclusive group of tribesmen engaged in a common ritual addressed to the supernatural. In all cults, the other elements of religion are instantiated: a set of common beliefs about the sacred and/or supernatural; a set of rituals designed to appeal to the supernatural; and a membership or community of worshipers who share the cult's beliefs about the sacred and supernatural and who engage in its rituals. Thus it is at the cult level of social organization that beliefs and rituals about the sacred and supernatural become integrated.

Frequently in the sociological literature and in lay terms as well, cults are considered to be small, charismatically led religious groupings which deviate from the more-established and larger church religions in a society. For example, religious groupings such as the Spiritualists, Bahai, Black Muslims, I Am, the Theosophical Society, the Father Divine Peace Mission Movement, and the early days of the Christian Science Movement are what sociologists usually label as cults. But in our terms, *cult* refers to *any* religious organization—no matter how large or small—that displays a concern for the supernatural and/or sacred, that shares beliefs, and that practices common rituals. Thus, cults can vary tremendously with respect to their size, degree of bureaucratization, existence of professional clergy, reliance on lay clergy, degree of centralization, stability of membership, and exclusiveness of membership (Wallace 1966, 84–101).[1] Religion in any society is, therefore, a distribution of cults; and except for the simplest societies, a variety of cult structures manifesting somewhat dissimilar beliefs and rituals is evident among a population.

In sum, then, the basic elements of all religious involve: (1) beliefs about the sacred and/or supernatural, or a realm lying beyond mundane activities and composed of beings and/or forces that are viewed as influencing on-going social action in a society as well as processes in nature; (2) stereotyped behaviors or rituals that arouse emotions, sustain beliefs, and provide links between the natural to the supernatural world; and (3) cult structures, consisting of a community of individuals who share beliefs about the sacred and supernatural and who engage in common rituals directed toward the sacred forces, entities, or beings of the supernatural.

SELECTION FORCES AND RELIGION

Religion is often a source of conflict and societal disintegration. But if this were its only consequence, it would never have emerged in the first place, nor would it have persisted to the present, even in the face of intense pressure for the secularization of social life. Religion was thus selected as a solution—albeit a most problematic one—to problems of organization revolving around (Turner 1972, 346–49): (1) reinforcing institutional norms, (2) legitimating tension-producing inequalities, (3) regulating social reproduction and placement, and (4) alleviating personal anxiety and tension. Each of these functions of religion is briefly examined.

---

[1] Sociologists have made a wide variety of typologies pertaining to the organization of religious status norms. Probably the most influential typology was Weber's two polar types of religious organization: the church and sect. These were developed in more detail by Weber's student Ernst Troeltsch ([1911] 1960), who viewed a *church* as a large, conservative, elite-based ascriptive and dominant religious organization. At the polar extreme to a church was a *sect*, which he viewed as a small, voluntary, quasi-rebellious religious order. Numerous amplifications of this typology have been made (Yinger 1970; Wilson 1969; Pfautz 1955; Becker 1950; Wuthnow 1988, 495). Generally, sociological typologies of religious organization include, from least to most organized: cult, sect, established sect, church, denomination, ecclesia (Salisbury 1964, 96–97; Moberg 1962, 73–99; Johnson 1960, 419–39). While useful in analyzing religion in modern societies, these distinctions do not allow us to grasp either the subtleties or complexity of traditional religious organization. Therefore, I have abandoned a sociological classification in favor of a more anthropological one (Wallace 1966). This classification will allow us to put in a comparative perspective modern religious organization. Thus, as noted above, cult structure is a generic term encompassing all *specific* forms of religious organization, whether a cult (in the sociological sense), sect, established sect, church, denomination, or ecclesia.

Religious rituals and values typically reinforce concrete norms guiding role behavior within the economic, familial, and political institutional spheres (Swanson 1960; Luckmann 1967; O'Dea 1970, 1966; O'Dea and Aviad 1983; Goode 1951; Durkheim [1912] 1965). Values give institutional norms special—perhaps even sacred—significance and thus increase the probability of conformity. Religious rituals, particularly in traditional societies, frequently permeate and circumscribe crucial role behaviors (Wallace 1966, 216–46). For example, among the Tikopia—a small, island society where fishing was one major economic activity (Firth 1936)—religious rituals assured adequate preparation of fishing canoes for often dangerous expeditions into the sea. The Tikopian natives viewed overhauling and caring for canoes as an extension of ritual obligations to the deities to secure food offerings. When work was performed as much for the gods as for human subsistence, the speed, energy, harmony, and coordination among workers increased greatly (Firth 1936, 90–95; Goode 1951, 107–9). Similar consequences of religion were evident in reinforcing and maintaining the Tikopian kinship system. For example, the patrilineal descent system of the Tikopians was reinforced by the fact that the dwelling of the oldest male ancestor was maintained as a temple for rituals to gods and ancestors (Goode 1951, 200), with patriarchal authority norms being reinforced by the exclusion of young women from certain religious rituals.

In more-economically developed societies, the reinforcing consequences of rituals for institutional processes decline, but religious beliefs—especially values—frequently have been the cultural underpinnings of many specific institutional norms. Indeed, when the religious code of the dominant religious cult in an industrial or post-industrial society is compared to the basic postulates and statutes of that society's legal system, it is clear that religion still exerts considerable influence on the normative system of a population. For law codifies many basic cultural values—especially those articulated by religions—and thereby mediates between religion and other institutional spheres.

In those societies where religion reinforces kinship norms, religion has profound consequences for regulating socialization and the eventual placement of the young in the broader society (Luckmann 1967). More specifically, religious rituals in many societies guide first the birth of a child and then mark with sacred significance his or her passage through adolescence, adulthood, and marriage. The religious rituals surrounding these status transitions, or *rites de passage*, regularize socialization and maturation, while impressing on their recipient the new normative rights and obligations attached to each new status. To exceed these rights or not to live up to the obligations becomes difficult when sanctioned by the supernatural. In this way religion helps assure commitment on the part of maturing actors entering new adult status positions. Among horticultural and early agrarian populations of the past, religious rituals were extremely elaborate and of great significance to the members of a society, whereas in industrial and post-industrial societies their impact tends to decline.

Societies revealing some degree of differentiation also display inequalities with respect to wealth, prestige, power, and privilege, thereby creating selection pressures for the legitimation of such inequality. Religion in pre-industrial societies not only had far-reaching consequences for legitimating political and other forms of activity, it also worked to legitimate the broader stratification system. This legitimating function reached its peak in the pre-colonial era in India, where the Hindu cosmology revolving around Karma and reincarnation became a justification for a rigid caste system of stratification. Those born orthodox Hindus (i.e., Brahmans) were entitled to elite caste positions, since the gods in controlling their reincarnation had placed them in an elite family. As Hinduism spread across India, non-Hindus were absorbed into inferior caste positions because the non-Hindu tribes were ritually "impure" and ignorant of basic Brahman beliefs. Although rarely as extreme as in precolonial India, religion in most traditional systems legitimated not only the institution of the polity but the broader stratification system in a society.

Moreover, as Max Weber ([1922] 1978, 491–2), recognized, religion's effect in supporting stratification varies for different social classes. For those high in the stratification system, religion legitimates their station as right and proper; for those lower in the system, religious beliefs typically hold out promises of a better station—or salvation—in the next life *if* beliefs are sustained and rituals practiced. It is this latter effect of religion that led Karl Marx ([1843] 1963, 441) to declare religion to be "the opium of the people" because it encouraged them to accept their situation in the present (with false promises for a better future). It is thus no coincidence that in the history of human societies, religion became more complex and concerned with control of earthly social patterns when stratification intensified. Guy Swanson (1960) found in his study of the emergence of high gods in fifty different types of pre-industrial societies, for example, that the supernatural becomes increasingly interested in everyday morality as the level of stratification increases. Similarly, Ralph Underhill (1975) developed a much larger sample of pre-industrial societies and found that the presence of a high god is related to societal complexity, a finding he interpreted in a Marxian tone as indicating that active high gods emerge when the economic system begins to generate stratification.

Even in more-industrial societies, studies have supported the notion that religiosity tends to be associated with political conservatism, a conservatism that legitimates political regimes and systems of stratification (Sanderson 1995, 483; Glock and Stark 1965). But since a smaller proportion of the population in industrial societies is religious, the effects of religion on sustaining stratification are reduced. Yet even though the direct influence of religion has declined, it is not difficult to see the religious roots of widely held beliefs that are often used to legitimate inequalities. For example, in the United States, the "Protestant ethic" is very much alive in Americans' distrust of the welfare system which "gives money to those who do not work" or in Americans' belief that those who "do not work" should not enjoy the same benefits as those who do. Or, to illustrate further, the intense identification of Americans' sense of self-worth with occupation and their concern with work and being "productive" reflect the continuing power of the "Protestant ethic."

Thus religion in all societies has consequences for social integration and control, whether through reinforcing institutional norms or legitimating inequality (Goode 1951, 222–23). Nonetheless, this fact should not obscure the potentially *disintegrative* consequences of religion for a society: New, emergent religious cults in a society can become a revolutionary collectivity. The sacralization of institutional norms can generate rigidity in behavior, which can become a liability when changes in the social and physical environment of a society require flexibility (O'Dea 1966). Religion can legitimate in the short run a ruthless political regime or oppressive stratification system, creating in the long run divisive and disintegrative strains in society, while generating disincentives for innovation (Childe 1953, 1952, 1951).

In all societies, people experience uncertainty, concern over the unknown, powerlessness, unpredictability, and anxiety. In providing a cosmology of the sacred and supernatural, religious beliefs have had the ability to alleviate or mitigate these multiple sources of tension; and in prescribing ritual behavior, religion has provided solutions to the individual and collective tensions among the members of a society. In horticultural and agrarian societies, where economic uncertainty was a constant condition of social life, these consequences of religion were extensive. In advanced industrial and post-industrial systems, where many economic uncertainties have been eliminated for at least some sectors of society, the alleviating consequences of religion are less far-reaching. But among many segments of the population in these societies—the poor, disenfranchised, the aged, and alienated—religion still provides an interpretation and answer to their fears and uncertainties. For example, many of the fundamentalist movements and small, sect-like cults emerging in industrialized and urbanized societies appeal to those who, for various reasons, cannot adjust to, or who feel marginal in, post-industrial social structures (Loftland and Stark 1965; Glock 1964). Yet, as has been clear in the United States, fundamentalists have become politically active, giving voice to those who feel marginalized and, thereby, reducing their sense of marginality. Moreover, in recent decades, studies in the United States have shown that fundamentalist beliefs need not be a reaction or barrier to broad participation in a post-industrial society (Wuthnow 1988, 484). Thus, as beliefs alleviate anxieties and manage tensions, they do not necessarily involve retreat from modernity but, instead, appear to give people a sense of meaning as they engage in the secular activities of a post-industrial society.

We are now in a position to define religion as an institutional system (Turner 1972, 349). *Religion is that structuring of activities revolving around beliefs and rituals pertaining to the sacred and/or supernatural and organized into cult structures which have consequences for reinforcing norms, legitimating inequality, guiding socialization and social placement, and managing variable sources of tension and anxiety in a society.* Despite the commonalities of all religion specified in this definition, the nature of beliefs, rituals, and cult structures has varied enormously, as human populations moved from hunting and gathering through horticulture and agrarianism to industrialism and post-industrialism.

BASIC TYPES OF RELIGIOUS SYSTEMS

There have been a number of attempts to delineate stages of religious evolution (e.g., Bellah 1970, 1964; Habermas 1979; Luhmann 1984; and Wallace 1966); and though each of these schemes is useful, Wallace's discussion of premodern religions will guide our review. To classify religions into types, we need to select some common dimensions that can serve as a point of reference for both comparing religions and recording their evolutionary development. Two such dimensions follow from the definition of religion presented above: (1) the nature of religious beliefs about the supernatural, and (2) the nature and organization of ritual activities in cult structures.

Simple Religions

Among hunter-gatherers, religion was comparatively simple. There could be beliefs about spirits and beings inhering in the empirical universe (sea, sky, plant life), but in many cases they were not perceived to exert extensive control over the world. Nor were they always worshiped as sacred in a highly intense way. There were no cult structures, save for the individual who may have practiced rituals that evoked feelings and emotions about spirits and beings.

Among hunter-gatherers who revealed a more-developed religion, part-time shamans emerged to act as mediators to the supernatural (Wallace 1966; Norbeck 1961). In these *shamanic religions*, a well-articulated value system was not part of the belief system, but the cosmology of these primitive religions displayed some degree of definition and complexity (Bellah 1964, 364–66). Supernatural beings were objectified and viewed as clearly distinct from the natural world, and some of these beings were believed to control and influence the worldly activities of individuals. Usually gods had specified and delimited spheres of influence. The relationships among gods could be the source of considerable speculation, often creating an incipient hierarchy or pantheon of relations among gods. Religious *myths* delineating the history of gods could also exist, but their complexity varied considerably.

This form of belief system can be illustrated by noting briefly some salient features of the traditional Eskimo or Inuit religion. The Eskimo pantheon comprised a varied mixture of lesser beings who were personified as the souls of preeminent humans and animals. Also, there were various minor and local spirits regulating the behavior of individuals. Usually particular kin groups had a set of ancestral souls and spirits with whom they had to reckon, and frequently some myths surrounded the emergence and persistence of these minor and local beings and spirits. Higher up in the pantheon were two primary gods—the Keeper of Sea Animals and the Spirit of the Air; but the mythology, division of powers, and the hierarchy of control among these higher, societywide gods remained somewhat vague and blurred. Thus the traditional Eskimo religious belief system marked a clear-cut distinction between at least some aspects of the natural and supernatural, but the internal differentiation of the cosmology into a complex and clear pantheon accompanied by supporting myths had only been initiated in this simple shamanic religion.

The fairly clear differentiation between the natural and supernatural in shamanic religions encouraged the development of rituals through which gods and humans interact. The locus of such rituals is the cult structure, but the cult structures in shamanic religions were loosely organized. Following Wallace (1966, 83–90), two general types of cult structures were evident: *individualistic cults* and *shamanic cults*. In individualistic cults, there was no categorical distinction between religious specialists and laymen, because members of the cult engaged in appropriate rituals addressed to the supernatural without a religious specialist as an intermediary. Shamanic cults displayed a more differentiated structure, with part-time religious practitioners serving as intermediaries between laypersons and the supernatural. These intermediaries assumed this status on the basis of family ascription, specialized training, and inspirational experience with the supernatural. General norms required that, for a fee, they act as magicians, witch doctors, medicine men, mediums, spiritualists, astrologers, and diviners. Depending on the society, the nature of religious beliefs, and the needs of the client, shamans could usually perform at least several of these services.

It is thus with shamanic cults that the first religious division of labor emerged in human societies. The shaman represented a religious specialist who was clearly differentiated from lay clients. But shamanic cults remained loosely organized, rarely revealing clear boundaries, places of worship, or stable membership. In fact, shamanic cults displayed a transient clientele who had little sense of religious community and who, despite sharing beliefs and rituals, had relatively low mutual identification and solidarity. Furthermore, few if any calendrical rituals were required of cult members; rituals were apparently performed only when needed.

Eskimo cult structure and organization reflected most of these conditions. Generally there were two individualistic cults and one shamanic cult organizing religious belief and ritual (Wallace 1966, 89). One of the individualistic cults was termed the "Spirit Helper Cult." Within this cult individuals sought the particular spirits, souls, and beings of their locale or of their kin grouping, for societal members patrilineally inherited certain Spirit Helpers who were seen as guiding and helping individuals in their daily activities and to whom appeals were made by wearing statuettes carved from walrus tusks, bags of pebbles, and remains of shellfish. To secure help from the spirits, individuals also had to also observe certain taboos, especially with respect to not killing the creatures being represented in this ancillary appeal. What is important about this cult is that there were no regularly scheduled rituals, with individuals seeking the help of their ancestral and/or local spirits by themselves. The second individualistic cult, the Game Animal Cult, had a more-clearly established set of ritual norms that cut across both local kin groups and larger communities. Certain societywide taboos existed, ostensibly to inhibit behavior that would offend major game animals—for example, the flesh of land and sea animals was never to be cooked together, since to do so would bring illness and starvation (Wallace 1966, 90). These and other norms were believed to prevent giving offense to the souls and spirits, the "Keepers," who controlled and regulated the supply of game on which the Eskimos depended for survival. Violations of ritual norms had to be openly confessed; and if violations on the part of one individual persisted, he or she was banished from the community. In this way, the community believed that it could avert potential disaster. Thus the Eskimos' Game Animal Cult displayed a more clear-cut structure than the Spirit Helper Cult because it was societywide and because it had distinct ritual norms whose violation brought sanctions from the community. But actual ritual behavior was still enacted by individuals without the assistance of an intermediary (hence, it remained an individualistic cult). The most complex cults among the traditional Eskimos were led by shamans who were seen as having a special ability to get the attention of a Spirit Helper. For a fee, the shaman would call on Spirit Helpers to assist clients suffering ill-health or bad fortune, with the shaman's task being one of discovering from a Spirit Helper which supernatural entity had been offended, which taboo had been broken, or which ritual had not been performed by the client. After making a diagnosis, the shaman underwent a spiritual trip to rectify the illness or misfortune. In the shamanic cult of coastal villages, there was one quasi-calendrical ritual ceremony performed by the shaman: his annual spiritual trip to the ocean's bottom to persuade and entice Sedna, the Sea Goddess and Keeper of Sea Animals, to release from her domain a sufficient number of animals so that the communities and villages could survive for the ensuing year.

In sum, then, shamanic religions—as exemplified by the Eskimo and other small groupings of hunter-gatherers—can be viewed as the most basic religious type, once some degree of religious evolution has occurred. The religious belief system, while distinguishing the sacred and profane as well as the supernatural and natural, does not display a clearly differentiated and systematized cosmology and value system. Structurally, cult organization evidences at most a clear differentiation between shaman and layman, although much religious activity still occurs within individualistic cults.

Communal Religions

Somewhat better-developed than shamanic are communal religions, which were typical of simple horticultural populations (Wallace 1966, 86–87). What

Table 6.1   RELIGION IN HUNTING AND GATHERING SOCIETIES

Belief system	Conception of a supernatural realm of beings and forces, but not clearly organized into a cosmology; some mythology; no clear religious value system
Rituals	Some calendric rituals, but most rituals performed ad hoc as needed; shaman directs some rituals, but many performed by individuals on their own
Cult structure	None that can be distinguished from band or its nuclear units; occasional "festivals" when bands come together

distinguishes communal religions from the shamanic religions of hunter-gatherers was not so much an increase in complexity of the belief system, but in the complexity of the cult structures. In addition to individualistic and shamanic cults were those that displayed a threefold division of labor (Wallace 1966, 87): lay participants; lay organizers, sponsors, and performers; and religious specialists (shamans and magicians). The rituals performed in these communal cults tended to be calendrical, with laymen organizing and often performing at least some of the prescribed rituals. Frequently, this organization of lay personnel began to approximate a bureaucratic structure, with regular technical and supervisory assignments for the laity. Still, no full-time priesthood or elaborate religious hierarchy could be said to exist (Wallace 1966, 87). Communal cults varied in size from very small to very large and encompassing the whole community; membership also varied and usually revolved around special social categories such as age and sex or around special groups like secret societies or kinship groupings. In these communal regions, however, the cosmology was only slightly more complicated than that in shamanic religions. The pantheon was a loosely structured conglomerate of supernatural deities and spirits, but the mythology surrounding these deities tended to be more elaborate than in shamanic religions. For example, among the Trobriand Islanders, there was a series of ancestral spirits whose genealogy was well known, but the hierarchy of relations and power among these spirits still remained somewhat vague and ambiguous. Moreover, the values of the belief system of communal religions were not clearly articulated or systematized, remaining implicit and uncodified into a moral code (Malinowski [1925] 1955). Thus, while the belief systems of communal religions were not greatly evolved beyond those of hunter-gatherers, the cult structure was considerably more complex than in shamanic religions.

As Wallace (1966, 91–92) documents or as Malinowski's ([1925] 1955) more extensive ethnography reveals, the Trobriand Islanders displayed the beginnings of two communal cults: the Technological Magic Cult and the Cult of the Spirits of the Dead. In the Technological Magic Cult, certain ancestral spirit-beings controlled economic activity. Hence, ritual deference had to be paid to these spirits with respect to the main types of economic activity among the Trobriand Islanders: gardening and deep-sea canoe fishing. No intermediary or spiritual helper was required to communicate with these ancestral spirits, but communal participation was somewhat calendrical, while rituals were supervised by magicians. The second communal cult structure of the Trobriand Islanders—the Spirits of the Dead—relied less on magicians and intermediaries than the Technological Magic Cult. Here, ceremonies and rituals were organized and run principally by laypersons. Their one major calendrical ritual was held at the end of the harvest and involved a prolonged period of food display, consumption, dancing, and sex. Aside from these two communal cults, the religion of the Trobriand Islanders was organized into shamanic cults with professional magicians and sorcerers causing and/or curing misfortune and illness for clients. Also, there were various individualistic cults requiring individual ritual activity with respect to such matters as love, protection from evil, lesser spirits, flying witches, and so on.

Communal religions thus display a level of structural organization beyond that evidenced in shamanic religions: Cult structures were more varied and began to evidence quasi-bureaucratic organization. Although the belief system was only slightly more elaborate than that among primitive religions, the mythology tended to be more extensive. Within communal religions, however, were the seeds of beliefs and cult structures that became increasingly conspicuous features of pre-industrial ecclesiastic religions, especially as societies became more stratified and hierarchical (Swanson 1960).

Traditional Ecclesiastic Religions

Traditional ecclesiastic religions were evident in advanced horticultural and early agrarian societies; they revealed a marked increase in the complexity of both the belief system and cult structure. In examining this type of religion, we will utilize the extensive ethnographic data on the traditional Dahomey of West Africa during its political independence (Herskovits and Herskovits 1933; Herskovits 1938), as well as Goode's (1951) and Wallace's (1966) secondary analysis of Dahomean religion. Dahomean religion is just a lesser-known example of a traditional ecclesiastic religion, such as the religions of ancient Greece, Egypt, Rome, and to some extent, Babylonia.

The most notable difference between the belief system of traditional ecclesiastic and communal religions is the extensiveness and complexity of the cosmology. With traditional ecclesiastic religions, there was an elaborate pantheon or group of pantheons as well as a relatively clear hierarchical ordering of the supernatural beings in terms of their power and influence. Also there was usually a creator god, a supernatural being who created both the natural and supernatural. The mythology of the cosmology was well developed and included episodes in the lives of gods, fraternal jealousies, sexual relations, and competition among various supernatural deities. In some traditional ecclesiastical religions, values began to be codified into a religious code of rights and wrongs—although equally frequently, religious values remained only implicit within ritual activity.

The traditional Dahomean religion displayed such a belief system. There was a female Sky God—Mawu or Mawu-Lisa (Lisa being the son of Mawu and yet often fused with her), although depending on the mythology, Mawu could also be a male. Mawu or Mawu-Lisa usually was believed to have divided the universe and world, because Mawu was the creator of all things— although other myths indicated that additional gods created certain things. Although some ambiguity existed concerning which god was the Creator, in most cases Mawu ultimately held the formula for the creation of humans, matter, and other gods. Although the mythologies surrounding Mawu or Mawu-Lisa were somewhat ambiguous, Mawu was almost always viewed as dividing the supernatural into three giant subpantheons pertaining to the Sky, Thunder, and Earth. For each of these subpantheons existed a host of deities with an elaborate mythology surrounding all of them. A fourth pantheon revolving around sea gods also existed, but its relationship to Mawu was less clear. Thus, the Dahomean pantheon was extremely complex, containing not only ambiguous but sometimes conflicting mythologies. However, despite these ambiguities, there were incipient hierarchies of power and influence extending from Mawu or Mawu-Lisa down to the gods of the various subpantheons. Also, though somewhat clouded, there was a creation myth about Mawu as well as some other gods in the subpantheon.

Religions such as the Dahomean were ecclesiastic because of a new form of cult structure, one displaying a professional clergy organized into a bureaucracy. These clergy differed from shamans in that they were not individual entrepreneurs; they differed from lay officials of communal cults in that they were formally appointed or elected as more or less full-time religious specialists (or priests). Relations among these priests usually became somewhat hierarchical in terms of prestige and power. These religious specialists of ecclesiastic cults also performed certain calendrical and noncalendrical rituals in established temple structures, with laypersons increasingly becoming passive respondents rather than active participants (Wallace 1966, 88). Furthermore these religious specialists began to exert tremendous nonreligious influence and perhaps authority in secular (as well as sacred) activities.

Although the Dahomean religion never spread far beyond West Africa, it displayed the incipient structural features of more-developed premodern religions such as Islam, Christianity, Hinduism, Buddhism, and Judaism. The Dahomean religion had numerous individualistic cults where members established ritual relations with various minor deities. The Dahomeans also had a shamanic cult—the Divination Cult—whose professional diviners discovered the proper ritual for certain crucial activities (harvesting, marketing, etc.) as well as illness and misfortune. Various quasi-communal cults—the Ancestral Cults—organized around kinship groupings were also in evidence, with kin members engaging in certain ritual activities, especially those surrounding death. But the distinguishing feature of the Dahomean religion was the emergence of an ecclesiastical cult. Each major pantheon in the belief system—Sky, Thunder, Earth, Sea—had a separate religious order or cult structure, and each of these cults possessed its own temple, professional clergy, and hierarchy of religious specialists. Thus, they represented different churches with related and yet separate cosmologies. What is most significant about the religious system was the quasi-bureaucratic structure of cults, since religious development into true world religions could not occur without this structural base.

Premodern Religions

Premodern is a label encompassing many of the religions (e.g., Christianity, Hinduism, Buddhism, traditional Judaism, Confucianism, and Islam) that emerged with advanced agrarianism and then spread to other agrarian populations[2] through combinations of war, conquest, missionary proselytizing,

[2] For a readable review of these and other "world religions," see Mathews (1991); Yates (1988). For even more detail in all religions of the world, see the fifteen-volume set compiled by Eliade (1987).

Table 6.2   RELIGION IN HORTICULTURAL SOCIETIES

	Simple	Advanced
Belief System	Conception of supernatural realm of beings and forces. No clear organization of supernatural into cosmology, but considerable mythology. No explicit religious value system or moral code.	Conception of supernatural realm of beings and forces. Increased organization of supernatural realm into levels and a hierarchical pantheon of gods and forces; extensive mythology often evident. Some indication of explicit values and moral codes.
Rituals	Clear and regular calendrical rituals, usually performed by individuals alone or in kin groupings, but at times led by shaman.	Regular calendrical rituals, often led by shaman and, in more complex systems, by full-time priests. Increased control and mediation of ritual activity by religious specialists.
Cult Structure	Explicit structures devoted to religious activity, involving: (1) division of labor among lay participants, lay organizers-sponsors, performers, and religious specialists (shamans, magicians, and others deemed to have special capabilities to mediate with supernatural); (2) explicit symbols and artifacts representing various aspects of the supernatural, and at times (3) specialized buildings and places where cult members meet to perform religious activity.	Explicit structures devoted to religious activity, involving: (1) clear division of labor between religious specialists (often full-time) and increasingly less-active laypersons, who assume role of worshipers; (2) hierarchy of religious specialists; (3) elaborate symbols and artifacts representing each aspect of the supernatural; and (4) specialized buildings and places (temples) for religious specialists to perform religious activity for laypersons.

and colonialism. Indeed, as a result of this diffusion and the organizational base that encouraged the spread of these religions, they are the dominant cults in most today's advanced industrial and post-industrial societies. Therefore, the label "premodern" only denotes their origins in the pre-industrial era. Frequently these religions have been imposed on—and to some extent amalgamated with—a more traditional indigenous religion, with the result that each society in which they are found has its own variant of the main religious strain. Furthermore, these dominant premodern religions often bear common origins, with one being a revolt or break with another: Christianity from Judaism, Buddhism from Hinduism, and Islam from both Judaism and Christianity.

The cosmology of premodern religions is greatly attenuated compared to that of traditional ecclesiastic religions, revealing a clear tendency toward monotheism or belief in one, all-encompassing god or supernatural force (Wallace 1966, 94–101). For example, Islam, Catholicism, Judaism, and Confucianism evidence clear tendencies toward monotheism (Allah, God and the

Trinity, God, and Tao, respectively, being the all-powerful beings and/or forces of the supernatural realm). Hinduism reveals a more ambiguous pantheon, however, as does its offshoot, Buddhism. Philosophical Hinduism (Wallace 1966, 94) is clearly monotheistic, with its all-encompassing supernatural being or force (the "One"), whereas Sanskritic Hinduism maintains an elaborate pantheon of gods including Siva, Krishna, Ram, Vishnu, and Lakshimi. The pantheon of Buddhism is similarly structured, with the world being guided by a series of Buddhas (or "Enlightened Ones").

Compared to traditional ecclesiastic religions, then, the mythology of the pantheon of premodern religions had become truncated. Robert Bellah (1964, 366) has called this the process of "de-mythologization," since little myth surrounds the creation of the all-powerful god and his court of relatives. Thus, the increasingly elaborate accounts of the jealousies, conflicts, rivalries, and genealogies typical of religious evolution up to this point suddenly began to decline at the premodern stage. For example, the myths revolving around Krishna and Vishnu, the historical sequences of Buddhas, the interaction of God and Moses, God and Jesus, Allah, the angel Gabriel, Mohammed, and so on are sparse indeed compared to the myths of the Dahomean and other traditional religions.

As Bellah (1964) emphasizes, one of the most distinctive features of premodern religions is the emergence of a series of *substantive beliefs* concerning the supernatural, revolving around the capacity of mortals to become part of this realm upon death. These beliefs emphasize for the first time the possibility of understanding the fundamental nature of both natural and supernatural reality (Bellah 1964, 367). For instance, Hinduism not only emphasizes the prospects for a better reincarnation in one's next life but also holds out the possibility of becoming a god; Christianity offers salvation in heaven after death; and Islam provides for the attainment of paradise after death. Also, it should be noted that premodern religious beliefs provide places for the unworthy—hell or a poor reincarnation, for example. Previous traditional religions had offered the chance for humans to maintain only a peace and harmony with the supernatural realm, but premodern religious beliefs now provided for the possibility of actually *becoming a part* of this realm.

Under these conditions, religious values become explicit, since conformity to these values increases the possibility of salvation after death in the supernatural realm. These values form a religious code spelling out appropriate behaviors for the members of a society: the Ten Commandments, the sayings of Confucius, or the Noble Eightfold Path among Buddhists being prominent examples. The significance of these religious codes is that they specify more than just stereotyped ritual behavior; they also place on individuals a set of diffuse obligations guiding everyday, nonreligious conduct. Yet these codes tend to emphasize worldly resignation and retreatism; for in order to secure salvation, conformity to religious law must not be too contaminated by worldly passions, actions, and events.

In sum, then, the cosmology of premodern religion began to shift toward monotheism, truncating its pantheon and attendant mythology, and highlighting substantive beliefs about the supernatural and salvation. Equally noticeable in these premodern religions was the emergence of a codified value system controlling both ritual and nonritual behavior and encouraging a kind of retreatism, or at least an acceptance of one's fate in this world.

The structural trends evident in traditional ecclesiastic religions thus were extended dramatically in premodern religions, as ecclesiastic cult structures increasingly came to dominate over shamanic, communal, and individualistic cults. Usually one large ecclesiastic bureaucracy with an extensive hierarchy of religious specialists became dominant: Catholicism in medieval Europe and in many parts of Latin America; Hinduism in India; Confucianism in pre-Communist China; Islam in the Middle East; and so on. The specialists within this bureaucracy could claim a monopoly on religious expertise and the right to perform major calendrical and noncalendrical rituals. They became permanent residents in large and elaborate temple structures and devoted all their time to operating the church bureaucracy. The influence of this dominant ecclesiastic cult and its bureaucracy was so great that religious elites had high levels of secular power, setting up a mounting tension in agrarian societies between religious and political elites (Bellah 1964, 368).

The church and state bureaucracies thus became clearly differentiated in the agrarian era, with the result that the legitimating functions of religion for the polity were no longer automatic and nonproblematic. Sometimes religious beliefs and the organization of a religious cult became the stimulus and locus for rebellious social movements, and so, because of their well-articulated and codified belief system and their high degree of bureaucratic organization, premodern religions could *potentially* become a major source of social change. As long as cult structures remained loosely organized in a communal or only incipient ecclesiastic form, they lacked the organizational resources to generate major social change in the face of a well-organized kin- or state-based polity. But as the religious bureaucracy became increasingly well organized, controlling financial and symbolic resources while demanding loyalty from the general population, its power to influence the course of events in societies increased. Still, despite their potential for instituting radical change, premodern religions historically have performed a conservative, legitimating function for the polity and other institutional structures in a society.

Yet within the institution of religion itself, considerable change could occur as lesser cult structures became ecclesiastically organized and began to challenge the beliefs and organization of the dominant ecclesiastic cult. Religious evolution has documented this process of revolt against the dominant cult again and again, whether it be Catholicism reacting to Judaism, Protestantism to Catholicism, or Buddhism to Hinduism. With further religious development, several dominant ecclesiastic cults (e.g., Catholicism and Protestantism in Europe) as well as subcults within these larger cults (e.g., the Protestant denominations) began to typify the structure of religion. Thus at their most advanced stage, premodern religions displayed several large ecclesiastic cult structures dominating religious ritual and activity in a society, but they also evidenced other forms of cult structures: communal, shamanic, and individualistic. For example, in India where Philosophical Hinduism dominates, religion in many rural village cults is still organized into communal cults and utilizes Sanskritic Hinduism and pre-Hindu beliefs and rituals. In these same villages also can be found various ancestral cults which represent a similar amalgamation of Sanskritic and pre-Hindu beliefs and rituals. Furthermore, there are shamanic cults of holy men (gurus and healers, for example) who perform necessary ritual activities for clients. And finally there are various individualistic cults where ritual activity revolves around seeking harmony with various personal guardian spirits. Thus premodern religions display considerable structural heterogeneity, with many different types of cult structures (ecclesiastic, communal, shamanic, and individualistic) whose size and relative influence vary tremendously. Premodern religions are a conglomeration of various cult structures, having similar but always somewhat divergent belief systems. The interplay—conflict, assimilation, accommodation, and conquest—among these various cults frequently makes premodern religions highly dynamic. Yet, when one large ecclesiastic cult dominates, a premodern religion will remain comparatively static—unless disrupted by nonreligious institutional influence.

Religion in Industrial and Post-Industrial Societies

Early Modern Religions   The Protestant Reformation marked the first emergence of what can be termed "modern religion." Until recently (and even now the matter is ambiguous), the great premodern religions of Islam, Buddhism, Hinduism, and Confucianism resisted change; and in fact, early reform movements within these religions lacked the widespread appeal or far-reaching consequences of the Protestant Reformation (Bellah 1964). Even today, under massive pressure from other institutional systems in industrial and post-industrial societies, these stable premodern religions are not easily changed. Yet, with industrialization, early modern religions can begin to shift to the pattern described below.

The cosmology of early modern religions becomes even more attenuated than that of premodern religions, especially under the impact of industrialization. The trend toward monotheism is more evident, and the cast of supporting gods and deities decreases. Myths become comparatively unimportant and are deemphasized. More revolutionary than these extensions of trends evident in premodern religions is the emergence of a new set of substantive beliefs about the supernatural and humans' relation to it. A clear separation of the natural and supernatural realms is maintained, but the premodern emphasis on the hierarchies within either of these realms is eliminated. God and humans stand in direct relation to each other, and mediating religious specialists (priests) are essentially excess baggage. Such substantive beliefs result in a reorganization of religious values, which still stress the importance of salvation but through a new route. For now, religious values emphasize the importance of individual faith and commitment to God, rather than ritual performance or conformity to strict ethical codes. Values also emphasize the

Table 6.3   RELIGION IN AGRARIAN SOCIETIES

	Simple	Advanced
Beliefs	Clear conception of supernatural realm of beings, and at times, forces. Relatively clear pantheon, hierarchically organized. Explicit mythologies as well as values and moral codes sanctioned by the supernatural and used to legitimate privilege of clergy and power of ruling elites.	Clear separation of supernatural and natural, but pantheons decline in favor of "universal religions" proclaiming one god or force in the universe. Mythology also declines and is simplified; moral codes and values become explicit part of simplified religious doctrines. Religious legitimation of elites still prominent, but religions seek to appeal to the "common person." Alongside spread of universal, monotheistic religions exist beliefs in magic and witchcraft tending to be localized in content
Rituals	Regular calendrical rituals, directed and led by full-time clergy. Considerable control by clergy of economic production, either through ownership of property or, indirectly, through ritualized rights to economic surplus.	Regular calendrical rituals, directed by full-time clergy, but rituals simplified and designed to appeal to mass audiences. Clergy still major property holder, but rituals increasingly separated from economic and political spheres, being directed instead to a force/god that can improve life now and in hereafter.
Cult Structure	Clear structures, housed in elaborate temples of worship supporting full-time. Bureaucratically organized clergy; explicit symbols, places, and times of worship evident. Cults often control not only economic but also much social and political activity.	Clear, bureaucratized structures in elaborate temples/churches. Times and places of worship specified, and symbols simplified. Cults still own property and exert political influence, but decreasingly so in the political arena. Alongside large universal religions exist smaller cults with different beliefs and ritual, though these tend to adopt elements of dominant religion.

necessity for God's work to be done in this world, which in Bellah's (1964, 369) words, becomes "a valid arena in which to work out the divine command." Moreover, a wide variety of secular beliefs ("capitalism," "democracy," "nationalism, "humanism," etc.) begin to compete with religious beliefs as providers of meaning, thereby increasing the competition between these "civil religions" and beliefs about the sacred and supernatural.

What distinguished the Protestant Reformation from reform movements in other premodern religions was that the new emphasis on individualism and de-emphasis of ritual and priestly mediation between God and humans became *institutionalized into strong ecclesiastic cult structures.* These structures were and are bureaucratized, with a hierarchy of religious specialists and with requirements of religious orthodoxy for lay members. Yet typical features of premodern ecclesiastic cults—such as compulsory membership, high authoritarianism, ritual emphasis, and elaborate hierarchy—were not evident in these early Protestant cult structures, such as Calvinism, Methodism, Pietism, and Baptism. Thus a curious accommodation between new religious beliefs within a somewhat watered-down form of ecclesiastic cult occurred during early modernization. The failure of other premodern religions to modernize resided not so much in the lack of reform movements similar to those that eventually spawned the Protestant Reformation, but rather in the incapacity to institutionalize these reforms into an ecclesiastic cult structure (Bellah 1964, 369). Still, early modern cult structures were not loosely structured or entirely permissive. On the contrary, the early Protestant cults required much orthodoxy and conformity to church rules, with this conformity extending beyond the church doors into everyday life. But within these cults, the de-emphasis on ritual, the decreasing role of the clergy as intermediaries, and the emphasis on individual relations between God and the person generated a whole series of contradictions between tightly organized ecclesiastic cults and a loosely organized belief system. With industrialization, these contradictions become increasingly evident to both the clergy and laity, resulting in a loosening of religious orthodoxy and cult structure as well as a further individualization of the religious belief system.

Modern Religion   The label "modern religion" is only a convenient term for describing religious activities in a few post-industrial, western societies with a Protestant tradition. Societies dominated by one of the large premodern religions do not display this "modern" religious type. And in societies that do, it exists alongside premodern and early modern forms of religion. Thus, what we are labeling "modern religion" is neither widespread nor even dominant in those post-industrial societies where it is found.

Modern religion is marked by the destruction of a coherent cosmology, as the supernatural mythologies and substantive beliefs all become increasingly ambiguous and unsystematic. Perhaps the most dramatic manifestation of the de-cosmologicalization of religion is reflected in the ambiguity over whether or not there is a god or a clearly distinguishable supernatural (Wuthnow 1988, 485). Bellah (1964, 370–71) has referred to this process as the breakdown of the basic dualism that has been central to all religions through history and throughout most of the world today. The belief in forces beyond humans' control remains in modern religions, but the clear-cut differentiation between the sacred and profane or supernatural and natural diminishes. Substantive beliefs begin to emphasize individualistic or personal interpretations of the nonempirical and sacred, with growing concern over searching for truths that fit one's actual conditions of living. To the extent that salvation remains a tenet within the belief system, it is likely to emphasize multiple and personal paths to life in another world, with these paths to salvation always involving enhanced adjustment and happiness in this world. These alterations of the cosmology are reflected in a new, emerging set of religions values. Rigid moral codes become less pronounced and are replaced by values directing worshipers to seek adjustment, happiness, and self-realization with others and the world around them (Bellah 1964, 363; Berger 1963; Luckmann 1967). Thus in modern religious belief systems, the elaborate cosmology typical of traditional ecclesiastical religions has crumbled, while the explicit and rigid moral code of premodern religions has become loose and highly flexible, emphasizing adjustment to the secular rather than to the sacred or supernatural.

With this flexible and indivualistic form of religious belief system, cult structures in post-industrial societies are altered, although the tight cult structures of premodern and early modern religions still persist and usually outnumber the more-loosely organized modern cults. In the near future, structures embracing the more flexible belief system of modern religions will remain ecclesiastical, but these ecclesiastical structures remain somewhat fluid, adjusting themselves to the needs of their clients. This is particularly likely as mass electronic media and market forces organize a significant amount of religious activity. Many subunits and organizations exist within any cult which cater to diverse groups of clients; and as the needs of clients change, the lower-level organizational units of the ecclesia servicing the membership will also change. Cults (churches, denominations, sects, etc.) come to provide more of a place or location where individuals work out their own solutions to ultimate questions about the cosmos and supernatural rather than a rigid orthodox structure where these solutions are prefabricated in the form of an established belief system and ritual pattern (Bellah 1964, 373; Lenski 1963, 59–60). This is increasingly the trend, especially among Protestant cults (denominations) in post-industrial western societies (Wuthnow 1994; Berger 1969; Lenski 1963, 59). These cult structures are a curious hybrid or cross between an ecclesiastic cult structure at their top and a more flexible, almost individualistic structure at their bottom or membership level. As media ministries proliferate, a further contradiction becomes evident, as conservative beliefs are marketed to a diffuse and mass audience whose members can remain isolated from one another, rarely engaging in collective ritual activity (Hadden and Swann 1981).

HISTORICAL TRENDS IN RELIGION

Tables 6.1 to 6.4 summarize in capsule form the long-term evolutionary and historical transformations of religion (Maryanski and Turner 1992). As becomes evident in reading the tables, one major transformation has been the building up of the cosmology during horticulture and early agrarianism, followed by its diminution. Movement through shamanic, communal, and traditional ecclesiastical religions involves an increasing codification and complexity of the cosmology: The number of deities in the pantheon, their degree

Table 6.4   RELIGION IN MODERN SOCIETIES

	Industrial	Post-Industrial
Belief System	Clear separation of supernatural and natural. Domination by universal religions proclaiming one god and/or force in their sparse pantheon and very little mythology, but still explicit codes of ethics and systems of values. New secular ideologies using referents to the supernatural further secularize religious beliefs, creating "civil religions" (e.g., nationalism, capitalism, humanism) that are not so much religious as advocacies of particular secular activities and social forms.	Same as industrial societies, but with further diminution of pantheon and mythology as well as some questioning of separation between natural and supernatural realms. Emphasis on personal interpretation of nonempirical and sacred in some cults. Less-pronounced and rigid moral codes in beliefs of some cults. Secular ideologies and "civil religions" compete with religious beliefs.
Rituals	Some calendrical rituals, certain of which lose their religious significance (e.g., Christmas gift giving); private rituals also encouraged. Mass media increasingly a vehicle for observing and expressing religious sentiments.	Same as industrial societies, except that religious rituals often supplemented/supplanted by secular rituals (e.g., "meditation," "daily workouts," "weekly therapy"). Mass media increasingly important as means for ritual enactment.
Cult Structures	Bureaucratized structures in variety of temples/churches (from large and grand to simple); times and places of worship specified but less regularly followed and/or enforced. Little political influence, except through capacity to mold public opinion. Some trends for consolidation of cults, counteracted in some systems by new, splinter cults. In democratic systems, cults may become political interest group/party lobbying for particular legislative programs.	Same as industrial societies, except that new national cult structures are created through market forces and mass media, particularly TV (in those societies allowing private TV), and cults increasingly involved in political lobbying and party activity.

of definition, the myths relating them and accounting for their emergence, and substantive beliefs about levels or planes in the supernatural realms all become more clearly articulated and codified into a comparatively unambiguous hierarchy of gods and supernatural forces. With the emergence of premodern religious forms, however, the number of deities decreases as a tendency towards monotheism becomes evident. Nonetheless, relations among supernatural beings as well as planes of supernatural existence remain clearly articulated. With emergence of early modern religions, these trends in cosmological development decelerate and begin to be reversed: Mythology becomes attenuated; the size of the pantheon decreases; and the various hierarchical levels within the supernatural realm are eliminated. And with post-industrialization, many cults further diminish the cosmology, as beliefs come to emphasize personal interpretations and relationships with the supernatural. And increasingly, religious beliefs about the sacred and supernatural must compete with "civil religions" revolving around secular beliefs dressed up in "god language" that provide meaning and purpose to individuals.

Similarly, religious values display a parallel curvilinear trend: From the shamanic to premodern stage, religious values become increasingly more explicit, culminating in the strict moral code of most premodern religions. This code persists with early modernization—although in a somewhat less compelling form. With post-industrialization, the rigid moral code in many cults becomes more relativistic as values stress a more flexible relationship between individuals and the supernatural as well as a more accommodating mode of adjustment in the natural world.

At the structural level, religious development entails an increasing bureaucratization up to the early modern stage: Shamanic religions display only individualistic and shamanic cult structures; traditional communal religions evidence communal cults with some degree of a division of labor among the lay membership; traditional ecclesiastical religions reveal cults with a bureaucratic structure revolving around a clear division of labor between laity and specialized clergy as well as a hierarchy of control among the clergy itself; premodern religions display an even more elaborate and extensive church bureaucracy with a high degree of centralization of its religious specialists, as is exemplified in the Catholic Church, which has a world bureaucracy culminating in the Pope as its head. However, early modern religions begin to decentralize their bureaucracies as smaller, geographically dispersed, and local bureaucracies begin to evidence only loose administrative ties to a central staff of clergy and as strict relationships of authority among units within the religious bureaucracy decline. And, as media ministries and alternatives to traditional ecclesiastic cults proliferate, the structure of cults undergoes further transformation, as membership often remains outside of the bureaucratized central headquarters of media-oriented ministries.

With these changes in beliefs and cult structures has come some degree of secularization among a greater proportion of religious cults. Of course, to speak of a trend toward secularization of religion represents a contradiction in terms, because religion revolves around the nonsecular—the ultimate, the cosmos, the supernatural, and the sacred. To a great extent religion has always been secular, since religious beliefs and rituals in traditional societies have had consequences for economic, political, educational, and familial structures and processes. But in traditional societies, religious rituals—whether calendrical, noncalendrical, or magical—have always made direct and strong appeals for the intervention of supernatural forces into everyday affairs. Many cults in modern religions decreasingly make such appeals. While operating on a supernatural or sacred set of premises, the actual role behavior of modern clergy in a myriad of secular activities such as social work, the leisure sphere, criminal corrections, youth programs, athletic leagues, marriage counseling, and group therapy frequently make little or no reference (much less an appeal) to the supernatural. Since the supernatural realm in modern religions has no clear-cut or elaborate cosmology or strict moral code, this is to be expected—especially as religion now must compete in a market-driven economy with many secular organizations. And when beliefs begin to emphasize the importance of each individual establishing his or her personal relationship with the ultimate conditions of life, direct and strong appeals of clergy for divine intervention become less appropriate. There is, however, only a trend toward increased secularization of religious activity, because if religious behavior completely lost sight of the supernatural and sacred premise, then it would cease to be religious. And if all cult structures became organized solely for secular activities, then the institution of religion would no longer exist. Twenty-five years ago, many analysts predicted this fate for religion, but these predictions were premature. The organization of rituals directed at the supernatural is still a most prominent form of human activity in even the most advanced post-industrial society.

These trends, portrayed in Tables 6.1 to 6.4, are thus only very approximate. Moreover, even if these trends are dominant, all types of religions can still be found within industrial or post-industrial societies. The transformations summarized in the tables do not so much *destroy* older religious forms, but rather they become more prevalent than these older forms. And in fact, older "folk religions," worshiping ancient gods and supernatural forces, have persisted even as premodern "universal religions" have diffused across populations and as these dominant religions have been transformed with industrialization and post-industrialization (Mensching 1959, 65–77; 1947, 137–48). Indeed, as we will see, this interplay among highly diverse religious types—some new, others very old—in contemporary societies is one of the most important dynamics of religion.

THE DYNAMICS OF RELIGION

Religion has changed in response to transformations in other institutions, as we will explore in the next chapter. But even as it has had to adapt to external institutional pressures, important dynamics internal to the religious institutional system operate in industrial and post-industrial societies. These dynamics revolve around religious movements producing diversity in beliefs, cults, and rituals.

This diversity runs a full range (Kurtz 1995, 167–209). On one end are "popular religions," where beliefs in such matters as the occult, astrology, lucky numbers, extrasensory perception, trances, mystical experiences, out-of-body experiences, powers of nature, and magic are still widely held and provide guidance for people over such fundamental issues as food, sickness and health, death and the dead, and transitions in the life cycle (Williams 1980, 65; Wuthnow 1988, 481). Such beliefs are organized in a wide variety of cults, from individual practitioners to secret societies, most of which are on the margins and fringes of religion in industrial and post-industrial societies.

At the other end of the religious spectrum are the established cult structures which dominate religious life in a society. Sometimes these are sanctioned by the state, but whether or not this is so is less essential than the fact that a vast majority of the population seeking religion belong to the cult structures of these established religions, all of which are the descendants of premodern religions in the agrarian era.

It is the in-between areas of these end points where the interesting dynamics occur. Successive religious movements in which new beliefs, rituals, and cult structures are invented take up much of this intermediate space, and the result in post-industrial societies is to increase religious diversity (Stark and Bainbridge 1985). Religious movements occur when subpopulations feel deprived relative to others in a society (Stark and Bainbridge 1980; Bainbridge and Stark 1979; Glock 1973) and when moral definitions of behavior and relationships are changing (Wuthnow 1988, 478). Under either or both of these conditions—especially when members of a subpopulation collectively experience deprivation and moral uncertainty, new religious beliefs are articulated, new leaders emerge, and new cults are formed. Multiple religious systems usually emerge under these conditions, setting them into competition over symbolic and ideological resources, financial resources, and members (Wuthnow 1988, 1987). This competition focuses beliefs and rituals while defining the boundaries of cult structures. In the end, some movements are more successful than others, thereby shifting the distribution and relative members of cults organizing the religious activities of a population. As a general rule, religious movements are more "evangelical" than established religions or popular religion. Through more cohesive cult structures and emotionally-laden rituals, they produce a number of potential outcomes. First, they can generate more fundamentalistic beliefs than established religions, which have been evolving less-rigid belief systems. Second, they can create entirely new beliefs and rituals. Or third, they can advocate a revitalization of the moral principles that have been lost. Each of these alternatives is briefly discussed below.

Religious fundamentalism advocates a strict interpretation of the texts in which beliefs were first written down. At the same time, it also demands a rigid morality, an adherence to rituals, and an intolerance for relaxing orthodoxy. In some societies, such as the United States, these sects are gaining membership for a variety of reasons: Their members' birth rates tend to be high; their emotional and evangelical appeal is often effectively packaged through the video mass media or through high-solidarity cults attracted to local communities, and their message responds to the sense of deprivation, marginality, and fears of moral decline among significant sectors of post-industrial societies (Marty and Appleby 1993). Not only in the United States, but elsewhere in the world (as in the Islamic nations), similar fundamentalistic movements are under way (Hiro 1989).

Religious innovations often spring from the same conditions that cause fundamentalism, but more typically, these advocate new religious beliefs rather than a renewed adherence to old ones. Historically this process has involved incorporating older religious ideas into a new set of beliefs. For example, Judaism, Islam, and Christianity ultimately involve variants and elaborations on the Book of Abraham; Buddhism was a reaction to Hinduism; and more recently, Mormonism involves an elaboration and change of ideas from Christianity. In more-industrial and post-industrial societies, the new religions can be conservative, but most are more liberal, advocating secular adjustment personal growth in their beliefs. Some, such as Scientology, are only marginally religious.

Revitalization movements involve efforts to recapture a way of life that has been lost through the articulation of beliefs and rituals. Relatedly, millenarian movements postulate a future state when things will be better and people once again will live in peace and harmony (Cohn 1957). These movements usually occur among those whose modes of existence have been uprooted by external forces and whose life is now insecure and anxious. Under these conditions, religious beliefs, rituals, and cults that promise hope of a return to the way it was—or, alternatively, to the dawning of a new millennia of happiness in the future—have widespread appeal. For example, in the latter part of the nineteenth century among conquered Native Americans, a number of millenarian movements emerged in which beliefs emphasized that the old ways would return and whites would be vanquished.

Thus, social change where moral definitions are altered and where people feel deprived are the breeding grounds for religious movements. These movements can go in many directions, but in the end they must compete for limited resources. Some are successful, as is evident for the great premodern religions (e.g., Hinduism, Buddhism, Christianity, Islam, Judaism) which still dominate the globe. Others die out. Still others find viable niches in which they can sustain cult structures. Thus, as long as there is social change in the broader institutional systems of a society, religious movements will emerge, compete, die, and selectively survive (Stark and Bainbridge 1985; Robbins and Anthony 1990).

CONCLUSION

At one time, many were predicting the demise of religion, or at the very least, its secularization and compartmentalization from the institutional mainstream. Yet, religion has remained a central force, even in highly secular, post-industrial societies. True, it no longer penetrates the political and legal systems as it once did in agrarian systems; nor does it dominate social life for most members of post-industrial societies. But it is still salient, and as can easily be seen, it is an important source of conflict in many societies of the world. Religion is thus a driving force in all societies.

Yet it is also a reactive force, having to cope with changes in its institutional environment. For as science and technology dominate economic activity, as political systems use legal-constitutional principles for their legitimation, as secular education for trade skills is extended to the masses, as kinship becomes nucleated and mobile in search of economic opportunities, and as medicine reduces uncertainty over health, the nature of religion must change. And this change, in turn, sets into motion many of the international dynamics evident in religion. Thus, to understand the nature of religion's operation in society, we need to explore the effects of other institutions.

Chapter
7

Religion in Institutional Context

The successive differentiation of new institutional systems—economy, polity, law, and education—from kinship has changed the nature of religion over the long course of humans' evolutionary history. Much like kinship, religion became increasingly elaborate with initial adoption of horticulture and agriculture; but with later agrarianism, religion simplified beliefs and rituals as the universal religions (Judaism, Christianity, Islam, Buddhism and, to a lesser extent, Confucianism and Hinduism) spread across the globe. Of course, even as these religions came to dominate, older religions, folk religions, and popular religions persisted; and at the same time, periodic religious movements have punctuated the period of hegemony of the premodern, universal religions. Thus, unlike kinship, religion has never reverted to its simple beginnings; indeed, religious diversity and ferment now prevail throughout the world. Much of what has occurred with religion in human societies represents a reaction and response to powerful institutional forces outside of religion proper. For in the end, with but a few exceptions, these forces have segregated and compartmentalized religion in industrial and post-industrial societies, reducing the power of beliefs and rituals while partially assuming many of the functions for which religion was originally selected in human history. We need, therefore, to analyze religion in its institutional context.

ECONOMY AND RELIGION

As a general rule, when the technology of a population facilitates the gathering, producing, and distributing of resources, the power of religion declines. Thus, among hunter-gatherers, who rather easily secured resources with little work, religion was not a dominating force. Similarly, among industrial and post-industrial populations, where securing sustenance has become less problematic, religion has lost some of its former salience. Religion exerted its greatest impact on social organization, therefore, when gathering, producing, and most importantly, distributing resources became problematic. Thus, as population size as well as inequalities associated with power and privilege escalated during advanced horticulture and agrarianism, the influence of religion was greatest. Only with the dramatically expanded capacities of industrial and post-industrial economies did this influence begin to decline.

Economy and Religion in Horticultural and Agrarian Societies

When the economy generates uncertainty and unpredictability, much of the anxiety associated with the potential inability to secure adequate resources can be alleviated by religious beliefs and rituals. Or, if securing resources is dangerous, then religion is often used to reduce the anxiety associated with danger. For example, Malinowski ([1922] 1955) noted that among the Trobriand Islanders, who engaged in dangerous deep-sea fishing, extensive magic (a form of ritual) was used to prevent disaster, mitigating much of the uncertainty and stress accompanying this dangerous economic activity. Even though technology had risen after contact with the West to a level eliminating the objective uncertainty of deep-sea fishing for the Trobriand Islanders, these religious rituals persisted—indicating that, once *institutionalized*, religious rituals persist even as the original conditions generating them have been greatly altered or even eliminated (O'Dea 1966, 10). In fact, the rituals may have actually increased the level of anxiety associated with economic tasks among the Trobriand Islanders (Radcliffe-Brown 1938), but the crucial point is that in the absence of higher technologies and associated physical- and human-capital formation, religion added a sense of certainty and predictability and that this continued to be the case because rituals had become institutionalized.

Even in more-advanced agrarian societies with an extensive technology, religious rituals had similar consequences. For example, among the Dahomeans (who displayed certain features of an early agrarian economy with a more complex market structure), religious rituals were intimately involved in cultivation, harvesting, marketing, weaving, woodcarving, and ironworking (Goode 1951, 88–89). Through rituals, Dahomeans made appeals to deities in order to assure the success of parties engaged in various tasks, despite the fact that considerable technology was utilized in all phases of the Dahomean economy.

With the emergence of a more advanced agrarian economy, however, the prevalence of religious rituals in economic processes began to decline. The accumulation of technology, which is concerned with the *secular*, displaced religious beliefs and rituals, which ultimately are concerned with the *sacred*. Religion increasingly became segregated from technology (Wallace 1966, 257–59), particularly when markets could provide secular services, such as insurance and banking, that alleviated much of the uncertainty in economic transactions in advanced agrarian economies.

Yet, as Marx recognized, religion was used to legitimate the inequalities that accompanied agrarian economic development. Inequality in the distribution of resources escalated even as the productive capacity of the economy increased (Lenski 1966; Turner 1984), thereby generating anxiety over whether subordinates in this system of inequality could receive sustenance and, at the same time, fueling their anger over poverty in the midst of privilege. Under these conditions, religion alleviated the anxiety over uncertainty, while legitimating the privilege of elites. Thus, as the purely economic basis for religion began to decline, it set into motion other forces that selected for the expansion of religion to reduce the anxiety and anger associated with inequality and stratification.

Moreover, as the productive capacity of the economy increased with advanced horticulture and agrarianism, there was now sufficient economic surplus to support more-elaborate ecclesiastic cult structures with an extensive professional clergy. This underscores the fact that economic development has had two seemingly contradictory consequences for religion: On the one hand, it increasingly excluded religious influence from the economy, per se; on the other hand, it provided the necessary economic surplus to support extensive ecclesiastic cult structures and generated the inequalities and associated uncertainties and anger which gave these ecclesiastic cults a role to play. With these more-elaborate cult structures of traditional ecclesiastic and premodern religions, systemization of religious beliefs and proliferation of the religious division of labor could occur. Without an extensive economic surplus, only shamanic and communal cult structures with shamans practicing magic were possible. However, once economic development accelerated, technological expansion forced major alterations of religious beliefs and cult structures. And so, as the economy decreased as the driving force for the emergence of religion, it created other conditions favoring the expansion and elaboration of religion.

Economy and Religion during Industrialization and Post-Industrialization

Industrialization and post-industrialization dramatically increase the output of goods and services; and in so doing, they potentially eliminate the specter of starvation and problems in securing sustenance. Of course, whether or not this potential reduces anxiety over sustenance depends on the level of inequality in the distribution of economic output and the capacity of the economy or other institutional sectors to employ all members of a population at a living wage. Moreover, the number of those left in marginal economic niches (where job skills and education create employment problems) or in cultural niches (where they feel out of synch with industrialism and post-industrialism) will influence the degree to which aggregate anxiety is alleviated. For most of the population in post-industrial societies, the economic anxiety that historically has caused people to be receptive to religion is considerably reduced; but for a sizable minority, economic or cultural marginality in the rapidly changing and credentially inflated economic system fuel anxiety and religious vitality. And the more prevalent is this latter segment, the more evident will be religious movements in all directions, whether towards fundamentalism, revitalization, or production of new beliefs and rituals.

Ironically, two of the most secularizing economic influences on populations—markets and mass media—can also contribute to the spread of religious movements. On the one hand, markets secularize a population by encouraging rational calculation of costs and benefits in terms of money and by encouraging concern with acquisition and materialism. But on the other hand, markets commodify everything, including the selling and buying of religion. Mass-media processes accelerate the marketing of religion by relatively low-cost access to the mass or specialized markets of potential consumers of religious messages. Indeed, markets and media condition members of a population to receiving advertising messages passively, and then, if receptive to the message, purchasing (or contributing) to its producers. As a consequence, virtually all potential market segments for religion can be reached and encouraged to participate in rituals without even having to enter a church. These media and market processes only work, however, in societies like the United States with private media systems; in those societies with primarily government-owned or controlled media, media marketing of religion will be less evident (unless the government sponsors an "official" religious doctrine).

Yet even as these market and media dynamics accelerate religious movements in post-industrial societies, the majority of the population remains, to varying degrees, committed to one of the modern offshoots of premodern religions or—as is increasingly the case—segments of the population drop formal affiliation with any religious cult. Even those affiliated with these premodern cults, as well as those attached to a religious movement, segregate religion from most of their daily activities and routines, because the economy requires that most work, markets, and purchasing be secular and rational. These economic forces produce a kind of diffuse secularism that pervades the orientations and behaviors of individuals; and in doing so, the economy segregates the more nonsecular orientations of religion from most daily activities. Moreover, because the economy of post-industrial societies is structured to generate, via profit-oriented and competitive markets, a constant expansion of technology or secular knowledge about how to manipulate the environment, the population is further conditioned toward a secular orientation in most spheres of activity. Indeed, market competition and advertising generate a "culture of technology," in which the population comes to expect constant technological change (even if it must be invented by advertising). This creates additional pressures for secular orientations. Much of this "culture of technology" reflects, and reciprocally feeds into, science as an emerging institutional system.

In a very real sense, science is a response to the same forces that drive religion: to understand the universe and to use that understanding to make life more predictable and certain. It should not be surprising, therefore, that religion and science historically have been interrelated—as perhaps was the case with early astronomy. But in the long term, religion and science eventually have come into conflict, since religion seeks to reduce uncertainty by requiring ritual appeals to the nonempirical, whereas science attempts to do the opposite by understanding the laws of nature governing the flow of empirical events. In the end, scientific knowledge increasingly challenges religious beliefs (White 1896), since the former relies on "demonstrable proofs, perceptible by any normal human" (Wallace 1966, 261), while religion relies upon faith in beliefs about the sacred and supernatural.

Initial conflicts between science and religion often were won by religious elites in agrarian societies, as was demonstrated by Galileo's famous "retraction" and "apology" for findings that contradicted religious dogma (i.e., that the earth was not the center of the universe). But there were powerful forces working in favor of science. First, early science often came under the patronage of elites who had the resources to protect its practitioners from religious persecution. In the case of Europe, status competition among elites over who had the best scientists gave scientists additional protection, while increasing incentives to produce secular knowledge (Turner 1995). Second, because of its potential utility in developing war technologies or in public-works projects, science often has been embraced by centers of power which, in agrarian systems, almost always have had an uneasy relationship with religious elites who represented an alternative source of power. Third and most important in the modern era, science and technological development in the economy have become linked, especially as markets for technology have emerged. As this occurs, the most dynamic force behind the spread of science is unleashed; for once science is attached to profits in markets, incentives beyond status competition among elites or war making by centers of power drive the expansion of new knowledge which can be bought and sold for profit. With these structural supports, science was able to overcome resistance by religion, although the history of agrarian populations reveals that religion was often able to prevail. Indeed, it might be argued that until science and economic technologies become linked in dynamic markets, science has remained particularly vulnerable to persecution by religious elites.

As science emerges as a distinct institution, increasingly tied to economy, it expands the secular knowledge base of a society. As it does so, religious beliefs about the sacred and supernatural, as well as rituals in cult structures directed toward the supernatural, become more segregated from the mainstream of secular activity. Moreover, elaborate pantheons of gods and myths about their activities and histories become less tenable and plausible as science increases the knowledge base in society. Rigid moral codes become outdated as secular knowledge is constantly changing and forcing individuals to reevaluate their changed circumstances. And so, a trend toward religious simplification which started before science was firmly institutionalized, is sustained by the spread of science. In the case of more-modern adaptations of premodern, universal religions, gods and pantheons become attenuated, moral codes become more flexible, distinctions between natural and supernatural become less distinct, and relations between humans and gods become more subject to individual interpretation. Liberal Protestantism, Unitarianism, Reform Judaism, and new quasi-religions such as Scientology (which also makes appeals to science) are conspicuous examples of these trends. And while the more traditional denominations of the world religions rarely go this far, there is a clear trend among established churches for simplification of beliefs and rituals. At the same time, however, among those most vulnerable to the expansion of scientific knowledge and its effects on educational "credentialing," job placement, and other life-chance forces various fundamentalist religious movements emerge and spread as a countertrend in a world increasingly dominated by the culture of science and technology.

Even as science and technology erode blind faith in religious beliefs and rigid moral codes, their effects on production and surplus income increase the wealth and affluence available to support cult structures. Thus, as religion is transformed by science and technology, its indirect effects on the economy help create the wealth that can sustain cults, although cults must increasingly compete in secular markets for this surplus income (a force which, noted earlier, further secularizes much of religion).

POLITY AND RELIGION

In horticultural populations, where distinct leaders began to emerge, political and religious leadership often overlapped. Those who performed religious rituals were also those who engaged in societal decision making. For example, among the Tikopia, village and clan chiefs represented a link between secular and sacred activities. As each chief served as the mouthpiece of the gods, leadership of secular activity was intermingled with religion.

Even in more-advanced horticultural or agrarian systems where an elaborate kin-based or clear state-based political subsystem had differentiated from the rest of society, considerable structural overlap between religion and polity persisted. Elite political positions were rationalized and legitimated as divine, while literate priests performed many of the administrative tasks of the state bureaucracy. Such a system as particularly evident in medieval China, where the emperor was worshiped as a god, while many key state administrators were religious specialists and experts. A similar situation existed in much of feudal Europe, with the literate clergy performing many necessary administrative tasks for the polity. But despite such overlap between state and ecclesiastical bureaucracies, strain and competition were inevitable between the secular concerns of the state and sacred focus of the church, even when the church continued to engage in secular activities such as profit-oriented farming or war making. Increasingly, as the state bureaucracy became involved in the secular tasks of allocating resources toward the attainment of goals, it began to usurp religious influence in the economy, family, education, and other spheres. And as the size of the state bureaucracy increased, this conflict between state and church intensified as each sought to claim not only the loyalty of the population but its material resources as well.

Yet premodern religions were nonetheless crucial to maintaining the legitimacy of the state-based polity. Even though the church bureaucracy and its specialists increasingly were segregated from the state bureaucracy, religion served as the major source of legitimation for the polity. Yet, because of the strain between religious and political elites, along with their respective bureaucracies, centers of political power had an interest in seeking an alternative basis of legitimation—a basis that the state could more readily control. Thus, the state encouraged new bases of political legitimation, such as law and civic culture. At this juncture, religion and the polity came into conflict, with religious leaders sometimes withdrawing legitimacy and/or encouraging popular revolts. The state, with its secularized administrative and military organizations, was usually in a much better position to endure in such a conflict—although political instability could persist for some time. Even with political instability, the church rarely was able to assume any degree of political power, and as a consequence, the church increasingly became segregated from, or subordinate to, the political system.

As agrarianism gave way to industrialism, the bureaucratized state became increasingly dominant. And except in rare cases, such as contemporary Iran, religion could no longer serve as either a principal legitimating or decision-making force. Incumbents are now recruited to and promoted in the state bureaucracy on the basis of secular expertise. The pervasive influence of the polity into an ever wider range of secular spheres—the economic, familial, educational, and legal—has reached a level equal to that of religion in more-traditional societies. With the ascendence of the polity in modern societies, religion now must accommodate itself to the state initiatives, rather than vice versa. Three patterns are evident (Vernon 1962, 252–53): The polity (1) supports some cult structures over others, (2) supports religion in general but displays no preferences, and (3) rejects religion and actively discriminates against all religions.

The first form of religious accommodation is most evident in societies with a state cult, such as the Church of England. In these cases, the state endorses and supports the religious activities of these churches, whereas in other modern societies the state church is less-formally acknowledged but still given preferential treatment. This pattern exists with the Lutheran Church in Sweden and Norway as well as with Judaism in Israel. During early periods of development in industrial societies, much religious tolerance and pluralism tend to become predominant, although one church can maintain its favored position.

The second form of accommodation is the separation-of-church-and-state pattern, most evident in the United States. This pattern was not intended (Williams 1970, 376); indeed, various cult structures originally established in the United States were hardly tolerant. For example, the Puritans came to America to set up a theocracy similar to that established by Calvin in Geneva, with church members holding secular authority (Vernon 1962, 255). Furthermore, religious persecution and killings were common in colonial America (for instance, Quakers were put to death by Protestants). But the sheer diversity of religious groupings in the United States eventually resulted in the separation-of-church-and-state doctrine and in growing religious tolerance. Yet such tolerance, it should be emphasized, grew slowly out of a long period of religious conflict and persecution. Moreover, even today in the United States, the separation is difficult to sustain as the "religious right" has increasingly mobilized in ways encouraging state sponsorship of religious doctrines, such as school prayer, abolition of abortion, and other "moral issues."

The third and rather rare pattern of religious accommodation involves the polity's attempt to eliminate religion or at least greatly attenuate it. This pattern was most evident in post-revolutionary Russia, where the state encouraged atheism. State persecution of all religion reached its peak during the late 1920s and early 1930s, when church property was confiscated and a seven-day workweek was established to discourage traditional sabbath services, with days off adjusted to fall conveniently during midweek (Vernon 1962, 260). But since the early 1940s, a more tolerant attitude of the Russian polity toward religion has been evident. With the fall of the Soviet empire in the early 1990s, a broad-based religious resurgence is under way, especially as public anxieties and fears about the viability of the system of societies emerging from the old empire escalate. Indeed, in the absence of a stable state, religion has great appeal to large masses within the populations of these precariously situated societies.

All these patterns of accommodation display a broad trend—the growing toleration of religion by the state and/or religious pluralism. This trend may not result in the complete separation of state and church or active state encouragement of religion, but it clearly reveals a growing acceptance of religion. The reason for increases in religious toleration is the state's clear supremacy in most industrial societies, where religion no longer represents a threat because it has become somewhat segregated from other institutional spheres or subordinated to the state in those spheres where both exert an influence. Yet, where the state is not so dominant (as has become evident in the aftermath of either the state's collapse in what used to be Yugoslavia or the state's incapacity to hold the Soviet empire together), religion has become highly salient as an ethnic marker and flashpoint of violent conflict. In the societies that eventually emerge from this conflict, the state and religion no doubt will be closely connected. Indeed, religion may exert considerable influence over the polity. Thus, the trend toward state domination and accommodation of religion is not universal, as the Iranian revolution documented and as virtually every point of religious/ethnic conflict in the world today would attest. When state power weakens, religion often fills the vacuum (Juegensmeyer 1993).

Still, in the stable states of advanced industrial and post-industrial societies, the state and the vast array of administrative linkages of the state to the economy, education, law, religion, and family make the question of competition between church and state simply nonexistent, or of very low intensity. Such a situation is the culmination of a long developmental trend toward the emergence, proliferation, and eventual supremacy of the state bureaucracy.

LAW AND RELIGION

Ultimately, law is concerned with controlling and coordinating social activities. As the scale and complexity of activities increase, bodies of codified law along with law-making, law-enforcing, and law-adjudicating agents and agencies have evolved as a clearly differentiated institutional system. Indeed, without such a system, there are limitations on how large a complex a society can become (Parsons 1971, 1966). Conversely, the smaller a population and the less complex its organization, the less intense are selection pressures for a distinct legal system. The relationship between law and religion must be visualized from this perspective: Much control and coordination in simple societies can be managed informally in face-to-face contacts and spiritually by ritual appeals to supernatural forces. In fact, law and religion were only partially differentiated in simple hunting-gathering or horticultural societies; and in these societies specific laws were intimately connected to religious beliefs (Hoebel 1954; Diamond 1951). Indeed, in such simple societies, supernatural spirits and beings were seen as responding with favor or disfavor to the mundane and specific behaviors and acts of mortals. This relationship between the supernatural and secular was usually codified into a series of religious postulates that represented the wills and dictates of supernatural spirits, beings, and forces, with members of a society required to harmonize their actions with the dictates of these religious entities. Religion was thus a very powerful source of social control and regulation in these societies, and most primitive legal systems laws were intimately entangled with religious dictates and practices. But regardless of the extensiveness of these interrelations, law always displayed some autonomy from religion.

Many religious dictates, when violated in simple societies, were sanctioned by the supernatural realm whose inhabitants would bring misfortune to an individual. For example, among the traditional Eskimos, violating a religious taboo was usually viewed as the cause of bad luck or hardship. To eliminate such misfortune required an Eskimo to consult a shaman, who pointed out the violations and served as an intermediary between the gods and the violator in order to relieve the hardship (Hoebel 1954, 261). This constantly reinforced association between violating religious dictates and bad luck maintained considerable order and control in Eskimo society, but when an Eskimo persistently violated a taboo, specific members of the community administered punishment. In this latter instance, legal sanctions rather than religious sanctions of guilt and fear were employed, indicating that excessive sin was to be treated as a crime and to be punished by mortals rather than gods (although in such cases law clearly embodied certain religious dictums). Moreover, many of the laws of even the Eskimo society bore little relationship to religion. Wife stealing and murder were wholly secular, because the legal rules concerning these crimes neither derived from religious dogmas nor overlapped with the jurisdiction of the supernatural (Hoebel 1954, 261). Thus, while interrelated with religion, even the most primitive legal system was also autonomous and encompassed purely secular crimes. Legal and religious norms thus represented overlapping but separate mechanisms of control and integration in highly traditional societies. As societies became more complex, this separation increased as a distinctive legal system began to evolve in response to increasingly complex problems of coordination and control.

As this separation occurred, law codified and incorporated religious dogmas—just as it had other cultural components, such as custom, traditions, and values. The emergence of an extensive body of torts (or civil, noncriminal laws) and the growing centralization and systematization of courts, police, and legislatures point to the influence of other institutions on legal evolution. These other influences emanated primarily from the polity and economy and, to a lesser extent, from the family and education. With the increasing commerce and exchange of advanced agrarian and, later, industrial and post-industrial economies, and with the emergence and expansion of the state, the law was used to integrate secular relations within the economy and to mediate between individuals and the developing polity. Since integrative problems stemmed from strains in concrete relations among individuals and organizations rather than from strains in relations between people and the supernatural, torts came to rival crimes as components of the legal system. Also crimes increasingly became redefined as violations of the public's and state's will rather than the dictates of supernatural forces.

In many agrarian societies, bodies of church law and adjudicating agents persisted, however. Much of this law embodied the moral codes of the belief system and specified appropriate ritual practices. However, a significant amount of such law was more secular, indicating what people should or should not do in daily transactions and providing for appropriate punishments for offenders and compensation for victims or aggrieved parties. When the state was weak and had to share power with religion, church law could be more significant for coordination and control than state law. Yet these bodies of church law were ultimately so infused with religious morality that they limited economic development and institutional differentiation; and in the end, selection for more secular bodies of law began. Still, until the development of Roman law, secular legal systems never developed beyond a certain point, apparently unable to throw off religion, tradition, and ascription as principles of social order and, hence, unable to develop, revise, and apply purely secular laws to all members of a population (Parsons 1971, 1966).

Once law broke through this barrier, it became more secular and developed into a system of *positive law*, which not only responded to new and complex problems of coordination and control but also to the need to reevaluate and reassess its premises and decisions. As this occurred, the last remnants of church law were subordinated to secular law, unless a religious movement (like that in Iran) could take state power and reimpose elements of traditional religious law. More typically in the history of advanced agrarian and industrializing societies, religious ideals were codified in abstracted but less-restrictive legal assumptions, with the vast body of law and its enforcement, enactment, and adjudication being purely secular and outside the purview of religion. Religious beliefs and rituals directed toward the supernatural were simply inadequate to provide the basis for integration and coordination in a highly differentiated social system. These integrative problems were too specific, secular, variable, and ever expanding. Courts enacting common-law precedents in response to specific sources of malintegration or legislatures enacting bodies of civil laws represented more rapid, efficient, and relevant solutions to these problems of coordination than did religious beliefs which are conservative and difficult to change.

And so, while religious values codified into moral codes could underlie and reinforce a myriad of specific secular laws, the church's codes, dogmas, and rituals ceased to have the same consequences for social control and coordination that they had in simpler societies. Such a decrease marked the growing compartmentalization of religion in modern societies.

Thus legal evolution might be viewed as a process of institutional invasion and succession of an emerging legal subsystem into a sphere which at one time was dominated—though never fully monopolized—by religion. Once law was firmly established, the legal system increasingly became involved in regulating economic activity, providing political legitimation, reinforcing crucial socialization norms within kinship, controlling education and corresponding *rites de passage*, regulating relations among individuals, and specifying relations between individuals and the state.

We should not, however, view law as completely displacing religion as a force for social control and integration. For many segments of the population in modern societies, religious beliefs and rituals are perhaps more salient than the laws, codes, and statutes of the legal system. Furthermore, religious overtones to the ideologies, beliefs, symbols, and pronouncements of spokespersons for social movements often emerge—as occurred in the United States with the anti-abortion movement of the 1990s or the civil rights movement of the 1960s. These movements reveal that religion, or at least a kind of religiosity, can have considerable power to unite and integrate masses in the population of industrial and post-industrial societies in their efforts to rewrite laws and alter their enforcement. Frequently the goals of these movements—such as the U.S. anti-abortion movement—confront and call into question legal structures and processes, yet these sporadic movements with religious overtones cannot be viewed as a major source of societal integration or control. When compared to the pervasive and paninstitutional influence of religion in pre-industrial societies, the segregation of religion in modern societies becomes abundantly clear. Indeed, religion exposes itself as an "outsider" when attacking more-dominant institutional systems.

EDUCATION AND RELIGION

In all probability, the first formal educational structures with clear-cut teacher and student roles were religious and involved imparting crucial religious beliefs. In horticultural societies, and in some hunter-gatherer populations as well, the pantheon, myths, substantive beliefs, values, and rituals of religion were clearly being stored by virtue of their more formal dissemination from one generation of specialized religious practitioners—such as shamans, diviners, witch doctors, and priests—to another. While much of such storage and dissemination occurred within kinship, formal education became more evident as cult structures grew and required professional religious specialists. Indeed, much of the power of the religious elites in agrarian societies came from their literacy and capacity to organize, codify, and present ideas that could dominate the illiterate. In agrarian China, for example, the bureaucrats of the emperor were selected on the basis of their literacy and knowledge about religion, because these generalized intellectual skills could be adapted for more-purely secular tasks in the state bureaucracy. And in Europe, almost all of the early universities were religious in character and orientation. Thus, the emergence and extension of education up to early industrialization was, for the most part, very much influenced by religion.

Beginning with late agrarianism and accelerating with industrialization and post-industrialization, however, the influence of religion on education declined, as the state sought to train its own bureaucrats and to establish a secular basis for its legitimation. Moreover, purely secular skills were now required in commerce; literacy was increasingly essential to industrial workers; science and technology became linked to military success and economic development; labor market competition in post-industrial systems set into motion credential inflation; and an ideology of education as a solution to economic and social problems became institutionalized in the minds of not only political decision makers but also the population as a whole. These and other forces have caused secularization and "massification" of the educational system which, rather than storing religious beliefs and then disseminating them to religious elites, begins to store and disseminate secular cultural components such as technology and a political culture and impart these secular idea systems to the masses.

And as this process of secularization and massification unfolds in industrial and most industrializing societies, educational structures come to have far-reaching consequences for storage and dissemination not only of vast secular culture but also for cultural expansion and innovation, for social placement of individuals in the society, and for social transformation of the society. These expanded consequences are a direct result of intensified pressures for technology, political indoctrination, and skills in the work force. As the culture of a society becomes secularized, school curricula in storing and disseminating culture also become increasingly secular. Even religious school systems impart mostly secular knowledge; and as the state gains the power to control and accredit these religious systems of education, further pressures for a standardized, secular curriculum mount. In some societies, such as the United States, religious schools are established deliberately to counteract these secular tendencies. Much of the emphasis in the United States for educational reform, like instituting a voucher system, comes from religious cults that seek to undermine the state's control of education and its secular slant.

Yet as the state controls the mass-education system, religion is further compartmentalized in several senses. First, it loses control of much socialization into the culture, taking a back seat to science, civics, and other secular belief systems. Second, it becomes irrelevant to social placement, careers, and life chances for most individuals whose futures are tied more to educational credentials than to rituals directed toward the supernatural. Third, it must adjust and adapt notions of God, the supernatural, salvation, myths, pantheons, and substantive beliefs to the predominantly secular training occurring in schools—a necessity that can simplify religion further by reducing the distinctions between natural and supernatural and by encouraging more individualized interpretations of the supernatural among variously educated members of a population. In the end, under these pressures for secular education, the influence of religion recedes, being increasingly confined to the private and personal sphere of each individual, who in most daily routines, pursues secular goals consistent with the opportunities that secular educational credentials provide.

KINSHIP AND RELIGION

In hunting and gathering as well as simple horticultural societies, religious rituals often were practiced in cult structures that overlapped with kinship units. With horticulture, the kinship unit, as determined by the descent, residence, and family composition rules of the broader kinship system, was not only the locus of religious rituals but also the source of ritual leaders. Thus, the maintenance of beliefs about the sacred and supernatural—both their transmission and reinforcement through ritual—was very much tied to kinship structures.

Even in more advanced horticultural systems where ecclesiastic cults dominated and where many religious rituals were performed outside kinship in temples by religious specialists, kinship socialization not only generated a committed membership, but also reinforced those rituals performed in temples through the performance of minor rituals—such as praying—by kinship leaders. Furthermore, perhaps the most vital consequence of kinship on a religion displaying ecclesiastic cults and religious specialists was financial: Members of kin groups donated the economic surplus needed to support nonworking religious specialists. Even where religious cults owned considerable property, the rank-and-file membership was always largely responsible for supporting a separate and autonomous religious subsystem. Usually the very act of giving such support was ritualized and rationalized by beliefs so that donating surplus reinforced commitment to a particular religious system.

The nuclearization of the family unit during agrarianism and, then, its further transformations with industrialism to more of a consuming unit for work performed outside the household has changed the relationship between kinship and religion. Kinship remains a source of financing cult structures and a place for such individual and collective rituals as prayer. However, its connection to cults is altered by the expansion of a market economy in which organized religion must compete with other, more secular service organizations providing pleasure, emotional support, and meaning to family members who have grown accustomed to a highly commodified world geared to individualized consumption in terms of idiosyncratic preferences. For some, this kind of market-driven world, where everything can be bought and sold, creates needs for the very kind of meaning that religion can provide—which is one of the reasons that religious social movements in post-industrial societies are evangelical and emotional. Yet even in this sphere, religion must niche-market itself and still must compete with alternative organizations that also can provide emotion and meaning (Iannaccone 1992; Turner 1972; Berger 1963).

Thus, there is no longer an automatic connection between kinship and religion, although successful churches such as Mormons and some fundamentalist cults effectively sustain the overlap between family and religious activity. Indeed, as they have had to compete, religious organizations have been highly effective marketers of religion inside cults themselves or through the media. Despite this effective marketing, however, religion must confront the facts that family members: (a) increasingly depart the home for work, school, and recreation; (b) conduct their daily routines away from one another; (c) participate in diverse but predominately secular cultures as they engage in their daily activities; and (d) come home to eat and sleep in households inundated by mass-media messages, most of which are secular. Thus, religious marketing must increasingly focus on "selling" to each individual, rather than to the family as a whole, its beliefs, rituals, and cult structure.

As a result of this need to sell itself in a market that becomes highly differentiated in terms of the needs and tastes of its individual consumers, religion becomes differentiated as particular cult structures engage in niche marketing (Berger 1963). Such market forces only operate in market-driven and media-saturated (especially private media) societies. And even in these societies, the vast majority of cult membership adheres to the belief and practices the rituals of the premodern universal religions. But this empirical fact does not obviate the market pressures on religion, as these traditional religions lose members who seek more-evangelical religious niches or who simply find religion a less-appealing alternative in the market.

In less market-driven societies, where government control of media is great, traditional religion can still hold the family as a whole—especially if economic and political instabilities increase anxiety levels. But even in these societies, the penetration of western marketing—and the accompanying commodity- and consumption-oriented culture, can begin to individualize family-member tastes across age and gender (to say nothing of class and region) in ways that will force religion to "repackage" and, hence, change itself to fit new family realities of industrial and post-industrial societies.

CONCLUSION

Religion was one of humans' earliest creations. Indeed, it appears to have emerged among Neandertals, a close hominid relative, or perhaps precursor, to present-day humans. Among most hunters and gatherers, some form of religion was evident, though undifferentiated from kinship and often somewhat vague in the minds of people. With horticulture and agrarianism, religion became a truly dominant institution, exerting a wide influence on all other institutional systems. And then, with industrialism and post-industrialism, religion became more segregated and compartmentalized from the secular orientations of other institutional systems. As a result of this compartmentalization, but also reflecting dynamics internal to religion, social movements simplified religious beliefs and rituals in later agrarianism. Today, the successors of these "premodern" religions still dominate the globe. Yet, within each society where these and other agrarian-era religions dominate, older religions persist. Moreover, there is a constant series of religious movements around fundamentalism, revitalization, and innovation of new religious beliefs, rituals, and cults. Thus, even as religion has become a less-dominant force in the institutional order, it is a key dynamic force in all human societies.

The changes in religion reflect the differentiation and expansion of other institutional subsystems: Law now provides and reinforces many institutional norms; education, state, and law regulate socialization and social placement; science provides interpretations of the meaning of events; and law, with the support of polity, manages the tensions generated by inequality. Yet the selection pressures that perhaps first led to the emergence of religion among Neandertals (that is, the anxiety and tension over life, death, and uncertainty) still exert pressures for its persistence. To be sure, religion must now compete with other secular structures in an area where it once represented the only solution. But as long as societies generate uncertainty, religion will remain a viable institution.

Indeed, industrial and post-industrial societies systematically generate pockets of anxiety, thereby creating potential constituents for religious movements or for continued adherents to the great premodern religions. Moreover, the very structure of religious cults, beliefs, and rituals often has encouraged proselytization of new converts—frequently through conquest and other coercive activities. When ethnic identities in contested territories are tied to religion, as has been the case in much of the former Soviet Union and in parts of the Middle East, it has become a flashpoint in intense and violent conflicts. Religion will, therefore, remain a powerful force in human affairs.

Chapter
8

Polity

*T*he first humans did not have government, or polity. Informal and equalitarian relations in band and kinship structures were sufficient for deciding what the members of the society should do, for mobilizing people in important tasks, for allocating resources, and for social control. But as populations got larger and settled down, problems of controlling and coordinating their members increased; and decisions over what the society as a whole should do and over how to distribute valued resources became more difficult to manage. These problems generated selection pressures for polity. Those growing populations that could not find a way to bestow power on certain members, who in turn would use this power to organize activities and to distribute resources, were soon extinguished by internal chaos or external conquest.

Thus, once human populations grew and became sedentary, a new era in human social organization was launched. As problems of coordination and control mounted, *power*—the capacity of actors to regulate the activities of other actors—had to be consolidated and used to make "binding decisions" about: (1) the coordination of actors, both individual and collective; (2) the allocation and distribution of resources among actors; and (3) the management of deviance by, and conflicts among, actors (Luhmann 1982, 143–44; Turner 1995).

These functions of polity can be seen as selection pressures that forced a population either to consolidate and concentrate power or to disintegrate. Yet the very process of consolidating and concentrating power is one of the most volatile forces of human organization, because it generates new problems of coordination among, and control of, those who resist their subordination to power or who resent the unequal allocation and distribution of valued resources. Polity is thus a necessary evil, one that humans only reluctantly adopted and one that generates enormous tension in human affairs (Maryanski and Turner 1992, 113–14; Johnson and Earle 1987, 160–93).

ELEMENTS OF POLITY

As noted above, power is the capacity of one actor or set of actors to regulate the actions of another actor or set of actors (Turner 1995). This capacity to regulate and control exists throughout complex social systems. However, as it becomes institutionalized as a polity, power acquires additional features, revolving around (1) the consolidation of its bases and (2) the centralization of its regulatory capacities (Turner 1995). Each of these is examined below.

The Consolidation of Power

Why are some actors able to regulate others' activities? Answering this question leads us to examine the *bases of power*, or the mechanisms by which some can control others (Turner 1995). There have been numerous efforts to specify these bases (e.g., Mann 1986; Blalock 1989; Collins 1975; Etzioni 1961). These efforts point to four fundamental mechanisms by which actors mobilize and use power: (1) the use of symbols, (2) the use of material incentives, (3) the use of administrative structures, and (4) the use of coercion.

The Symbolic Base of Power   A polity always seeks to mobilize and use cultural symbols to legitimate its right to make decisions and, thereby, regulate the actions of others. As we saw in the last chapter, religious beliefs often were used to legitimate the rights of the leaders in a polity to control others. Later the legal system and its broad philosophical tenets often are employed. Equally frequently, emotionally charged symbols about a population's history, territory, or nationhood can be employed to legitimate rights to control others. The more consensus exists over key symbols, the greater is the intensity of people's feelings about these symbols; and the more effective is a polity's use of symbols, the greater is its power to regulate. Conversely, the less consensus over symbols, the less emotionally involving are these symbols, and the less competent is the polity in using them to justify itself and its actions, the less will be the power of the polity and the more it will need to rely upon other bases of power.

The Material Base of Power   A polity always seeks to provide material incentives (e.g., money, land, jobs, and other sources of satisfaction) in order to assure conformity to its decisions and dictates. Conversely, a polity will impose disincentives or punishments (i.e., taking away of material sources of satisfaction) for nonconformity. Of course, a polity must first have control of enough material resources to make their manipulation effective. But once this control exists, the selective bestowing and taking away of these sources of material well-being become powerful tools in getting others to do what the polity desires.

The Administrative Base of Power   To use power means that it must be administered. Decisions must be made, implemented, and enforced. And as populations get larger, these administrative activities escalate, and dramatically so. Once a *system* of decision-making, order-giving, monitoring, and sanctioning exists, it becomes more than just a tool for imposing power, the administrative system itself becomes a base of power. For an in-place structure of control has the capacity to regulate independently of other bases of power.

The Coercive Base of Power   Ultimately, power resides in the capacity to force physically conformity by others. Yet, this is a capacity that can only be selectively used, because coercion always generates resentments; it is a very costly form of social control. If a polity frequently must employ coercion, this fact reveals that the polity has not effectively mobilized the other bases of power and that it is incurring high costs in maintaining social order.

A polity is most effective when these bases of power are *consolidated*, or brought together and balanced so that no one base is utilized excessively. An effective polity, therefore, is: (a) legitimated by agreed-upon and emotionally arousing cultural symbols, (b) able to control and effectively manipulate important material incentives, (c) organized into a coherent administrative structure, and (d) capable of selectively but infrequently using coercive force. Maintaining this balance, however, has never been easy—which is the reason that the institutionalization of power in polity is such a volatile and dynamic process, as we will see shortly.

The Centralization of Power

A polity centralizes as well as consolidates its bases of power. To varying degrees, the key decision-making or leadership positions of a political system are concentrated among a delimited set of actors. The smaller this set relative to all political decision makers in the polity, the more *centralized* is power. Although the degree of centralization of power can vary enormously, a polity cannot be said to exist unless some degree of centralization of the bases of power occurs. A feudal monarch, kin-based chief, and elected president in a democracy may vary in how much power they directly control, but they all represent positions in a political system where power is concentrated. A system where not even a minimal degree of centralization has occurred usually reveals conflicting centers of power and considerable instability (as when, for example, a series of feuding warlords controls different regions of a society). Conversely, when power is so concentrated that rule is arbitrary and promotes high degrees of inequality (as in most agrarian monarchies), the balance among the bases of power becomes distorted toward the coercive and administrative side (Tilly 1990). As a result, material resources are exhausted through exploitive taxation without redistribution, leading to the escalation of inequalities and resentments which eventually delegitimate the symbolic base and that mobilize coercive opposition to centers of power (Weber [1922] 1978; Skocpol 1979; Goldstone 1990; Tilly 1990).

Much like consolidation, then, the stable centralization of power is difficult to create and sustain. Too much centralization increases inequalities and resentments (Lenski 1966; Turner 1984), whereas too little prevents effective consolidation of the bases of power and invites multiple and typically conflicting centers of power. Centralization of power is thus as volatile and dynamic as the consolidation of power.

We are now in a position to define polity as an institution: *A polity is a societywide system for consolidating and centralizing power in order to make and implement binding decisions with respect to coordinating activities among individual and collective actors in a population, allocating and distributing resources among actors, and managing deviance by, and conflicts among, actors.* Because the consolidation and centralization of power inevitably impose constraints on actors, while differentially allocating and distributing resources among them, the emergence of polity was not so much welcomed as accepted as a necessary evil.

TYPES OF POLITICAL SYSTEMS

The emergence and elaboration of polity historically has been tied to development of the economy for a very simple reason: To support a distinct political system requires an economic surplus (Lenski 1966; Turner 1984). For without the ability to release leaders and their administrative staff from the necessity of supporting themselves, the size, scale, and scope of polity are limited. Moreover, since low-productivity societies will not be able to sustain large populations, there are less-intense selection pressures for separating a political system to coordinate population members, to regulate the allocation and distribution of resources, and to manage conflict and deviance. But as societies began to grow in size, there were mutually reinforcing effects among increasing population size, production, and power. Larger populations have had to produce more and, in the process, generate the surplus to support political leaders, who were needed because a growing population presents more logistical problems of coordination and control. As production and polity expanded, the population could grow further, thereby creating additional problems of production, coordination, and control, which initiated yet another cycle of economic and political development.

Polity in Hunting and Gathering Populations

In most hunting and gathering populations, a polity did not exist because it was not needed. Leadership tended to be somewhat ad hoc—arising if required for a specific purpose, but soon dissipating. Among some hunting and gathering populations, a headman was differentiated, but as is typical, his powers were very limited. For example, among the !Kung-san of Africa, the headman's main duties revolved around directing migrations and some economic activity while performing certain necessary religious ceremonies for the society's welfare (Fried 1967, 87), but these leaders possessed no sanctioning power or capacity to use force.

Among some hunting and gathering populations, however, a more visible leader could be found. This was especially likely when hunter-gatherers began to settle down, usually near waterways or bodies of water where fishing could provide an ample economic surplus to support the "Big Man," who took power in order to coordinate economic activities, promote defense, negotiate peace or wage war, and regulate exchange. The Big Man became the village spokesperson with outside groups, negotiating trade, performing ceremonies, striking political agreements, and waging war. Internally, the Big Man often "owned" the land or had rights to its economic outputs; and he usually had the right to distribute the resources to other members of the population or, frequently, to sponsor prestige-giving festivals and engage in trade with other populations (Johnson and Earle 1987; Maryanski and Turner 1992, 114; Sahlins 1963). Thus, if a stable surplus existed and if a population grew, even hunter-gatherers could begin to consolidate and centralize power. But in a real sense, this development was premature, because normally hunting and gathering populations were small, nomadic, and leaderless. When they were able to produce a stable surplus and, thereby, become more sedentary, hunter-gatherers began to approximate simple horticultural populations in economic productivity and population size, but not the horticulturalists' extensive use of the descent rule to form kinship systems. Thus, Big Man societies have been an evolutionary cul-de-sac, but they point to the basic conditions that cause polity to emerge. These conditions were more consistently evident with the spread of horticulture among the world's populations.

Kin-Based Polities in Simple Horticulture

As human populations grew and settled down, the descent rule of kinship was used to create a way of organizing this larger population. The first true polities were thus lodged in unilineal descent structures, with the leaders of the descent group—whether a lineage, clan, or moiety—being the political leader for that grouping. As descent groupings came into conflict, or at least competition, some of these groupings were more successful than others. As a result, the head of the dominant grouping, usually a clan or moiety, became the chief or paramount chief among other local heads or chiefs, with the latter assuming the role of the paramount chief's lieutenants. When this process occurred historically, polity was no longer tied to each village but began to consolidate villages into a larger political system (Kirch 1980).

The bases for this kind of centralized polity involved a consolidation of: (1) coercion by fellow kinsmen and their allies; (2) symbolic legitimation through the beliefs and rituals of communal and, later, ecclesiastic cult structures; (3) use of kinship rules of descent, authority, and residence to create an administrative structure; and (4) extraction through taxation or tribute of the material surplus produced in economic activity and then its redistribu-

Table 8.1   POLITY IN HUNTING AND GATHERING SOCIETIES

	Nomadic	Settled or Semisettled
Centralization of Decision Making and Leadership	Some individuals may be followed because of their prestige and expertise, but no compulsion to conform to directives. Most decisions are made by individuals or by nucleated kin groups.	Sometimes, settled hunting and gathering populations developed "Big Men" who possess power to direct activities.
Consolidation of Bases of Power:		
Material Incentives	None for most hunter-gatherers	In Big Men systems, leaders often use their control of trade, land, and economic surplus to manipulate others.
Symbolic	Those with prestige often can get others to follow them.	Same as nomadic, although Big Man systematically seeks to garner prestige through manipulation of material incentives.
Coercion	Not utilized in most hunting and gathering societies.	Big Man and his allies or kindred in semisettled populations often use coercive force.
Administration	None	Big Man and his allies or, at times, his kinsmen can become a "quasi-staff" among more-settled populations.

tion (often with some skimming to support the privilege of elites in more-advanced horticultural systems).

In simple kin-based polities, this consolidation of power was highly effective, although the use of the kinship system to organize social life inevitably created strains among kinfolk forced together by descent and residence rules and subordinated to one another by descent and authority rules (Maryanski and Turner 1992, 91–112). If this kin-based polity sought to conquer its neighbors and extend its territorial holdings, the balance in the consolidation of power began to change as further strains on the kinship system mounted in efforts to use kinship principles to control the larger territory. For when larger territories were conquered, their surplus often was extracted and their peoples subordinated in terms of coercion rather than religiously legitimated kinship rules. New patterns of political control were adopted as the inadequacies of kinship to rule became increasingly evident. Chiefs now became kings; and the reliance on coercion and extraction of surplus without full redistribution to those who produced it escalated inequalities and, thereby, made the legitimation of privilege more problematic. Moreover, the administration of power now involved more than kindred, who may still have held the elite positions in the polity but who had to turn over the tasks of administering coercion, extracting surplus, and controlling tensions to nonkin. As this process occurred in human history, the beginnings of the

Table 8.2   POLITY IN HORTICULTURAL SOCIETIES

	Simple	Advanced
Centralization of Decision Making and Leadership	Headman or chief at village level empowered to make decisions in consultation with other kinsmen and, perhaps, religious specialists. At times there is a paramount chief who, in consultation with village heads, makes decisions for larger network of villages.	Explicit king or chief empowered to make decisions for all communities and kin units, sometimes in consultation with local village/kin leaders and religious specialists.
Consolidation of Bases of Power:		
Material Incentives	Headman can extract economic production of kin units but also must redistribute economic output in ways that enhance his power.	Developed taxation system that the king or chief can use to manipulate conformity from other elites who, in turn, control villages and kinsmen
Symbolic	Prestige that comes from redistribution by chief, kinship descent and authority rules as they define leaders, and sanctioning by supernatural beings and/or forces.	Prestige that is attached to king and chief, but less reliance on redistribution and more on pomp and ceremony of office. Religious beliefs become as important and often more important than kinship rules (descent and authority) for legitimation of king or chief.
Coercion	Chiefs have coercive capacity, enforced by their allies and kinsmen.	Dramatically escalated coercive power, often from a standing army of kinsmen and nonkin recruits. In highly advanced systems, a professional army.
Administration	Chiefs and paramount chiefs have staff comprised of allies and kinsmen. Lineages, clans, and at times moieties become administrative conduit of decisions.	Kinship begins to be replaced by more-bureaucratic system of administration, but kinship and village leadership still an important conduit of administration.

state became evident (Carneiro 1987; 1981; 1970; Service 1975; Evans et al. 1985).

Advanced Horticulture, Agrarianism, and the Emergence of the State

With the greater economic surplus provided by more advanced horticulture and full-scale agrarianism, the consolidation and centralization of power began to shift. Power was now concentrated in a monarch; and the bases of power were consolidated in a somewhat new pattern. Coercion was organized in a more clear-cut militia or standing army in order to control conquered territories, thwart hostile actions by the nobility, and repress peasant uprisings. Legitimation came from religion, but the emerging conflict between religious leaders and the nobility created selection pressures for new bases of legitimation in tradition and law. Administration increasingly was turned over to nonkin functionaries, who were organized in quasi-bureaucratic structures. Material incentives were used primarily to keep the nobility in line with the monarch's wishes, creating vast inequalities between the nobility and the rest of the population—particularly the peasants who produced the surplus that was extracted to support the power and privilege of the monarch and nobility (Lenski 1966; Turner 1984).

Once this pattern of consolidated power existed in human history, it tended to increase inequalities, because the need to coerce potential dissidents and the escalating requirements for administering the appropriation of material surplus were expensive, thereby increasing the costs of running the state and, hence, the need to extract ever more surplus to meet these costs (Fried 1978, 1967). Given the problem of legitimating this inequality as tensions with the ecclesiastical cults of religion mounted, the reliance on the coercive and administrative bases of power further skewed the consolidation of power away from the symbolic base and the use of material incentives toward coercion and tight administration (Turner 1995).

Industrialization, Post-Industrialization, and the State

Industrialization has generated a sufficient economic surplus to support a large bureaucratic state in which power is, to varying degrees, centralized and which reshuffles the four bases of power toward somewhat diverging patterns of consolidation. In democratic states, where incumbents in the decision-making bodies of government (the chief executive and legislative bodies) are selected in contested elections by the members of the population who enjoy political freedoms and citizenship rights, the consolidation of power revolves around four factors:

1. Minimal and selective use of coercion.
2. Symbolic legitimation in terms of secular legal principles usually embodied in a constitution.
3. Manipulation of material incentives through tax and redistribution policies for a broad array of the population.
4. Reliance on an extensive administrative bureaucracy whose officials are recruited and promoted for their expertise and whose heads are ultimately responsible to the elected executive and to members of representative bodies.

In less-democratic or totalitarian states, where contested elections are not held or, if held, are mechanical confirmations of decisions made by those who hold power, the consolidation of power is skewed toward:

1. Extensive use of coercion or threats of coercion.
2. Legitimation in terms of secular constitutional principles that are frequently ignored by those holding power. (A religious variant, such as that in Iran, is for legitimation to come from religious doctrines that are also subject to manipulation.)

Table 8.3   POLITY IN AGRARIAN SOCIETIES

	Simple	Advanced
Centralization of Decision Making and Leadership	Hereditary monarchy composed of king and other nobility organized into state bureaucracy composed of military officials, administrative bureaucrats, and at times, religious officials	Hereditary monarchy, organized into coercive state bureaucracy, begins to transform relations between king and Nobility in favor of ever more centralized control by monarch. Less delegation of decision making to nobility
	Consolidation of Bases of Power:	
Material Incentives	King uses nobility to extract economic surplus from estates of nobility in accordance with taxation formula. Manipulation of tax formulas and monarchical patronage to elites are common tactics for manipulating conformity	Heavy taxation of peasants, nobility, and growing merchant/artisan sectors to support growing state bureaucracy, army, public-works projects, and geopolitical activity. Use of patronage, franchises, and subsidy to other elites as mechanism of social control, coupled with strategic expenditures on public works (roads, ships, ports, and other infrastructural projects)
Symbolic	Prestige of nobility, per se, but heavy reliance on religion to legitimate power. Success in geopolitics becomes increasingly important source of symbolic manipulation of conformity. Less emphasis on redistribution as sources of legitimacy	Prestige of nobility, per se; complete abandonment of redistribution to mass of population as source of legitimation. Growing tension with religious leaders over religious basis of legitimation. Increasing appeals to "nationhood," "ethnicity," and other secular symbols
Coercive	Very high capacity for coercion by king's army, village and city police, and by armies of nobility	Very high capacity for coercion by king with a fully professionalized army, system of town and city police, with less reliance on armies of nobility
Administration	Feudal system of relations among monarch, nobility, army, and workers, coupled with administrative army of king's bureaucrats and, at times, religious officials	Reliance on feudal system of relations continues, but ever more control exercised by state bureaucracy, either directly through bureaucratic system (enforced by laws, courts, police, and army) or indirectly through franchise to other elites

3. Selective use of material incentives to "buy off" the masses (through state-run job, education, and recreation programs) and to support the privilege of elites.

4. Extensive intrusions of the state bureaucracy into the daily affairs of actors, coupled with high degrees of regulation of other institutional systems.

Industrialization creates pressures for democratization and the corresponding profile of consolidation and centralization of power, under several conditions: First, a relatively free and open market system encouraging the entrepreneurial activity must exist. Second, a large bourgeoisie who are willing to mobilize politically to support their interests in market-oriented activity must be in place (Moore 1966; Szymanski 1978). Third, a large industrially oriented working class that, despite opposition by the bourgeoisie (who want to keep wages down by politically disenfranchising workers), must be able to mobilize politically to press for the right to vote (Rueschemeyer, Stephens, and Stephens 1992). Conversely, when markets are not well developed, when the bourgeoisie is small relative to the land-owning aristocracy of the agrarian era, and when the industrial working class is small or politically inactive, a more totalitarian form of state is likely to emerge with industrialization (as was the case for Russia and its satellites, Eastern Europe, Germany in the West, and most of Latin America, Africa, and Asia). However, as these less democratic societies have sought to compete in the world system by expanding their free markets, encouraging entrepreneurship, and developing a working class, pressures mount for the democratization of the state—although it is not clear that these pressures can always shift the pattern of centralization and consolidation of power toward a more democratic profile. China and Russia will, for example, be interesting test cases as they undergo transformation to market-driven systems.

These transformations in the pattern of centralization and consolidation of power are summarized in Tables 8.1 to 8.4. Although the changes in the polity summarized in these tables are, in an ultimate sense, reflective of economic surplus available to support the polity, many of the dynamics of centralization and consolidation of power inhere in other forces unleashed with a growing economic surplus and an in-place political system. We should, therefore, review some of the underlying forces that have changed the nature of government over the long run of human evolutionary history.

THE DYNAMICS OF POWER

The Self-Escalating Nature of Power

Polity originally emerged as a visible institutional force when populations grew and settled down, thereby escalating problems of coordination and control (Turner 1995; Maryanski and Turner 1992; Carneiro 1973, 1970, 1967; Fried 1967; Johnson and Earle 1987; Earle 1984). Once leaders possessing power came into existence, the dynamics of power were initiated. When set into motion by population growth, consolidation takes on a life of its own,

Table 8.4   POLITY IN MODERN SOCIETIES

	Industrial	Post-Industrial
Centralization of Decision Making and Leadership	Disappearance of monarch, except as figurehead in some societies. Centralized state bureaucracy of civil servants, sprinkled with patronage, and clear tendency toward election of legislative and executive decision makers, although the number of parties and freedom of the electorate varies enormously	Same as industrial societies, except for dramatic increase in democratic systems, in which legislative and executive leaders are selected in elections, with varying degrees of true competition among candidates. Varying patterns of centralization of legislative, administrative, and judicial functions of government
Consolidation of Bases of Power:		
Material Incentives	Extensive system of progressive income (and at times, wealth) taxation, coupled with systems of sales and property taxes. Manipulation of taxes themselves for distinct subpopulations, or redistribution of tax revenues to targeted sectors of the population become common bases for manipulating the material base of power. The welfare state emerges	Same as in industrial societies, with increasingly complex system of taxation and redistribution through tax subsidies or tax expenditures and direct budgetary expenditures on targeted sectors of the population. The welfare state expands, although there is considerable variation in its size and scope
Symbolic	Decreased reliance on religious symbols and increased reliance on secular reliance on secular symbols: ideologies and democracy, citizenship rights, constitutional and legal principles, ideologies of welfare activities, nationalism, and beliefs associated with geopolitical activities	Same as industrial with growing reliance on secular systems of symbols
Coercion	Very high capacity with professional army and police, used strategically and, to greatly varying degrees, constrained by laws	Same as industrial with legal constraints on coercive actions increasingly evident
Administration	Vast state bureaucracy controlling virtually all institutional spheres, staffed increasingly by professionals certified by educational credentials and regulated by civil service system of promotion	Same as industrial societies, with some efforts (often unsuccessful) to "privatize" activities previously controlled by administrative system

because as legitimating symbols, coercive capacities, manipulation of material symbols, and administrative forms are brought together, the short-term interest of those involved in each of these bases of power is to expand their base. Controllers of symbols want to attract growing numbers of followers; forces of coercion wish to increase their readiness; administrative factions want to extend their prerogatives; and holders of material resources want to have more. Thus, as the bases of power are brought together, or consolidated, there are pressures for the mobilization of ever more power. This process began slowly in human history, primarily because the size, densities, and diversity of the population did not push consolidation over the critical threshold. But once this threshold was reached, usually with advanced horticulture, polity became an increasingly distinctive institutional system (Easton 1965). As polities have grown, however, maintaining balances among the bases of power has proven ever more difficult.

Difficulties in Balancing the Bases of Power

Governments rarely achieve stable balances among the four bases of power—symbolic, coercive, material, and administrative. As holders of any one base seek to extend their influence, the bases of power often come into conflict. For example, those who hold material wealth rarely are willing to give this control of the material riches of the population over to the state. Those who control coercion are often frustrated by what they perceive as the incompetence of the administrative wing of the state. Those who control important symbols, such as religious leaders, typically resist the state's efforts to develop alternative symbols. And those who run the administrative apparatus fear the coercive branch of the state, while seeking the material resources of others to sustain their operations and the systems of symbols to legitimate these operations. The history of all societies, therefore, has been littered with the debris left over from the conflicts among those holding differing bases of power.

Still, without some balance, even if somewhat distorted, polity cannot function. As a consequence, disintegration of a population can follow. Users of power recognize, at least implicitly, that they must control all bases if they are to lead effectively. Thus, many of the dynamics of power revolve around contests among those from one base trying to dominate the others. The controllers of religious symbols sometimes win, as in Iran. At other times the forces of coercion win, as is evident in virtually any nation experiencing a coup d'etat. Less frequently, holders of material wealth win, as was the case in Shakespeare's *Merchant of Venice*. Generally in the long run, it is the civil administrators who come to dominate the state—at least in its day-to-day operations. In fact, the long run of human history is a documentary on how power has become ever more concentrated and centralized in the administrative base, which has then sought to maintain some pattern of accommodation to the other bases of power that are not directly under its control.

The Centralization of Power

As power is consolidated, pressures emerge for its centralization, because as actors holding different bases compete, the winners come to control the losers. Thus, built into the very process of consolidating power is its centralization—whether as a headman or elected prime minister. Centralization of power, however, presents problems in maintaining balance among the bases. If symbolic leaders hold the most power, then the centers of controlling coercion, administration, and material incentives will be distorted by the need for symbolic orthodoxy. If the coercive base wins, then all other bases will be directed toward facilitating coercive repression. If controllers of material wealth dominate, then the other bases will be used to augment and further concentrate material wealth. And, if the administrative base overly dominates, then a dreary world emerges in which everything is administered bureaucratically. But we should note that this last scenario seems most stable and, hence, least volatile and out of balance. For this reason, selection has favored the administrative base, tempered by and integrated with the other bases (Weber [1922] 1978). Indeed, the great accomplishment of democratic forms of government has been the particular blending of the bases of power: (1) the effective use of administrative structures, whose ultimate leaders are elected, to control the coercive base; (2) the secularization of symbols legitimating the administrative and coercive components of government and, at the same time, restricting the use of administration and coercion (Weil 1989); and (3) the sharing of control of material resources and incentives between the state and other actors outside the state.

Production, Distribution, and Power

As noted earlier, increased production and market distribution create wealth that can be used to sustain the polity. But aside from this enabling capacity, production and distribution create active selection pressures for the expansion of the state. The state's basic dilemma is how to tax surplus wealth in a way that mitigates against the hostility of those who must pay and, at the same time, to use these taxed resources to address the problems of coordination and control generated by expanded production and market activity. Rarely has this dilemma been resolved without generating conflict, but it has been the basic problem that all polities have had to manage, or face the disintegrative consequences. Centers of power in agrarian societies simply taxed their populations to the point where other elites' privilege was threatened and, indirectly, the well-being of peasants who depended on the resources of these elites was undermined. In agrarian systems without a large commercial class, the resulting conflict was typically intraclass, with elites fighting one another for resources and privilege and with peasants "revolting" to restore the old order under which they at least had some security. With commercialization of the agrarian economy, however, the conflict became increasingly interclass, as the commercial class's wealth posed threats to traditional landed elites. Moreover, in order to meet their tax obligations as well as their needs for privilege, elites began to impose on peasants more profit-oriented practices, such as higher rents, demands for larger shares of harvest, and even displacement from estates (Lenski 1966; Lenski, Nolan, and Lenski 1995, 205–207; Kautsky 1982; Goldstone 1990).

Industrial and post-industrial polities have taxed and redistributed wealth in ways that have reduced hostilities and allowed for government to address the problems of coordinating productive and market processes in ways that encourage economic innovation and growth (Turner 1995).

Inequality, Stratification, and Power

When power is consolidated and concentrated, inequalities increase (Lenski 1966; Moore 1977), for power is not only a resource in itself, it can be used to extract the resources of others. Those who can coerce, symbolically control, materially manipulate, or administratively dictate are all in a position to increase their resources at the expense of others. Those who come out on the short end of these power dynamics are rarely content. Indeed, they are almost always hostile and, hence, are a potential source of internal threat.

This existence of hostility and internal threat typically has had the ironic consequence of mobilizing ever more power to control the threat, which leads to more inequality, internal threat, and concentration of power to manage the escalated threat (Turner 1995, 1984). If this cycle is continually ratcheted up, the society can fall apart as hostilities build to the point of open revolt by either peasants or traditional elites (McCarthy and Zald 1977; Tilly 1978; Davies 1962). The constant peasant revolts, coupled with periodic rebellion by some nobility, of agrarian societies—especially those with a growing commercial class—were a good indication that these highly stratified societies were at the high end of this cycle (Goldstone 1990; Tilly 1990). Conversely, whereas the comparative stability of advanced industrial and post-industrial societies indicates that they have found a way, at least for the present, to keep this cycle somewhat in check. With industrialization, then, comes some efforts at redistribution of wealth through the activities of the state (Lenski 1966). Thus, if the power of the state can be used to extract resources from the more privileged segments of the society and, then, redistribute these in education, health care, welfare, and other benefit programs for the masses, then the tension associated with inequality can be mitigated. Much as the headman in a simple horticultural society had to redistribute most of what he took from others, so the modern state must redistribute to sustain its legitimacy and viability. But still, inequality persists in these more-developed societies; and hence, power remains concentrated to manage the hostility that is inevitably generated by such inequality. This management can take many forms—administrative cooptation through social programs (e.g., welfare, medical care), ideological manipulation (e.g., nationalism or scape-goating of particular sectors of the society), material buy-outs (e.g., subsidies, tax credits, special tax rates), or strategic coercion (e.g., selective enforcement of laws, massive mobilization of armed forces at flashpoints of conflict). No matter what the profile or configuration among these forms, power is more concentrated as a consequence. Power and internal threats arising from inequality are, therefore, inevitably interrelated.

Geopolitics and Power

When distinct populations or societies come into conflict, they centralize power so as to mobilize and organize resources to deal with the conflict (Webster 1975). Whether this centralization has involved giving power to a Big Man in a settled hunting and gathering population, clarifying descent and authority rules among lineages of horticulturalists, or creating an army of mass destruction, external conflict with other populations will always concentrate power. Even less severe forms of conflict, such as economic competition, will consolidate and centralize power to manage more effectively the competition.

And once power is concentrated to confront conflict, its symbolic legitimacy becomes more dependent on being successful in the conflict (Weber [1922] 1978). Political leaders have thus faced an interesting dilemma: They could gain power through external conflict and through creating a sense of external threat, but they would set themselves up for an erosion of their symbolic base of power if they were to "lose" in the external confrontation. When centers of power are seen by the population, or some of its strategic segments, to "lose," then other bases of power—coercion, administration, or material manipulation of incentives—often must be mobilized to compensate for symbolic delegitimation, thereby setting into motion the conflict-producing cycles of inequality and internal threat discussed earlier. Thus, as Skocpol (1979) observed, revolutions were more likely to occur in agrarian societies *after* the loss of a war in the geopolitical arena. Less-intense forms of conflict, such as economic competition, might produce less-dramatic delegitimating forces, but government is still under pressure to "explain" why it has failed.

Democratization of Power

It appears that the process whereby decision makers are selected has become more democratized, although this is, at best, a very uneven and variable trend in the world's societies. Internal conflict and threats, such as that in the former Yugoslavia or Soviet Union, inevitably decrease the chances for democracy; and external geopolitical threats—whether real or manufactured by elites—are often a reason for suspending democratic processes. It is nonetheless clear that all post-industrial societies are comparatively democratic and many industrial and industrializing societies are beginning to move in this direction—but again at a highly variable and episodic pace.

Before examining why democratization of polity occurs, we should define some of its essential features:

1. The rights of citizens to vote for key decision-makers in free elections.
2. The existence of parties who place candidates and policies before voters.
3. A distinctive arena of "politics" in which issues are debated and in which parties and individuals supporting candidates are willing to confine their disagreements and conflicts to this political arena.

4. A willingness by all participants in the arena of politics to abide by the results of elections.

These features of democracy, however, depend on a delicate balance among the bases of power.

At the symbolic level, government must enjoy a diffuse legitimacy in the eyes of the population—that is, a legitimacy that transcends specific issues and disagreements about government's actions (Turner 1995; Weil 1989). This diffuse legitimacy needs to be based on secular idea systems—nationalism, constitutional principles, historical traditions—rather than religious beliefs, which can arouse intense and uncompromising orientations. With diffuse, secular legitimacy, government is not held accountable for each and every action with which segments of a population may disagree. Without this reserve of legitimacy, each decision or action by government can become a potential stimulus to delegitimation.

In terms of a coercive base of power, force must be used only periodically, for if each decision by leaders must actively mobilize coercion, or threat of coercion, resentments soon accumulate to the point that delegitimation will occur. To paraphrase Edmund Burke, "no nation is ruled which must be perpetually conquered."

The use of material incentives by government must be viewed in a general sense as "fair" (whether this is actually so is less relevant than the *perception* of fairness). Specific uses of material incentives can be viewed as unfair and as a debatable point in the arena of politics. But in a global and general sense, the public must see government use of material incentives as basically and fundamentally "fair." Taxing policies, redistribution, and subsidies must also be perceived as in the national interest. Without these perceptions, the use of incentives becomes, itself, a source of resentment which undermines the symbolic base of power and often prompts the overuse of the coercive base of power by polity to compensate for its loss of legitimacy—a tactic that only inflames resentments.

Finally, the administration of decisions must not be seen as a spoils and patronage system. Instead, the public must perceive that, whatever the merits of specific administrative programs, the administration of these programs is designed for their implementation. It is when the public perceives administration as corrupt and as a source of privilege for elites that it becomes a source of resentment. Even if administration is seen as inefficient or as implementing flawed policies, it generates less resentment because these issues can become points of debate in the arena of politics. However, if administration is seen as yet another source of inequality, resentments dramatically escalate.

Maintaining this broad profile among the bases of power as they support and sustain the features of democracy listed earlier is difficult, and especially so when internal inequalities or external enemies create perceptions of threat that distort the balance toward a coercive-administrative profile of power. For once coercion is overused, it bends administrative processes to its ends and, thereby, begins to limit the rights of citizens as voters, the activities of opposition parties, the integrity of a separate arena of politics, and the willingness of participants in politics to abide by the results of elections or even to allow elections to express the preferences of the public. Democracy is thus a most delicate political dynamic—one which, since humans left hunting and gathering, has only recently reemerged in the institutional order.

CONCLUSION

As long as human populations were small, the consolidation and centralization of power were unnecessary. But once the consolidation became essential to social order, achieving viable balances among its bases—symbolic, material, coercive, and administrative—has proven difficult in the history of the world's societies. Imbalances in favor of coercion, administration, manipulation of incentives, or symbolic intensity have created distortions that have generated resentments and internal conflict. And even when some degree of balance prevailed, particular sectors of the population always resented the use of power, often forcing centers of power to distort balances in order to address these resentments.

The history of all known populations that have moved beyond hunting and gathering is, therefore, one of consolidation and centralization of power—often followed by some deconsolidation and, in many cases, complete collapse of the polity. Power thus has always had a dialectical quality, being built up and then creating the internal contradictions and imbalances that have caused its deconsolidation. For as power is consolidated and centralized, it creates the very conditions that make less polity viable: Concentrated power escalates inequalities that generate resentments that throw into imbalance the bases of power; concentrated power enables larger populations to be organized but eventually beyond the capacity of polity to manage; concentrated power often is used to engage in costly and unsuccessful geopolitical conflicts that can bring a regime down; and concentrated power creates the very conditions—consolidation and concentration—that invite the holders of power to attempt further concentration which eventually aggravates all of the other conditions listed above.

Recently, a kind of "end-of-history" argument has been proposed, arguing that a long-run convergence of the world's societies toward a postindustrial profile and democratic forms of government will somehow suspend these dialectical forces and will, thereby, achieve a permanent and self-correcting balance among the bases of power. In this scenario, redistribution through the tax and subsidy programs of the welfare state mitigates against the resentments and internal threats that come from inequality as well as perceptions of injustice and corruption; and movement after the end of the Cold War toward resolution of external economic and political conflicts decreases the imbalances that come from external threats. Although the achievements of democratic forms of government, in a relatively short span of human history, have been rather spectacular, it is not clear that these balances among the bases of power mark so much an end of history as merely a chapter in the evolution of human societies since hunting and gathering.

There are clearly forces at work that can make polity less benign. One is the fact that the use of power is *always* resented by some who become potential sources of conflict. Another is persisting inequalities that generate conflict. Yet another force is the persistence of religious-ethnic symbols as bases for conflict-group formation. And one that never goes away is points of geopolitical tension among societies in every part of the world which inevitably generate a less-benign polity.

Thus, the history of polity is not at an end. The dialectics that inhere in the consolidation and centralization of power into polity are still very active, as they have been throughout human history since hunting and gathering. These dialectics not only inhere in the very nature of power and its formation into polity, but also in the dynamics of those other institutions in the socio-cultural environment of government. It is to this latter topic that we turn in the next chapter.

Chapter
9

Polity in Institutional Context

*P*olity is a decision-making and implementing system, establishing societal-level goals and, then, drawing upon the material and symbolic resources of other institutional systems to realize these goals. Political systems thus depend on other institutional spheres in order to maintain each base of power, as well as balances among these bases. In a sense, power is consolidated and centralized into polity in order to draw upon the organizational outputs of other institutions; and it is this fact that makes an understanding of the influence of other institutions on polity so important.

ECONOMY AND POLITY

Without the capacity to generate economic surplus, a distinctive polity cannot exist. Thus, the most basic effect of the economy on polity is producing the surplus that enables political leaders and their staffs to consolidate and centralize power. The greater the economic surplus produced, the more power potentially can be mobilized in a society (Lenski 1966).

For hunter-gatherers, there was little surplus to support a distinct political system; and only with a more-settled existence did Big Man systems of leadership emerge, usurping and distributing the surplus. With horticulture, descent and authority rules of kinship organized the appropriation and redistribution of economic surplus. As this surplus increased with expanded production, the scale and scope of these kin-based polities also grew, often becoming less kin-based and moving into state formation. Because agrarian economies could produce more than horticultural systems, a larger monarchical state system could be supported. With industrialization and the vastly expanded capacity for generating a surplus, the state bureaucratic system became fully institutionalized, extending its influence into virtually all spheres of activity.

Yet, the economy not only enables and facilitates the consolidation of power by providing the surplus on which polity survives, it demands such consolidation in order to mobilize, regulate, control, and distribute human and physical capital, technology, and property in ways that sustain the viable organization of the economy. We shall examine some of these key pressures from the economy on the polity below.

Appropriation and Redistribution

When economies generate a surplus beyond the subsistence needs of the population, problems of who is to get how much of the surplus escalate—often into violent confrontations. There is, then, intense selection pressure to resolve rising distributional problems; and these pressures are one important reason for the emergence of polity. For ultimately, the leaders of government—from Big Man and chiefs through monarchs and dictators to parliaments and prime ministers—make decisions about the allocation of economic surplus. As the surplus grow with economic development, the complexity and scale of these allocation decisions correspondingly increase.

Allocation depends upon the consolidation and centralization of the bases of power so as to have the capacity to appropriate economic surplus and, then, the administrative facility to redistribute what is expropriated. Big Man and horticultural chiefs usually redistributed all or most of what they collected in order to gain prestige and honor (thereby consolidating their symbolic claims to power). Such "generous" redistribution was also encouraged because much of the surplus could not be stored (it would simply rot) into accumulations of great wealth. With advanced horticulture and agrarianism, surplus could be stored and hoarded. Moreover, the new productive outputs that come with mining and metallurgy, marketing and trade, masonry and building, and many other advances of these economies allowed for vast wealth to be accumulated and for great privilege to be enjoyed by elites. With industrialization, some redistribution of appropriated surplus to the larger masses occurs, thereby reducing somewhat the extreme inequalities of the agrarian era (Lenski 1966).

The inequalities generated by the extraction of surplus and its redistribution to the more privileged sectors of the society force the further consolidation and centralization of power in order to manage and control the growing resentments and internal threats. This turn of events, as we noted in the last chapter, only makes government more costly, more biased toward coercion and, hence, more in need of additional extraction of revenues to support itself. Yet, in usurping surplus, governments develop *systems of taxation* that institutionalize the appropriation process in terms of taxation formulas and by administrative offices for tax collection. For most of human history, this system of taxation was very simple, as when a headman received ritualistically the economic output of kin units and then gave it back to them. But as the economic output increased, as the functionaries in polity grew in size, as the expectations for wealth and privilege of elites escalated, as the military adventurism of elites expanded, and as public-works projects (canals, bridges, roads, ports) supported by government multiplied, the formulas of taxation and their administration become more complex, eventually being specified by laws in an emerging legal system and administered by a larger-scale state bureaucracy. Thus, the very process of creating a taxation system increases: (a) the administrative base of power in order to rationalize the collection of taxes; (b) the coercive base in order to enforce the compliance of taxpayers; and eventually, (c) the legal system in order to articulate and adjudicate ever more complex formulas of taxation.

In creating a system of taxation, government also begins to formalize definitions of property and property rights. For example, a horticultural chief may theoretically have "owned" all land, but he had to allocate gardening plots to kin units in return for their economic outputs, which he then redistributed back to them. In all of this expropriation and redistribution, definitions of property and property rights are being established. And once this process is started, it continues so that almost all resources, technologies, physical capital, and even human capital become defined in terms of property or rights to property. When defined as property, it is but a short step to viewing these elements of all economies as commodities that can be bought and sold in markets. Without establishing a system of taxation, then, notions of property and commodities would be very limited. When systems of property rights become institutionalized in tradition and law, the scale of government can expand because there is more property to be taxed and commodities to be accumulated. Historically, there often has been a lag between new definitions of property and taxation formulas, as was evident in most feudal systems where the output of manorial estates was taxed even as new sources of more-liquid capital were being accumulated by the bourgeoisie in their market activities. Indeed, until the wealth of the bourgeoisie and the wages of workers were seen as taxable property, the size and scale of the state were restricted.

As definitions of property and tax formulas have become more clearly articulated, the state's extraction of economic surplus has become more varied. Moreover, the capacity of the state to extract liquid capital has given it the ability to finance ever more projects and to expand its horizons. In human history, much of this financial ability has gone to pay for war and military adventurism. Military conquest can, if successful, increase wealth (through plunder and pillage). But if unsuccessful, war drains the capital resources of a society and makes it vulnerable to both internal and external threats. Military activity can also bias technological development away from domestic production, which can put societies engaged in economic competition at a competitive disadvantage. (This is why such societies often go to war with their economic competitors.) For example, the Cold War between the United States and the Soviet Union seriously distorted the economies of both societies toward military ends with the result that, in the case of the former Soviet Union, the domestic economy soon stagnated, whereas in the United States, the diversion of technology as well as human and physical capital to the military enabled more domestically oriented economies like Germany and Japan to challenge the dominant position of the U.S. economy in the world system. Thus, the taxation-expenditure formulas of government come to have significant consequences for: (a) the level and nature of technology, (b) the total amount of physical capital in the economy, (c) the distribution of this physical capital across sectors of the economy, and (d) the nature and profile of skills among human capital as well as their distribution across sectors of the economy.

Coordination of the Economy

As the economy grows, a larger population can be supported; conversely, population growth places selection pressures for increased gathering, producing, and distributing. Population size, per se, escalates the logistical problems revolving around the coordination and control of the larger population. When accompanied by a larger number and diversity of economic units engaged in gathering, producing, and distributing, the logistical loads escalate that much further. These mounting logistical loads for coordination and control of the economic activity of a larger population represent selection pressures to consolidate and centralize power.

At first in human history, this consolidation involved giving headmen, Big Man, and chiefs rights to coordinate basic tasks, as when the chief assigned gardening plots to kin units or when the Big Man engaged in negotiation and trade with neighboring communities. Later, as power became more consolidated and centralized under a king or monarch, power was increasingly used to regulate all economic elements—property, technology, and physical and human capital. With industrialization and post-industrialization, whether in market-driven or state-managed economies, the administrative branch of government (and, if necessary, the coercive branch as well) have been involved in coordinating and controlling not only all elements but all phases of the economy—that is, gathering, producing, and distributing.

Thus, as logistical loads mount for coordinating larger-scale economic processes, the involvement of government as an entrepreneurial force in the economy increases, even when the public and key corporate actors see such governmental involvement as undesirable—as is the case in the United States, where public opinion is decidedly antigovernment. The impetus for this government involvement in state-organized societies comes from many sources:

1. The need to define and enforce property rights of actors involved in the economy and, of course, the government's interest in taxing such property.
2. The need to finance infrastructures that no single economic actor alone can afford (e.g., roads, rails, airports, canals, ports, bridges, communication systems).
3. The need of economic actors, such as private corporations, to have their rights and responsibilities specified and enforced.
4. The need to adjudicate conflicts between economic actors.

5. The need to enforce contracts among economic actors.
6. The need to manage the supply of liquid capital.
7. The need to control tensions between those with rights to human and physical capital (i.e., labor-management relations).
8. The need to redistribute economic output to create infrastructures for the development of human capital (e.g., schools).
9. The need to mobilize and stimulate technological development (e.g., institutes of science and higher systems of education).
10. The need to control gathering and production for societal goals (e.g., military conquest, corporate success in world system, full employment).
11. The need to even out the oscillations of markets or to restrict excessive speculation in metamarkets.
12. The need to control and manage the utilization and depletion of stock resources (e.g., oil, minerals), living resources (e.g., soil via the microorganisms that sustain its fertility), and ecological balances.

The needs number into hundreds, and each represents a selection pressure, or a logistical problem, that is not readily resolved within the economy itself. As these pressures have mounted individually and collectively, they have brought government into the economy. In so doing, the nature of consolidation and centralization of power is transformed.

Initial involvement of government in economic coordination was relatively limited, assigning tasks and redistributing outputs in a comparatively egalitarian manner. In this process, the chief heightened his symbolic base of power, instituted the manipulation of material incentives, created the first administrative system, and held the threat of coercion as a possible sanction. From this simple beginning with horticulture, however, polity in agrarian systems coordinated economic actors, with the intent of extracting resources to support the privilege of elites. But in the process, polity (a) built the incipient administrative system for tax collection and for public expenditures, (b) developed effective strategies for material incentives in order to control elites, (c) created a permanently mobilized coercive force, and (d) initiated the process of using more secular symbols for legitimation.

During industrialization, the "needs" of the economy for coordination have escalated dramatically beyond those for even the most advanced agrarian population. This has resulted in the trends evident in agrarian systems accelerating toward a larger administrative base, a more effective coercive base, a highly active material/manipulation base, and virtually complete reliance on secular symbols and law as a base of legitimation. Moreover, the balances among these bases have been reconsolidated toward the administrative-material/manipulation side, employing law and secular symbols more than coercive force to carry out the coordination of economic activities. These trends are most evident when pressures for redistribution are great and when economic growth and development are major societal goals. Conversely, they are less prominent when external and internal threats are high, when economic growth must overcome active resistance by old agrarian elites, and when basic entrepreneurial structures (e.g., corporations, free markets) are not prominent. Under these conditions, industrialization can cause a shift to the administrative-coercive bases of power—as was the case in the Soviet Union before its collapse in the 1990s and as has been the situation in much of Latin America during the twentieth century. But with further economic development, a tilt in the balances toward administrative-material/manipulation bases can occur as distributive forces in markets become increasingly dominant.

Distribution and Exchange

Markets, Wealth, and Power   Exchange of goods and services in markets places special burdens on polity. Among hunter-gatherers and simple horticulturalists, barter was most typically conducted by individuals. However, in both Big Man systems and kin-based chiefdoms, political leaders could control negotiations, because these leaders soon learned that wealth is generated through exchanges and, in their particular case, prestige or honor as well. In more agrarian populations, the importance of market exchanges for the polity became manifestly evident, although their most pervasive influence on government was to come only with industrialization. But we can nonetheless see in agrarianism the seeds of market forces.

Open markets become crucial to the polity because they generate wealth both directly and indirectly. By creating places and opportunities for demand to be expressed, markets offer incentives to produce new kinds of goods and services for profit, thereby developing wealth in the form of profits for producers and market middlemen as well as the myriad of services that emerge with open markets (e.g., banking, insuring, and accounting). Monarchies in agrarian societies were often reluctant or shortsighted in taxing the wealth generated in markets because markets could also erode the traditions and conservative symbols on which the privilege of elites resided. Markets and commercialization also create a new class of bourgeoisie who posed threats to traditional elites, creating a dilemma for polity over how to manage potential class conflict. Moreover, though markets could generate wealth for agrarian elites by enabling them to sell surplus output from their manorial estates, the feudal structure of these estates consumed much of what was produced. Nonetheless, some landed elites recognized the potential for the commercialization of agriculture. For example, some of the British landed aristocracy saw that by throwing peasants off the land and hiring labor they could make a higher profit in markets and, hence, generate more wealth for themselves. Once this commercialization of agriculture occurred in Europe, it began to dismantle the last remnants of the feudal system, often by escalating interclass conflicts among peasants, landed elites, emerging bourgeoisie, and political elites. With this connection between wealth and market transactions, especially as it generated interclass conflict, polity began to have a special interest in markets not just to support raw privilege but also to generate revenues for material manipulation of incentives, for financing armies, for extending administrative functions, and for legitimation through control of the secular symbolic media of markets, money, and law.

Markets and Reconsolidation of Power   The reliance on markets thus changes the balances among the bases of power. Though far from a universal trend, markets tend to shift the balances toward an administrative manipulation of material incentives profile, as is examined below for each of the four bases of power.

The wealth emerging from markets is a special kind of wealth—liquid capital that can be easily taxed and used by the polity to manipulate materially key segments of the population. The dominant historical pattern was to tax land and its products, spending the surplus to subsidize elite privilege. But the capacity to generate liquid wealth was limited by the nature of property. With industrialization and expanding market activity, the income and wealth generated in differentiated markets (rather than fixed forms of property of agrarian systems) began to provide more of the revenues used by polity to finance projects and strategically provide subsidies. For example, schools, roads, media, and other infrastructural investments are a way of buying the loyalty of the masses, whereas specialized subsidies like building airports, canals, and ports or purchasing products (from airplanes, and other military hardware to office supplies) subsidize combinations of owners and managers of specialized interests (e.g., airline companies, defense contractors) and the larger masses who garner wages from these companies. Without the vast and liquid wealth generated by markets as profits and wages, government is limited in its taxing abilities and, therefore, in its capacity to manipulate material incentives. But with markets, wealth is generated and can be taxed. At the same time, selective and targeted government purchases in the market can provide one mechanism for manipulating material incentives. Markets thus represent a powerful force for reconsolidating power around the manipulation of material incentives.

Still, money can be taxed and used to buy coercive power. Indeed, markets generating liquid wealth enable polity to professionalize its coercive force and, as a consequence, to rely less on volunteers and conscripts. At first, some polities used their newfound access to wealth to purchase mercenaries. But mercenaries were too professional and neutral, they lacked the necessary loyalties to regimes; and they were expensive as well. Thus, political leaders learned that armies composed of a mixture of career professionals, conscripts, and volunteers represented a more loyal and less expensive way to mobilize coercion. Similarly, at the regional and community level, professional police forces proved to be highly effective when funded directly by the state. Without liquid wealth generated by markets to purchase for wages these coercive personnel, the reach of the state was limited and often challenged by regional sources of countercoercion (e.g., warlord, clan, tribe, ethnicity). And even with a professional army, the mobilization of less-professional but more-committed regional counterforces to the state can be effective—as Russia is learning in her post-empire days. At the intersocietal level, the conduct of war is often decided in favor of the less-professional army whose members are more committed—as the United States learned in Vietnam, the Soviets in Afghanistan, and the British in colonial America.

Indeed, markets are more than a source of wealth that can be taxed and used to finance coercion; increasingly they have become a source for the distribution of coercive capacities—sometimes against the state. There is now a world-level market, both open and covert, in the sale of coercive implements. This market is making it possible to mobilize countercoercion against the state in any society, even the most developed. Markets are capable, therefore, of eroding the state's efforts to maintain a monopoly of coercive force. Of course, the very emergence through market activities of countercoercive threats forces the state to mobilize even more-coercive power and to crack down administratively on market activities. Markets, then, are very much involved in determining the degree of reliance of the state on coercive force.

A state cannot bureaucratize effectively or extensively its administrative functions without the capacity to pay its bureaucrats (Weber [1922] 1978). If kin or other loyalties are the basis for recruiting administrators, the state cannot be large. Markets enable the state to tax liquid wealth and wages for purchasing in a labor market the incumbents of the state bureaucracy. Indeed, the purchase of labor for government jobs not only expands the administrative capacities of the state, it also gives the state one more channel for manipulating material incentives through strategic and selective purchases of labor in the marketplace.

Moreover, once market forces influence the recruitment and placement of administrative incumbents, competition for slots can lead to an upgrading (in terms of education, skill, and other attributes) of these incumbents—especially in societies like the United States which have an excess pool of educated labor. These market pressures for professional upgrading are, however, mitigated by civil service systems that tend to emphasize seniority over skill in placement and promotion of personnel. But the net result is still a general upgrading of competence in the administrative base of power. While people in industrial and post-industrial societies often complain about the competence and efficiency of bureaucrats, the latter are a dramatic cut above those state administrators in less developed societies who have been recruited in terms of nonmarket criteria, such as tribal or regional affiliation, religious background, or other ascriptive considerations.

Markets also transform the symbolic base of power, in two ways: (a) through the growing reliance on the money and other neutral media of exchange; and (b) through the proliferation of laws to regulate market transactions.

As societies industrialize, markets come to utilize money or its equivalents as the only criterion for assessing value in exchange transactions; and as this criterion expands to transactions in virtually every sphere of social life, the stability of money as a marker of value has important consequences for legitimating centers of power. Increasingly, the capacity of money to denote value in exchanges determines the extent to which members of a population perceive that the polity is operating efficiently and effectively. If the value of money decreases through inflation—that is, the purchasing power of money declines—then members of a population experience a net loss of value and gratification in their market exchanges and, consequently, in their life's routines. As a result, the general public and strategic economic actors come to blame the polity for their loss of purchasing power. Thus, as the economy becomes market driven, the potential instability of money becomes an increasingly important consideration in making political decisions. Indeed, the legitimacy of the government depends more and more on its ability to maintain stability in the purchasing power of money in markets.

For this reason, government seeks to regulate the supply of money in market-driven systems. When too much money is in circulation, its purchasing power declines, setting into motion inflation which erodes the legitimacy of government. Conversely, if money retains its value or even increases in value through deflation, then government is seen as sustaining the life-styles of the masses, encouraging the profits of strategic economic actors, and protecting the wealth of the privileged. The dilemma for government is how to balance its own desires to print and spend money in order to realize its many goals and to manipulate incentives for a wide range of actors, on the one hand, with the tendency in market systems for too much money in circulation to cause inflation and, eventually, delegitimation of government, on the other hand. This dilemma pulls government into the regulation of the money supply in an effort to maintain the supply below the demands for spending, both inside the governmental sector and outside in the private sector. Rarely can government achieve this balance, however, and as a result, inflation is a chronic problem in market-driven economies.

Still, if government can keep inflation somewhat in check and if it can facilitate economic growth in ways that keep the growth of profits and wages ahead of inflation, then it can retain legitimacy. But if inflation begins to exceed profits and wages, thereby reducing corporate and individual well-being, then a political regime will experience a loss of legitimacy. For example, the rampant inflation of pre-Nazi Germany was an important force in delegitimating the Weimar Republic and in making the population receptive to Hitler. Similarly, the chronic inflation in most of Latin America has contributed to the political instability of some countries in this region. Even in the United States, where the diffuse legitimacy given to government provides some breathing room, inflation has led to rapid shifts in the control of government by Democrats or Republicans. Thus, the specter of inflation pulls government into the economy, creating new laws and systems of administration to maintain the purchasing power of money. If these efforts fail, then an important source of symbolic legitimation is lost, because in the end, money is a symbol of value. As its purchasing power declines, so do perceptions of government's effectiveness and efficiency.

Just as government must be perceived to be effective in sustaining the value of money, so must its use of bodies of law and the court system be seen as maintaining honesty and fairness in market transactions. As markets buy and sell everything as a commodity, it becomes essential to regulate exchanges along a number of fronts, including: the assurance that agreements and contracts will be honored; the protection of consumers from fraud, misrepresentation, and harm; the perception that markets, especially labor and consumer-goods markets, are not exploitive or predatory; and the assurance that, in general terms, market transactions operate to benefit the society as a whole. The tendency of markets, if left alone, to do just the opposite forces government to intervene in order to keep unregulated markets from eroding the public's sense of fairness and equity. Thus, the ever-present potential for abuse in markets stimulates the expansion of legislative, administrative, adjudicative, and enforcement activities by government. And in so doing, government's legitimacy is increasingly tied to perceptions that laws regulating market transactions promote fairness and honesty. Markets thereby become a major force in shifting the symbolic base of power to secular symbols embodied in the legal system.

World-System Markets and Power   The extension of markets to the world system level has greatly complicated their regulation, because goods, services, money, and other financial instruments are now exchanged instantaneously in metamarkets driven by information systems somewhat beyond the direct control of national governments. Maintaining balances of trade, integrity of money, viability of corporate actors, security of labor markets, and flows of physical and human capital all become problematic when world-level markets operate outside the control of a central source of political power. At times, governments seek to strike world-level trade agreements or establish monetary policies, but since each government must respond to the domestic demands of economic actors and the public as a whole, these agreements are fragile and typically difficult to sustain in the long run. As a consequence, world-level markets are hard to control, even though they affect the legitimacy of governments and the viability of domestic economies. For example, polity experiences a loss of legitimacy if government is seen as too accommodating with its trade partners (as is certainly the case with the United States government and its trade imbalances with Japan); if government is seen to allow capital and jobs to flee to sources of lower-priced labor, if government is seen to let technologies be captured by foreign corporations, if government is perceived to let its currency lose value in world money markets (thereby driving up the price of imported goods and services), or if government is believed to let foreign capital investment exploit domestic labor, resources, and businesses. If these perceptions are correct, the viability of the domestic economy declines, thereby eroding further government's capacity to extract economic surplus and effectively govern a society. As a consequence of these troublesome realities of the modern world, then, government inevitably expands the administrative base of power in an effort to gain some control of its fortunes in the markets of the world system.

RELIGION AND POLITY

In hunting-gathering and simple horticultural societies with more-egalitarian patterns of decision making, religious ritual and beliefs were often interwoven with most major decisions in the society: when and where to hunt; when to move on; or, in the case of emerging horticulturalists, when and where to plant and harvest. The communal hunting and planting rituals associated with major decisions in these simple societies reaffirmed religious beliefs, and in so doing, made rituals even more effective in mobilizing people to engage in necessary behaviors. They also alleviated much of the uncertainty and anxiety arising from these behaviors (Wallace 1966, 110–27). Sometimes these rituals were performed by special practitioners such as a shaman; at other times kin leaders doubled as religious practitioners. Thus one of the major consequences of religion on political decision making in very simple societies was to mobilize the members of the society and to confer legitimacy to leaders. Since decision makers in these systems had a limited capacity to use physical force or coercion, invoking the gods and performing rituals reaffirming beliefs became effective and often necessary bases of power.

With the emergence of a kin-based polity in full-blown horticultural systems, the legitimating consequences of religion for decision making became even more significant. Societies with kin-based polities displayed a clearly visible locus of power and decision making, for heads of kin groups exerted real control over their kinsmen. If paramount chiefs existed, the head of one kin grouping had decision-making power over the heads of other kin groupings in the society. Religion often provided the necessary legitimation of these power differentials (Parsons 1966). Although this legitimating consequence of religion could take various forms, leaders were often considered gods or at least as having special powers of communication with the gods, and they usually were charged with preserving the society's religious dogma and traditions, frequently becoming important religious practitioners in a society. Because religion was an influential and compelling force in these early horticultural societies, the domination of religious roles by political elites enabled them, if they wished, to legitimate inequality by making it seem the mandate of the gods. To rule by divine right thus represented a major basis of power in most pre-industrial societies.

In more-advanced horticultural and agrarian systems, where an extensive administrative bureaucracy existed, literate religious practitioners often performed many of the administrative tasks requiring expertise in the political bureaucracy. In systems where both extensive political and religious bureaucracies existed (as in feudal Europe and China), considerable overlap between the emerging secular state and ecclesiastical bureaucracy was evident. But as both the state and church bureaucracies developed, a clear segregation between the institutions of polity and religion ensued (Wallace 1966, 261). Usually, but not always, religion still legitimated the right of elites to hold and wield power, but eventually a basic conflict between the more sacred concerns of religion and the secular focus of the emerging state became marked. This conflict was aggravated by the state's growing dependence on the wealth generated by secular commercial activity and by the interclass conflicts that escalate with commercialization of the economy.

To the extent that the state and religious bureaucracies were separated and to the degree that the state came to have a monopoly on societywide power and decision making, the religious bureaucracy and its leaders soon became subordinate to the state and its elites—though rarely without considerable conflict. This separation of religion and polity became even more distinct as administrative and military officials in the state from nonelite families assumed important decision-making positions and as the commercialization of the economy eroded older class and status-group distinctions.

With the development of a true state-based polity, a legitimacy vacuum sometimes could emerge. Religious elites attempting to regain lost influence often withdrew religious support from the state—or, more often, the extensiveness of the state's secular tasks made religious or sacred legitimation increasingly inadequate and/or inappropriate. Historically, as the extensive secular activities of the polity became divorced from the sacred concerns of religion, the polity sought new sources of legitimation. These new sources of legitimacy did not always immediately replace the fading capacity or willingness of religious practitioners to justify the extensive secular agenda of the state. Thus, the existence of a legitimacy vacuum helps to account for the instability of early state-based polities—especially those like almost all agrarian societies that revealed high levels of inequality.

Much of this necessary legitimation could come only with the creation, codification, and transmission of a civic culture (Almond and Verba 1963). A political culture of predominately secular beliefs, values, ideologies, traditions, rights, duties, myths, and heroes can enhance the polity's symbolic base of power and, thereby, give it the right to engage in extensive secular tasks. Robert Bellah (1967) has referred to this civic culture as it emerged in the United States as a "civil religion," a term that has double meaning because it denotes both the development of a secular political culture and the assumption by this culture of the legitimating functions formerly performed by religion in more-traditional societies. This civil religion revolves more around law, order, rights, and duties than around God, the ultimate, and the cosmos. To the extent that the supernatural is a component of this civil religion, individuals and government are required to carry out the will of supernatural forces in *this* world (Bellah 1967, 4–8).

A more dramatic example of the emergence of a civil religion could be found in post-revolutionary Russia, where the new regime created, codified, and transmitted an entirely new political culture with all the trappings—(ritual, beliefs, symbols, myths, saviors, etc.) of more-traditional religions (Wallace 1966, 262). The Communist party became the ecclesia Marx and Lenin emerged as the sacred figures; the tombs of leaders became sacred places; the hammer and sickle became the sacred symbols; the works of Marx, Engels, and Lenin became the sacred texts; and so on. In Russia, the rapid emergence of a civil religion—or in our terms, a civic culture—was dramatic and highly effective in legitimating in just two generations a new state-based polity, although the millions killed during the Stalin purges would indicate that coercion as much as symbols dominated balances of power. In other modernizing societies, nationalism represents an attempt by the polity to create a civic culture rapidly. However, in the short run, this culture rarely fills adequately the legitimacy vacuum created by the emergence and expansion of the state and the decline of religion. Indeed, as in the case in Iran, religious leaders sometimes can recreate a religious culture when a previously secular civic culture has failed to legitimate a regime's rule.

Thus, it seems unlikely that most modernizing polities can shift from a religious to a secular basis of legitimation without an interim period of tenuous legitimacy and stability. Securing new sources of secular political legitimation while establishing some degree of institutional integration between the polity and religion historically has become a source of tension, strain, and conflict in social systems undergoing the transition to an industrial economy.

In the end, as state-based polities have sought to legitimate themselves with secular symbols, eventually they have been able to exercise tremendous control and influence over organized religion. But is the reverse true? The effects of religion on state-organized political processes vary enormously. For example, religion in western European societies does bestow very diffuse and weak legitimacy on the polity; and religious beliefs, rituals, and symbols frequently are incorporated into the predominantly secular political culture of industrial and post-industrial societies. But even in systems that supposedly have religious political parties, the religiosity of such parties is often rather minimal. It would be difficult to determine, for example, just what goals and programs of the Christian Democratic party in Germany are specifically Christian, or for that matter religious, since economic or bread-and-butter issues tend to dominate the party platform. In Italy and France, where Catholicism and the Catholic Church traditionally were allied to the ruling elite, such established state religions led to the emergence of anticlerical political parties (Glock and Stark 1965, 203), and recent trends indicate an increasing irrelevance of religion for both these clerical and anticlerical political parties in Europe.

In contrast, religion has become increasingly salient in the party politics of American society, as a "Christian Coalition" of right-wing and fundamentalist cult structures has become highly organized to exert influence on electorial processes at local, state, and national levels. Indeed, religious activists have challenged legally sanctioned policies, such as abortion and bans on school prayer, and in the process have eroded the legitimacy of the state and its two dominant political parties. To the extent that this attack by religion is on the legal system—especially the laws and courts which sustain policies about which the religious right disapproves—the legal system as the dominant source of institutional legitimation for the state suffers further erosion of its capacity to provide a symbolic base of power to the American polity. Just how far a well-organized religious movement will go in altering U.S. electoral processes remains, at this moment, an open issue.

Thus, religion can still be a potent force on polity in the contemporary world, as is dramatically illustrated in American electoral politics or in much of the Middle East. In this religious activism, the legitimacy of the polity is often questioned when it fails to make decisions in accordance with religious leaders' wishes. And, because of the worldwide trade in sophisticated arms, religion in this and other parts of the world often represents a potential source of countercoercive power which places even greater pressure on the polity to implement the goals of religious leaders. Thus, religion can become not only a source of erosion in the polity's symbolic base of power, it can also pose challenges to its coercive base.

LAW AND POLITY

In hunting and gathering as well as simple horticulture, law was a recessive institution, being fused with kinship, religion, and the emerging polity. At times, it became possible to see a glimpse of a separate legal system, as when a council of elders heard the evidence and directed kinsmen to force an offending person to pay compensation for violating a rule. In this example can be found the three basic elements of law: laws, adjudicating structures, or courts; and enforcement capacities. And if elders had decided that this case required a new or revised rule, then the fourth element—the legislative function—of all legal systems would surface. With advanced horticulture and agrarianism, the emerging and developing state began to establish a more permanent legal system. Once a legal system was sufficiently differentiated from its political origins, it exerted independent effects back on the political system that had created it (Luhmann 1985, 1982).

As polities have consolidated and centralized power over humans' evolutionary history, the basis of legitimation has shifted from religious to secular symbols. For horticulturalists and early agrarianism, religious symbols were sufficient, but as polity became more distinct as an institutional system and increasingly intrusive in regulating social action, it inevitably came into conflict with religion, which, as was emphasized above, could be a potential source of rival power, even in the contemporary world order. Polities thus began to seek alternative bases of legitimation to justify the need, or desire, to intrude into ever more spheres of social activity.

As this process has unfolded, law has become a new legitimating base of power. For law to be an effective source of legitimation, however, it must possess three features. First, it must codify in some form the emotionally charged values, traditions, and religious dogmas of the population into secular tenets. Second, it must help to establish a civic culture that provides basic postulates and principles for law enactment and enforcement. Finally, it must create a system of law-enacting (the legislative function), law-managing (courts), and law-enforcing (police) structures that members of the population perceive as fair and honest.

These three criteria have proven difficult to meet, especially in agrarian systems where polity historically supported vast inequalities. However, even in these agrarian systems, there was clear movement toward embodying traditions in secular tenets, creating a civic culture, and promoting (usually through symbolic manipulation) perceptions of fairness and honesty among agents and agencies of the emerging legal system. Still, the legal systems of agrarian populations rarely met these criteria fully; and so, it should not be surprising that the polity's legitimacy was always tenuous in the eyes of the peasant masses of these systems, especially as the polity also had to confront rival sources of power from religious organizations and as the commercialization of the economy created new cleavages for interclass conflict.

Even industrializing societies have experienced crises of legitimacy because the legal system has failed either to codify traditions or to create a civic culture that resonates with all sectors of the population and, more fundamentally, because the legal system has been perceived as corrupt, dishonest, and unfair. Many countries of the Third and Fourth World today have failed in their efforts to construct a legal system that codifies traditions, creates a civic culture, and fosters perceptions of honesty and fairness. As a consequence, the symbolic base of power for these polities is problematic.

A legal system must become somewhat autonomous from polity and capable of self-reflection as well as self-correction if it is to operate as a base of symbolic power (Luhmann 1985, 1982). If the legal system is seen merely as a tool of oppressive application by elites and those in power, it can become a secular source of *delegitimation*. How, then, does an autonomous, self-reflective, and self-corrective legal system codify traditions, promote a civic culture, and stimulate a sense of honesty and fairness?

Whether embodied in a constitution, as in the United States, or in well-established common-law traditions, as in England, the postulates of a civic culture must be given a kind of "sovereignty" in that they cannot be arbitrarily violated by centers of power or sectors of the public (Luhmann 1982). To create such sovereignty, centers of power must "give up" the right to decide what ultimately is right or wrong as well as what the relation of citizens to the state is to be. They must turn these rights over to an autonomous legal system that can legislate new laws, provide mechanisms for their adjudication, and enforce decisions arising out of adjudication. Relatedly, this autonomous legal system not only must embody those higher-order postulates, it must have the power to decide which laws enacted by political bodies are consistent or inconsistent with these higher postulates. Most importantly, the legal system must have the right to enforce the conformity to laws, whether those produced by legislative bodies within the polity or those emerging as precedents from adjudication in the courts of the legal system itself. If these basic conditions of "sovereignty" are met, then the legal system can begin to operate in ways that legitimate the polity and thereby strengthen its symbolic base of power.

Yet, sovereignty alone is not sufficient; the legal system must also be perceived as effective in resolving points of dispute and conflict as well as in managing deviance. Some of this effectiveness comes from the capacity to adjudicate disputes and deviance within reasonable time periods. In handling the "work load," the legal system very much determines its own legitimacy and, indirectly, its capacity to legitimate the polity.

Another part of the effectiveness of the legal system comes from its responsiveness to changing conditions and its corresponding ability to generate new laws for managing altered conditions in the society. This responsiveness is always a delicate balancing act because new laws cannot be perceived to violate broad legal postulates of the civic culture, which, by its very nature, is conservative. Moreover, because the legislative bodies of the polity often must be the source of these new laws, there is no guarantee that politicians will act responsively or responsibly.

Still another part of effectiveness of a legal system is a body of procedural laws (specifying how actors in the legal system are to act) that guides the interpretation, implementation, and adjudication of substantive laws. Procedures must be seen not only as efficient but also as fair. The legal systems must be able to develop bodies of procedural law that reflect higher legal postulates embodied in the civic culture and, at the same time, that can respond to the caseloads as well as the changing nature of cases being adjudicated by the legal system.

When a legal system has sovereignty and autonomy as well as effectiveness, it becomes a potent force for legitimating polity. This kind of legal-system is most likely with democratization of the polity; and so, legal system legitimation of polity is fully operational only in a very small portion of the world's societies. Without these legitimating effects of the legal system for polity, the balances among the bases of power will remain slanted toward administration-coercion, because in the absence of a secure symbolic base of power, administrative regulation and threats or actual use of coercive force must prevail over the manipulation of material incentives. As China, present-day Russia, the satellites of the old Soviet empire, and the emerging nations of southeast Asia continue to industrialize in a more market-driven profile, the legal systems of these societies will need to change in order for their political systems to receive full legitimacy. Indeed, in cases like Russia, where the economy has been given a rapid "shock treatment" of market-oriented capitalism, the legal system does not display either the sovereignty or effectiveness to legitimate the new, less-domineering political forms in this society. In contrast, China may be able to make the transition to a new legal system, but if it does not, then the legitimacy of government will be questioned—especially with the escalating needs to adjudicate the increased caseloads that come from market-driven economies.

KINSHIP AND POLITY

Among hunter-gatherers, decision making occurred within nuclear kinship units, and at times informal leaders emerged to suggest the best course of action for each family as well as the band as a whole. When a Big Man system emerged among more-settled hunter-gatherers, he could call upon those related by blood and marriage to help him enforce decisions. However, such was not always the case, because personal alliances were often as important as kin ties in maintaining power. Still, even in very simple societies, kinship was a locus of decision making; it was typically the unit to be guided by decisions; and it was a potential source of support and even coercive backup to leaders.

Moreover, there was also a latent effect of kinship—one that becomes increasingly significant as polity developed. It revolved around socialization of commitments among members of a population to whatever decision-making system that may have existed in these simple societies. Socialization imparts not only skills, but motives, orientations, shared histories, and other capacities that are obviously important in sustaining the culture of a population. Most of these socialization effects were hardly noticeable with hunter-gatherers, occurring automatically in the normal routines of daily life. However, they became increasingly important as polity emerged as a distinct institutional system within kinship, and absolutely paramount as polity differentiated from kinship.

Thus, aside from occasional Big Man systems, polity first evolved as a structured and stable social form within the unilineal descent systems of horticulturalists. As polity eventually began to differentiate from kinship with advanced horticulture and agrarianism, the socialization functions of kinship became more important for imparting commitments to the polity. Thus, the two basic connections between kinship and polity have revolved around providing: (1) the structural locus for early political formations, and (2) the necessary socialization of commitments to polity. When (1) was most evident, (2) was hardly noticeable, being fused with the normal socialization of the young into the rules and rituals of the kinship system; but when (1) declined and gave way to nonkin political formations, (2) became very noticeable and critical to maintaining commitments to the symbolic base of emerging state power

The Emergence of Kin-Based Polity

When humans settled down and began to support larger populations through horticulture, problems of coordinating activities and controlling deviant acts escalated, forcing the consolidation and centralization of the bases of power. But early horticulture could not generate sufficient surplus to support a separate polity, even under mounting selection pressures for power. The solution was to build on the nuclear units of hunter-gatherer bands, linking nuclear units into extended families, families into lineages, lineages into clans, and clans into moieties, in terms of descent, residence, authority, and marriage rules. This solution resolved two sets of selection pressures at once—one concerning how to pool and coordinate economic labor or human capital and the other how to regulate and control all social activity.

The descent rule, specifying whether the male's or female's family was to be more important, was the key to this system because it set the parameters for other rules, such as marriage, residence, authority, and family activity. To convert a unilineal kinship system into a political system, all that was necessary was an authority rule within the extended family units, lineages, clans, and moieties. Once this rule existed alongside a descent rule, it became possible to organize decision making: Heads of the largest kin units in the system—whether lineages, clans, or moieties—became political leaders, and those down the authority hierarchy became lieutenants. And, if larger kin units, such as clans or moieties, were connected, eventually the leader of one would become a paramount chief and the others his lieutenants or council of advisors. Thus, the unilineal descent systems of horticulturalists could provide a relatively simple solution to selection pressures for coordination and control of a larger population.

But they did so at a cost of forcing kindred to live together in often uneasy patterns of proximity, with the result that great tensions erupting into feuds and fights were frequent in these kin-based systems. Indeed, perhaps one reason why horticulturalists were almost always at "war" with their neighbors may have been to deflect some of this internal tension outward so as to avoid internal collapse. (However, it could be argued that the mobilization of capital and technology toward constant war may have kept populations at a horticultural level of economic development.) Whether to control the heightened internal tension or to organize effectively for external conflict, there was selection increasingly clear lines of authority—leading to a more distinct political system lodged within the structure of kinship.

Large numbers of people could be organized in such systems of kinship. But eventually with some advanced horticultural populations such as those in China and Meso-America, and certainly with the emergence of agrarianism in the Middle East, southwest Asia, and Europe, kinship became inadequate to structurally house and organize larger numbers of people. As a result, selection began to favor new political formations which eventually evolved into a state. In its feudal form, the state often was composed of the remnants of the old kin-based system, as in hereditary monarchies. But the jealousies, rivalries, and other tensions among leaders in these systems, coupled with patterns of conquest, led to a gradual erosion of kinship in favor of a nonkin state, organized more in terms of bureaucratic than kinship rules and principles. As this process of differentiation of kinship and polity unfolded historically, the problem escalated of how to produce loyalty to the nonkin state.

Kinship, Political Socialization, and State-Based Polities

When kinship and polity are separated, the problem of how to reconnect them magnifies. This problem of reconnection revolves around political socialization, in which members of a society internalize the symbols that make them loyal and committed to the political system, thereby providing the polity with its symbolic base of power. Because family interactions precede interaction in other socializing agents (e.g., schools and workplace), because the social ties among family members are emotionally intense, and because these ties endure over long periods of time in a child's formative years, the effects of family on political socialization can be profound. At a minimum, children learn something about the salient markers of politics (emblems, flags, insignia), the broad aspects of political-cultural history, the diffuse sense of satisfaction or dissatisfaction of parents with "politics" and "leaders," and the basic contours of how the political system operates.

In many developing societies, however, this political socialization can be accompanied by socialization into older, traditional kinship loyalties which can stand in opposition to state policies. For example, in many areas in

Africa where western colonial powers imposed a state on previously warring tribes organized more on kin-based principles, the old tribal animosities have prevailed, making socialization into the political culture of the state less important than that of the tribe. For example, this became painfully evident in Rwanda in the 1990s and a few decades ago in Nigeria. There are many variations on this breakdown of political socialization into alternative cultural symbols. For example, as evident in both the rebalkanization of Yugoslavia and the diversity of claims to sovereignty in the post-Soviet Union, other symbol systems—ethnic, regional, and religious—have been more salient in family socialization than the symbols of the coercive-administrative state. Thus, a history of conquest and colonization often places kinship (and its capacity for generating loyalty and commitment) at cross purposes with the state.

Even in areas such as most of Latin America, where state-based polities have endured for long periods of time, where fewer ethnic groups or kin-based tribes were thrown together, where cultural unity in language and religion has occurred, and where old kinship systems have broken down, family socialization often works at cross purposes to the state. Much of this socialization reflects anger and frustration over class and regional inequalities, but the symbols of old ethnic and kin ties often are evoked as vehicles for mobilizing and venting this anger over inequality.

Even in the advanced post-industrial democracies of North America, Europe, and Japan, political socialization in kinship often is problematic. In the United States, for example, the decline in party affiliations of the electorate, the dramatic drop in the percentage of the population voting, the diffuse sense of anger toward the political system, and the distrust of politicians all signal that political socialization has not been automatic. Curiously, and perhaps fortunately for political stability in America, this disenchantment is overlaid with a diffuse emotionality about what American society should be, an emotion that is easily aroused by the flag and other symbols (such as the Vietnam memorial). Such emotional responses argue for the effectiveness of family socialization at a deeper emotional level in generating loyalty to the state.

Because family socialization cannot be reliable in generating the commitments that provide polity with its symbolic base of power, political systems create and use the schools to indoctrinate the young into the civic culture and arena of politics. Indeed, in terms of managing people—whether their political commitments or their work skills as human capital in the economy, state-based polities increasingly rely on education to realize goals and consolidate power.

EDUCATION AND POLITY

Education and Polity in Industrializing Societies

Education does not become a visible institutional form until late agrarianism, and even there the system of schools was devoted to training religious practitioners, privileged elites, and other limited categories of people. Indeed, education became yet another resource that was unequally distributed, and thus created additional status-group distinction between elites and nonelites in terms of their speech, tastes, and demeanor styles. The vast mass of the population in agrarian societies remained uneducated, illiterate, ignorant, and poor.

With industrialization, however, the extension of the educational system to the larger masses begins; and among late industrializing societies, polity is typically committed to using mass education as a tool for economic development by virtue of increasing the skill levels of human capital. Education is also used for creating, promoting, and transmitting a coherent political culture to people from diverse social classes, regions, ethnicities, and kin groupings. Since family socialization in these transitional societies can subvert the development of a societywide political culture, state-based polities often massify the educational subsystem in order to counteract the effects of family socialization. For unlike the family, educational structures can be manipulated by the centralized polity. Thus, the classroom frequently becomes the principal center for transmitting a political culture, along several fronts.

One front is straightforward classroom indoctrination: Built into the curriculum and textbooks of the school system in modernizing societies is an explicit goal of instilling a unified political culture. Such indoctrination involves selective, partial, and biased presentation of history, myths, legends, and current events. And although classroom indoctrination occurs in all schools, it is most visible in societies where a state-based, modernizing polity is attempting to unify diverse populations and regions, while legitimating its right to possess societywide decision-making prerogatives.

Another front for transmitting a political culture is classroom ritual that supports a particular political culture. Saluting the flag, saying a pledge of allegiance, singing patriotic songs, honoring national heroes, celebrating important events, and exposing students to patriotic symbols, pictures, and sayings of leaders are typical examples of the political ritual life in school classrooms (Dawson and Prewitt 1969, 155). In systems attempting to create and transmit a unified political culture where none has existed before, the amount of time and resources devoted to classroom ritual will be great. Rituals can be effective in two ways: First, since rituals involve *actual behavior* with respect to selected cultural components, they can arouse and instill emotional commitment (Hess and Torney 1967, 100–12). Rituals can invoke emotion toward an existing polity even though young students may not fully understand the words and symbols involved in a ritual. Second, since such rituals as saluting the flag, pledging allegiance, and singing national songs are done in a *group* context, they become more compelling in the minds of young students (Collins 1988; Dawson and Prewitt 1969, 157). When effective, ritual can instill commitment to the tenets of a particular political culture. But frequently, rituals become mere formalities external to individuals and unconnected to the polity—especially when family socialization does not reinforce the political culture enacted in a ritual.

Yet another front for transmitting political culture is the authority and, at times, charisma of the teacher. Because the teacher is often the first nonkin adult to whom the young are exposed for a long period of time, he or she takes on special significance in the mind of the student. Moreover, at times in the schools of developing areas, teachers become dominant community or village leaders and wield influence extending beyond the classroom. Because of teachers' authority and prestige in these areas, they can exert tremendous influence both on students and their parents. Since these teachers are usually paid by the polity, they can be relied on to impart a particular political culture both to students and their parents. In the larger urban centers of developing systems, however, where schools are more bureaucratized and where teachers are less prominent in the community, teacher charismatic authority declines, especially as children get older.

Beyond these specific paths of influence, education can have more general and diffuse consequences for political processes associated with the effects of schooling on political involvement and awareness. For example, Almond and Verba (1963, 175–85), in a classic comparative study of five nations, found that the educated in traditional systems, compared to their noneducated counterparts, displayed more awareness of governmental processes, more concern with political campaigns, more insight into the impact of government on the individual, more opinions on political matters, more willingness to engage in political discussion, more desire to join organizations such as political parties, and more confidence in their capacity to influence the government. Thus in establishing mass public education for indoctrination purposes, the polity also generates a politically knowledgeable and involved public—a situation that often has the ironic consequence of encouraging antistate activities or, at least, new public demands upon the polity. In the long run, these expressions of discontent or demands can lead to the formation of effective political parties or factions within a one-party system which can mark the beginnings of political democratization (Lipset 1960, 27–82).

As education is used to indoctrinate, polity seeks to rely increasingly on the symbolic base of power. Moreover, to the extent that education is defined by the masses as a vehicle for their betterment, the creation of a state-run, mass-education system is a form of manipulating material incentives and associated symbols emphasizing the possibilities for a better life. And to the degree that the state becomes increasingly involved in education and seeks to extend its reach, polity creates a large, centrally run administrative structure which begins to shift its administrative base of power to provisions of human services. In turn, these consequences on the noncoercive bases of power of running a state school system can decrease the reliance of the state on its coercive base, although only to the degree that political indoctrination is effective or to the extent that mass education is associated with material improvement in the lives of the masses. For without economic growth and some, even modest, redistribution of resources by the polity, the inequalities of the more agrarian era persist into the industrial era, sustaining old tensions between elites and the masses which education cannot indoctrinate away. Even with economic growth, however, older systems of inequality can be maintained (with each class' standard of living increasing in lockstep) or even aggravated (with usurpation of resources by the state or exploitive practices by economic actors). If such is the case, the state's reliance on educational indoctrination becomes that much greater.

Another ironical outcome of using education to promote economic development concerns higher education. The more educated people are, the more reflective and potentially critical they become of political regimes. Even when the state sponsors a higher-education system, there is a tension between imparting factual knowledge and, at the same time, maintaining control of students' political commitments. When developing countries send their students to the colleges and universities of advanced post-industrial systems, these problems of maintaining thought control can be even more vexing for the state, especially as students become accustomed to the democratic civic culture of these societies. Indeed, many try to stay in their host country, and among those who return (such as Ho Chi Minh, who was educated in Paris), a cadre of political critics can establish a potentially confrontational beachhead in their native country.

Thus, for developing polities which are making the transition to a more fully industrial profile, education can be a double-edged sword. On the one hand, it is essential to overcoming more-traditional forms of political socialization in kinship and in creating a new state-oriented civic culture. But on the other hand, it can hold out promises of a better life that go unfulfilled, and it can make the population more knowledgeable, cosmopolitan, and unwilling to accept the despotic tendencies of these transitional states.

Education and Polity in Advanced Industrial and Post-Industrial Societies

In advanced industrial and post-industrial systems, there is rarely a need to create a new political culture, since political stability has existed for a sufficient period of time for a body of myths, traditions, heroes, lore, and ideologies to have emerged and become codified into a civic culture. Moreover, though exceptions abound, there are comparatively few, if any, competing political cultures deviating from the dominant one. Under these conditions, transmitting political commitment as well as salient cultural components presents less of a problem for modern than for modernizing polities, since commitment tends to emerge as a by-product of family socialization. For once the family generates commitment and initiates transmission of a stable political culture, the polity need not regulate and control school political socialization to the extent typical of traditional modernizing systems. Furthermore, though political socialization always occurs, especially at lower educational levels, it tends to be less deliberate and intense. The cognitive as opposed to emotional aspects of the political culture are given more emphasis. School textbooks and curricula are more likely to present objectively (but never completely so) knowledge of civics, governmental structures and processes, and the way that good citizens participate in government (Coleman 1965, 220–26). But inevitably, certain political ideologies, myths, values, beliefs, and other components of the political culture slip in the backdoor in any curriculum. Still, the ritual life of the classroom in schools of advanced societies is likely to be minimal, routine, and considered boring by both teachers and students. Teachers, as professionals, are more likely to attempt to remain objective, avoiding partisan issues such as conservatism or liberalism, party allegiances, or the like. However, they do impart many of the assumptions of the political culture—sometimes unconsciously. For example, in the United States assumptions revolving around the sanctity of the two-party system, free enterprise, basic freedoms, and other aspects of American political culture are transmitted by teachers—even those attempting to remain objective.

Thus even though political socialization in schools is comparatively low-key, it is extremely effective. This is largely because school socialization on the whole reinforces rather than counteracts family socialization. Indeed, school socialization into a civic culture is often so effective that it becomes a source of disenchantment with the political process which does not "measure up" to the somewhat idealized standards learned in schools. Of course, some degree of idealization of political processes is probably necessary for people to develop diffuse commitment to the polity; however, at times students are overprotected from political realities. Later, when confronted with these realities as adults who have "bought into" the textbook portrayal of the political system, citizens can become disillusioned and alienated. Since exposure to political realities through contact with the mass media is inevitable in a comparatively democratic country, overprotection and then rapid exposure can intensify feelings of disenchantment and outrage. To the extent that this process is built into the socialization of the young, we can expect considerable disaffection from politics as an inevitable outcome of effective political socialization during the early school years, and media-led disenchantment in later years.

Still, the intensity of emotions that citizens feel about the contradictions between the ideals and realities of politics vary considerably. In the United States, a high level of disaffection occurs, whereas Europeans experience significantly less. Part of the reason for these variations is the great difference between the mass media in the United States, where a vast array of private media outlets engages in a great deal of political criticism, and the media in most European countries, where much of the media tends to be owned and operated by the state.

CONCLUSION

Polity is the regulator of a society, and it coordinates activities in other institutional spheres. Reciprocally, these spheres provide the resources on which power is built, in two senses: First, the "demand factor" or "selection pressures" generated by institutions require government to intervene in order to resolve problematic issues. Of course, once government has mobilized to intervene, it often regulates more than is necessary, generating resentments and, at times, stimulating the formation of counterpower. Second is the "resource factor," or the outputs that other institutions provide for the polity as it consolidates power. The manipulation of the material-incentive base of power comes from economic surplus, as does the capacity to support and sustain both the coercive and administrative bases. In simpler systems, the administrative and coercive bases of power come from the structure provided by unilineal kinship systems. And depending on the complexity of the society, the symbolic base of power comes from a combination of religion, law, kinship, and education.

It is this dynamic reciprocity that makes maintaining balances among the bases of power difficult. For as polity draws resources from other institutions, it also must regulate activities in these institutions. And as individuals and collective actors give resources—from paying taxes to generating political loyalty—they also must give conformity and accept constraint by those who have mobilized power. In giving resources *and* compliance, however, they often become resentful. Thus the consolidation and centralization of power are delicate balancing acts between over- and underregulation of other institutional spheres, which, on the one hand, create selection pressures for regulation and, on the other, must give up their resources in order for polity to consolidate and centralize the power that allows for such regulation. Since power, once consolidated and centralized, typically seeks to garner more power, the balances inevitably become skewed toward overadministration—thereby generating resistance by actors in various spheres. Such resistance can begin to undermine the bases of power (minimally the symbolic but eventually the material and coercive as resistance becomes intense), forcing polity to skew its consolidation and use of power even further toward the coercive-administrative side. Thus, the dynamics of power inhere in its effects on other institutional systems as they provide the resources by which power is consolidated.

Chapter

10

Law

As human populations have grown and differentiated over the long course of human history, problems of coordination and control have escalated. These problems represent selection pressures for developing new ways to resolve burgeoning disputes among individual and collective actors, to control rising rates of deviance, to enforce increasingly diverse agreements among parties, to legitimate the growing concentrations of power, to mitigate against the episodic conflict potential of inequality, to codify cultural ideals and values into a workable set of rules for an ever more-differentiated population, to specify the relations between those in power and those subject to power, and to somehow manage many other problems of coordination and control that can tear a society apart. Indeed, it is problems like these that have led to the disintegration of human populations as coherent societies, indicating that solutions to these selection pressures often have been ineffective, or just temporary stopgaps in the face of disintegrative forces (Turner 1995).

One response to these selection pressures has been to consolidate and concentrate power. But power creates its own integrative problems, which set into motion additional selection pressures to find a mechanism for legitimating power and inequality while coordinating and controlling members of a population. For those populations who remained viable in their environment, the solution to these selection pressures has been the evolution of law.

Among simple hunter-gatherers, law was recessive because many of the problems of coordination and control could be managed through face-to-face negotiation among members of small bands. As populations became larger and more differentiated, however, new problems of coordination and control emerged. Moreover, power became more consolidated and centralized, which, in turn, increased tension-generating inequalities. Under these conditions, the visibility and scope of the legal system grew more essential in the face of rising disintegrative pressure. By late agrarianism and early industrialization, then, the legal system had become one of the most essential institutional complexes in human societies. Our goal in these two chapters is to understand this development of law as a human response to the ever-present potential for societal disintegration.[1]

BASIC ELEMENTS OF LEGAL SYSTEMS

A legal system comprises a number of basic elements (Turner 1980, 1974, 1972): a body of rules or laws, a capacity to manage disputes in accordance with laws, a set of procedures for creating new rules or eliminating old ones, and an ability to enforce laws. Let us examine each of these elements in more detail.

Body of Laws

Laws are special kinds of rules, above and beyond the day-to-day normative agreements among individuals. Not only do they specify what is appropriate or inappropriate; they also indicate that these rules should be obeyed and that a failure to do so invites intervention by third parties (Malinowski 1922; Moore 1978; Hoebel 1954, Turner 1980). A body of laws consists of two fundamental types of rules: First, there are *substantive rules* for (a) regulating relationships among members of a population and (b) defining deviant behavior and, then, controlling it. Second, there are *procedural rules*, indicating just how third parties can cause substantive rules to regulate what are viewed as important relationships and what are defined as deviant acts.

Though the differentiation of laws from regular norms, along with the distinction between substantive and procedural laws, would have been difficult to discern in most hunter-gatherer populations, these features of laws surfaced from time to time, indicating that an implicit legal system was buried just beneath the surface of daily activity. As societies moved beyond hunting-gathering and became larger and more complex, these characteristics in the body of laws came to the surface and began to regulate ever more aspects of social life (Turner 1980; Schwartz and Miller 1964).

The body of laws in a population always instantiates, to some degree, the traditions, values, customs, institutional norms, and other cultural systems of a population—especially its elite elements who are most influential in deciding what the laws will be. Yet to the degree that the body of laws only represents the culture and interests of the powerful and privileged, it will be less likely to be effective in regulating, controlling, and coordinating the larger mass of the population. As a consequence, coercive force or the threat of

---

[1] The approach taken in this chapter is functionalist, but with a conflict theory slant. I draw from my own work (Turner 1980, 1974, 1972; Fuchs and Turner 1991) and William M. Evan's (1990, 222–23) theoretical model. Also, elements of Black's (1993) theory. For reviews of theoretical approaches to the sociology of law, see: Rich (1977), Selznick (1968), Reasons and Rich (1978), Vago (1994), Evan (1990, 1980, 1962), Chambliss (1976), Black and Mileski (1973).

its use more than the moral imperative of law will be used to control members of a society. In hunting and gathering populations, law was very much fused with custom, tradition, values, and culture (Lowie 1966; Gurvitch 1953); and hence, it was effective when needed. In advanced industrial and post-industrial societies, law also tends to reflect broadly held cultural customs, traditions, values, beliefs, and institutional norms which are amalgamated into a "civic culture," which, in turn, is translated into broad legal postulates (both substantive and procedural) guiding the formation and adjudication of laws. It is the societal types between these beginning and current end points of societal development—that is, from advanced horticulturalism through agrarianism to early industrialism—that the most discordance between the body of laws and the culture of the broader masses can be found. For in these societies inequality has been greatest, with the powerful and wealthy often using law as a tool to exploit the masses economically and to control their protests (Marx 1965; Pashukanis 1978; Cain and Hunt 1969; Davis 1962; Duke 1976).[2] It should not be surprising, therefore, that these societies are subject to periodic collapse from within and, because of internal strains, to conquest from without.

Management of Disputes and Deviance

A legal system develops mechanisms for dealing with disputes and deviance in accordance with laws. Such management involves appeals to a third party who listens to claims and, then, in accordance with an interpretation of law, renders a judgment of who is at fault, why, and what should be done to the offending party. These are the essential features of a court and, in particular, the key role of judge; but in most societies of the past, these features of courts were not well developed (Black 1993, 97–122). For example, in a review of anthropological ethnographies, Katherine Newman (1983, 50–103) develops a typology of "court" systems in pre-industrial societies. In some hunter-gatherer societies, there was no third party available for resolving disputes. In slightly more developed societies, third parties of high-prestige individuals were available but were not defined as necessary by procedural rules and were not given any power to reach a verdict (only the giving of "advice" was possible). In somewhat more-developed hunter-gathering systems, disputants were supposed to approach third parties, or their representatives were to do so, but these parties still could not make binding decisions (they could only suggest compromises that would activate informal, interpersonal pressures by band members on disputants). In still more developed hunter-gatherers, Big Man systems, and in simple horticultural populations, mediation could involve true adjudication by leaders or councils of elders rendering decisions or verdicts that were binding on the disputants, who increasingly were represented by others (such as fellow kinsmen acting as "lawyers"). In

---

[2] The conflict tradition in sociology has dominated much analysis; see, for example: Chambliss and Seidman (1982), Quinney (1974), Black (1993). The approach taken here might be viewed as a kind of functional-conflict approach.

subsequent evolution of horticultural systems, councils became more restricted to elites, and chiefs now had increased power to render verdicts, with the more complex of these systems having an appeals process from local councils/chiefs to paramount chiefs and restricted councils of elites. In advanced horticulture and agrarianism where a state existed, a system of courts, often with full-time judges and bureaucratic organization, would emerge. From this base, industrial and post-industrial societies now reveal a structure of courts revolving around: (a) the statuses of judges, juries or panels, lawyers/barristers, and litigants/defendants; (b) the division of adjudication into criminal and tort (civil) systems as well as into specialized administrative, military, and other restricted forms of adjudication; (c) the full bureaucratization of record keeping and other administrative functions; and (d) the hierarchical ordering of courts culminating in a supreme tribunal.

Thus, the evolution of courts and related functions has occurred incrementally and slowly in human history. Political leaders and elites have been reluctant to turn their decision-making power over to an increasingly autonomous legal system. But as the volume and diversity of disputes and the rates of deviance have escalated, elites had to create adjudicative structures or watch their societies disintegrate (Turner 1980, 1974; Parsons 1962; Bredemeier 1962). As this process occurred, courts often had to articulate new laws or mandate their enactment in order to manage emerging problems and points of coordination and control.

Creating New Laws

There is always a legislative element in a legal system whereby particular parties are given the right—indeed, often the mandate—to enact new laws as circumstances require (Evan 1990; Turner 1980, 1974, 1972; Lloyd 1964; Davis 1962; Sawer 1965). Among hunter-gatherers, prestigeful persons could suggest new rules, but they had no capacity to impose them on others. It was not until some degree of power was consolidated and concentrated in kin heads, village chiefs, and councils of elders that a true legislative function existed in which new laws could be enacted. As power became increasingly consolidated, this legislative function was more pronounced, especially as the complexity of social relations and rates of deviance increased. Eventually, legislative bodies are elected by the citizenry in industrial and post-industrial societies, but this transition occurs only with late agrarianism; and even with industrialism, legislative bodies are often little more than "rubber stamps" for those holding dictatorial power. Thus, except in those legal systems that allow some court decisions to serve as law making (as is the case in the United States and England but less so in continental Europe [Vago 1994, 10–13]), the legislative process remains within the polity.

Enforcement of Laws and Court Decisions

Ultimately, if laws and court decisions are to have the capacity to coordinate, regulate, and control, they must be obeyed. Historically, moral persuasion, informal sanctions, shaming, and other noncoercive techniques could operate effectively on members of small populations revealing minimal differentiation in terms of age and sex categories and inequality with respect only to prestige and honor. As populations became larger and more complex, however, laws and decisions had to be enforced, by coercion if necessary (Newman 1983). Since the polity rarely relinquishes its claim to a monopoly of force—indeed, it seeks to legitimate through law and ideology its right to have a monopoly on the use of force—the enforcement of laws and court decisions comes from the polity rather than the courts. Courts can have enforcement agents of their own, but these never rival the coercive force of political leaders. As long as the capacity to make decisions on disputing parties or to force deviants to change their behavior overlapped extensively with polity—as is the case with chiefs, kings, and councils of elites who fill both court and legislative functions—there was little conflict between the emerging legal system and the more developed political system. Enforcement simply came by edict of political leaders. But when there is a separation of courts from decision makers and when legislative bodies have some autonomy from political leaders in the administrative branch of government, a potential dilemma emerges because legislators and judges have no real coercive power. Instead, they must draw on the coercive power of political leaders at the top of the administrative system to enforce laws and court decisions. And if conflict between these leaders and the emerging legal system occurs, the autonomy and viability of the legal system can be undone by political fiat backed by coercive force.

Thus, historically, as the legal system has differentiated from the polity, it has remained partially embedded in the polity and had to rely on the latter's coercive base to enforce decisions and judgments. This reliance has included the capacity of the court and legislative systems to have their decisions against political leaders and administrators backed by the coercive base of power lodged in the very polity that is being regulated by laws and court decisions. Only where a viable civic culture exists—one infused with accepted legal postulates about the relationship between the state and the population—has the legal system been able to exert this influence on polity. In return, for giving the legal system this autonomy, law provides polity with much of its symbolic base of power.

A number of selection pressures have led humans to develop legal systems (Turner 1972, 214–15): (1) structural coordination, (2) legitimating power and inequality, and (3) preserving, codifying, and integrating cultural symbols. We will examine further each of these selection pressures.

Actors in a population, whether individuals or corporate units, must be minimally coordinated. Law has major consequences for establishing, maintaining, or reestablishing coordination in a variety of ways. First, the legal subsystem specifies and enforces appropriate action in crucial areas of interaction among actors. Laws, courts, and enforcement as well as administrative agencies regularize interaction and give it predictability. Second, law also provides procedures for settling disputes and conflicts when they arise.

The legal subsystem provides an alternative to violence and vengeance by allowing disputing parties to settle their conflicts in courts. In this way law, restores coordination when it breaks down. Finally, law checks deviance that could pose a serious breakdown in coordination and control. By specifying what is deviant and providing negative sanctions for such deviance, the legal system controls behavior in critical spheres. Such control facilitates coordination by increasing conformity and hence the predictability of social action.

The legal subsystem legitimizes power, giving some the right to control others and, in the process, giving elites wealth and privilege. Sometimes inequality is explicitly written into laws and enforced by courts and police, but frequently the legitimation is subtle: Police differentially enforce the same laws for the rich and poor; the wealthy have the knowledge and financial resources to press effectively their interests in courts; and administrative agencies in the legal system push the interests of the rich more than the poor. Thus, once a legal system exists, it always legitimates and reinforces inequality and stratification.

Every society has a cultural system, or storehouse of customs, traditions, values, lores, beliefs, technology, and dogmas. Much of this cultural inventory, especially basic values and beliefs, is reflected in the codes and statutes of a legal system (Weber [1922] 1954). For example, basic American values of equality, justice, humanitarianism, and individualism are preserved and codified in the Constitution, as well as in a large number of national and state codes and statutes. Similarly, before the collapse of the Soviet Union, basic values of collectivism were codified in the Soviet constitution and legal system, while being imposed on Soviet satellites (which was one of the reasons for the low levels of legitimacy given to the polity by its western and southern satellites).

But law does more than preserve and codify; it integrates values and other cultural components into concrete and specific structural situations. Law specifies in certain crucial situations just exactly how values, beliefs, customs, and traditions are to be realized in day-to-day interaction among actors (Luhmann 1982). This relationship between law and culture can be highly dynamic in any rapidly changing society where new values, beliefs, and ideologies often come into conflict with the old, thereby forcing legislation and court decisions to reconcile changing values not only with each other but with concrete interaction situations that are affected by the conflict (Gurvitch 1953). If reconciliation of these sources of cultural conflict is impossible, as is often the case, the disintegrative potential of a society increases. Thus, the legal system of a changing society seeks to resolve many—but never all—of the conflicts resulting from a lack of cultural integration, especially as these conflicts disrupt basic social relations (Friedman 1969a, 1969b). For example, in the United States at the turn of this century, the values of rugged individualism and laissez faire came into conflict with emerging values of collectivism and social welfare. The conflict was particularly acute in labor-management relations as labor sought to bargain collectively with management determined to preserve old laissez faire values. In the long run, a host of labor-management laws partially resolved this integrative crisis. Similarly, in the face of widespread poverty, conflicts between American values of rugged individualism, on one side, and humanitarianism on the other were mitigated by the emergence of a host of welfare laws at both the national and state levels (although Americans still remain highly ambivalent about welfare to the poor). Similar examples of the integrative impact of law on culture and society can be found in all societies, especially those undergoing rapid cultural and social transformation.

As problems of structural coordination, legitimating power and inequality, and integrating culture have escalated in human history, law has been used as a "solution," at least temporarily until the disintegrative potential in these problems overwhelms the legal system and centers of power. Nonetheless these functions of law—however imperfect and transitory—are important in defining law as an institution: *Law is a system of rules and rule making, rule mediating and interpreting, and rule enforcing that overlaps with polity and yet reveals varying degrees of autonomy from polity. It has consequences for resolving problems of structural coordination, legitimation of power and inequality, and cultural preservation, codification, and integration.*

TYPES OF LEGAL SYSTEMS

Law has been very much connected to the evolution of polity, the advance of societal complexity, and the rise of inequality. Since all of these forces are ultimately outcomes of economic processes, the basic types of legal systems that have existed in human history can be grouped into those typical of hunting and gathering, horticulture, agriculture, and industrial and post-industrial societies.[3]

Legal Systems among Hunter-Gatherers[4]

Some hunter-gatherers did not have all elements of a legal system, because rules invoking the possibility or appropriateness of third parties to

---

[3] This review of different types of legal systems draws from many sources, including: Weber [1922] 1954; Sawer 1965; Vago 1994; Lloyd 1964; Evan 1990, Bohannan 1968, 1957; L. Friedman 1977, 1975, 1969a, 1969b; W. Friedman 1959; Selznick 1968; Rich 1977; Reasons and Rich 1978; Pospisil 1978, 1974, 1958; Parsons 1966, 1962; Bredemeier 1962; Hoebel 1968, 1954; Kuper and Kuper 1965; Lowie 1966; Gurvitch 1953; Llewellyn and Hoebel 1941; Malinowski 1926, 1922; Newman 1983; Schwartz and Miller 1964; Gluckman 1965, 1955; Diamond 1971, 1951; Kroeber 1926; Lambert 1956; Schapera 1930; and Fock 1974. For a nonsocial-science review of types of legal systems, see: David and Brierley 1985.

[4] We are fortunate that early anthropologists were trained originally as lawyers and, hence, had an interest in law. For example, Sir Henry Maine, Johan Bachofen, and John McLennan were originally law professors (Hays 1958, 32–40), initiating a long tradition of anthropological analyses of law. See, for illustrations, Aung (1962), Barton (1969), Bohannan (1957), Firth (1970), Fock (1974), Gluckman (1965), Hart (1961), Haydon (1960), Kroeber (1926), Lambert (1956), Lowie (1937, 39–53), Moore (1978), Newman (1983), Pospisil (1958), Rattray (1929), Smith and Roberts (1954).

resolve disputes would have been hard to find. These systems generally had rules that allowed for self-redress by an individual for perceived wrongs. For example, among the !Kung-san of Africa, one of the last remaining hunter-gatherer societies, "when a dispute arises between members of the band . . . the only remedy is self-help" (Schapera 1930, 152); and a person may seek "vengeance" for serious offenses. Yet individuals in these self-help systems typically possessed a sense of proportion about the seriousness of an offense and the intensity of the self-help response. For instance, illicit sexual relations would be viewed tolerantly, perhaps only inviting a weak rebuke, among some hunter-gatherers, but among others, adultery was viewed more severely (Newman 1983, 60). Among the Mataco of South America, infidelity gave the injured party the right to impose sanctions, but if jealously led to murder of the offending party, this act was considered too extreme and invited a harsh penalty in the form of an avenging "blood feud" by the victim's family (Fock 1974, 224–25). In fact, the original infidelity was forgotten because of the greater severity of murder.

Other sanctions among hunter-gatherers included shaming rituals by the band against offenders, rituals to send illness to offenders, contests designed to humiliate offenders, and other less physical forms of retaliation (Newman 1983, 59–65). Yet, at times, the punishment for violations of the law or loss of a dispute could be quite physical. For example, among the Australian aborigines, an aggrieved "plaintiff" and his kin could hurl spears at the "defendant," who was armed with a shield. When the defendant was wounded, the punishment was over (Sawer 1965); and while the defendant did not usually die, he nonetheless was hurt, often severely. Evident in these examples is the existence of rules carrying special significance and sanctions for their violation as well as explicit procedures for enforcement of violations of these rules through self-help. Such is a legal system at its most elementary level; and it is from this primordial base that legal evolution must have begun many thousands of years ago.

A somewhat more-developed legal system among hunter-gatherers involved the intervention of a third party—the beginnings of a judge and court—into the self-redress process. The third party was usually a high-prestige man who could be called on to advise disputing parties about what they should do. But he did not have the power to make them follow his advice. Nonetheless, his prestige and his capacity to shame litigants (over their disrespect of the customs and codes of the people) gave him considerable influence.

At times, this advisor role could be expanded to that of mediator, in which the third party negotiated settlements between relatives of the litigants, who acted as "lawyers" for the disputing parties (Kroeber 1925, 89; Newman 1983, 70–73). At other times, the third parties were the representatives of the litigants themselves, who came to constitute a primitive court. For example, among the Yurok of California (Kroeber 1926), an individual feeling cheated by another would engage the assistance of two nonkinsmen, as would the other charged with the offense. These assistants would then assume the status of judge, or as they were known to the Yurok, "crossers."

Procedural laws indicated just how these "crossers" were to behave; and after hearing the evidence offered by the litigants and their pleas pertaining to substantive law, the "crossers" would render a decision in accordance with a rule of punishment known by all (Hoebel 1954, 24). Here was a primitive court, *analytically* very similar to those in modern systems: The litigants were their own lawyers, but clear-cut judge statuses were created to interpret grievances in light of unwritten laws.

A somewhat more-developed system of mediation was found in Big Man societies, where there was some capacity to dictate solutions to disputes by withholding material incentives or by using coercion. These types of legal systems were far less prevalent than the advisor and self-help pattern, but data from enough of them indicate that once some power was consolidated, the legislative component of law clearly emerged. For example, Llewellyn and Hoebel's (1941, 127–28) reconstruction of the Cheyenne Indians—who had reverted from horticulture back to hunting and gathering with the arrival of the horse in North America and with their relocation onto the plains—provides a good illustration of what transpires with Big Man system, or in the case of plains Indians, with chiefs (who were, in essence, Big Men rather than heads of unilineal kin units). To go on the warpath, a Cheyenne warrior borrowed, without asking, the horse of another Cheyenne warrior. When the horse was not returned, the aggrieved warrior went to a court (as a litigant) composed of "warrior chiefs" (high-prestige warriors) who sent for the culprit. The "defendant" confessed, agreed to restitution, and even offered to make the aggrieved warrior his blood brother. The matter as a court action was then settled, but the chief or Big Man then assumed legislative role, proclaiming: "Now we shall make a new rule. If any man takes another's goods [note: not just horses, but any goods] without asking, we shall go over and get them back for him. More than that, if the taker tries to keep them, we will give him a whipping." Thus, new substantive and procedural laws were enacted by the chief, as both judge and political legislator.

Among hunter-gatherers, then, we can see the beginnings of a legal system. A body of laws existed, although only just distinguishable from other normative agreements. There also was an incipient distinction between substantive and procedural laws indicating, respectively, what was violated and how violations were to be managed. There could be no court in purely self-help systems, save for the "court of public opinion." However, once advisors were used and once individuals or their relatives made a case to the advisor, the positions of judge, litigants, and lawyers could be found in their most rudimentary form. Enforcement was mostly self-help among hunter-gatherers, but it was action constrained by rules that "punishments must fit crimes." The law-making or legislative component was the most recessive component of the legal system of hunter-gatherers, although decisions or advice given by mediators was remembered and used again to settle similar violations of rules or disputes among parties. And when a Big Man emerged—as the case of "chiefs" among the Cheyenne—power was consolidated and more explicit law making and enforcement ensued.

Table 10.1   LAW IN HUNTING AND GATHERING SOCIETIES

	Nomadic	Settled or Semisettled
Body of Laws:		
Substantive	Few laws that can be distinguished from day-to-day norms, but norms do specify proscriptions and pre-scriptions.	Same as nomadic, but some norms will be more "rulelike" because of Big Man's or headman's claims to property, trade, and other prerogatives.
Procedural	Some norms specify what is to be done when violation of important norms occur.	More likely to be rules specifying what is to be done with violation of important rules, especially those involving headman's prerogatives.
Legislation of Laws	No explicit body or person to legislate rules, although high-prestige individuals may suggest rules.	Headman is, at times, likely to try to legislate new rules, although his capacity to get conformity is based on his prestige and personal charisma.
Courts:		
Judge	No one is authorized to manage violations of rules, except for those who feel that their rights have been violated. Prestige leaders at times may offer suggestions about how to resolve disputes.	Same as nomadic, although Big Man may assume role of advisor and make suggestions about how to resolve disputes. At times, these suggestions carry moral authority.
Jury/Council	None	None, although at times Big Man and his allies can act as a council that con-siders disputes and grievances.
Enforcement of Laws	"Redress" system of enforcement, in which harmed individuals must seek compensation or punishment on their own. Most disputes resolved by simple face-to-face discussions. Violence in the form of feuds and revenge can occur, but is rare be-cause unresolvable disputes usually lead to a breakup of the band.	Most disputes resolved by normal face-to-face discussion. Aggrieved parties, even with favorable advice from Big Man, must still use redress and seek enforcement of rights on their own. Feuds and revenge are more frequent, but usually mediated by the Big Man.

Legal Systems among Horticulturalists

The legal system among simple horticulturalists was often much like the advisor-mediator system of hunter-gatherers. A greater potential for law making existed, however, because power was being consolidated in kin-heads, village chiefs, councils of elders, and religious specialists. For exam-ple, the chiefs of the Bantu-speaking Tswand of South Africa possessed con-siderable law-making authority. They could lay down edicts and declare old laws obsolete (Schapera 1956). To illustrate this power of law making, Hoebel (1954, 278) relates that in 1934 a young married man died childless. According to kinship rules, the young man's unmarried younger brother was supposed to take up with the widow and "seed" her children, but he would not do so. Therefore, his father took up sexual relations with the widow—substituting for the derelict son. This situation did not sit well with his wife, who appealed to the district council (she is now litigant, the council is now a court of law) to have her husband stopped. The council ruled against her, saying that her husband's conduct was in accordance with "ancient right and custom" (i.e., laws), but the district chief overruled the council, declaring the custom obsolete. The chief thus assumed the status of "appeals-court judge," as well as that of legislator by declaring the old rule outdated. When the father refused to obey the chief's declaration, he was punished severely (clearly, the chief's edict was a law, because it was enforced).

Horticulturalists also evidenced a more explicit court structure and, in many cases, a system of courts. For example, among the Kikuyu, disputes within a family were settled by the father. And if members of two families in a dispute could not come to a satisfactory resolution, the family heads of all kin groups within a clan sought to do so. However, if the two disputants came from different clans, a council of elders of all the clans within the village—constituting a kind of village council—settled the dispute. And if the disputants were also from different villages, then an intervillage council would act as a court. Thus, we can see that various courts were being assembled in accordance with spheres of jurisdiction as dictated by descent and resident rules.

As simple kin-based horticulture began to move toward a state-based system, councils of elites, forming a kind of ruling oligarchy, assumed many legislative and court functions (Kuper 1971; Newman 1983). Membership in these councils was based on family wealth as much as descent and authority rules, and their capacity to manipulate material incentives or purchase coercive force made their edicts and decisions truly enforceable.

Both kin-based and wealth-based systems revealed a paramount chief who had the right to hear disputes, make decisions, proclaim new laws, and enforce laws and decisions. There was a wide variation in this pattern, however. At times, the paramount chief oversaw just a few villages and his powers were not great, but at other times, the paramount chief was, in reality, a king of a nation. Max Gluckman's (1965, 129–272) description of law and politics in old tribal societies captures much of this variation, but the critical point is that the largest of these kingdoms came close to constituting a true state system. In these prestate, advanced horticultural populations, the legal system was differentiated along several lines. First, the legal system evidenced distinct levels, from village through region to nation. At each level could be found explicit laws, legislative bodies, courts, and enforcement capacities by local heads and chiefs. Second, at the national level, the elements of the legal system were more elaborated, consisting of more explicit rules, permanent legislative councils of the king or paramount chief, standing courts staffed by administrators and officials, and dramatically expanded enforcement capacities. This more elaborated system often articulated only loosely with local legal systems, but the increased administrative activity at the national level often involved overseeing lower-level laws and decisions. However, unless local disputes threatened the power and privilege of national elites, the two systems could operate somewhat independently.

With true state formation in advanced horticulture, the legal system changed by virtue of the concentration of coercive force. As Fried (1967, 237) points out, rules within and outside of kinship were now enforced by central rulers; and the state began to manage ever more activity. As it did so, the state developed larger bodies of law, both substantively and procedurally. It expanded courts and related officers for managing the courts, from judges to administrative record-keepers. And it established enforcement procedures, ranging from fines and other material deprivations, through imprisonment and banishment, to outright execution. In this process, the body of laws became more codified, especially as writing was developed and used to record the law (Weber [1922] 1954; Diamond 1971, 40–41). These codes, such as the imperial codes of the Inca empire or the Chinese empire at its moments of dynastic unification, specified crimes and threats against the state; and they began to be applied more uniformly. Local laws and codes still persisted, as did local adjudication, as long as it did not interfere with the imperial code's intent to maintain elite privilege, state finances, and state control of coercive power. But the groundwork for more-advanced legal evolution had been laid with state-based horticulture: Rules increasingly were written down and codified in formal and systematic ways; and while local rules existed alongside the codes of the state, conflicts between the two were resolved in the state's favor, further codifying and systematizing the body of laws. Legislative activity existed, once again, at multiple levels, but the council of elites began to look more like a deliberative legislative body. Courts at the state level were supreme. While their articulation with local adjudicative processes was loose, they often evidenced differentiation of full-time, professional judges, lawyers, and administrative record-keeping staff. They also had the potential, if desired or needed, to protect the interests of elites or the state, to intervene in local courts and, thereby, begin the process of court integration. Most significantly, laws and court decisions were no longer advisory; they were backed by the extensive coercive capacity to impose fines, confinement, or death on litigants. With agrarianism, these features of the legal system were to develop further.

Legal Systems in Agrarian Societies

The level of development of the legal system in agrarian societies was very much related to the level of state formation. As coercive, administrative, and material incentives were consolidated into a quasi-bureaucratic state, the state used its power to regulate and control ever more activity in the population. Thus, law became essential as a mechanism for exercising this control and for legitimating the often blatant and self-interested use of power by

Table 10.2   LAW IN HORTICULTURAL SOCIETIES

	Simple	Advanced
	Body of Laws:	
Substantive	Highly variable, from fairly complex system of rules governing family, property, and contracts to very few rules outside those outside those of kinship and normal day-to-day demeanor and ritual.	Complex system of rules governing family, property, contract, and other civil matters; but also bodies of laws specifying relationship of individuals, kin-groups, and other corporate actors to the emerging state, or in some cases, fully developed state. Laws increasingly are written down, often by religious scribes, and more likely to be codified as a system of rules. Religious prohibitions and prescriptions often will be important elements of law
Procedural	Highly variable, but most systems have some understanding about how parties are to resolve disputes by bringing in advisors or mediators or by making appeals to local chiefs or councils of elders or councils of elders or elites.	Clear rules about what is to be done to resolve disputes. Rules increasingly specify how parties are to make appeals to courts controlled by representatives representatives of the state.
Legislation of Laws	Chiefs or councils can suggest new rules that arise from disputes.	Paramount chief, king, councils of elites, and at times, councils of religious leaders can all make new rules that are binding and enforced. Court decisions by judges or political leaders frequently involve stating new precedents and, hence, new laws. At times, religious elites can pronounce new laws that are accepted by the state.

Table 10.2 *Continued*

	Simple	Advanced
		Courts:
Judge	Chief often will serve as an advisor or mediator of conflict in order to arrive at an acceptable compromise.	Kin leaders, local chiefs, paramount chiefs, and kings all can serve as judges serve as judges. In some systems, full-time judges can be found.
Jury/Council	Elders or elites can serve as either advisors or mediators who help in developing a compromise over a dispute.	Councils of elders at the local level, councils of elites at more regional levels can serve as juries. At times, religious councils can impose decisions with respect to religious doctrine.
Lawyer/ Representative System of Courts	Relatives of parties in dispute may seek to represent the claims of their kinsmen to advisors and mediators. Paramount chief and councils may, at times, serve as an "appeals court" for decisions made by kin-heads and local chiefs.	Disputants are frequently represented by kindred or by legal specialists. Relatively clear system of local, regional, and appeals courts composed of local chiefs, regional political leaders, and paramount chief or king as well as their respective councils of elites. Religious courts can, in some systems, exist alongside more secular courts, as can various tribunals of secret societies, merchants, and other groups of actors. Criminal and civil courts may be differentiated.
Enforcement of laws/Court Decisions	Kin and individual feuds and violent revenge can often occur outside the legal system. Court- and judge-suggested "redress" is still common, although chiefs and councils strive to reach compromises that all parties and their representatives find acceptable. Much enforcement involves shaming, ignoring, and otherwise treating guilty parties as undesirable.	Redress is now virtually gone. Revenge and feuds that take place outside the legal system are still frequent but less tolerated by the emerging state. Efforts are still made to reach mutually acceptable compromises, but ultimately coercive force can be, and often is, used to enforce laws and court decisions.

political elites. Historically, population growth stimulated economic development, and vice versa, which in turn increased the state's interest in regulating activities and legitimating its use of power—especially as this power was used to increase inequalities.

Added to these pressures for law were the differentiation of economic activity, the expansion of markets and the resulting increase in the volume of exchange transactions, the constant need to increase tax revenues to support state adventurism and privilege of elites, and the frequent need to sort out relations and transactions (e.g., citizenship, tribute, taxes, administration, etc.) with conquered peoples. To the extent that, in A. S. Diamond's (1951, 303) words, "the law of a people is the instrument by which its orderly activity is maintained and protected," the sheer amount of increase in such activity with agrarianism forced the development of law. Wherever political control of territories could be achieved, law became an instrument of this control. This control was embodied in written codes which, to varying degrees, constituted a system of rules for regulating key classes of human activity: marriage, inheritance, property, contract, crime, disputes, taxation, state-church relations, and the like.

The culmination of this development of systematic codes was Roman law, although less-systematic systems could be found in the various consolidations of power in Egypt, Persia, Greece, and small states in the Middle East as well as in Japan, India, and other agrarian societies of the East. By extending "citizenship" (to all "free men") and applying the law consistently and more or less equally to citizens, a system of laws emerged in Rome specifying rights of persons vis-à-vis government and rights of individuals to one another (Parsons 1966, 88). Beginning with the Roman emperor, Justinian, and during the sixth century C.E., a system of codes was legislated and, over the centuries, expanded. The intent was to create a comprehensive body of enacted laws that could regulate and control all essential activities among citizens. No agrarian system went this far in creating a centralized body of laws. Indeed, most simply adapted and adjusted old local codes in an ad hoc manner of issuing degrees and establishing precedents from court decisions. But in all agrarian systems, considerable attention was paid to writing down the legal codes and, in some manner, trying to systematize them into a more coherent whole.

As agrarian societies moved to an advanced profile, the legislative body tended to get larger, with more debate about what the laws should be. In some cases, such as the city-states of Greece and later Rome, a limited form of "election" or "competitive selection" to such legislative bodies as senates, councils, and forums occurred. However, these selection processes were only among elites and, hence, far from representative of the population as a whole.

The court systems of agrarian societies became more developed as the body of laws to be interpreted and applied to increasingly diverse contexts expanded. At first, even in the developing Roman system, the officers of the court were part-time and comparatively unprofessional. But as the body of laws became codified and as legislation continually added to this body, a system of courts became more integrated, moving from local tribunals to state-level courts; and the officers of the court—from judges, administrators, and scribes—were increasingly full-time and professional. If a strong body of enacted laws existed, as was the case in Rome and those societies that adopted Roman civil law, courts were primarily involved in interpreting existing laws. In other societies, such as England and societies like India, Canada, Ireland—and America that adopted the English model during their agrarian eras—no coherent body of enacted laws was developed initially. Instead, court decisions at the national level created common law precedents that became part of a body of laws, but the ad hoc nature of these court decisions produced a less coherent and systematic form of law than that originating from legislative enactments within government. In both systems, a hierarchy of courts developed in order to either impose top-down civil law to the local level, or to pass up for review and validation or invalidation court precedents from the local level. Moreover, the involvement of courts in an increasing number and variety of actions and transactions generated further pressures for their integration into a coherent hierarchy, which, in turn, worked to increase the coherence in the body of laws and its legislative enactment.

Enforcement of law and court decisions became more decisive in agrarian populations. The increased economic surplus that could support the coercive base of power, coupled with the need of polity to regulate and intervene in a wider array of actions and transactions, worked to expand not only the total amount of coercive power available to the polity but, more importantly, the use or threat of coercive power to enforce laws and court decisions. With advanced agrarianism, therefore, came coercive policing, torture, prisons, and executions; and these means of enforcement gave more-material sanctions, such as fines, penalties, and compensation in civil matters, an imperative force. Indeed, agrarian polities tended to overuse coercion in order to repress resentments over inequality, to control deviance, to regulate disruptive actions and transactions, and to compensate for weak symbolic legitimacy. Such violence by the state escalated as the expansion of markets and the commercialization of the economy created or escalated interclass tensions, all of which increased internal threats to the polity.

This overuse of the coercive element marked the great weakness of agrarian systems. If coercion rather than bodies of law, legislative enactment, legal precedent, and court adjudication were to determine what people must do and what the relationship between state and citizenry was to be, the legal system lost its capacity to create a civic culture in which broad principles—incorporating values, beliefs, and customs—legitimated the centers of power in society. Indeed, when the rule of law was easily suspended in the name of short-term crisis management or pursuit of privilege by those controlling the coercive base of power, its effectiveness as a basis for legitimating power and inequality, for preserving and integrating culture, and for coordination was reduced. As agrarian leaders faced fiscal crises, demands of noble elites, mass protests from peasants and slaves, external threats, and new social constructions like markets that aggravated interclass and intra-class conflicts, these leaders often subverted through arbitrary edict and coercion the very legal system that had enabled them to consolidate power (Turner 1995). This dismantling of legal development helps explain why agrarian systems, and empires composed of agrarian societies, were constantly built up, only to collapse under disintegrative pressures from the very forces that led to legal development—forces such as needs for coordination and control, legitimating power and inequality, and preserving as well as codifying culture. These forces overwhelmed political systems whose military reach and the imbalanced consolidation of the coercive-administrative bases of power had exceeded the capacity to govern and sustain the symbolic base of power provided by law.

Legal Systems in Industrial and Post-Industrial Societies

The Body of Laws   Bodies of law in modern legal systems are extensive networks of local and national statutes, private and public codes, crimes and torts, common-law precedents and politically enacted civil laws, and procedural and substantive rules. One of the most distinctive features of modern law is the proliferation of public and procedural laws, especially that type we can call "administrative law." With expansion and then bureaucratization of both the polity and legal subsystems, much law is designed to regulate and coordinate activity within and between bureaucracies as well as between individual incumbents, on the one side, and governmental and legal bureaucracies on the other. Another feature of law is the increasing proportion of civil to common law, for with the consolidation and centralization of power, legislation becomes a more typical way of adjusting law to social conditions. Common-law precedents from court decisions remain prevalent and actually increase even in systems with long histories of civil law. Yet as a codified system of law emerges, civil law as a proportion of all laws dominates over common law in all industrial or post-industrial societies.

As enacted laws come to dominate, the expanding body of laws constitutes a better-defined system, in which clear hierarchies of laws—from constitutional codes to regional and local codes—become increasingly evident. There is some degree of consistency in these hierarchies of laws, although many ambiguities remain, especially in societies like England and the United States with long common law traditions. As law develops a more consistent internal structure, it becomes more autonomous and differentiated from culture. Laws still preserve basic values and ideologies, thereby having many consequences for reconciling conflicts among cultural components. But the body of laws is more autonomous, possessing its own distinct logic. This autonomy is amplified as the practitioners of law—lawyers, judges, and police—become more professionalized, since professionalism inevitably generates its own norms, values, and traditions, which often deviate significantly from those of the broader society and culture.

Table 10.3   LAW IN AGRARIAN SOCIETIES

	Simple	Complex
Body of Laws:		
Substantive	Highly variable, but there will be explicit rules, often written down, concerning (a) what is defined as a crime, (b) what is the relation among individuals, kin-groups, and other corporate actors, and (c) what are the prerogatives of the state and the obligations of actors to the state.	Same as simple systems, but the body of written law is much larger and more systematic, although the degree of systematization will vary greatly. Religious laws can exist alongside secular laws. Laws increasingly reflect broad legal postulates that embody the general values of a population but more typically the culture and interests of elites.
Procedural	Clear rules about how to resolve disputes and how parties are to present grievances to courts. Some rules about how officers of the court are to behave, but these vary in salience and in the capacity to generate conformity by court officials.	Same as simple systems, but more-complex and binding rules on parties, especially court officials.
Legislation of Laws	Officials at city, regional, and national level have some capacity to pronounce edicts. Ultimate authority to legislate rests with king and council of elites. At times, forums and other bodies of elite representation may exist and have legislative functions. Court decisions increasingly can become part of law, although the ratio of court-generated to political elite-generated law is highly variable.	Same as simple systems, but forums of elites are more likely to be actively involved in legislating new laws; and in the advanced stages before industrialization, legislative bodies of nonelite representation sometimes can be found. Court decisions become an increasingly important source of common law in many systems.

Table 10.3 *Continued*

	Simple	Complex
	Courts:	
Judge	Political leaders at all levels of government can still double as judges, but increasingly there is a cadre of full-time judges who are more likely to have been formally educated in the law.	Except at the highest level, where the king and elite council may operate as judges, courts are staffed by full-time professionals, although at the local level, judges may be part-time. But increasingly, all judges are educated in the law, both substantive and procedural.
Jury/Council	Juries still tend to be dominated by councils of elites at local, regional, and national levels.	Same as simple systems, but emergence of ad hoc juries composed of nonelites and peers becomes evident.
System of Courts	Emerging system of local, regional, and high-level (supreme) courts.	Relatively coherent system of courts, with increasingly clear rules about procedures for making appeals to higher-level courts, culminating with the monarch and his or her council.
Bureaucratization of Courts	Expansion of court activity increases number and differentiation of personnel, thereby prompting bureaucratization of courts. Differentiation among civil, criminal, and administrative courts.	Full bureaucratization of courts
Enforcement of laws/Court Decisions	Enforcement of laws and court decisions is increasingly performed by full-time agents. Feuds and revenge are punished by enforcement agents because they violate criminal laws.	Same as simple systems, but more complex and formal system of enforcement at local, regional, and national levels. Enforcement agents increasingly are organized bureaucratically as police, sheriffs, and military. State claims legitimate use and monopoly of coercion and, therefore, punishes all other actors who use coercion. Much enforcement is administrative in character, as bureaucratic extensions of the state monitor and manage actions and transactions of individual and collective actors in the society.

Still, even as the details of the body of laws become somewhat detached from culture, the broad legal postulates and associated civic culture of the legal system reflect the traditions, customs, and values of the population. And where they have not, as in the aftermath of the Russian and Chinese revolutions, the polity purges dissidents and engages in massive resocialization and indoctrination of the population. As long as these broad postulates are considered legitimate, the larger body of laws will also be seen as legitimate, at least in the diffuse sense of legitimacy discussed in Chapter 8.

Indeed, as the complexity of laws increases, there is no option but to turn the specifics of law over to professionals trained in the law and to focus the public's attention on broad legal principles and precedents. However, when professionals in the legal system act in ways that generate disrespect from the public—a phenomenon that appears to be occurring for lawyers in the United States—there is a corresponding loss of respect for the body of laws and, eventually, for the broad legal (constitutional) principles on which it rests.

The underlying principles organizing a body of laws have an enormous influence on the nature of law as well as on how the legal system will operate. Legal scholars often note four basic types of legal systems, evidencing distinctive types of laws (see Vago 1994, 10–13, for a summary):

1. The Roman civil law system in which comprehensive laws are enacted by political bodies.
2. Common legal systems based on case law, relying on precedents set by judges in deciding on a case.
3. Socialist legal systems based on socialist principles of:
   a. providing for people on the basis of their needs
   b. using the state to define, interpret, and provide for people's needs.
4. Islamic or religious law, where the sacred texts provide the basic guidelines for all laws, law enactment, and court decisions.

As noted above, civil law becomes more prominent in industrial systems, even those with long traditions of common law.

Most interesting are socialist and Islamic systems. In the case of former socialist states, such as Russia, the body of laws was ill-suited for a market-driven, contract-oriented, and profit-making economic system. Profits as well as private property and private ownership of economic units were repressed for most of this century by the legal system in favor of collective ownership or, in reality, state ownership. Thus, today the existing body of laws, as well as the principles of the civic culture that were imposed by heavy-handed indoctrination and enforced by Joseph Stalin's purges, are simply not designed to regularize market transactions or to redefine individual freedoms vis-à-vis the state. The result has been chaos, corruption, and violence in Russia in an effort to regularize actions and transactions in a new, market-oriented system. Indeed, the "Russian mafia" of illegal syndicates controls much of what occurs in market transactions, because without a viable body of laws, selection forces work to create order through the use of informal "laws" and "rules" of organized criminal syndicates.

The Islamic system of law poses fewer problems because the economies of these societies are not highly industrial, save for the extraction and export of oil. The religious nature of the body of laws will create problems for further modernization, however, since traditional sayings, acts, and proclamations, coupled with "the word of God" in the Koran, limit what can be legislated and what common-law precedents can be set in the courts. Indeed, the nature of law is more reminiscent of simpler economic forms, such as horticulture and early agrarianism, than of a modern commercial system. Still, this system has proven viable in coordinating activities and transactions in the Islamic world, although much of this viability is the result of the capacity of oil profits to insulate these populations from patterns of full-scale industrialization and internal market development that might clash with the restrictions of religious-based legal codes.

Legislation of Laws   In industrial and post-industrial societies, legislative bodies within the political subsystem increase in size and power, becoming responsible for the vast majority of law enactment in the legal subsystem. Just how free the legislatures (or assemblies, congresses, parliaments, or equivalent bodies) are to enact law differs greatly from society to society, depending on answers to questions like the following (Turner 1972, 238):

a. How established is the constitution of the legal system? The more established the constitution—as in the United States, but not in England—the more constraint on law enactment.
b. How many and how powerful are the higher courts of the legal system? Do they have the power to interpret the constitutionality of laws? To the extent that they do, constraint on legislators is increased.
c. How extensive and effective are the enforcement agencies of the legal system? The more extensive and effective, the greater are the law-enacting powers of the legislature.
d. How extensive, professional, and integrated is the court system in a society? The more courts are an integrated and institutionalized mechanism for applying laws, the more effective law enactment can be.
e. How strong are custom and tradition in society? How much value and ideological consensus is there? The stronger custom and the more consensus over values and ideology, the greater is pressure on legislatures to enact laws not deviating too far from these cultural components and the associated civic culture.
f. How responsive to public opinion must the legislature be? Are legislatures elected in free elections? If so, law enactment must reflect more clearly the fads and foibles of public opinion and sentiment.
g. And most importantly, how autonomous from the political rulers in a highly centralized polity is the legislature? To the extent that power

lies with a small number of elites, the greater is the political constraint on legislatures.

All of these conditions affect the legislative processes in modern societies. By establishing the weights and relative influence of each factor, predictions about exact legislative structures and processes can be made for each particular legal system.

Despite all the potential variability, several overall generalizations about legislation in modern systems can be made: Legislation is not piecemeal but comprehensive. Law enactment increasingly tends to cover large areas where disputes and integrative problems are evident (or at least perceived as problematic by legislators and political elites), thereby making bodies of civil laws a more prominent part of the legal system, even where—as in England—a long tradition of common law exists. Once legislative enactment becomes prominent, a more consistent and stable body of laws emerges; and though laws will always contradict and overlap one another in any legal system, comprehensive enactment tends to generate a discernible *system* of laws. With the emergence of a stable legislature, comprehensive law enactment can become a mechanism of social change, establishing new structures and relationships, especially when effective court and enforcement systems exist to force and maintain the changes dictated by laws.

Courts and Adjudication   Modern courts reflect the complexity—and resulting integrative problems—of industrial and post-industrial societies. With the high degree of differentiation, there are many more disputes and considerably higher rates of deviance than in traditional societies. By necessity, then, the courts come to have growing consequences for mediating and mitigating conflicts, disputes, deviance, and other sources of malintegration—especially as kinship, community, and religion no longer exert the pervasive influence and control typical in pre-industrial societies.

The roles of court incumbents (e.g., judge, lawyer, litigant, juror, and administrator) become more distinct and clearly differentiated from one another, and the positions of judge and lawyer become highly professionalized and, hence, licensed, sanctioned, and guided by professional organizations. As the volume of codified law in any particular area expands, court officials become specialists, dealing only in certain types of cases such as family, tax, bankruptcy, real estate, corporate, or criminal law. Since modern courts must handle a tremendous volume of cases, creating vast administrative problems, administrative statuses (clerks, bailiffs, stenographers, and public prosecutors) proliferate, specialize, and become heavily bureaucratized.

Just as the structure of courts becomes increasingly differentiated and specialized, so do the courts themselves, with particular courts—like their incumbents—often mediating only certain kinds of disputes. For example, in the United States, courts usually can be distinguished in larger urban areas along at least domestic (family and divorce), criminal, and civil (or more accurately, torts) lines. Probably the distinctive feature of courts in industrial and post-industrial societies is that they constitute a clear-cut system of community, regional, and national mediation and adjudication structures. The jurisdictions of each court are better articulated (Parsons 1962) and the hierarchy of control is less ambiguous than in agrarian and early industrial legal systems. Cases unresolved in lower courts are argued in higher courts, with these courts having the power to reverse lower-court decisions.

One of the serious problems facing modern courts is case overload. Courts cannot properly handle the volume of cases needing mediation and adjudication. One of the consequences of this fact is that litigants often settle out of court in order to avoid delays created by case overloads and backlogs. Such proceedings further the normative obligations on lawyers, who must negotiate for a client out of court as often as plead and argue a case inside the court. Another problem endemic to modern courts is a result of bureaucratization. Bureaucratization tends to make the process of adjudication somewhat invisible—for behind the vast hierarchies of bureaucratic offices much hidden mediation occurs that is not carried out in accordance with procedural laws or made public. Since modern legal systems usually attempt to implement some view of "justice," such proceedings can severely threaten this implementation. In fact, administrative bureaucracies are often judge and jury without many of the procedural (and professional) safeguards required within a courtroom. Yet, with extensive court backlogs, this kind of "administrative mediation" is perhaps necessary in modern legal systems.

Enforcement   The enforcement of laws and court decisions in modern legal systems is performed by a clearly differentiated and organized police force. In most industrial and post-industrial societies, there are several different kinds of enforcement agencies, with separate and yet somewhat overlapping jurisdictions—typically, a trilevel system consisting of a community-based force, another district or regional force, and a national police force. Each police force possesses its own internal organization, which becomes increasingly bureaucratized; and between forces there are relatively clear lines of communication, power, and control.

Police forces at all levels are heavily bureaucratized because of the volume and complexity of their functions in modern legal systems. Moreover, police forces are guided by many procedural laws—especially those we labeled administrative—laws, that regulate and control the way in which enforcement can occur. But since police bureaucracies are large, they can hide many violations of these procedural laws; and because they can do so, the police can maintain considerable autonomy from laws, courts, and even the political bodies supposedly controlling their activities. These facts always pose the problems of unequal or arbitrary enforcement of laws, denial of due-process rights (and all industrial and post-industrial systems, even totalitarian ones, articulate such rights), and concealment of illegal police action.

Enforcement of laws often is a more purely administrative process in industrial and post-industrial societies. Indeed, the administration of laws becomes as important as the coercive enforcement of laws, as is evidenced by the growing number of regulatory agencies in modern societies. In the United States, for example, agencies such as the Federal Communications Commission, Federal Trade Commission, Federal Reserve Board, Food and Drug Administration, Federal Aviation Agency, Environmental Protection Agency, and others oversee and regulate conformity to laws. These agencies cannot be considered a police force in the strict sense, but they do enforce laws—calling in police and courts if necessary. Much law enforcement in modern societies is of this kind: administrative agencies interpreting laws for various system units while constantly checking on these units' degree of conformity to laws. The emergence and proliferation of these strictly administrative enforcement agencies continue the bureaucratization of law enforcement in the legal systems of advanced industrial and post-industrial societies. In a sense, administrative enforcement underscores the basic structural dilemma of all legal systems: The legislative and enforcement components are lodged primarily in the polity, which can come into conflict with more-independent adjudicative (court) components.

TRENDS IN LEGAL SYSTEMS

Tables 10.1 to 10.4 summarize the differences in the legal systems among hunter-gatherer, horticultural, agricultural, industrial, and post-industrial populations. Emerging from these descriptive summaries are several distinct trends which should be highlighted.

Bureaucratization

Because of the pivotal place of law in modern societies for coordinating action, the legal subsystem becomes necessarily large, and size inevitably generates administrative problems which are partially resolved through bureaucratization. Not only is there bureaucratization of courts, police forces, and various administrative or regulatory agencies, but similarly, as legislatures increase in size, they too become vast administrative hierarchies. One consequence of this trend is for each bureaucracy of a modern legal system—courts, police, and legislatures—to achieve considerable autonomy from other elements because what occurs within each bureaucracy can be hidden. Such autonomy can protect and insulate the respective components of the legal system from excessive manipulation by either the public or political elite. However, this autonomy from supervision and control also enables courts, police, and regulatory agencies to engage in de facto legislation—independent of the legislature and political elite. Within and behind the vast maze of bureaucratic offices in the courts, police, and regulatory agencies, differential and preferential enforcement, or lack of enforcement, of laws can be hidden—a trend that amounts to law enactment, since only some laws are enforced. For example, the common process of "copping a plea" in U.S. courts violates the spirit of American procedural law. But by

Table 10.4 LAW IN MODERN SOCIETIES

	Industrial	Post-Industrial
	Body of Laws:	
Substantive	Written body of laws organized along one of four patterns: (a) civil law, (b) common law, (c) socialist law, (d) religious law. Each type has rules that denote crimes, specify relations between actors and the state, and mediate relations among actors. All systems reveal general legal postulates that reflect a mixture of cultural values and traditions of the masses and elites, as these have led to the articulation of a "civic culture".	Same as industrial, except that a combination of the "civic culture," broad legal postulates, and electoral political pressures exert more constraint on the body of substantive laws.
Procedural	Clear body of rules, specifying how all agents in the legal system are supposed to act as well as how disputants are to prepare and present cases in courts. Procedural laws, specifying rights and duties of all actors in the system, increasingly are used to guide the formulation of substantive laws.	Same as industrial system, except that procedural laws are even more constraining on substantive laws.
Legislation of Laws	Elected representatives at most levels of government enact new laws, although the degree of freedom and choice in "elections" varies. The nature of representative bodies differs, but often two elected bodies of legislators jointly enact laws. Except in civil-law systems, court decisions also contribute to body of law.	Same as industrial systems, except that elections are more likely to be free and, because of active and diverse political parties, to offer a wider range of choice among potential candidates.

Table 10.4 *Continued*

Courts:

	Industrial	Post-Industrial
Judge	Increasing separation of position of judge from political offices, although judges are constrained by the state, and vice versa. Professionalization of judges in terms of education, experience, and competence, although in those systems where judges are elected (usually at local levels), both separation of judges from politics and professionalism decline. Depending on system of law, judges have autonomy and power, with most power given in common-law systems, somewhat less in civil and social systems, and even less in religious systems.	Same as industrial, except that judges are more autonomous from political or religious centers of power.
Jury	Juries of peers, judges, and experts become common, replacing juries dominated by elites. Councils of advisors and elites disappear as major court agent.	Same as industrial.
Lawyers	Full professionalization of legal profession, with examination systems and sanctioning associations.	Same as industrial.
System of Courts	Clear hierarchy of courts, from local to regional to national; system of appeals up to supreme tribunal of judges. Clear differentiation of criminal, civil, administrative, and military courts (and at times, other courts, such as maritime courts).	Same as industrial.
Bureaucratization of Courts	Full bureaucratization and professionalization of courts, involving use of educational credentials, examinations, and civil service systems for placement and promotion, although if judges are elected, professionalization suffers.	Same as industrial.
Enforcement of laws/court decisions	Differentiated by geographical jurisdiction (e.g., local, regional, state, nation) and by function (investigative, coercive, spying) at each level. Fully professionalized. Enforcement agents often become an active vested interest in the political arena.	Same as industrial systems, except procedural laws are more likely to be invoked, often creating conflicts between enforcement agents and courts/legislatures imposing procedural constraints. Such conflicts often cause police, sheriffs, troopers, and other enforcement agents to become political lobbies.

threatening delays, expense, and the risks of court trials, court officials can coerce defendants to plead guilty to a lesser charge. American police have been likely to treat violators of laws in an urban ghetto much differently from white, middle-class violators of the same law in suburban communities. Thus, differential social-class enforcement of laws amounts to police enactment of new substantive and procedural laws (Black 1993, 1976).

Similar processes occur behind the vast administrative bureaucracies of other modern legal systems, particularly for those societies without a democratic political tradition and civic culture. While bureaucratization is inevitable and necessary for the reasonably smooth functioning of a legal system, it grants legal structure considerable autonomy, and in some cases, excessive license.

Professionalization

Professionalization involves specialized training, regulation by professional associations, and the utilization of expertise for the welfare of clients. Professionalism in legal systems first emerges as courts become prominent and distinguishable elements. By the Middle Ages in Europe, lawyers' behavior involved the roles of *agent*, representing a client in court in various legal matters; *advocate*, pleading a case before a judge and perhaps jury of peers; and *jurisconsultant*, advising, teaching, consulting, and writing. The final criterion for professionalization is an active regulatory professional association. In modern systems, lawyers usually are regulated by such associations. Furthermore, because judges in most modern legal systems are lawyers, judge statuses can be considered quasi-professions in all respects except the formal regulatory capacity of the association. However, much informal regulation still can occur through judges' contacts with periodicals and members of the legal profession.

Once the profession of law becomes established, legislators in law-enacting bodies tend to be drawn from the profession; and to the extent that this occurs, law-enacting structures become indirectly professionalized. This professionalization of the legal system occurs for several reasons. First, modern legal systems are complex, with vast bodies of substantive and procedural laws. Such complexity necessitates considerable expertise and competence of court and legislative personnel, a necessity that can be achieved best through extensive professional education. Second, professionalism also stabilizes law—giving it a tradition that is passed from one generation of professionals to another. Though the laws of a legal system constantly change, they are best altered by courts and legislatures in light of existing traditions and precedents—a necessity that, once again, can be achieved by expert training. Third, since so much legal activity occurs outside courts and legislatures in administrative hierarchies, considerable knowledge and expertise are required to carry out administrative adjudication. As a consequence, professional staffing of the bureaucracies and professional counseling of individuals negotiating within the bureaucracy become requisites for the smooth functioning of a modern legal system.

In all industrial and post-industrial legal systems, then, legislative, court, and administrative structures always possess a high proportion of professional incumbents. The last element of the legal system to professionalize is the police, but as procedural laws begin to take hold, some professionalization of police forces occurs through training in specialized academies. Professionalization of the police probably increases its enforcement effectiveness—but for which client: the state or the police themselves? Since professional norms usually emphasize flexibility in the name of service for the client, it makes a great deal of difference just whom the police define as a client. If the client of the police is the state, then individual rights guaranteed under procedural law will be violated in service of this client—a fact that is best illustrated in most totalitarian societies, where a highly professionalized police force views the state as its client. If the police themselves become their own client, as they develop collective-bargaining agreements and associations in pushing their interests, the enforcement of law becomes biased toward the interests of the police.

Systematization and Centralization

Law in modern societies is a system, indicating a high degree of interrelatedness among its component parts; and as law develops it comes to constitute more of a system. A national system of codified laws setting general guidelines for state, regional, and local laws emerges. While laws at each level display some autonomy from one another, they begin to approximate a reasonably consistent and coordinated body of rules. Courts also become systematized, with the jurisdictions of local, state, regional, and national courts becoming clearly delimited; and they begin to form an explicit hierarchy of control and decision making. Enforcement structures similarly evolve clear boundaries of jurisdiction with a clear hierarchy of power and control.

Much of the systematization of the legal system is a reflection of the consolidation and centralization of power. Until the exclusive use of force can be concentrated into a legitimate political structure, legal-system development will remain somewhat disorganized at a national level. Nor can law become a system until clear legislative bodies emerge. Without a national legislature, law remains tied to the scattered common-law precedents of local and regional courts, enactments of local legislatures, or the arbitrary dictates of local or regional centers of power. Once national legislative enactment of laws exists and once there is a centralized source of force to back such enactment, a comprehensive body of rules and courts to mediate them can develop. Conflicts, traditions, anachronisms, and gaps in the law can be remedied by enactment of civil codes and statutes. These comprehensive codes and statutes help standardize both the procedures and substance of court and police actions into a more integrated whole. And once mediation and enforcement agencies have a common set of procedural and substantive laws guiding their actions, consistency in enforcement and court processes across diverse regions can occur.

A major force promoting systematization and centralization of the legal system is the polity's use of law to effect social change. Law becomes the means for implementing the plans and programs of the polity. For example, in Russia after the communist revolution, legislative enactment drastically changed not only the structure of laws, but the courts, police, and administrative agencies. These changes were deliberately made to effect basic changes in conditions of production, transactions, and the nature of legal ownership and contract (Friedman 1959). Law also radically changed the kinship structure by making marriage more of a legal contract, by creating "on paper" egalitarianism among men and women in and out of the family (although in actual practice relations in Russia remained highly patriarchal), by removing much of the stigma of illegitimate births, and by the legislation of liberal abortion laws. Utilizing legislation in this way necessitates centralizing police, courts, and administrative agencies, because these must become integrated and centralized in order to enforce, administer, and mediate the new programs of the polity. To have courts, police, and other legal structures decentralized would make societal planning through legislation ineffective.

Systems without this capacity to centralize and coordinate their legal subsystems cannot implement planned social change through legislation. There are, however, many limitations on how much the legal system can be used as an agent of planned social change. These limitations can be seen in answers to the following questions:

1. How much do changes deviate from custom, tradition, and deeply held values? The more deviations, the greater will be resistance to planned change through law enactment.
2. How drastic are the structural rearrangements demanded by new laws? The more drastic, the greater resistance will be.
3. In what structural areas are changes legislated? It is probably easier to legislate change in the economic and educational spheres than in either the familial or religious spheres, where values, traditions, and emotions run deep.
4. How much force does the polity possess, and how great is its capacity to apply that force? The more the polity has the sole possession of force and capacity to use it, the more it can overcome cultural and structural resistance to legislated changes.

These trends—bureaucratization, professionalization, and systematization along centralized lines—appear ubiquitous in industrial and post-industrial societies. Some legal systems, such as those in Continental Europe, evidenced these trends early in their development, because they adopted the Roman tradition of civil law. In other systems, such as in England, the use of common law worked against these trends, at least for a while. Yet eventually, as the integrative functions of law increase with general societal development, all legal systems can be expected to display a high degree of bureaucratization, professionalization, systematization, and centralization.

CONCLUSION

From very modest beginnings, law has evolved into a complex system that regulates just about every facet of social life in post-industrial societies. Indeed, it has become the principle integrative structure of a society, preserving, codifying, and translating key cultural symbols into specific rules, defining what is deviant, and coordinating transactions among actors. As we have seen thus far, law influences the operation of economic, kinship, religious, and political institutions. And we will see in Chapter 13 that it influences education as well. Each differentiated institutional complex—from economic to educational—of a modern society could not operate without law; nor could relations among institutional subsystems proceed smoothly. In the absence of law, then, a large and differentiated social structure is not viable. Furthermore, if a specific legal system proves incapable of managing internal actions and relations within an institutional subsystem, as well as external relations among institutional subsystems, social structures and the cultural codes that guide them begin to disintegrate.

Conversely, law exists because of pressures generated by the operation of institutions and the inequalities that institutional subsystems generate. When institutions remain undifferentiated and simple, law is not needed most of the time. But as institutional growth and differentiation occur—that is, as economy, kinship, religion, polity, education, and newer institutional complexes like science and medicine separate from one another and begin to elaborate their structure and culture—law becomes ever more essential (if a population is to remain organized). And add to these selection pressures those concerning the inequalities that institutional growth and differentiation inevitably produce, and it is clear that law becomes ever more critical to maintaining order.

Of course, in maintaining order, law generates its own disintegrative pressures. When law coordinates contracts that exploit others; when it legitimates an oppressive polity; when it differentially punishes criminals by social class; when it selectively enacts or enforces laws in terms of ascriptive criteria, such as gender and ethnicity; when it protects the privilege of elites; when it sanctions an unfair system of taxation or is perceived to do so, then the legal system may generate the seeds for its own destruction and the broader society that it seeks to keep together.

In the end, law always fails, because all known societies have collapsed or have been weak enough to be conquered. But out of the rubble of a former society organizing a population, new institutional systems are built up into a new society or a series of new societies. And as these institutional systems are constructed, law once again becomes a means for their integration, however problematic and temporary. Thus, to understand legal systems, we need to review the specific pressures from other institutional complexes that determine the nature of a legal system.

Chapter
11

Law in Institutional Context

As economy emerged as a distinct institution from kinship, as religion arose, as polity consolidated power, and as education massified, and, today, as still-emerging institutions like science and medicine grow in influence, each has created problems of internal control and coordination as well as problems of external articulation with its institutional environment. These problems represent selection pressures on law, for ultimately law becomes the mechanism for maintaining the viability of an institution and the larger institutional system of which it is a part. To understand the dynamics of law, therefore, requires a review of how other institutional systems affect the organization of legal systems.

ECONOMY AND LAW

Until the economy can generate a stable and predictable level of surplus beyond the subsistence needs of a population, its effects on law will be minimal. Among hunter-gatherers rules may have specified rights to property (arrows, spears, bows, temporary huts, a hunting kill, etc.) and even may have indicated how exchanges were to occur, especially among more-settled hunter-gatherers. Even when more-mobile hunter-gatherers could generate a temporary surplus, such as when the !Kung-san had a large kill, rules for the distribution of this kill were invoked (who saw it first, who tracked it down, and whose arrow was fatal). Thus, as soon as surpluses began to emerge, selection for rules to regulate and coordinate distribution became evident. Still, only with a consistent surplus that could support more stable leadership (the beginnings of polity) and which could be used in exchange distribution (the beginnings of markets) did the effects of economy on legal systems become pronounced.

As gathering-producing increased to the point of generating a surplus, two forces were unleashed. First, the surplus could be used to support a more distinctive polity which engaged in appropriation of the surplus and, to varying degrees, redistribution of what it had appropriated. Second, exchanges among individuals and collective actors—such as lineages and clans, villages, and later corporate units—became possible. This second process created intense selection pressures for regulation and coordination with respect to the definitions of what property could be exchanged as well as what the rules of exchange were to be. For if what one "owned" or had "rights" to own could not be defined and if the material obligations of parties exchanging property could not be agreed on, conflict was inevitable. To avoid this conflict, the needed regulation came from the differentiation of tort laws (laws about relations among actors) from criminal laws (laws specifying deviant acts by actors). If power had been consolidated and centralized to a sufficient degree, then these different kinds of laws may have been legislated within polity, although historically, agreements regulating exchange often have been created by parties to the exchanges. Merchant laws in feudal Europe, for example, remained outside the politically controlled legal system for many centuries (Turner 1972); and only later, through a long series of common-law decisions in local courts and through waves of consolidation of power, did these torts become part of the formal legal system. Or, among similar economies, such as the horticultural patterns of the Trobriand Islanders, individuals who did not meet their exchange obligations were often punished by families who would systematically exclude the individual from access to economic resources (Malinowski 1926). Thus, whether sanctioned by a polity or left to the parties themselves, exchange activity caused torts to emerge. The first historical records of torts, as distinct from crimes, are from the Egyptian legal system sometime before 4000 B.C.E. Although the exact reasons for their existence can never be known, torts probably emerged in response to the trading activities among the seminomadic groups of this region. Somewhat later, in Mesopotamia, the Codes of Hammurabi dating from 2100 B.C.E. contained numerous sections dealing with commerce—deeds, sales, loans, deposits, bills of lading, agencies, and partnerships (Davis 1962, 81). Once these torts existed as a body of laws distinguishable from crimes, selection pressures for their adjudication and enforcement must have increased, leading to the differentiation and development of court systems, which, in turn, created pressures for the enforcement of court decisions.

The effects of these legal processes back onto economic processes are worth highlighting. The key feedback effect is the capacity to differentiate torts from crimes and, then, to adjudicate decisions in courts and enforce these decisions. If such capacities exist, they facilitate exchange and, more indirectly, stimulate gathering and producing. For without the capacity to regulate, coordinate, and organize exchange, economic development was limited. However, once this entrepreneurial effect of law on economy was firmly in place, it stimulated the growth of gathering, producing, and distributing. This relationship between the law and economy can be exemplified by China in its pre-industrial phase. Although China was as technologically and culturally developed as feudal Europe, it did not industrialize until this century. Hence, one of the great mysteries of history is why China did not industrialize before Europe. Part of the explanation apparently lies in the Chinese legal system, which had extensive laws as well as court and police structures but not a codified body of torts. The imperial code of medieval China was a criminal code and did not concern matters of trade, commerce, transactions, exchanges, contract, and property, which were left to local customary law and did not become incorporated into the national legal system until this century. Without torts, a major roadblock to economic development existed in China despite its advanced technology (Weber [1922] 1954; Sawer 1965, 55–60; Lloyd 1964, 241–42; Davis 1962, 80–81).

Subsequent economic development through agrarianism, early industrialism, and post-industrialism has similarly revolved around the effects of expanded economic exchange on law. Escalating exchange has caused: (1) torts to expand dramatically; (2) courts to differentiate into diverse kinds of administrative and civil courts which adjudicate breaches, disagreements, defaults, and conflicts over exchanges and contracts; and (3) enforcement capacities to expand and differentiate with respect to the amount of coercion, restitution, and regulation to be imposed by agencies of the state. Torts have come to specify an ever-greater range of property and property rights, such as copyrights, patents over technologies, and environmental hazards. Torts have also come to regulate ever more types of exchanges of capital, goods, services, and eventually labor disputes and contracts. For without this entrepreneurial input from law, the basic elements of an economy—technology, physical and human capital, and property—cannot be effectively coordinated, thereby stagnating the economy and, more importantly, creating potential arenas of conflict over property, property rights, contractual obligations, fraud, corruption, misrepresentation, and other contentious issues.

Because the legitimacy of polity and its ability to consolidate power rest on the use of law to control and regulate critical social relations, political systems have sought actively to develop law in ways that resolve these potential arenas of conflict. For as Chapter 8 emphasized, law becomes an important tool for the consolidation of power, but only when the population perceives the legal system to be effective and legitimate, thereby giving polity a vested interest in developing a legal system that can provide entrepreneurial functions for the economy.

POLITY AND LAW

As long as polity was fused within kinship, as was the case in most horticultural populations, the rules of the kinship system also operated as the laws of an implicit legal system. Of course, as we saw in the last chapter, kin-heads, chiefs, paramount chiefs, councils of elders or elites, kin representatives, and other political embellishments of kinship systems could legislate new agreements in addition to kinship rules. And they could sit as courts and enforce the decisions rendered. Still, it is not until a kin-based system of governance began to shift toward a state-based system that the effects of polity on law began to accelerate.

If the polity simply codified existing traditions and customs, the law could be an effective source of coordination, control, and legitimacy. But, if the polity used laws to exploit, if this use had to overcome well-established local traditions and systems of common law, or if this usage went against a kin-based system of adjudication, then law was likely to be considered as illegitimate by population members. As a consequence, the capacity of state-imposed law to regulate and coordinate was correspondingly diminished. This ineffectiveness of state-imposed law was particularly evident, for example, when European colonial powers consistently attempted to impose European legal traditions on the indigenous legal systems of Africa. Illustrative of this problem are the Kuba of what was once called the Congo. The Kuba possessed a tribal and territorial legal system which persisted long after colonial law was introduced, because the Kuba system was more relevant and effective in regulating the traditional activities of the indigenous population. In providing stability and regularity to action, the Kuba legal system remained legitimate in the eyes of the Kuba tribesmen, despite the best efforts of colonial authority to impose its own system on the native population. Indeed, the persistence of local laws could reach extreme proportions, as among the Tiv, where it was considered immoral for a tribesman to adjudicate a case in a state-run court (Bohannan 1964, 202–3). To cite another example, the attempt by the post-revolutionary Russian polity to restructure through law basic family and community relations in its Mongolian territories proved a disastrous failure (Massell 1968), since the laws bore little relation to existing structural arrangements, although these cultural and structural sources were, in the end, only constraints rather than complete roadblocks to legislative initiative by the polity. The state—through its monopoly on force as well as control over educational socialization—could legislate social change. For example, as was the case in the old Soviet Union, a combination of legislative enactment of new laws, state indoctrination into a new Soviet culture, and the threat or use of force allowed the Soviet polity to restructure radically through law a whole new series of social relationships (in pursuit of the goals of socialism, military power, and economic development). Yet the rapid collapse of the Soviet Union in the 1990s indicates that the legitimacy given to Russian law was never great. Indeed, customary law was still used to adjudicate many cases, especially since in principle (but often not in fact) the Soviet empire was a "voluntary union" of "independent" republics which could retain some of their older legal traditions.

Nevertheless, if the state desires to increase regulation and control, increasingly it will do so through law; and the more centralized is the administrative apparatus of the state, the more it will seek to differentiate laws with respect to torts versus crimes as well as private versus public (state-related) disputes. The state will seek to enact more-comprehensive bodies of civil law, thereby increasing the ratio of civil to common laws and, indirectly, clarifying the relations among torts, crimes, private, and public laws. Moreover, court systems are often expanded by the state to serve as a mechanism

for, and symbol of, individual and collective actors' rights to redress grievances, thereby deflecting or diminishing potential hostility toward the state
and, in the process, legitimating the polity.

Thus, as laws are used to regulate and coordinate, they must be adjudicated in courts. The more complex and differentiated the body of laws used
by polity to implement policies and plans, the more developed will be the
court system—evolving into a centralized hierarchy of local, regional, and
national courts with clear jurisdictions and procedures for appeals. Such is
especially likely to be the case when power is highly centralized.

As court decisions are rendered, they must be enforced. Ultimately,
enforcement is only possible because centralized states seek to monopolize
and mobilize coercive power. Still, enforcement is often somewhat diffused
among a variety of regulatory agencies, which can even have their own
administrative courts. For example, in the United States, the coast guard,
the Postal Inspectors, the Bureau of Alcohol, Tobacco and Firearms, the military police of each service, and the Federal Bureau of Investigation are all
adjuncts to administrative agencies, and most have their own tribunals.
Although more-centralized legal systems reveal a less-diverse pattern, much
enforcement of laws occurs within bureaucratic agencies rather than
through direct military or police coercion.

As the body of differentiated laws, the adjudicative capacities of court
hierarchies, and the ability to enforce decisions all expand, they can facilitate
the growing autonomy of a legal system and the creation of a civic culture
that translates traditions, customs, values, and beliefs into broad legal postulates. Reciprocally, this system of postulates shapes the content and form
of new laws, the adjudicative decisions of courts, and the enforcement of laws
and court decisions. The capacity of the civic culture to have these effects
depends not only on the extent to which it embodies the culture of the larger
population, but also on the degree to which a common civic culture can be
instilled into the members of a population through family socialization and
state-controlled school indoctrination. Moreover, if the legal system is seen
as efficient and, by and large, fair in adjudication and enforcement, then this
perception helps establish a common civic culture.

The reciprocal effects of law on polity were, of course, analyzed in Chapter 9 on the institutional environment of polity, but several are worthy of special mention here because they influence subsequent legal development. If a
civic culture can be developed and seen as legitimate by the general public,
then there is an increase in the diffuse legitimacy bestowed on the polity in
general and, thereby, on its capacity to regulate and coordinate. This civic
culture also can lead the public to impute to the body of differentiated laws
as well as the system of courts a generalized sense of fairness, which, in turn,
furthers the political legitimacy of the state. Another reciprocal effect of law
on the state comes from the differentiation of laws and courts in regulatory
agencies; these agencies and bureaus become important tools for regulation
and coordination that strengthen the administrative and symbolic bases of
state power. And, if enforcement of law and court decisions can occur

through bureaucratic agencies that are viewed as somewhat distant and autonomous from the military—which is ultimately the polity's coercive base of power—then the resentments that enforcement inevitably generates will be deflected somewhat from the core leadership positions of the state, and the state will not be perceived as overusing its coercive arm.

If these reverse causal effects from law strengthen the power of the state by providing it with increased legitimacy, regulatory and adjudicative mechanisms, and enforcement capacity, the polity is then in a better position to develop the legal system further as a means to expand the scope of its regulation and coordination of activities by individual and collective actors. This expansion is limited, however, because at a certain point the state will be perceived as overregulating. When this threshold is passed, the legitimacy of state actions will be called into question. And, if the state persists in overregulating, its bodies of law, courts, and agents of enforcement can become targets for delegitimation. As this process unfolds, the symbolic base of political power rapidly collapses and decreases the state's ability to use effectively or efficiently the legal system for regulation and control. As the legitimacy of the state erodes, the legal system becomes less viable and, in fact, it can become the symbolic target for dissatisfaction with polity as a whole.

RELIGION AND LAW

In hunting-gathering societies that evidenced beliefs in the supernatural and included ritualistic cults, the effects of law and religious beliefs on control and coordination were intermingled. Members of the population saw supernatural forces, beings, and entities as responding to the behaviors of individuals, with the result that individuals sought to harmonize their behaviors with the perceived will of the supernatural. For example, among the traditional Eskimos, violating a religious taboo was usually viewed as the cause of bad luck or hardship; and to eliminate such misfortune required an Eskimo to consult a shaman who pointed out the violations and served as an intermediary between the gods and the violator in order to relieve the hardship (Hoebel 1954, 261). This constantly reinforced association in the minds of individuals between violating taboos and bad luck maintained considerable order and control in Eskimo society, but when an Eskimo persistently violated a taboo, specific members of the community punished the individual. In this latter instance, legal sanctions rather than religious sanctions of guilt and fear were employed, for excessive sin was considered a crime and punished by humans acting as legal agents rather than as emissaries of the gods (although in such cases law clearly embodied certain religious dicta). Many of the laws of even the Eskimo society, however, bore little relationship to religion. For instance, wife stealing and murder were wholly secular, for the legal rules concerning these crimes neither derived from religious dogmas nor overlapped with the jurisdiction of the supernatural (Hoebel 1954, 261). And so, while interrelated with religion, even a simple legal system like that of the traditional Eskimos revealed some autonomy and encompassed purely secular crimes. Legal and religious norms thus represented overlapping but separate mechanisms of control and integration in highly traditional hunting and gathering societies of the past.

As horticulture emerged in human history, the will of the supernatural became more likely to be codified into a series of religious postulates, often embellished by myths and beliefs about gods in a pantheon. These postulates constituted a kind of religious code of law, violation of which brought supernatural sanctions and, at times, secular enforcement by fellow cult members. In agrarian systems, religious values and beliefs were even more salient as cult structures became larger, better organized, more politically powerful, and increasingly wealthy. Indeed, literate scribes of the cults often wrote down bodies of "church law" and, at the same time, the laws of the emerging state as well. Church officials even may have assumed the role of "judges" in religious tribunals. When the state was weak or unstable, as was the case through the "Dark Ages" of western Europe, church law was often a more significant source of societal integration than secular law. Even today, in countries like Iran and other Islamic societies, bodies of religious law, often adjudicated by religiously oriented cleric-judges, regulate and coordinate much activity.

There are limits, however, to the capacity of religious law to control and coordinate actors in a population. As populations have grown and as economic development has ensued, secular problems of control and coordination have escalated. These problems have stimulated the initial development of new bodies of common-law precedents established by local courts and, later, the evolution of the state and the gradual imposition of a state-controlled legal system. During advanced agrarianism, considerable conflict and confusion in the legal system could exist as bodies of church law, local common law, and state-mandated law, as well as their corresponding agents of adjudication and enforcement, existed side by side.

At this point that problems of integration have arisen, stemming from rising rates of deviance, from new economic relations revolving around coordinating physical and human capital in new forms of exchange, and from new relations of individuals to the emerging state. Thus, selection has favored the segregation of religious law, tribunals, and dogmas from secular actions and interactions. This transition rarely has been smooth, because organized religion has been reluctant to give up its power. And yet, unless the emerging state-based polity can segregate religion institutionally from much secular activity, legal evolution has been thwarted. In the end, polity usually has prevailed; and religion has been given special privileges by polity in exchange for providing diffuse symbolic support to government. Often, this support has become part of the civic culture and, in secularized form, part of the legal postulates guiding the development of bodies of common law and civil law. For example, the basic constitutional postulates of the American constitution—freedom, equality, and individual rights—represent secular incarnations of Protestant religious ideals. Once this segregation of religion was under way, new bodies of common law and state-initiated civil law, expanded systems of secular courts, and state-controlled enforcement all could develop.

As they did so, they have fed back on religion. Typically, the "place" of religion, in terms of its rights and privileges, has been specified by laws and perhaps by broad legal postulates—thereby institutionalizing the segregation of organized religion. As this institutionalized segregation has occurred, law and polity have been better able to develop institutional autonomy and, in so doing, to provide a secular basis for control and coordination of the activities of individual and collective actors. Yet such segregation of religion and imposition of secular control often have been resisted. This trend was evident in the Islamic Revolution in Iran, and is becoming clear in the United States, where the "Christian Coalition" or "Religious Right" in America, is making efforts to inject highly charged religious value premises into secular law. Thus, even in a post-industrial society, an uneasy standoff often occurs between the legal system and organized religion.

EDUCATION AND LAW

As legal systems have developed, whether by common-law precedents or state-initiated civil law, the knowledge and expertise requirements for incumbents in the legal system have increased. In simple hunting-gathering and horticultural systems, this expertise was acquired through kin-based socialization. But as legal development of written and codified bodies of laws was initiated in advanced horticulture and agrarianism, the effects of education on the legal system became ever more pronounced. For with a large body of written laws forming a legal tradition, education of judges, lawyers, administrators, and legislators has occurred—initially and for some time in apprenticeships, but eventually, in higher-education structures. In applying the increasingly complex body of laws to specific cases or in establishing common-law precedents, judges must possess legal training if decisions and precedents are to display some degree of consistency with existing laws and social conditions. Lawyers advising clients and advocating their cases in courts also must have considerable knowledge of substantive and procedural law. And while this knowledge can be acquired informally and through experience, formal, professional training of lawyers becomes necessary if the legal system is to develop further. Also, just as the administrative bureaucracies of a developing economy have required expertise as a means to enhanced efficiency, so have the court and legislative bureaucracies. Finally, emergence of a consistent body of civil laws (enacted law) has been dependent not only on a large number of educated and professional legislators but also on extensive law schools and libraries which can guide and assist lawmakers. Thus, it is no coincidence that in virtually all advanced horticultural systems, such as China, or agrarian systems like India, Europe, and the Middle East, the rise of higher-educational systems was correlated with the development of law as a profession (Ben-David 1971), although much training in law up to post-industrial societies often came from apprenticeships as much as training in formal school structures. To illustrate further, the reemergence of civil law in France under Napoleon, and later in other parts of Europe, can be attributed partly to the well-developed French law schools and the legal scholars in them (Lloyd 1964).

An extensive legal profession must be in place for a legal system to become more fully developed and autonomous. Moreover, attached to higher education, professional schools preserving the legal tradition while socializing future incumbents of the legal system become increasingly advantageous, for several reasons:

1. The laws of a modern legal system are complex, requiring considerable expertise in applying them. Judges therefore must be well versed in many areas to adjudicate cases properly.
2. Lawyers must be capable of advising and pleading cases in accordance with a complex body of substantive and procedural laws as well as the proliferating body of administrative laws.
3. Legislators must have access to legal advice in law enactment in order to preserve some consistency among laws.
4. Court officials and administrators must have legal training to record, store, and implement court proceedings.
5. Officials in administrative agencies and tribunals must be capable of applying and adjudicating a host of administrative laws, because, without some degree of professional expertise in this vast legal network, bureaucratization would generate more chaos than it resolves.

Furthermore, systematization as well as centralization of laws, courts, legislatures, enforcement, and administrative agencies would be impossible without at least some formal training of participants in the legal system. Thus, without formal education, especially university-level education, and professionalization (in both the universities and occupational system), there would be few of the common legal conceptions, practices, precepts, or traditions underlying and supporting these trends typical of modern legal systems.

Aside from the effects of higher-level professional education on facilitating the internal development of legal systems, mass education at lower levels has far-reaching consequences for generating diffuse commitment to law among the general population. If a legal system is to be effective, people in a society must have some willingness to obey laws, adhere to court decisions, and accept law enforcement and enactment. Mass-educational socialization through instruction in history, lore, civics, and government generates commitment to the traditions and values reflected in laws as well as specific structures of the legal system (Almond and Verba 1963). Furthermore, formal education probably generates cognitive awareness of legal structures and processes, and such awareness helps maintain the legitimacy of the legal system by making it familiar and less intimidating to the members of a society. Yet it does not appear essential for a populace to be educated on the details of the legal system. This is illustrated by a study of public awareness of the U.S. Supreme Court in the 1960s (Murphy and Tannenhaus 1968), which showed that most people were ignorant of the functions of the Court at even the most elementary level, despite the fact that the 1960s marked one of the Court's most activist periods. Educated respondents were somewhat more likely to be aware of the Court's functions in American society, but only a little more so. Furthermore, only a minority of respondents in this study could name specific cases or landmark decisions of the Court—including such change-producing decisions as school integration, reapportionment, and criminals' civil liberties. Of those who could, most disagreed with the Court's decisions. Yet when asked about the legitimacy or right of the Court to do what it was doing (even if they were not sure just what that was), an overwhelming majority answered in the affirmative. Thus, ignorance of and even disagreement with a prominent and visible legal structure can be coupled with a commitment to that structure.

Educational socialization thus has perhaps its most significant impact on law not so much by communicating the details of enactments, decisions, and enforcement, but rather by indoctrinating citizens into the broader civic culture which bestows diffuse legitimacy on the legal system. Thus, in the United States, where educational emphasis is on civics and government and the underlying values and constitutional principles of government, a considerable amount of diffuse legitimacy is generated for the legal system. Much the same occurs in other industrial and post-industrial societies.

KINSHIP AND LAW

As the major agent of socialization, especially of basic values and beliefs, kinship always has important effects on law. This influence of socialization has varied from imparting commitments to the basic cultural values and beliefs that undergird the postulates and rules of the legal system to the more-specific nuances of the laws, adjudicating procedures, and enforcement processes. In general, the simpler the legal system, the more details of this system are imparted, whereas as legal systems become more complex, family socialization imparts commitments to the basic values of the civic culture that eventually becomes the guiding framework of law. Thus, among hunter-gatherers and simple horticulturalists, socialization in kinship also involved imparting knowledge of basic rules, procedures for their mediation, and perhaps enforcement, whereas among industrial and post-industrial populations, family socialization can impart only the basic cultural premises on which a very complex legal system rests. And for populations between these extremes, family socialization has shifted over time with more advanced horticulture and agrarianism to increasingly general premises and away from the specifics of law. If local or religious legal systems have remained viable, however, many of the details of local laws, courts, and enforcement have continued to be learned within kinship. For often, even as a state-initiated system of law has been expanding, local codes, tribunals, and enforcement activities have stayed intact for long periods of time during advanced horticulture, agrarianism, and, at times, during late industrialization when pockets of individuals have been left by polity to fend for themselves.

Historically, kinship also has had more than socialization effects on law in kin-based political and economic systems. Here, the rules of the legal system were often the same as kinship norms, or at least circumscribed by these norms: The courts were built from kin leaders and councils of kin elders; the representatives of litigants were fellow kin members; the enforcement of laws and decisions were by kindred; and even a court hierarchy of appeals was based on hierarchies of kin lineages and chiefdoms. Thus, in these horticultural societies, where unilineal descent shaped other kinship norms, the structure of the legal system paralleled the structure of kinship groupings created by descent, authority, residence, and activity norms.

As law began to differentiate from kinship, however, it abandoned the structural template provided by kinship (and religion as well) and, instead, began to follow the mandates of polity in the face of an increasing volume and variety of new problems of control and coordination. As law became structurally free of kinship, the importance of family socialization into the cultural underpinnings of the evolving legal system was to become increasingly significant for sustaining diffuse commitments to law.

CONCLUSION

Law is a unique institution because of its effects on integrating activities within and between other institutional complexes. For without law, the differentiation and development of other institutional systems will prove to be inviable (Bredemeier 1962; Parsons 1962). Yet, the emergence of law can also escalate integrative problems when it remains too closely embedded in centers of political power. Under these conditions, law becomes a tool for preserving the privilege of elites and, at the same time, a target for the anger and frustration of the masses. Although this elite bias in law never goes away—even in democratic post-industrial societies—law becomes a more balanced system, integrating diverse segments of the population and providing legitimacy to the polity.

The critical breakthrough for legal systems is their capacity to achieve autonomy from polity as well as from other institutions like religion and kinship and to develop their own internal systems for adjusting law to social conditions. Once this differentiation occurs, law historically has become a force for further differentiation and development of the institutional order. As long as law is tied to polity or enmeshed in kinship and religion, the scale and complexity of societies will be limited. But as law becomes autonomous and yet responsive to the problems of control and coordination that complexity generates, it becomes a driving force behind human evolution. Law enables the complexity of large post-industrial societies to remain viable, because it can intervene into each institutional complex—economy, kinship, polity, education, religion, and such emerging complexes as science, medicine, arts, and sports—and provide mechanisms for coordination and control.

Thus, the evolution of law has been primarily a response to the demands of its institutional environment. Conversely, if law has proven capable of meeting these demands, this environment can develop and differentiate further and, thereby, place new demands on law. The legal systems of most historical societies eventually have collapsed under this burden or been usurped by centers of coercive and administrative power. Hence, there is little reason to assume that current legal systems in post-industrial societies will not, in the long run, encounter a similar fate under the ever-escalating demands of law's institutional environment.

Chapter
12

Education

For most of human history, people have learned what they needed to know through participation in familial, economic, religious, political, and legal activities. They learned by watching or doing, and occasionally, by explicit instruction. Almost imperceptively and, indeed, often episodically, learning gradually changed, at least for some in society. Future shaman, magicians, priests and other religious practitioners became apprentices to those already practicing this vocation. Somewhat later came apprenticeships in trades, crafts, arts, and closed professions or guilds. Much of this training was embedded in kinship, although nonkin apprentices would often learn their trades in a family. Similarly, families involved in commerce would teach their children how to read, write, and calculate. And at times, low-prestige private schools would emerge to teach the basics of literacy to some of the masses seeking careers in commerce and government. Private tutors gave elites the cultural capital—languages, classics, literature, history, poetry, and other nonvocational knowledge bases—necessary to separate them from the masses and middle classes. And over time, private and elite preparatory schools began to house and train the children of elites. Eventually, true universities were to emerge—at first to train literate members of the middle classes in professions such as law and medicine, and later, to instruct elites in nonvocational fields of learning.

Still, most instruction occurred through apprenticeships, family instruction, and private tutoring, right up to the beginnings of the industrial era. Then education began to grow and to extend its influence to an ever-wider range of the population. During this explosion of instructional activity, the institution of education became clearly differentiated for the first time in humans' long-term evolutionary history. This sudden growth and differentiation of education is what we seek to explain in this and the next chapter.

ELEMENTS OF EDUCATION

The institution of education, as distinct from general socialization and learning, involves several basic elements: (1) a system of formalized instruction,

(2) an explicit curriculum, and (3) a pattern of ritualized passage. As education has become increasingly differentiated as a distinct institutional system, these three elements have become correspondingly more pronounced.

Formalized Instruction

Education involves two distinct status positions: teacher and student. The more explicit the distinction between teacher and student, and the more formally organized their interaction in terms of time and place of instruction, the more they are part of the institution of education. For most of human history, however, learning was not institutionalized in a distinct educational system. Among hunter-gatherers or simple horticulturalists, adults might have paused or set aside a time for formal instruction in handcrafts, ritual, or other activities. And on these occasions, the institution of education could be seen, but only as a fleeting activity buried in other institutional systems like kinship, economy, or religion. But with advanced horticulture and agrarianism, we see more-permanent instructor-student relations in apprenticeships for a wide variety of crafts, private tutelage of elites, religious instruction for future members of the priesthood, merchant family instruction in literacy and arithmetic, closed guilds requiring specific periods of instruction for professionals, and even private schools—ranging from places for acquiring literacy to universities imparting high culture or professional skills. Under these conditions, education has become more formalized, marking its first beginnings as an institutional system.

Explicit Curriculum

Education as an institution revolves around a curriculum, or subject matter that is to be taught by teachers to students. Again, for most of human history, the curriculum remained buried in the ongoing socialization of the young and the learning of adults in their daily lives. But as instruction became more explicit in apprenticeships, tutelage, guilds, families, and schools, the formalization of the teacher-student relationship also involved a more clearly stated and delimited subject matter—an emerging curriculum that could be trade skills, literacy, arithmetic, or languages and cultural markers of elites. As the curriculum of formalized instruction became more clearly defined, then, education was further differentiated as an institutional system.

Ritualized Passage

Throughout history, most formal instruction, even that revolving around a curriculum in schools, did not involve mandatory attendance, grades, examinations, or degrees (Collins 1977). Rather, students' observable proficiency in a skill was an indicator of their progress. Yet the beginnings of what eventually became the capstone to a fully differentiated educational system could be found when apprentices were declared practitioners, when guilds admitted their trainees to full membership, when student-priests became full-fledged priests, when low-status schools pronounced that a student could read, and at other points of passages that denoted progress through a curriculum. As education became institutionalized, these points of passage were ever more ritualized along several dimensions: (a) attendance at formalized instruction became more mandatory, (b) proficiency was more subject to grading and examinations, and (c) progress through the curriculum was denoted by standardized degrees or other markers of progress. The more ritualized is formal education along these dimensions, the more it is institutionalized.

In sum, then, the emergence of education as a distinctive institution revolves around formalized relations between teacher and student, explicit and delimited curricula, and ritualized passage through a curriculum. Until the beginnings of the nineteenth century, the vast mass of the population in human societies remained untouched by the institutionalized system of education. Indeed, it had been a recessive institutional form—often barely, or only episodically, distinguishable from activity in the more-developed economic, kin, and religious institutional systems. Thus, although education is now a prominent institutional form in most human societies, this visibility of education is very recent.

SELECTION PRESSURES FOR EDUCATION

Through the agrarian era, education tended to be either (1) practical and oriented to acquiring necessary economic skills through apprenticeships, low-status primary schools, and family socialization, or (2) nonvocational and concerned with acquiring cultural capital through private tutors, elite preparatory schools, and universities, in order to mark status differences among strata in the system of inequality (Collins 1977; Bourdieu 1984; Bourdieu and Passeron 1977). Education began to change when the developing state sought to use education to instill a civic culture legitimating its hold on power and to train bureaucrats. Surprisingly, economic changes associated with industrialization were less-important forces on education because most occupational skills could be acquired through apprenticeships and on-the-job training. Indeed, even today, some have argued that education has less to do with acquiring vocational skills than it does with marking social status and maintaining political loyalties.

Thus, the forces that have operated to expand education have emanated primarily from the state, the system of inequality, and only secondarily from the economy. These forces are, of course, intimately connected, since the polity, economy, and system of stratification have mutual effects on one another. As these mutually interconnected selection forces have played themselves out historically, and most particularly, in the industrial and post-industrial era, education has come to have a number of important effects on maintaining a viable society. Some of these are examined below.

Social Reproduction

As education has evolved as a formal system of instruction (in schools), imparting a particular curriculum, and establishing a highly ritualized passage through the system, it has had important effects on reproducing members who can participate in, and fit into, other institutional spheres. This reproduction occurs along economic, political, and cultural dimensions.

Economic Reproduction   The more developed an educational system, the greater is its effect on imparting trade skills, cognitive knowledge, interpersonal skills, and motivational dispositions appropriate for participation in the economy. Marxist-inspired approaches are most likely to emphasize that schools reflect the needs of a capitalist economy for pliant workers whose cognitive orientations, motivational dispositions, and interpersonal skills enable them to sustain capitalist social relations. These analyses emphasize one of two possible arguments. The first is a "correspondence" argument, that the structure of the school mirrors the nature of the workplace, in which emphasis is on obedience to rules, deference to authority, punctuality, and external evaluation (e.g., Gintis 1972; Bowles and Gintis 1976; Anyon 1980). The second is a "cultural" argument, that the school becomes an arena for ideological conflict, but one in which the dominant social class imposes its norms, values, beliefs, morality, goals and, thereby, "colonizes" the minds of the young so as to make them committed to reproducing economic relations (Carnoy and Levin 1985, 1976; Carnoy 1989; Giroux 1990a, 1990b, 1981). More-moderate approaches make the argument that schools respond to perceptions—by school administrators, policymakers in the state, teachers, and at times, parents—of what is required of human capital, providing the differential training for filling economic positions requiring different skills.

In a sense, all of these arguments are correct, to a degree. Education *does* reproduce economic relations through its effects on the motivational, interpersonal, trade, cognitive, and evaluational aspects of students' personalities. Whether this is "good" or "bad" is, in reality, an evaluation of the economic and educational systems—an evaluation that typically produces errors in analysis. Where these approaches also err is in their assumption that economic forces determine how education is structured. The beginnings of mass education occurred historically before full-scale industrialization, and hence, this economic change cannot have been the original cause of educational growth. More important, it appears, are political pressures—although, at times, efforts at expanding education to the masses have come from religion (as was the case with the Protestant Reformation, or more generally, when religion has interest in exposing the masses to religious texts).

Political Reproduction   Modern systems of education have been created by the polity as it has responded to various pressures. The state began to finance schools in the agrarian era in order to expand literacy among those who might become its bureaucratic functionaries, but such initiatives did not massify the educational systems. Rather, as states have sought to consolidate their symbolic base of power, they have supported schools to impart the "civic culture" (values, goals, beliefs, histories, mythologies, heroes) which is used to legitimate power (Ichilov 1990; Boli, Ramirez, and Meyer 1985; Ramirez and Boli, 1987; Anyon 1980). These efforts by polity revolve around imparting to individuals a conception of themselves as "citizens" who will contribute to the goals of the polity and, at the same time, who will enjoy as consumers the benefits of state actions (Ramirez and Boli 1987, 154). In so doing, the state has attempted to blend its symbolic and material incentives bases of power, thereby reproducing relations of power in the society.

Cultural Reproduction   Obviously, schools impart both the economic and political culture of society. In fact, much of the effect of economy and polity on the curricula and instructional system of the schools in a society is through cultural symbols that are blended both with the broader societal culture and the specific professional-bureaucratic culture of the school system itself (Gramsci 1972; Apple 1988, 1982a, 1982b, 1979, 1978; Giroux, 1990a, 1990b, 1981). Much of what schools teach is cultural—language, science, history, art, music, literature, civics, mathematics; thus, the schools are involved in reproducing the culture of a society. Although this culture is influenced disproportionately by the forces of production and power, culture also reflects the history of a population as well as its class, gender, and ethnic divisions, its institutional systems, and its other structuring forces (e.g., geography, population size, urban profile, etc.).

In fact, schools often become battlegrounds among representatives of different subcultures—political, ethnic, regional, class, gender, religious—who intensely debate pedagogy, curriculum, credentialing, and other features of the school structure and culture. Thus, depending on the forces being mobilized in the schools' environment, the schools at any given time impart ever shifting aspects of culture. Nonetheless, schools remain a principal source of cultural transmission in late agrarian, industrial, and post-industrial societies.

Cultural Storage

To reproduce culture, schools must first store this culture and then pass it on. When culture is unwritten, it cannot be highly complex, because of the limitations of human memory. As a consequence, formal education is less necessary as a mechanism of either storage or cultural reproduction. But, once a written language exists, the capacity to expand systems of symbols is dramatically escalated. As the production of culture expands, it no longer can be stored in the minds of people. Culture must now be assembled in texts, computer algorithms, files, and other compilations; and these compilations of symbols must, in turn, be stored in a way that they can be retrieved (Turner 1972). Though much storage and retrieval occur outside educational structures, education nonetheless becomes an important cultural warehouse. The collective knowledge of instructors, libraries, computer facilities, and research staffs houses much of a population's culture. Moreover, this culture is stored in ways that it can be retrieved, if desired or needed, and passed on to new generations via the social reproduction activities of the educational system.

Social Placement

Educational systems always have had effects on the placement of individuals in the broader social structure. Such placement operates at two different, though increasingly interrelated, levels: (1) membership in status groups, and (2) incumbency in occupational positions. In advanced horticultural and agrarian societies, low status primary schools that taught the rudiments of literacy, apprenticeships and guilds that gave individuals a craft or profession, and kin-based instruction that imparted the necessities for commerce were all involved in placing individuals in the larger occupational structure. The specific occupations of these nonelites became a master status for their membership in a status group—whether merchant, artisan, government scribe, or priest—that could be distinguished by life-style, demeanor, speech, and other forms of cultural capital. In contrast, the private tutors, preparatory schools, and scholastic tracks of universities were involved in sustaining the distinctiveness of elites without reference to a vocation. Thus, there was a clear separation between status-group membership based on occupation and income, on the nonelite side, and status-group membership based on acquired culture, on the elite side. Indeed, education in music, poetry, rhetoric, history, classics, literature, and other nonvocational pursuits, coupled with the demeanor styles that such nonvocational pursuits generated, became an important marker and gatekeeper of class divisions between elites and nonelites (Collins 1977).

Much of the early growth of educational systems came not so much from efforts to achieve a better vocation, but rather from a desire of nonelites to claim greater prestige because of their educational achievements. Often children of wealthy merchants were sent to school or were given private tutoring in a self-conscious effort to emulate the cultural styles of elites, whereas at other times education was used by less-affluent people to gain an increase in respectability (Collins 1977). In a few instances (as among the philosophes in eighteenth-century France), education has been used to mobilize new cultural symbols which challenged those of the elites. (Indeed, the teachings of the philosophes legitimated the French Revolution of 1789, while becoming the broad principles behind the American Constitution.)

Vestiges of this division between education for status group membership remain even in post-industrial societies. Examples include education in "prep schools," as well as Ivy League and other elite private colleges, in the United States; and "public" schools (really private schools), as well as Oxford and Cambridge Universities in the United Kingdom. But in the more recent history of education, the distinctions between education for entrance to status groups and occupations have become blurred. As middle and lower classes have sought "cultural capital" as a source of prestige and respectability, and as the state has expanded education at all levels, the same educational credentials affect both vocational placement in an occupation or profession and status-group membership. This crossover effect began slowly—for example, when top government officials in England are recruited from the ranks of elite school graduates, or when the law and business schools of Ivy League and other elite universities feed the upper echelons of corporate law and business. But once this connection between educational credentials and occupation is established for elites, then nonelites can begin to pressure the state to provide those same educational opportunities facilitating higher occupational and status-group memberships.

If the stratification system and its corresponding series of status groups have remained strong, then a "sponsored-mobility" pattern, where the young are sorted early into vocational or college-bound tracks and schools, will be most evident. Such a system gives enormous advantage to the children of elites, who have the resources to sponsor their performance in schools and examinations. In contrast, if strata and status groups are more fluid and flexible, then a "contest-mobility" system prevails, providing many more opportunities to greater varieties of young people to pursue higher education and delaying as long as possible the sorting of students into college-bound and vocational tracks. As we will see, there are always political pressures toward a "contest-mobility" system as individuals seek the credentials that afford access to better occupations and higher status-group affiliations. This connection between advancement in schools and occupation as well as status-group membership becomes increasingly visible as employers (initially, the state and educational system itself as an employer, but eventually economic employers as well) begin to use credentials as the main criterion for hiring.

As these placement effects of a growing educational system develop, the system itself becomes more ritualized in marking passages, since grades and test scores increasingly are used to determine how far students can go in school and, hence, where they will be placed as adults in society. As passages becomes ritualized, the possession of educational credentials becomes the primary resource of the young in highly competitive labor markets. And, as the labor market and credentialing activities of the educational system become ever more interdependent, the social-placement consequences of education become more pervasive and profound.

Conflict Management

The expansion of the educational system and the use of credentials issued by this system in labor markets have had profound effects on the management of conflicts emanating from the inequalities inherent in the stratification of a population. Much class and ethnic conflict is now transformed and transmuted into debates over access to the cultural capital and credentials offered by the educational system. Thus, access to schools rather than transformations in economic and political arrangements is more likely to become the salient issue when educational credentials, job placement, and status-group membership become associated. As this deflection of tension occurs, potentially more-serious conflicts are avoided, or at least mitigated when they come. In this deflection conflicts also become more ideological (Gramsci 1972; Apple 1988; Giroux 1990a, 1990b), focusing on inclusion of ethnic cultures and their histories, on special programs to help the culturally disadvantaged, on better pedagogy in order to reach effectively more diverse student populations, on the fairness of the testing system, on teacher cultural biases, and on a host of related issues that skirt around more basic class, gender, and ethnic inequalities.

It is these mitigating effects that bring polity into education. If the schools can be expanded and if their incumbents can come to believe that access to an education is more equally distributed, then those who do not perform well in the system can be stigmatized for their personal failings or limitations, while the broader patterns of societal stratification can escape criticism.

One does not need to view this process critically or cynically, because expansion of education does increase opportunities for mobility by nonelites—*if* the labor market is able to place credentialed graduates in positions corresponding to their educational attainment. Of course, when the educational system produces a surplus of credentials relative to jobs, then the conflict potential is escalated, although only if graduates blame the economy or polity. In fact, because of their inculcation into the economic and political culture, graduates frequently do not protest or mobilize for conflict; instead, they often blame themselves or migrate to countries with a more robust labor or human capital market. Thus, ironically, societies whose economies cannot absorb their overeducated graduates become exporters of educated labor to more developed societies, as has been the case, for example, with India (at least until its recent economic growth).

Social Transformation and Change

Educational systems are almost always viewed by the state as a vehicle for implementing social change. Indeed, developing societies in the process of industrialization expand the educational system not only in order to create "new citizens" but also to raise the skill level of human capital so as to stimulate further economic development. There is now a world-level ideology associating education and social progress (Ramirez and Boli 1987), an ideology that has encouraged the rapid expansion of educational systems in all parts of the world. This expansion has also been encouraged and financed by such transsocietal sources of funding as the World Bank, which propagates the ideology that economic growth and education go hand in hand and which also advocates a particular model of how education should be structured. As a consequence, there is a convergence in how schools are organized in the developing world.

Polity in fully industrial and post-industrial societies also uses the educational system to implement social changes. For example, as noted above, special programs in schools are often used to increase equality of opportunities for formerly disadvantaged groups. More indirectly, polity can fund "Big Science" in research universities in an effort to develop new knowledge that will be adopted in change-producing technologies.

Thus, because polity can control schools, and because schools are involved in the socialization of citizens and human capital as well as in the production of knowledge and symbol systems, the state views the schools as a vehicle for implementing policies. Other institutional systems—kinship, religion, and economy—are less-easily managed, or are managed at unpredictable costs and with uncertain outcomes, by state intervention. Therefore, the state is more likely to use an institutional system that it can control to generate social change.

At times, however, education is used to generate social change that is not sanctioned by the state. This more "subversive" use of education can occur in private schools (although these usually support the status quo because they are generally funded by elites and religion), in state-financed schools removed from administrative supervision, and in schools where democratic ideals of the broader society create a normative climate emphasizing "academic freedom." An instance of this latter pattern is found in American higher education, where classrooms often are used for political mobilization and ideological conversion of students against social inequalities and/or against supporters of the status quo (e.g., corporate America, government). If such transformative efforts actually threaten the state, however, use of the material base of power (cutting off funds, for example) and even the coercive base are likely to ensue.

Education is the last of the core institutions to differentiate in human history, and we are now in a position to define education as an institution, distinct from the learning that occurs through activities in other institutions. *Education is the systematic organization of formal student-teacher instruction, revolving around an explicit curriculum and involving ritualized student passage, which has consequences among the members of a population for social reproduction, cultural storage, social placement, conflict management, and social transformation.*

TYPES OF EDUCATIONAL SYSTEMS

Tables 12.1 and 12.2 illustrate the status of education as a recessive institution up to, and including, advanced horticulture. Up to this point, most education was informal and, if formal, confined to instruction for scribes, war-

Table 12.1   EDUCATION IN HUNTING AND GATHERING SOCIETIES

Instruction	Most learning comes by observation and practice; occasional instruction by adults within family and band units.
Curricula	Hunting and gathering technologies, religious beliefs and rituals, band-kinship history.
Ritualized Passage	Typically a ceremony marking general transition from childhood to adulthood.

Table 12.2   EDUCATION IN HORTICULTURAL SOCIETIES

	Simple	Advanced
Instruction	Most learning by observation and practice, yet frequent episodes of explicit tutelage of young by elder kin.	Same as simple system, except there are explicit patterns of apprenticeship in crafts. Also, a clear training period for religious practitioners, warriors, and scribes. Clear school structures evident. Tutors also prominent for political and religious elites.
Curricula	Technologies, religious beliefs and rituals, kinship history and traditions.	Same as simple system, except now various patterns of apprenticeship and school structures impart literacy, arithmetic, religion and history, military skills, religious rituals, crafts, and arts.
Ritualized Passage	Transition to adulthood, always marked. Transitions to age cohorts, to warrior status, and to new positions in kinship marked after a period of instruction.	Same as simple, except that clear ceremonies marking completion of apprenticeships and, at times, school-based education are now evident.

riors, religious practitioners, and craft apprentices. With agrarianism (see Table 12.3) came explicit school structures for training. This shift often constituted the beginnings of a hierarchical system from primary to university-level education, for a select few: those who would be government officials (often in church-sponsored schools, or private primary schools), religious practitioners (although their training frequently occurred in religious schools), military officials (again, often in separate military academies), commercial entrepreneurs (although much of this education was by tutors or kin members outside of schools), and members of emerging professions such as law and medicine. Elites were still taught by tutors; and if they entered private secondary- or university-level schools, instruction was nonvocational, emphasizing aesthetics over all other skills. Religion still exerted an enormous influence on education; in fact, if religion were as bureaucratized and as powerful as the state, religious instruction would dominate all levels of the educational hierarchy (Collins 1977). As states gained power relative to religion, however, education became more secular. Still, the vast majority of the population remained illiterate, learning what they required in family and apprenticeships.

Industrialization dramatically changes the educational process, not so much because of demands for new kinds of human capital (which can perform industrial activities without formal education in schools), but more because the state seeks to consolidate its symbolic base of power through instruction into a civic culture. However, the correlation between universal literacy and

Table 12.3   EDUCATION IN AGRARIAN SOCIETIES

	Simple	Advanced
Instruction	Apprentice-master teaching in all trades and crafts. Private tutors for children of elites. Some schools for imparting literacy. Military academies. Kin-based instruction for commerce. Religious instruction for priesthood. In a few cases, higher-education structures for emerging professions and nonvocational elite instruction.	Same as simple system, except primary schools more prevalent (both private and state-financed), secondary schools for elites, and beginnings of universities for professions (law and medicine) and for nonvocational training of elites. Private tutors for children of elites is still the dominant form of instruction, and for religious priesthood. A vast majority of population never goes to school and is illiterate. System of church schools for admittance to priesthood or positions in government bureaucracy can also exist.
Curricula	Depending on instructional venue, economic technology, literacy and counting, military skills, religious beliefs and rituals, commerce, and crafts are taught.	Same as simple system, but primary, secondary, and university-level schools will have a diverse curriculum revolving around writing, arithmetic, history, languages, geography, and classic literatures.
Ritualized Passage	Ceremonies marking completion of apprenticeships, military training, and religious training.	Same as simple system, except that some school structures will tend to have grades, examinations, and graduations.

schooling that exists for early industrializing societies, most of which are now post-industrial, has become translated into a worldwide ideological belief that economic development follows from expansion of the education system. Hence, currently industrializing societies now seek to develop an educational system for economic reasons—whether or not there is a real basis for this faith in education's power to generate economic development (independently of technology, physical capital, and entrepreneurship). As the state takes over education, it initiates a number of dynamic trends revolving around extending education to the mass population in the name of increasing equality of opportunities. As it does so, the entire educational process is bureaucratized; and as bureaucratization occurs, grading, examining, sorting, and tracking of students emerge as the means to "rationalize" assessment of students' performance. Credentials marking movement through the educational hierarchy increase in salience as determinants of changes in labor markets and status groups. The dynamism in these trends is examined below.

Table 12.4   EDUCATION IN MODERN SOCIETIES

	Industrial	Post-Industrial
Instruction	Learning now occurs in bureaucratized and hierarchical system of primary, secondary, and university-level schools (some private, but mostly state-sponsored). Nearly universal primary and secondary education. University-level instruction for a minority. Private tutors exist for specific skills but decline as a base for instruction.	Same as industrial, except university-level instruction reaches a larger proportion of secondary school graduates, but this is highly variable (ranging from 25% to 65% of secondary school graduates).
Curricula	Basic skills in reading, writing, and arithmetic. History and civil culture. Vocational skills in secondary schools for some; university-oriented curriculum in literature, mathematics, science, arts, history, and social sciences for others.	Same as industrial, with increased emphasis on science, computer-based skills.
Ritualized Passage	Extensive and incessant system of grades and examinations, punctuated by periodic graduations and movements to educational tracks.	Same as industrial, except that there are efforts to mitigate against the discriminatory effects on the disadvantaged of grading, testing, and tracking systems. Also, increased efforts to provide disadvantaged with cultural and financial resources necessary to compete in school hierarchy.

DYNAMIC TRENDS IN EDUCATION

Massification

By almost any measure—years of schooling, proportion of population completing primary and secondary schools—education now reaches a greater percentage of all the world's populations. In 1950, about 60 percent of the young enrolled in primary schools, a figure which is an average between the 100 percent figure for industrial and post-industrial societies and 44 percent for the poor, still-industrializing societies of the Third and Fourth World. By 1975, this average had climbed to 86 percent, and by the 1990s it was over 90 percent (Ramirez and Boli 1987, 152; UNESCO 1994). Secondary education (junior high school and high school) showed a similar increase, from about 11 percent in 1950, to 41 percent in 1975, and well over 50 percent in the 1990s. Even college-level education expanded—although more of this increase occurred among industrial and post-industrial societies than in those still industrializing. Indeed, in societies like the United States and Canada, over

60 percent of secondary school graduates at least begin college. (For most other post-industrial societies, the percentage is around 30–35 percent.)

This dramatic extension of education has occurred because of two basic factors: (1) the world-level ideology, uncritically accepted by most political regimes, that the education of human capital is a key to economic development, and (2) the desire of political regimes to socialize the young into a legitimating civic culture (Braungart and Braungart 1994). Thus, the massification of education is a political process, one initiated and financed by government (Meyer, Ramirez, and Soysal 1992).

This massification of education presents a number of dynamic dilemmas. First, it may not be possible for other elements of the economy (technology, physical capital, and entrepreneurship) to keep pace with the education of human capital, which may become overeducated for the economic positions available in the labor market. The result can be an educated, restive, and resentful subpopulation who blames the state for its plight. Second, education, especially higher education, tends to enhance critical thinking, in ways that can be directed at the polity, especially if the polity is perceived to violate the ideals of the civic culture learned in schools. These two dilemmas can become volatile when combined; and thus, massification of education rarely resolves either the economic or political problems of developing nations. Indeed, massification can aggravate them. In fact, authoritarian leaders in industrializing societies often have reduced funding for schools, fired teachers, and closed universities because these are seen as threats to traditional elites. In South America, for example, military regimes were most likely to work against massification—although as these regimes have given way to more-democratic forms of government, massification has resumed (Brint 1996; Hanson 1995; Levy 1986).

Equalization

Accompanying the massification of education is typically an ideology of equalization, in which the schools are to give all future citizen rights to achieve their aspirations in a fair and open process. Old patterns of ascription and inequality are now to be eliminated as performance in schools is to determine how one will fare in the labor market and, ultimately, in status-group membership. The problem with this ideology is that it never can be realized in practice, because: (a) students bring to schools varying advantages and disadvantages associated with family socialization and family resources, (b) schools themselves always vary in terms of the resources that they can provide students, and (c) older patterns of ascription (by gender, ethnicity, region, class) are not eliminated in schools.

This difficulty of realizing in practice what is preached in educational/political ideologies can be a volatile force in a society, because individuals' escalated hopes and aspirations must confront the reality of an uneven playing field. This confrontation can disproportionately escalate people's sense of deprivation in ways that may potentially lead them to be willing subjects in mobilizations against polity. Indeed, education can become yet another way of sustaining older patterns of inequality; for as educational credentials become tickets to entrance into occupations and status groups, those without the ticket become resentful. Such is especially likely when education was perceived by lower class- and status-group members as a way to become economically and socially mobile.

Evaluating, Sorting, and Tracking

All educational systems today engage in systematic processes of (1) evaluating performance of students (through grades, teacher assessments, and standardized examinations) and then (2) sorting students into different tracks of education, leading them into varying niches in the labor market. There is, however, a great deal of variability in how and when sorting and tracking occur.

In older societies with a long agrarian history, where secondary and university education were for the hereditary aristocracy and the upper bourgeoisie, with some sponsorship of exceptional lower-class students in secondary schools and universities (Turner 1960), evaluation, sorting, and tracking of students toward either vocational careers or university-level studies occur early. In societies with a less-entrenched aristocracy, whether because of its displacement through conflict or because of the newness of the society itself, testing and sorting come later in a student's career. Among post-industrial societies, Germany and the United States are at the extreme poles of these differences (Brint 1996). Germany tracks students into different schools early, whereas the United States does so very late; and even if American students are tracked into vocational programs, they can still enter a college or university. Other post-industrial societies, such as Japan, Sweden, France, Italy, Canada, and Australia fall between these poles, with most moving toward the American pole, although both Sweden and England remain like Germany in severely limiting college enrollments.

Less-developed societies send far fewer students to universities, primarily because of comparatively low secondary enrollments and because of the relative scarcity of universities. Sorting occurs early, sometimes by default as poorer students drop out of school after their primary education, and at other times as a result of examinations in which they are at a disadvantage when competing with sons and daughters of higher social classes.

Even in the most open systems—such as those of the United States, Canada, and the other English-speaking democracies outside of England—the grading, sorting, and tracking processes tend to follow class boundaries, because people of higher classes have more of the relevant cultural capital and financial resources to sponsor their children in school. Still, in most postmodern societies, there are efforts for compensatory education (special classes, scholarships, and other mechanisms for helping children from less-advantaged environments) but these still must overcome serious obstacles stemming from the lower cultural capital of parents and early socialization by family and peers.

Because educational credentials become increasingly critical to placement in an occupation and to gaining access into status groups, political pressures always exist for making the system more open and fair. But just how this political pressure changes tracking varies enormously. In Sweden, for example, these pressures led to intense efforts to find talented students from lower-class backgrounds early in their school careers and, then, to help them pursue a university-oriented secondary career. Nonetheless, the percentage of all students actually entering college still has remained rather low in Sweden. In England, the exam system was modified and pushed back in a student's career, and the "red brick" university system was expanded (that is, universities other than Oxford, Cambridge, and perhaps the London School of Economics). Nonetheless, the rates of college entrance still remain much lower than most other post-industrial societies. In the United States, the university and college systems were expanded dramatically with the creation of "land grant" universities from the 1860s onward and with the emergence of community colleges in the second half of this century. Furthermore, the testing and tracking systems were pushed back further in a student's career; and the consequences of tests and grades on a student's ability to enter college were less determinative (except for elite universities). In addition, government and universities in the United States established a wide variety of special loan, scholarship, and admission programs for students from disadvantaged backgrounds.

Credentialism and Credential Inflation

The demand to reduce the effects of early testing, sorting, and tracking on access to colleges and universities has had the ironic consequence of encouraging credentialism and credential inflation (Collins 1979; Dore 1976). Potential employers now give more credence to the credentials themselves and view them as accurate markers of ability. As a result, alternative ways of assessing workers' abilities are abandoned in favor of their educational credentials, as these are brought to a highly competitive job market. In turn, this credentialism has produced "standardized membership categories," such as high school graduate, college graduate, or post-graduate, which gloss over the wide variations in abilities and knowledge of individuals in these categories (Brint 1996). A more damaging effort has been to exclude from portions of labor markets those who do not have credentials that put them into a standardized category. The disadvantaged are most likely to lack credentials. Therefore, pressures by disadvantaged subpopulations to open access to credentials—which, in turn, helps to spawn credentialism—can backfire for those among the disadvantaged who fail to get these now-mandatory credentials.

Another ironic consequence of political pressures for access to credentials is credential inflation. If virtually all members of a post-industrial society belong to a standardized membership category like "high school graduate," and if credentialism diminishes efforts to assess the wide variations in knowledge and talent of people in this category, the credential loses its value in the labor market. This forces students to seek additional credentials, such as a "college degree," to distinguish themselves. If enough individuals get this new credential, however, it too loses value, forcing those who want to distinguish themselves in a labor market to seek even more educational credentials.

One effect of such credential inflation is that the disadvantaged are the least likely to have the resources to continue the pursuit of additional credentials. Another effect is the overproduction of credentials and standardized categories like "college graduate," with the result that workers must seek jobs that do not require the skills associated with such credentials. Indeed, as more and more credentialed individuals must take jobs formerly held by those with fewer credentials, the latter are pushed out of these jobs, thereby deflating their credentials further. Since these displaced individuals are likely to be from lower and disadvantaged classes, credential inflation hurts them more than those who have the resources to stay in the credentials race. Yet another effect of credential inflation is to raise pressures for the credentials to be defined as "entitlements," regardless of whether or not students have earned them. A high-school degree is now a virtual certainty for any student who stays in school in post-industrial societies; and the "grade inflation" in universities of many societies like the United States makes getting a college degree considerably easier than previously.

Bureaucratization

Massification of education inevitably generates bureaucracy as a means to coordinate and control a large-scale activity. Equalization of education also generates bureaucracy as a means to implement, administer, and monitor programs that further equality of opportunity. As the state initiates both massification and the ideology of equalization, it furthers bureaucratization of the educational system, since states always seek to create bureaucratic structures to consolidate power and to regulate their institutional environment.

This last force is perhaps the most significant, because when states have been centralized, they have extended their administrative base of power over other institutional spheres—especially those crucial to consolidating the other bases of power: symbolic, coercive, and material. Thus, when states have sought to impose a new civic culture, or revitalize an old one, they massify and bureaucratize the educational system. When they have needed committed military officers and mass conscript armies in order to expand their coercive base of power (as was the case in early eighteenth-century Japan, Denmark, and Prussia, or early twentieth-century Russia) they have massified and bureaucratized the school system (Collins 1977). When states have sought to provide material incentives as a base of power, they have often done so indirectly by providing educational opportunities that, in turn, will bring material payoffs to graduates.

Once bureaucratized, an educational system shifts towards grading, sorting, and tracking, because bureaucracies are record-keeping structures.

The goal is to rationalize instruction, keep records on performance, and promote on the basis of performance. And once this organizational form is imposed on educational systems, grades, tests, required sequences, set time periods, and certification become prominent. Historically, this change occurred in advanced agrarian societies, like China, and agrarian societies such as Japan and the Roman Empire, once the state bureaucratized the educational systems (Collins 1977), although not to the degree of contemporary societies because education was still oriented to elites. With industrialism and post-industrialism, however, the state massifies the system and, hence, extends the educational bureaucracy and the accompanying emphasis on grades, tests, sequences, and certification. With these as organizational tools, sorting and tracking are inevitable, despite emerging political pressures to provide equalities of opportunities through delaying or weakening the criteria (grades and examinations) used to sort and track students.

Centralization

Educational systems vary enormously in the degree of centralization of the bureaucracy at the national level. Highly centralized systems, such as those in post-industrial France, Sweden, Japan, and most industrializing societies, will vary in how much they each spend as a whole on education. But within a given society, per-student expenditures will tend to be equal across the entire student population. In contrast, highly decentralized systems—like that in the United States, where much financing and control is local—spend widely varying amounts on students. For example, affluent school districts in Texas spend as much as nine times more on students than poorer districts. Between these extremes are societies like Germany and Canada where education is centralized at regional levels (e.g., provinces, states); and in these systems, expenditures on students are approximately the same within regions but can vary across regions.

   Thus, the degree of centralization has important effects on the equality of expenditures for education. With the exception of the United States, where beliefs in "local control" of schools are intense, political pressures for equalizing expenditures on students and, presumably, equality of opportunities for students bring the state into financing schools. Once financing passes to the national level, so will administrative control over the "pursestrings." Centralization of educational systems is, therefore, a general tendency, unless powerful ideological pressures such as those revolving around ethnicity (as in the French-speaking Quebec province of Canada) or politics (such as power beliefs in "state rights" and "local control" in America) override efforts to pass financing and control of schools to the national government.

Professionalization

School bureaucracies are complicated by the fact that instructors define themselves as professionals who have a higher obligation, above and beyond the bureaucratic mandates of the schools. There is often a tension between the professionalism of instructors and the bureaucratic demands of the school system to process and promote students in standardized ways. This tension is complicated because the "clients" of this profession and the school bureaucracy are nonadults (at least up to the college or university level) who do not directly "purchase" a school's and a teacher's services and who are not readily able to evaluate the competence of the services received. Furthermore, these clients are usually not in a position to "take their business elsewhere." The end result is for the school bureaucracy to have a level of control over its clients that resembles a coercive bureaucracy, such as a prison, but this bureaucratic control is mitigated by and often in conflict with the professionalism of teachers. At the same time, teachers often are unionized, which makes them contracted workers pulled toward the imperatives of a union bureaucracy as much as a profession.

This mix of conflicts is further confounded by the size of teaching as a profession, or as a unionized group of workers. For example, teaching is by far the largest profession in America, with some 4.4 million members; and if college instructors are added, the profession comprises well over 5 million. As a large interest group, teachers can exert considerable political power in democratic societies. When teachers "strike," they disrupt other institutional systems such as the family (which must reorganize its scheduling) and the polity (which needs schools to push its political agendas). Yet despite this potential power, teachers rarely exert as much power as much smaller, high-prestige professions like medicine and law, or even as much as industrial unions. Part of the reason is that professionalism and the helplessness of their clients make teachers reluctant to strike as an industrial union would. Another part is that professional teachers' organizations are often not well organized as an effective lobby in national politics—although in some countries, such as the United States, teacher organizations have begun to exert an influence on national politics. Still, the potential for mass political influence by teachers exists; and if it were mobilized, it could disrupt the state's control of education.

Privatization

Through the agrarian era, virtually all schools were private; but as the state began to finance education, the proportion of private schools declined—even in societies like Spain and France with a long tradition of Catholic education. At the primary and secondary levels of education, societies rarely have over 10 percent of the student population in private schools. At the higher-education level, societies vary in their number of private colleges and universities. The United States has many, whereas Germany and most European societies have virtually none; England and Japan have a few (in England, the separate colleges of Oxford and Cambridge are private, but each of the universities as a whole is public); and in most developing nations, universities are almost exclusively public.

For most of the world, therefore, the historical trend has been toward government-financed and administered schools. Only in the United States does a large private sector of education exist; and it should not be surprising, therefore, that advocacy for creating open competition between public and private schools is intense (through such mechanisms as vouchers that parents would use to pay for their choice of schools, public or private). But only in societies with intense ideological commitment to local control of schools, or where religion is still a dominant force, will this long-term historical trend away from government-controlled schools be challenged.

CONCLUSION

Although it was the last of the institutions examined in this book to differentiate as a distinctive system, education is now at the center of the institutional order. In a sense, education has forced its way into this order, pushing on and assuming functions of other institutions. These institutions in the environment of education, thus, have had to adjust and adapt to the expansion of education—especially when this expansion has been backed by the state in its efforts to consolidate power. Even if schools become antiestablishment in their mission, they threaten the power of the state and bring state regulation into education.

Thus, the institutional environment of education presents an interesting set of dynamics. Education has been pushed by the state; and as systems of education have grown, other institutional systems all have had to accommodate education. Yet, these institutions also have exerted their own influence on the emergence, development, and operation of education. The evolution of education came late as an institutional system, and as a result, it developed within an already-differentiated institutional order. Despite its influence on changing this order, education also had to adapt to existing institutions, as we shall explore in the next chapter.

Chapter
13

Education in Institutional Context

*A*s education institutionalized, it had to do so in an environment of established institutions and existing patterns of societal stratification. The profile of education, thus, has been determined by pressures from its institutional environment and from forces of stratification. In particular, as we will come to appreciate, polity has had the greatest influence on education—especially as the polity has sought to consolidate power and to mitigate the potential for the mobilization of counterpower that always inheres in a system of inequality and stratification.

POLITY AND EDUCATION

Historically, when centers of power began to consolidate the administrative, symbolic, and coercive bases of this power, they took an interest in the educational system. The historical patterns have varied considerably, but there is one clear relationship: As the state has emerged and consolidated its administrative base of power through the creation and expansion of bureaucracy, it has begun to exert control over education and to use education to sustain not only the administrative bureaucracy but also the symbolic and coercive bases of power. The more bureaucratized the state became and the more it sought to regulate education, the more the system of education itself has taken on a bureaucratic form, emphasizing grades, examinations, promotions, and certification.

Randall Collins (1977) offers a number of interesting examples to illustrate the variations in this general pattern. For instance, beginning with the Han dynasty and particularly in the T'ang dynasty of China, (618–907 C.E.) the bureaucratic unification of China under the emperor led to the use of an examination system for promotion within, and for honor outside, the imperial bureaucracy. The examinations were given every few years, and the goal of the examinees was to pass initially the district exam, then the provincial exam, and finally the metropolitan exam. Only a small percentage were allowed to pass each exam, but those who did rose in the imperial bureaucracy and received growing honor and prestige. Such a system created a market for education and private tutelage, mostly of elites, because only they could afford the costs involved. The system proved very effective in controlling those elites who might form a counterbase of power. To take another example from the Tokugawa regime in Japan (1600–1850 C.E.), when a centralized bureaucratic state had succeeded in unifying a formerly fractured feudal system, the regime effectively neutralized the aristocracy by requiring them to spend time in court rituals and by making education of elites compulsory. Moreover, local lords were required to create schools for the samurai, the hereditary warrior class, with rank among the samurai corresponding to the length of time spent in school. Within the central bureaucracy, administrative decisions required elaborate and highly stylized forms of written requests, which could be learned only in schools. Another illustration of how the bureaucratized state begins to use education comes from the later periods of the Roman Empire (300–400 C.E.), when the state became more centralized and bureaucratized as it sought to mitigate the slow disintegration of the empire. During this period, the state increasingly was monitoring the schools, regulating their teachers and curriculum (although this process was cut short by the full collapse of the empire).

This effort to regulate schools, either directly or indirectly by creating markets for education, revolves around the bases of power:

a. Schools have been used to train literate bureaucrats of the state to sustain the administrative base of power.
b. Schools have been used to generate loyalty to the state in order to promote the symbolic base of power.
c. Schools have been employed to train a loyal military, or to occupy elites who might otherwise mobilize their own countercoercive forces, as a means for maintaining the central state's coercive base of power.
d. In more recent times, schools have organized in ways to make access to material well-being in labor markets dependent on credentials in order to maintain an effective manipulation of material incentives as a base of power.

Each of these uses of schools by the state is examined in the sections that follow.

Education and the Administrative Base of Power

Bureaucracy requires literacy and, hence, education. Religious bureaucrats—often fused with those of the state in agrarian systems—often were trained in schools created by religion or the religiously-oriented state. In medieval Europe between 1050 and 1300, for example, the church sought to consolidate political power by expanding the education of church bureaucrats; in the process, the university system emerged as a means for sorting those who would assume high ranks in the papal bureaucracy. This effort was to fail, but it underscores the interest by centers of power in regulating its incumbents through education. This is best illustrated in the seventeenth and eighteenth centuries by the rigidly bureaucratic Prussian state, which was one of the first states to create a compulsory elementary system of education and which used its universities to recruit state officials. Similarly, in France somewhat later, the state created military and engineering schools to bypass the aristocracy and church schools in recruiting administrators.

This pattern of using schools to recruit administrators continues to the present day. Schools are financed by the state and organized in hierarchical form, using grades, examinations, and certificates (diplomas) to label performance. On the bases of these labels, almost all of the incumbents in the state's administrative bureaucracy will be recruited for careers in "public service." Indeed, much as they did in schools, state bureaucrats will work their way up the organizational hierarchy on the basis of grades for job performance, civil service-type examinations, and certifications or classifications of rank in the bureaucratic hierarchy.

Education and the Symbolic Base of Power

The symbolic base of power is perhaps the most elusive, and for most of humans' evolutionary history, religious symbols have been used to legitimate power. Reliance on religion, however, makes polity dependent on a potential rival for power. Thus, as soon as polity has been able to break its dependence on religion, it has sought alternative symbols to legitimate itself. These symbols often carry religious content, but polity typically has attempted to create a more secular, civic culture that embodies traditional values and customs but also contains more specific beliefs about power, nationhood, and politics.

The first public school systems were, in essence, created to impart a civic culture and, thereby, to legitimate polity. With exceptions such as England, which delayed building state schools until the end of the nineteenth century, these systems were constructed in late agrarian societies before extensive industrialization. (However, many of these societies—Prussia, Germany, France, Russia, Denmark, and America, for example—were on the verge of industrializing.) The schools, though, were built more in response to political than economic demands as polity sought to unify diverse subpopulations into a common civic culture. Similarly, today polity in developing societies will massify education in an effort to generate commitment to a new civic culture; and if a society has experienced conflict (riots, revolution, coups d'état) in forging itself, polity will place great emphasis on education in creating "new citizens"—as was the case with Russia and China in their post-revolutionary periods, the United States after the Civil War, Vietnam after the defeat of the south, and many former military-dominated regimes of South America.

Education and the Coercive Base of Power

In agrarian societies, education often was employed by polity as a diversionary device to occupy those nobility who might mobilize counterpower. Thus, for example, in Tokugawa Japan, the long-term education of the samurai and the requirements for high-ranking nobility to stay in educational programs until their mid-thirties were effective in diverting the nobility's attention.

At other times, education has been used by polity to train its military force. The first state-sponsored public schools were created in the early eighteenth century by Denmark and Prussia, followed by Japan in the later part of the century, as these societies sought to create mass conscript armies (Collins 1977). Much of this education focused on the political culture, making students receptive to their conscription into the military. Long before recruitment of mass armies, polity often had created military academies for training officers of the coercive force. Indeed, nonreligious, state-sponsored education first emerged in most advanced horticultural and agrarian societies as a way to train those who would direct the state's coercive base of power. The descendants of these academies still exist in industrial societies; West Point and Annapolis are well-known examples in the United States, and similar academies can be found in most developing societies.

As the state has grown, the training of diverse arms of the coercive branch of government has also grown and has differentiated into specialized academies and colleges for all kinds and levels of coercive activity. These range from national military academies, through specialized war colleges and post-graduate training in all aspects of coercion, to regional and local police training facilities. In the United States, these specialized schools are often accompanied by military and police tracks within colleges and universities.

Education and the Manipulation of Material Incentives as a Base of Power

The polity always seeks to manipulate material incentives in ways that encourage conformity to its directives. Government historically has engaged in manipulation through taxation, budget expenditures, and subsidy programs; but sponsorship of education has become an indirect means of manipulating material incentives. By financing public school systems and, moreover, by offering financial assistance (e.g., scholarships, loan programs) for those continuing their education beyond secondary school, polity can manipulate the material aspirations of the public. In so doing, it also symbolically manipulates the population in ways that support political regimes (e.g., "work hard in school and you can have a better life" in the society controlled by the polity).

Indeed, polity can have a vested interest in credentialism, and even credential inflation, because it keeps students in schools where they are exposed to the civic culture legitimating the polity and because it keeps the younger generation, who are the most likely to be restive, occupied in pursuit of careers in the existing system (rather than some alternative). Contemporary governments thus actively push the ideology of education, arguing that the society as a whole, as well as its individual members, should seek education for their material betterment.

This kind of symbolic manipulation works as an effective material incentive as long as labor markets (a) use educational credentials to hire and promote workers and (b) can absorb the graduates of school systems and give them jobs roughly corresponding to their educational credentials. If these two conditions are met, the educational system becomes an important mechanism for manipulating material incentives. Conversely, when these conditions are not met, polity will have created an educated, critical, and potentially restive subpopulation of unemployed or underemployed citizens who may call the legitimacy of government into question.

Education is also effective as a form of material manipulation because it places the burden for success or failure on the individual, thereby mitigating individuals' tendencies to blame government for their misfortunes in life. If education is defined as "the key to success" and if polity makes it "equally available to all," then failure to receive material benefits by the deprived sectors of the society (who are always at a disadvantage when competing in schools and who drop out early in the credentials race) becomes defined as "their own fault" rather than as the product of a system that denies the deprived access to material well-being. At the very least, some of the sting of failure is deflected and displaced from the political system to the individual when the polity has successfully propagated the perception (almost always inaccurate) of open access to the schools that will provide for material success.

In sum, then, education and the consolidation of power in the state always have been linked. As the state bureaucratizes and seeks literate incumbents, as it trains a military, as it searches for nonreligious symbols of legitimation, and as it provides material incentives indirectly through credentialism and labor markets, state sponsorship and control of education grow. At first, this sponsorship is limited—often involving little more than creating a market for the educated. But as the state expands in late agrarianism and early industrialism, it not only finances the system but seeks to control what is taught. In fact, education becomes one of the critical tools by which states maintain power.

RELIGION AND EDUCATION

Training of priests was initially an apprentice-form of education, but as the organization of cult structures became bureaucratized with advanced horticulture and agrarianism, more-formal training in religiously-oriented schools, academies, seminaries, monasteries, and similar units ensued. For as religious values and codes became written, literacy among priests was required; and as bureaucratic hierarchies for organizing worship emerged, literate bureaucrats were necessary. These pressures for the education of those in the religious bureaucracy were particularly intense when the religious and political bureaucracies overlapped. For example, Collins (1977) notes that when the Maurya regime (300–200 B.C.E.) conquered India and sought to displace the caste system with Buddhism, it relied on the monasteries to train literate Buddhist monks as administrators. A more successful Buddhist-based bureaucracy endured in Tibet in the seventh century C.E., in which the monasteries held most of the property, engaged in most of the commerce, mobilized much of the military, and provided all of the educated administrators of government. In this theocracy, the high lamas undertook a long period of education in the monasteries before assuming their positions and pursuing their careers in the political-religious bureaucracy. As noted earlier, other examples come from medieval Europe between 1050 and 1300 when the papal bureaucracy expanded, creating a market for university-educated bureaucrats who held degrees in theology and canon law.

Thus, many of the first signs of distinctive institution of education came from efforts to organize religion bureaucratically, often in combination with a desire by religious elites to exert political power. In the end, with exceptions like medieval Tibet or present-day Iran, the state would win out in this contest and use education to consolidate its more secular bases of power. Still, religion often has created parallel systems of education. The Catholic system of primary, secondary, and university-level schools is the most prominent example of a parallel system that enrolls significant numbers of students in those societies where Catholicism is a prominent religious force— the United States, Spain, Italy, France, the Netherlands, Latin America, and parts of Africa.

In addition to constructing parallel systems of education, religion also engages in short-term religious training as a supplement to the regular educational system. "Sunday school" is the best example of this approach, although such education can extend to several days a week and to school and vacation periods. These "schools" are, however, narrowly focused on indoctrination into religious values, codes, and cosmologies, although some engage in indoctrination into broader social issues. For example, Catholic "Sunday school" in Poland before the collapse of the Soviet empire often focused on secular social and political issues. A Sunday school in many fundamentalist Christian cults in America is decidedly activist on social and political issues, such as abortion, "family values," and other moral issues that frame the political agenda of the "Christian Coalition" in the United States.

For most of the nineteenth and twentieth centuries, religion has been involved in the initial education of those in the less-developed world. The "missionary school" often appeared long before state-run schools reached the rural populations of the undeveloped and developing countries of the Third and Fourth Worlds. These schools often sought to mix religious indoctrination, western culture, and basic skills. As states in these societies have consolidated power, however, they often have discontinued this form of education—or, at the very least, restricted it to outlying populations. Yet, in some of those societies where a missionary school system was in place, the system still exists as a parallel system to that run by the state.

In the end, however, religious education is rather limited in all societies when compared to the vast public systems financed by the state. Even in societies with parallel religious schools, the percentage of students in these schools rarely exceeds 10 percent of the total student population. Moreover, the state exerts some control over this parallel system in accreditation rules, which require certain topics be taught to a particular standard established by the state. Thus, while religion is still very much involved in education, its activities are secondary to those of the state.

ECONOMY AND EDUCATION

For most of human history, the skills necessary for economic activity were learned through informal apprenticeships with parents or other relatives. With advanced horticulture, more-complex skills in crafts and arts, or special skills like shaman and priest, could be learned in more formal and, at times, secret apprenticeships. Even very advanced skills in agrarian systems—such as law, medicine, architecture and engineering—were often acquired in apprenticeships. Indeed, the skilled artisans who produced the first machines to be used in the Industrial Revolution had never gone to a school. Thus, right up to, and even into, industrialization, most crafts were learned outside of formal schooling; and as is illustrated by England as it went into full-scale industrialization, the level of education among the masses of industrial workers was very low. Industrialism did not require skills beyond those that had been acquired in the agrarian era; indeed, it often demanded lower skill levels.

The expansion of education, therefore, was stimulated less by economic demands than by political pressures to consolidate power (and at times by religion). Yet once education was extended to larger masses, the economy did begin to exert some influence on its organization. Initially, it helped to have literate workers in the emerging factory system, who could read plans and directions. Also, as the factory system expanded, workers needed a whole host of personality attributes, such as interpersonal styles of specificity and neutrality, which were more efficiently acquired in formal education structures. Furthermore, since work was now performed in factories, working adults were away from home, with the result that their children could no longer learn work skills by parental tutelage (Clark 1962). In this situation children, often left the home and mastered in schools those minimal work skills necessary for their participation in the economy. With further expansion of the factory system and the resulting increase in economic production, new kinds of administrative, distributive, and service roles became more prominent. Frequently, these roles were organized bureaucratically; many involved professional training; and most required not only literacy but also specialized and often high-level expertise in a wide variety of areas. The emergence of these types of positions was both dependent on, and perhaps an impetus to, the expansion of higher-education structures. For only in undergraduate, graduate, and professional schools could some of the expertise needed to play these new economic roles be acquired.

Economic conditions requiring expertise not only stimulated the expansion of higher education during industrialization, they also resulted in its secularization when dominated by religious interests. Furthermore, the elitist and aristocratic profile of traditional education became altered toward more pragmatic and vocational concerns and increasingly away from maintenance of traditional status groups. Yet, such secularization was almost always troublesome. For example, the emergence of more vocationally oriented universities during the industrialization of Europe and the United States was not automatic, for professional and vocational training were included in the curriculum only as a last resort. The University of Berlin in the nineteenth century was foremost a scholarly structure, with professional and "official classes" only a secondary concern. The modern British university as a professional school began with the foundation of the University of London (Halsey 1967), but professional training was still largely a twentieth-century occurrence. Even to this day, the less-vocational and more-elitist Cambridge and Oxford dominate the British higher-education system. In the United States, the Morrill Act, creating land-grant colleges, failed to integrate completely education with the economy; and even today at the undergraduate level, professional and vocational training are still resisted in favor of the liberal arts. More-technical training has been added to the curriculum not by revision of the undergraduate curricula but by the extension of formal education into graduate school. Societies currently undergoing industrialization usually fare somewhat better in this process, since there is less likely to be a long genteel or religious tradition dominating higher education.

Aside from shifting requirements for human capital, the technological demands of industrializing economies also can stimulate the expansion of higher education. Industrialization relies on the constant infusion of technology; and societies that are to keep pace with this demand often expand research and development facilities in higher education. For example, the graduate lab assistant, researcher, researcher-teacher, and researcher-consultant have become prevalent roles in higher education as the technological requisites of an industrializing economy have become built into the curriculum and research programs of colleges and universities.

These pressures on education in industrial economies become more intensified as the economy moves toward a post-industrial stage of development, because positions in the economy become service-oriented. Those requiring high levels of professional or technical expertise stimulate expansion of higher education, particularly professional education. But many of the service positions in post-industrial societies do not require great skill or education. Nevertheless, because of credentialism and credential inflation, both employers and potential employers perceive that even routine service jobs require educational credentials. As these perceptions spread and, indeed, are propagated by polity as an ideology, public pressures to equalize opportunities to education (especially college-oriented tracks in secondary schools and university admissions) intensify—often independently of any realistic demands from the service sector of the economy.

Thus, there is no doubt that industrial and particularly post-industrial economies create demands for educated human capital, especially in service-oriented, high-skill, technical, and profession slots. Yet much work in post-industrial economies is routine and, if anything, unskilled. However, because of the competition in the labor market, coupled with polity's need to massify and equalize educational opportunities, the educational system expands to provide more skills to greater numbers of individuals. Secondary-education systems tend to become somewhat more open to those segments of the population previously excluded (by early examinations), and the higher education system in at least some societies also tends to become more open to a larger portion of the student population.

LAW AND EDUCATION

As a late-emerging institutional system, education confronts problems of becoming integrated with previously differentiated institutions—economy, kinship, religion, and polity. Some of these integrative problems are addressed by the legal system as conflicts periodically emerge. One potential conflict between kinship and polity comes when the polity massifies public schools and requires, through compulsory-education laws, that all children attend school (up to a specified age). This conflict is most acute in developing societies, where children's labor in kinship is lost to schools. But in the end, the polity usually prevails if it has the resources to make education available to all its citizens and to enforce truancy laws.

Another point of conflict is between polity and religion, especially as polity has expanded the public education system and has imposed a state-mandated curriculum that is sustained by laws, court decisions, and threats of coercion. Except in theocratic states like Iran, where there is no conflict, the state usually prevails, forcing church schools to meet curricular requirements specified by laws. Still, there is always a potential conflict between the secular orientation of the state and the more sacred concerns of the church; and this point of conflict is often adjudicated in courts. For example, in the United States, the issue of public-school prayer, sex education, and the teaching of evolution continue to be debated in the legislative arena and to be challenged in courts. The legal system thus keeps this conflict from erupting into more-intense forms of disruption.

As education is perceived to be the key to economic success, yet another point of conflict is between those who are advantaged and disadvantaged in the larger stratification system. Because of their cultural capital and financial resources, the affluent and wealthy are able to perform better in schools than the poor; and because schools increasingly become the arbitrators of life chances, many class and ethnic conflicts are fought over gaining access to educational opportunities. The legal system has been crucial in mitigating the severity of this conflict by enacting legislation, adjudicating grievances in courts, and enforcing laws and court decisions that have sought to open opportunities and to reduce the discrimination—the deliberate and blatant as well as the subtle and inadvertent—that inevitably come when the disadvantaged must compete with the affluent in the educational system. In the United States, for example, laws about school integration, bilingual education, use of intelligence tests, premature tracking, and biased college-admissions policies have sought to reduce the disadvantages of poor minorities. But this battle is rarely resolved, because ultimately it concerns which sectors of a society are to gain access via the marketability of educational credentials to valued resources—jobs, income, prestige, and status-group membership.

Thus, as education becomes an important mechanism by which polity consolidates power vis-à-vis other institutional systems, and as education becomes a significant arbitrator of life chances, it potentially comes into conflict with other institutions or it becomes an arena of conflict over inequality. In both cases, law is critical to reducing the intensity of this conflict.

KINSHIP AND EDUCATION

As kinship has lost some of its socialization and social-placement functions to education, a potential conflict emerges—one that is usually resolved by political action and legal system response. And by mature industrialism and post-industrialism, the kinship system has accommodated itself fully to the reality that it must send the young to school and that the school will assume socialization and social-placement functions formerly under the control of kinship. Still, the conflict can persist—especially in a society like the United States, where "local control" of schools is both an ideology and, for most school districts, a fiscal reality. Here, the curricula, teaching methods, and organization of the school can come under scrutiny by family members who, through local groups such as Parent Teacher Associations or advocacy groups like the Christian Coalition, can exert pressure on the school bureaucracy. In most societies, where the state's control of education is more centralized, this conflict between the needs and interests of family and the curriculum of the schools rarely arises. However, in the United States, the tension between what adult family members think should happen in schools and what the professionalized teachers and bureaucratized administrators believe should occur can be intense, often erupting into local political battles. Indeed, some parents have gone so far as to pull their children out of school in "home schooling" programs, often for religious reasons but also for other ideological disagreements with the school system. Yet the United States is the exception in this capacity for kinship to politicize the schools.

More universal is the effect of kinship on the resources that students take to the school classroom. Since family socialization precedes school socialization and continues through secondary school, students' performance in schools and, hence, the credentials that they will ultimately receive are greatly circumscribed by the kinship system. The resources of kindred—financial, cultural, and social—also will have a profound effect on how well their children perform in the school bureaucracy; and in general, this effect is positively related to the parents' social-class position. Because of this relation, schools tend to operate in ways sustaining the social-class position of family members across generations, although this impact can be greatly mitigated by political pressures from disadvantaged sectors of the population to increase opportunities for children from lower-class backgrounds. But, as noted earlier, the ironic effect of increasing the number of formerly excluded pupils who possess secondary and college credentials is to decrease the value of these credentials and, thereby, to force individuals to go further in the credentials race—a race that becomes ever more burdensome on those who lack the financial resources to persevere.

CONCLUSION

As the last institution to emerge and differentiate, education has had to accommodate itself to an existing institutional environment. It has taken functions away from kinship; it has had to become separated from its religious origins; it has been used to consolidate political power; and it has become increasingly regulated by the legal system.

Current ideologies see education as the key to economic prosperity. But as we have seen, education as a distinctive institutional system historically has been more involved with religion, status-group membership and stratification, and most importantly, the consolidation of political power. Even today in both the developing and post-industrial worlds, the ideology of education continues to emphasize the relation between economic and educational processes. Yet much of this relationship is somewhat illusory, because a great deal of the demand for education comes not so much from needs for precise types of skills in the economy but from credentialism and credential inflation.

Credentialism and credential inflation result from the ideology of education and demands by lower social classes for access to what is perceived to be the principal arbitrator of life chances. Thus, just as when elite status groups sought to differentiate themselves from nonelites, education is very much involved in societal stratification. As such, it will continue to be an arena of conflict.

Chapter
14

Fundamental Interchanges in the Institutional Order

THE EVOLUTION OF COMPLEXITY

There was little need for an institutional order among hunting and gathering populations; the requirements of hunter-gatherers could be met easily by small bands of nuclear families wandering in search of resources. Institutional activity was, in essence, folded into kinship, where it could typically be performed without undue strain on the time and energy of band members. When populations became sedentary, however, they also began to grow; and with this growth came new selection pressures for more-elaborate social structures. At this point in humans' long evolutionary history, distinctive institutions began to become visible inside and outside of kinship. Most institutional activity was performed within the elaborated kinship system of horticulturalists, because creating a more complex kinship system to house and organize economic, political, religious, legal, and educational activity was the easiest way to respond to selection pressures for structures that could support and sustain a larger population.

Although kinship provided much of the organizational setting for other institutions among hunter-gatherers and early horticulturalists, economic activity within kin structures was to become the driving force of human evolution and institutional differentiation. For ultimately, the capacity to support the differentiation and elaboration of social institutions is dependent on gathering, production, and distribution. At first, nuclear units in bands could serve this purpose. Later, among horticulturalists, more complex kin units connected by a descent rule could coordinate gardening activity and the distribution of outputs. But eventually, new and differentiated economic structures—especially nonkin corporate units and markets—began to develop with advanced horticulture and agrarianism. As this development occurred, the economy was freed from the restrictions of kinship, which by its nature, is a conservative institution. Yet for thousands of years, human populations could not get past the barriers imposed by agrarianism. By fits and starts, new technologies, new forms of physical capital, new skills among human capital, new entrepreneurial mechanisms, and new systems of property were slowly emerging, to be sure. Nonetheless, the vast inequalities in agrarian systems made them unstable. Societies would develop to a point of potential breakthrough to a new form of economic organization, but in the end, they would collapse back under the pressures of internal conflict and fiscal crises. Even evolving market structures, which by their very nature are highly dynamic, could not make the breakthrough to a new economic form. When this breakthrough finally came in western Europe, it forced all institutional systems to adapt to these changes, accelerating the process of institutional differentiation.

Along with economic activity within kinship, religion was one of humans' first institutional systems. Although not all hunter-gatherer populations had strong beliefs about the sacred and supernatural or structures organizing rituals directed at supernatural forces, most did—at least in some incipient form. By the time human populations settled down, religious activity was prominent in these sedentary societies. Much of this religious activity was conducted within kinship structures, but separate religious practitioners were also evident, even among hunter-gatherers and always among horticulturalists. Religion was thus beginning to differentiate from kinship early in humans' long evolutionary history. And as it did so through horticulture and agrarianism, it increased in complexity, elaborating the cosmology of supernatural beings and forces and creating ever-larger and more-elaborate temples to house leaders of cult rituals. Then, with advancing agrarianism, a sudden simplification of religion began. The cosmology became more simplified, lay persons could participate more in religious rituals, hope for a life hereafter among the gods themselves became a possibility, and cult structures became organized for proselytizing new converts. These new religions spread over the world and are still with us today as the dominant religions, although older cult structures also exist alongside the descendants of these agrarian religions.

As religion differentiated, however, it had to accommodate the expanding secular economy and the emergence of a distinct system of political power. The struggle with centers of secular power was long, typifying advanced horticulture and agrarian systems. But in the end, polity has generally been able to segregate—at least to a degree—the sacred concerns of religion. Yet even in the more modern world, this segregation is often overcome as religious movements exert political influence or, as in parts of the Islamic world, take the reins of power. Thus, the long-term evolutionary trend was for religion to elaborate and gain power through the agrarian era, only to be pushed from the institutional order by secularizing forces in market-driven economies and by pressures mobilizing state power. Religion nonetheless has persisted as a dynamic institution, even in the most advanced post-industrial societies.

With expanded economic production, coupled with a growing population, selection favored the development of the polity. Concentrations of power were required to coordinate and regulate the larger social mass. Those populations that could not consolidate and concentrate power were selected out, falling apart from within or being conquered from without. At first, polity was housed in the elaborate kinship system of horticulturalists; but with agrarianism and even advanced horticulture, a distinctive state system emerged, organized around an administrative bureaucracy and backed up by the mobilization of coercive power. Religion was at first the major source of legitimation for these new centers of power; but over time, law and a broader civic culture became an even more-significant source of legitimation, except in the few remaining theocracies. With concentrations of power, inequality increased dramatically as those with power extracted the resources of others. Power thus created enormous tension within human societies. Moreover, it was used to conquer other societies. With polity, then, came not just the capacity to coordinate and regulate, but also the ability to exploit and destroy. Over time with industrial and post-industrial production, the democracies of the early industrializing societies have been used (and often imposed) as a template in many of the late industrializing societies, although this path to democratization is hardly smooth or clear. But there are powerful economic forces, especially free markets and information systems operating at a world-system level, that may force liberalization of power toward more democratic forms.

Law was, much like other institutions, buried within kinship during the hunting and gathering as well as horticultural eras. But early on, even among hunter-gatherers, it is possible to see rules that were applied to problematic situations and that were enforced, if only by public opinion and threats of sanctioned revenge. These rules and their application represented the first signs of legal-system differentiation from kinship. As problems of coordination and control escalated with population growth and increased production, selection pressures mounted for a system of rules, adjudicative procedures, and enforcement capacities to manage these problems. As polity and religion evolved into more-complex forms, law was typically affiliated with both, and only when polity became dominant over religion did law become clearly differentiated. Even then, however, law often was used as a tool by the powerful to sustain their privilege. When law could become more autonomous from polity, separating its adjudicative functions from centers of power and placing legislative and coercive functions under the review of courts, it could facilitate rapid differentiation of other institutional systems. Once a relatively autonomous legal system was in place, new rules and adjudicative procedures could respond to, as well as facilitate, institutional differentiation, elaboration, and coordination.

Among the institutions examined in this book, education was the last to differentiate. For most of human history, education was performed in kinship and, if it existed as a separate structure, it was confined mostly to elites. Only slowly did schools imparting secular content begin to reach the masses, although early religious movements such as the Protestant Reformation accelerated the development of education. Only well into industrialization did polity create a national school system to promote indoctrination into a civic culture, to impart trade and interpersonal skills to human capital, and to develop and disseminate new technologies. Today, political leaders in industrializing societies often view education as the key to economic development and political stability, since it performs such critical functions for political legitimation and for developing human capital. As education has differentiated and elaborated, many of the socialization and social-placement functions from kinship have been assumed by schools; and it has come to have increasingly far-reaching consequences for the economy (as a source of human capital and technology) and polity (as a source of political legitimation).

In sum, then, the long-term evolutionary history of humans has revolved around the differentiation of distinctive institutions from kinship—economy, polity, religion, law, and education. Other institutions such as medicine and science are still in the process of differentiating, although it could be argued that they are now fully differentiated systems of the institutional order. The differentiation of institutional subsystems of this order presents problems of how to integrate these discrete subsystems. That is, how do the various institutions that have become distinctive systems fit together? Over the long course of evolution, the relations among the systems of the institutional order have changed somewhat, as each new institution became differentiated and as some institutions, such as economy and polity, have become more dominant. Indeed, we have tried to document these shifting patterns of interrelations among institutions during societal evolution. However, beneath these shifting patterns of relationships are certain fundamental relations among institutional subsystems. As a way to close this analysis of the institutional order, we should examine these more-fundamental and generic patterns of interconnection among institutions.

KEY DYNAMICS AMONG SOCIAL INSTITUTIONS

In societies where the institutional order is fully differentiated, it becomes possible to see the basic nature of the connections among the separate institutions comprising this order. As long as institutions were fused with kinship or overlapping in their structure, the nature of the interchanges among them was obscured. But with some degree of separation in their structure and functions for society, their consequences for one another become more readily apparent. These consequences constitute interchanges, in the sense that each institution provides for the others certain resources on which their operation depends and, conversely, receives from these other institutions resources that shape its workings. Table 14.1, on pages 278 and 279 summarizes these interchanges. In the sections that follow, we discuss each of the interchanges summarized in Table 14.1. It may be useful to refer periodically to the table in order to keep in broader perspective the complex web of interconnections among institutions.

Economy and Polity

For much of human history, societies had economies but no polity. The consolidation and concentration of power were neither possible nor necessary among small bands of hunter-gatherers. But as problems of coordination and control escalated, selection favored the emergence of the polity, or government. From this point in human societal development, the relationship between economy and polity has been fundamental to the viability of a society. What, then, is the basic relationship between polity and economy?

At the most generic level, this relationship revolves around physical capital. A political system cannot become complex without a stable and sufficient economic surplus to support political leaders. Thus, the productivity of the economy determines whether or not a polity can exist and just how elaborate it can become. Without forms of liquid capital to finance political functionaries and to enforce decisions of leaders, a political system remains merged with kinship. At times, Big Man systems can develop among settled hunter-gatherers, but their leaders always confront the problem of extracting surplus and then redistributing it in ways that maintain their prestige. And, when the use of coercive force becomes necessary, they often must call upon their kindred and related allies. Thus, even Big Man systems are not wholly differentiated from kinship. Nor are they particularly stable, because, in a sense, they are premature: The economy has not developed to the extent that it can support and sustain a distinct political system.

The emergence of money—the most liquid form of capital—dramatically accelerates political development because it enables administrative functionaries in the polity to be paid with a resource that can be used elsewhere. Moreover, an effective coercive force is best mobilized when its key members are paid professionals. Equally important, money becomes an increasingly important basis for consolidating the symbolic base of power. If money retains its value, it becomes a symbol of the effectiveness of a political regime; if money loses value or is unstable, its instability highlights the ineffectiveness of the political regime. Finally, without money, the amount of manipulation of material incentives is limited. True, a polity can grant lands, let out franchises, and bestow honor that can indirectly give elites material benefits; but without money, material manipulation is limited to land, favors, and honor, which—though highly rewarding—are not as flexible as material manipulation in terms of money. Indeed, if nonmonetary manipulation cannot, ultimately, bestow money on those receiving lands, franchises, and other favors, its effectiveness as a source of manipulation is reduced. Thus, the capacity of the economy to generate physical capital, and most significantly, liquid physical capital like money, determines how the administrative, coercive, symbolic, and material-incentive bases of power are mobilized.

Once a political system develops, its policies have effects on the level of physical capital available to the economy. These effects operate on a number of fronts. First, the taxation and appropriation policies of the polity determine how much liquid physical capital can be retained for reinvestment in gathering, production, and distribution. These policies operate both directly and indirectly. Taxation of productive output or the capital used to generate such outputs, such as land in an agrarian system, directly reduces the amount of capital available for reinsertion back into the economy. More indirectly, taxation policies influence incentives for innovation, capital investment, and entrepreneurial activity. When taxation policies create disincentives for hard work, capital investment, innovation, and entrepreneurial creativity, they decrease gathering, producing, and distribution processes. Second, the expenditures of polity on infrastructural projects—roads, ports, canals, airports, information systems, and other projects—greatly influence the level of activity in the economy. If the appropriated monies are used in this way, rather than to support elite privilege and geopolitical adventurism, then taxation policies become strategies for capital reinvestment in accordance with the goals of the polity. However, such infrastructural projects are often designed for defense and war making; and under these conditions, they have a less dynamic effect on economic productivity, unless they facilitate conquest and plunder of capital from other societies. Third, geopolitical policies, from conquest to open trade, influence how much access to resources and markets in other societies is possible, which in turn determines the level and profile of gathering, producing, and distributing processes. Relatedly, the boundary-maintenance activities of polity beyond sustaining their physical integrity also determine the level and nature of capital—for example, when government imposes protective tariffs, institutes export-import subsidies, and employs similar procedures for monitoring the flow of goods and services across borders.

Polity has a number of indirect effects on other economic elements, all of which ultimately influence the amount of physical capital available as private wealth or, more importantly, as sources of investment in gathering, producing, and distributing. With respect to property, it is the coercive arm of the polity—as it overlaps with the enforcement wing of the legal system—that sustains definitions of property. With respect to human capital, the investments of polity in education can dramatically reshape the pool of human capital available to the economy. With regard to technology, taxation policies influence the incentives for technological innovation; furthermore, direct investments in research and science, or subsidies through the tax code, can have important effects on the amount and rate of technological development. And finally, with respect to entrepreneurial activity, polity is always involved in coordinating human and physical capital, technology, and property systems in an effort to increase productivity that it can then appropriate.

These additional effects do not, however, obviate the basic relationship between economy and polity. For in the end, it is physical capital that is being exchanged in the many transactions of economic and political actors. The productivity of the economy—particularly its capacity to generate liquid capital—determines the size and shape of polity, whereas the policies of polity affect how much physical capital is available for gathering, producing, and distributing processes.

Economy and Kinship

Until the economy fully differentiates from kinship during agrarianism, kinship remains the primary entrepreneurial structure for organizing technology, human and physical capital, and property rights. As differentiation between economy and kinship occurs, however, the more-basic and fundamental relationship between these institutional systems is exposed. This relationship involves the exchange of human capital from kinship in return for consumer goods and services from the economy (Parsons and Smelser 1956).

In simple economies, the provision of human capital to the economy also involves the technological knowledge that individuals have learned, as well as the physical capital (such as tools and implements) that labor brings to the economy; the rights to property contained in kinship rules; and the entrepreneurial consequences of unilineal descent for organizing all of these elements of an economy. As other structures emerge to provide technology, to pool physical capital, and to organize economic activity, kinship retains its functions as the provider of human capital to the economy.

Socialization in kinship generates the commitments, interpersonal skills, and initial knowledge base for labor to be inserted directly into the economy. Or more indirectly, it supports and sustains the movement of the young through educational structures, which in turn impart much of the skill and knowledge (or at least the credentials) necessary for participation in the economy. Whether directly or indirectly through its effects on school performance, kinship is nonetheless the key source of human capital. In kinship future human capital is born; in kinship early socialization establishes basic behavioral patterns; and in kinship the resources and support necessary for school performance ultimately reside.

As kinship and economy differentiate, kinship is transformed from both a producing and consuming unit to one revolving primarily around consumption. The members of the family, and the family as a whole, generate the demand for consumer goods and services. Much of this demand is direct, as when families purchase basic consumer goods or services in a market. But much of the demand is less direct, as goods and services are produced for other economic units, which in turn provide families with basic consumer goods and services. Even when economy and kinship are not differentiated, this fundamental relationship between the two institutions is paramount. Economy would not even exist unless members of families required life-sustaining commodities. Thus, the initial selection for economic organization came from the biological needs of kin members. As economy and kinship become more elaborated, this fundamental connection becomes somewhat obscured as kinship serves as the entrepreneurial basis for the economy. But the more the economy differentiates from kinship, the more apparent is this underlying relationship between the two institutions.

Economy and Education

Much like the kinship system, education provides human capital for the economy and, in societies where research is performed in universities, some technology as well. Reciprocally, the effects of economy on education tend to be somewhat indirect. One effect is via the polity: As productivity increases the amount of economic surplus, some of this surplus is used in industrializing and industrial systems to finance education—particularly as the polity seeks to generate a legitimating civic culture and to stimulate economic development. Another effect is through the labor market in more-developed economies where educational credentials are used to sort and place human capital. Such usage generates a market demand for the expansion of the educational system, generally through political pressures on polity to extend educational opportunities but also through direct purchases by consumers of both private and public education structures (creating consumer demands for education at all levels and in all forms).

The effects of education on economic development are somewhat ambiguous, but generally, investments in educating human capital do not pay off unless there is a corresponding investment by the private and public sectors in physical capital, technology, and entrepreneurship. Thus, expansion of the educational system is driven by perceptions of the population and political leaders that the education of human capital will inevitably increase economic productivity. Indeed, the expansion of the educational system is as much driven by an ideology stressing the relationship between economic and educational development and by political necessity to meet the populace's demand for signs of new opportunities as by real labor-market demand in the economy.

Yet, in the long run, advanced industrial and post-industrial economic development cannot occur without formal education of human capital that can be coordinated with higher levels of technology and complex forms of physical capital. Moreover, as the scale and scope of education expand, the educational system becomes a major economic actor. For example, the combined income of those working within the educational establishment or those involved in building the physical structures of the educational system generates a tremendous demand for consumer goods and services, which in turn stimulates the economy.

The basic relationship between economy and education is thus somewhat similar to that between family and economy. Education is a source of human capital for the economy; and the economy provides the resources via the polity to expand the educational system as well as many of the consumer goods and services necessary to build and maintain the educational infrastructure. As the labor market begins to utilize educational credentials for sorting and placing human capital, and as both the general population and the government perceive a relationship between education and economic growth as well as personal prosperity, the economy begins to generate a high demand for expanding the educational system.

Economy and Law

Law remained a recessive institution for much of humans' evolutionary history, although all societies have revealed rules that were subject to adjudication and enforcement. But law frequently was evident only in an ad hoc manner, at moments of crises and conflict. Still, the effects of even these incipient legal systems on coordinating and regulating social relations were clear, even in very primitive form. With differentiation of the economy from kinship, and then its elaboration into a more complex and dynamic system, economy begins to evidence severe problems of internal coordination and control. Exchange in markets is perhaps the key dynamic, because once relatively free and open markets emerge, selection pressures are intense for new rules governing exchange; property; the relationship between human capital and those who employ it; physical-capital formation; and eventually, the rights to and uses of technology. Thus, the fundamental relationship between economy and law revolves around entrepreneurial problems inherent in economic differentiation and the capacity of law to provide an array of external entrepreneurial services to the economy.

Even when law and kinship rules overlap, the entrepreneurial consequences for the economy of implicit bodies of law (within kinship rules) are evident. These rules define property rights, specify what human capital is to do, indicate uses of physical capital, and regulate the application of technology. Such entrepreneurial functions become more explicit as market systems emerge and as the economy begins to differentiate from kinship. Once the rules of unilineal descent no longer organize economic activity, there is intense selection pressure to create new rules. Sometimes these cannot be created, and conflict destroys the economy or significant portions of the economy. At other times in history, informal and formal "merchant laws" have emerged as a way to regulate exchange and to sanction those who do not abide by the rules. Eventually, the developing polity becomes involved in regulating economic activity, because as emphasized earlier, the viability of the polity depends on the productive outputs of the economy. This process of political intervention is rarely smooth. But over time, polity uses the legal system as a tool for regularizing and coordinating relations in the economy.

Until an autonomous legal system is in place, however, economic development is inhibited because there is no coherent and consistent force to define property rights, uses of physical and human capital, or access to technologies. As markets become increasingly dynamic, selection for this external force escalates. Through a series of crises (ranging, for example, from definitions of the rights of corporate actors, through labor-management disputes and concerns over concentration of capital in oligopolies, to concerns about the environment and genetic engineering), pressure is placed on the legal system to provide rules, adjudicative procedures and, if necessary, enforcement capacities to resolve and regularize these crises. Thus, inherent in a dynamic economy is a constant demand for external regulation by law. And despite conservative ideologies like those in the United States stressing free enterprise and laissez faire, the reality is that the economy constantly generates new crises of entrepreneurship which cannot be managed by economic actors themselves.

As a result, the body of tort law in a society expands, the civil court system grows, and the legislative activities within polity or in separate administrative bodies accelerate. In societies without this capacity to use tort laws effectively in regulating a market-driven economy (such as in Russia in the post-Soviet Union period), the economy often remains chaotic, with regulation coming from corruption, threats, and coercive activities of criminal syndicates. There is, then, nothing inevitable about the evolution of law to meet these entrepreneurial demands of the economy; indeed, economies have often stagnated or fallen apart. Yet because the economy is so vital to the viability of polity and the members of kinship units, pressures to develop and use laws come from these other institutional sectors.

Polity and Law

As polity becomes differentiated from kinship, problems of consolidating power become more complicated. Without kinship rules to organize administrative tasks, to provide enforcement coalitions, to regulate the distribution of material incentives, and to legitimate the use of power with the symbols of kinship, all of these bases of power must be rebuilt and reestablished. Rarely is this a smooth process, especially when polity must compete with well-organized religious cult structures for power. The polity eventually creates, or usurps from religion or economic actors, a system of laws that (a) enables it to legitimate itself with secular symbols, (b) provides broad rules by which to administer decisions and manipulate material incentives, and (c) gives the polity the right to use coercive power. Law thus emerges not only from economic demands for entrepreneurial resources but also from the need to consolidate the bases of power in order to control and coordinate activities in the broader society. Conversely, once law exists as a distinctive system, it provides support for the legitimating, administrating, manipulating (of material incentives), and coercing activities of the polity.

This support is, however, contingent, limiting the actions of the polity by rule and court decision. Should a government ignore the law, as is often the case in the history of human societies, political regimes undermine the law's all-important capacity to provide a symbolic bases of legitimation. Thus, the basic relationship between polity and law revolves around a legal system's capacity to provide contingent support for the consolidation and use of power and a polity's need for a system of rules, adjudicative procedures, and enforcement capacities that can facilitate this consolidation and use of power.

This basic exchange is complicated by the fact that the legal and political systems overlap. The legislative process of law making resides primarily in the political system, as do many of the enforcement capacities of the legal system. This overlap often leads political leaders to use, in an arbitrary fashion, the legal system for their own narrow purposes. To the extent that polity uses the legal system in this way, it becomes less effective as a resource in consolidating power for polity and as a mechanism of societywide integration and coordination. The law, in essence, simply becomes a cynically imposed tool for the use of power.

The key problem in the relationship between polity and law is thus one of how to create and sustain a relatively "autonomous" legal system at the very same time that the elements of the law remain partially lodged in polity. Historically, relatively few societies have ever been able to achieve a balanced interchange where an autonomous legal system provides contingent support for polity in its consolidation and use of power, on the one side, and where the polity provides resources for maintaining a system that will limit how power is to be exercised, on the other. The key event is for the polity to give up some of its power to the legal system in exchange for secular legitimating symbols and rules for guiding the use of power. Polity rarely has been willing to do so voluntarily, but demands from economic actors or rumblings from the discontent in a society often have forced the polity's hand.

Once the polity has given over some of its power, the legal system must, in return, provide the primary basis for legitimation of polity (often expressed in a Constitution) as well as the flexibility to generate new rules for guiding the use of power as changing circumstances dictate. Law must become "positive law" in two senses. First, the legal system must create procedural rules to regulate legislation, adjudication, and enforcement of laws. If these procedural rules are accepted by the population, then they further legitimate polity and, at the same time, guide the implementation of political decisions. Second, the legal system must have the capacity to change laws as new demands for coordination in the society emerge, but such changes must be performed in accordance with procedural law. If laws become enshrined and too conservative, they lose the ability to coordinate flexibly social action, and eventually, rigid legal rules begin to erode the legitimacy of the polity. So, a positive legal system, if it is to be effective, must have the capacity to legislate new rules, or alternatively, to adjudicate them from court decisions. These two conditions are, in historical reality, difficult to achieve; and only the political democracies of the contemporary world have come close to meeting them.

As societies become differentiated, selection pressures mount for an autonomous and positive legal system to manage problems of coordination among diverse institutional subsystems, and the many actors in these systems escalate. Once the rules of kinship can no longer provide the basis of coordination and once the power of religion to dictate daily routines declines, an alternative source of coordination and controls is needed for a society to remain viable in its environment. The consolidation and centralization of power is the easiest route to developing this alternative source of control and coordination, but soon the abuse of power erodes its legitimacy and effectiveness in regulating social activity. As a result, legal systems are expanded, and in a few historical cases, they have become sufficiently autonomous to provide both legitimation of polity and the tools for the effective administration of power and enforcement of political decisions. In turn, because these legal systems are effective, the polity has been willing to provide the resources to sustain the system and, most importantly, to grant it a certain degree of autonomy.

Polity and Kinship

Among hunting and gathering bands, polity is hardly noticeable. Only with settled gatherers does clear leadership begin to emerge, typically in the form of a Big Man system. As polity becomes distinctive, and even when lodged in the kinship systems of horticulturalists, the basic exchange between polity and kinship also becomes clear. Kinship produces political loyalty in exchange for the allocation of power and authority within kinship (Parsons and Smelser 1956).

As the principal agent of socialization—indeed, for most of human history, the only agent—kinship imparts basic values, beliefs, and commitments to the young. In this process of socialization, members of a society can acquire commitments to leaders, or at least to the broader system of consolidated power. In horticultural systems, where the descent and authority rules also determine the distribution of power, political commitments were the natural by-product of socialization and generally gave to senior kin the right to power. When there is a clear structural division between kin units and those holding power, however, the socialization of political loyalties is not so automatic. In fact, even among horticulturalists, feuds within clans and lineages or between them also make the socialization of loyalty problematic. However, the problem becomes even more obvious with a clear differentiation between polity and kinship. The situation is aggravated further as the consolidation and centralization of power are used to perpetuate vast inequalities; under these conditions, kin socialization can not only fail to impart the appropriate loyalties, but actually can work to produce the opposite. Revolutionaries often are raised in kin structures that are unsupportive of political regimes, and to the extent that socialization works against imparting political loyalties, it destroys the symbolic base of power so necessary to the polity.

This vulnerability of government to the erosion of its symbolic base of power frequently propels its intrusion into the family system. There are, of course, limits as to how far polity can intervene in the private lives of family members, but at a minimum, the polity and legal system operate to define marriage and dissolution rules as well as the distribution of property among family members. In this way, power and authority are also allocated to the family as a whole (as a legal corporate unit with rights, obligations and responsibilities) and to its individual members. For example, for much of the agrarian era, wives in many societies could not own property, hold contracts, litigate in court, or exercise their political will (through voting or other means of political expression). As a result, the polity and the legal system allocated power disproportionately to men. In more recent years, polity has extended the rights of women in the family, although these vary enormously even in political democracies (as a comparison of the industrial powers of the West and Asia would make clear). Nonetheless, as polity and law have redefined the rights of women, shifts in authority relations within the family become possible.

The polity changes the allocation of power in the family for a simple reason: to accommodate potential shifts in political loyalties. If, for example, wives are politically restive or if members of lower-class families are dissatisfied, the potential for socializing disloyalty increases. Of course, even as socialization erodes the symbolic base of power, the other three bases can typically compensate—at least for a time until the pressures on the government to change the allocation of authority increase to the point where they overcome the other bases of power. Indeed, those who have power within kinship often will be supportive of the political system that supports their family authority, even at the cost of tension with other family members.

It is this dynamic and potentially troublesome exchange of political loyalty for authority in kinship that often leads the polity in industrializing societies to expand the educational system as an alternative to exclusive reliance on family socialization. Here, the goal is to impart a political culture to the young that reaffirms the symbolic base of power; and if family socialization supports the reaffirmation, then polity further consolidates its symbolic base of power. Alternatively, if family socialization contradicts educational socialization, then polity will have difficulty in legitimating itself in terms of a political culture.

Polity and Education

Historically, political regimes have not encouraged the education of the masses, either because they could not afford it or, more typically, because they considered it a threat to the system of privilege and status-group membership of elites. Indeed, up to the industrial era, most education was privately financed and acquired, with the vast majority of students coming from elite families. When polity has become involved in education, it almost always is designed to create political loyalties and firm up its symbolic base of power. In return, as polity establishes a state-run bureaucratic system of schools, it reallocates authority among key socializing agents.

The use of education to create political loyalty is a complicated process in post-industrial, industrial, and industrializing societies. Obviously, the civics curriculum of schools imparts the (distorted) history of the society, requires classroom rituals (such as pledges to the flag) directed at affirming political loyalty, creates historical heroes who symbolize the political culture, and presents the rudiments of the legal system supporting the polity. Less directly, the polity uses the expansion of primary and secondary education to the masses (and eventually higher education as well) as a sign that economic opportunities are increasing. In this way, the polity also manipulates the material aspirations of the populace. In return, the government expects loyalty from citizens whose opportunities for a better life are increasing. If, however, people's aspirations are raised beyond the capacity of the economy to absorb and reward its increasingly educated population, then much of the effort of civics training by schools can be undone. Moreover, the literate population is now in position to receive and communicate written messages questioning the policies of the political regime.

Another less direct effect of polity on education comes from its capacity to employ in the state bureaucracy the educated labor pool. It is no coincidence that governmental bureaucracies are often bloated as the state seeks to absorb its educated members and, in the process, co-opt them and make them loyal to the political system. Such employment practices often divert capital from the economy and thereby act as a drag on productivity, although the purchasing power of state bureaucrats creates market demand, which in turn stimulates production. In the end, despite the depletion of liquid capital involved, the state often has little choice but to employ its educated work force in order to affirm that opportunities are increasing—especially when the economy cannot absorb a significant portion of credentialed human capital.

Thus, the polity's investment in education is often a high-stakes game of diverting capital from the economy to education in an effort to increase political loyalties. In making this investment, polity is reallocating power and authority to agents of socialization. For as education becomes compulsory and as opportunities for success are determined by educational credentials, some of the authority of parents and control of family over children is lost and reallocated to the schools. Education thus can become a threat to the traditional authority system of kinship, leading parents to pull their children out of school. In the long run, however, the growing use of educational credentials by employers in the economy overcomes the threats experienced by parents who also desire expanded opportunities for their children. Yet, until the economy can absorb large portions of the better-educated population, the creation of the education system will not dramatically shift power and authority from family to schools. And even when this shift does occur, schools do not supplant kinship; rather, children typically are subject to increased regulation by virtue of the interpersonal authority of the family and the bureaucratic authority of the schools. In creating a school system, however, the polity has reallocated authority to socializing agents who are more reliable than the kinship system in imparting political loyalty.

Law and Kinship

Kinship provided the template for much of the legal system through horticulture; the substance of laws as well as their adjudication and enforcement followed the rules of kinship and designated kin as judges and enforcers of rules. Still, even when heavily fused with the kinship system, elements of laws, adjudication, and enforcement also were evident outside the template of kinship. As kinship has become nucleated and law increasingly autonomous as an institutional system, the basic exchange between law and religion has become more evident. The legal system provides the rules, as well as their adjudication and enforcement, that define and control family organization. In exchange, family provides the socialization of commitments to the general tenets of the legal system. This interchange always existed, even when law and kinship overlapped; but the exchange has become more pronounced as kinship and law have differentiated. Moreover, as the influence of religion on the institutional order has declined, law has taken over many of the tasks formerly performed by religion. Furthermore, the polity has a clear interest in controlling the family as a source of political loyalty. To realize this interest, governments have used the legal system to define and organize family and, in the process, have usurped many of the functions formerly performed by religion.

As the legal system has increased its integrative consequences for the society as a whole, it has developed specific laws, courts, and enforcement procedures for regulating the basic functions of the family, such as sex, marriage, biological support, reproduction, dissolution, and social placement of the young. In many societies, separate bodies of laws and courts devoted exclusively to family processes have evolved. But whether or not such separate systems of family law have emerged, the legal system regulates family organization and activity by specifying rules about sex and premarital sex (often ignored and violated), marriage, dissolution, child care and support, child and spousal abuse, family authority (via gender-oriented laws), and child placement (via compulsory-education laws and their consequences for acquiring credentials and jobs). And as rates of family dissolution, child and spousal abuse (or at least awareness of these), and out-of-wedlock childbirth have increased throughout the developed world, but especially in the West, the legal system has sought to intervene further into kin activities.

Such intervention is possible because family socialization, as reinforced by school indoctrination, generally supports the rights of the legal system to regulate institutional activity. The broad philosophical tenets of the legal system, as well as a smattering of knowledge about substantive bodies of laws and courts, are learned in family interactions. Schools provide a more structured indoctrination into the civic culture that ultimately frames the legal system, but family socialization is crucial in reinforcing commitments to the legal system. As a consequence, with each new "crisis" of the modern family, legal intervention is either demanded (as with child and spousal abuse) or at least tolerated. However, highly contentious issues, such as rights to abortions, often undermine the legitimacy of the legal system (by those who view the law, whichever side it falls on, as "immoral"). This intervention, and even the controversy that the legal system can generate, only serve to highlight the exchange between law and family whereby law regulates and controls basic family processes and family provides diffuse commitments to the legal system.

Law and Education

Even before law was clearly differentiated from kinship, socialization of commitments to both the broad legal tenets and the specifics of law was essential. Conversely, the process of socialization was assured by the rules of kinship. As law became increasingly differentiated and autonomous from kinship, the basic nature of this exchange remained the same, except now it was an exchange between two distinct institutional systems. Educational socialization in schools generates commitments to the broad civic culture framing the legal system, as well as some knowledge of specific laws, court decisions, and enforcement precedents. Reciprocally, law regulates the formation and operation of school structures, both state-mandated and private.

Since law has become the basis for the consolidation of the symbolic base of power, the state has an active interest in assuring that members of the population are socialized into the tenets and procedures of the legal system. Thus, a large portion of the curriculum in both public and private schools is devoted to history and civics, as these have influenced, and been influenced by, the operation of the legal system. Moreover, as the law becomes complex, education is increasingly involved in the training those who legislate, adjudicate, and enforce the law. Initially, much of this training is by apprenticeships to practitioners, but over time, formal credentials are required of many incumbents in the legal system. For example, law degrees for those who advise legislators (and, informally, for many legislators as well) and those who are involved in adjudication (judges, attorneys, and barristers) are generally required, as is specialized training (often in state-run academies) for those who enforce the law.

Law regulates the educational system by defining the obligations of public and private schools; and with industrialization and post-industrialization, law increasingly specifies the minimum years of schooling that all citizens must have. Moreover, as educational credentials become both the symbol and reality of economic opportunities, the legal system often is used by segments of the population to gain rights to educational opportunities. For example, in the United States, court decisions, legislative enactments, and presidential or executive orders all have been involved in increasing the access of minorities and other subpopulations who have been the victims of discrimination in education (as well as in other institutional spheres). Indeed, as educational credentials become the defining criterion for opportunities, pressures on the legal system to guarantee these opportunities mount. The legal system thus moves beyond establishing minimal requirements; in post-industrial societies, it increasingly defines the rights of individuals in gaining access to all levels of the educational system.

Polity and Religion

Throughout much of humans' evolutionary history, political and religious leaders have overlapped; those who held political power often were religious elites. Yet, more typically, there was some differentiation of political and religious functions; and this division became increasingly evident as societies grew in complexity. Indeed, advanced horticultural and agrarian societies generally experienced conflict and tension between religious and political elites and their corresponding organizational systems. In the end, the state-based polity won this contest, with some notable exceptions, such as contemporary Iran. Throughout evolutionary history, however, the basic exchange between polity and religion has remained fundamentally the same: Religion provides contingent support to government, offering a symbolic basis of legitimation for the polity; the polity provides religion with a certain autonomy to control nonsecular symbol systems and to organize the population in cult structures. In a few cases (such as the Soviet Union's unsuccessful attempt to create an atheist society), the state has discouraged religion. But more typically, the state and religion have reached a compromise, with the state using some religious symbols for legitimation, and religion supporting such usage of its symbols in exchange for the right to organize ritual activities.

With a few exceptions, such as the theocracy that emerged in Tibet and some societies of the Middle East, the exchange between polity and religion has evolved toward less reliance by the polity on the legitimating symbols of religion. Because religion can mobilize emotions and because of past war making by religious organizations in many societies, the state has sought alternatives that it can control more readily. The development of a legal system is the most obvious of these alternatives, because such a system provides the polity with a secular basis of legitimation (again, except in a few societies with a religious legal system). States generally attempt to develop a civic culture which may include some religious symbols and mythologies, but which for the most part is secular, emphasizing the history, heroes, legal principles, and other secular matters that highlight the centrality of the state. In this process, religious beliefs still can provide a diffuse legitimacy, but often religious symbols are restated in a more secular form so as to become integrated into the civic culture.

As religion becomes somewhat segregated from direct legitimation of the polity, the state still allows religious organizations some autonomy and often protects them through the legal system. In this way, religion is co-opted in supporting political regimes. However, religious cults often have been actively involved in political movements (as in the U.S. civil rights movement of the 1960s or in the current political mobilization of the Christian Coalition). Such activism, however, usually is practiced within the legitimate arena of politics and in accordance with the rules of the legal system. If such activism exceeds these boundaries, then the state, if it can, typically crushes religious activity that could undermine the legitimacy of polity. Thus, when religion ceases to offer contingent support to the symbolic base of power, the polity often begins to invade the autonomy of religion. The state usually prevails in this contest, but as the revolution in Iran underscored in the 1970s, religion sometimes can win this contest.

Religion and Law

Religious ethics and codes always have been partly fused with secular laws. But as a distinct legal system has emerged, this fusion has become less obvious; at best, religious symbols provide some of the moral premises on which more-secular laws are based. Through agrarianism, however, religious law was often more dominant than emerging secular law. And even in some contemporary Islamic societies like present-day Iran, religious law remains central. However, as problems of coordination and control have escalated with population growth and increased production and as states have sought a secular basis of legitimation, legal-system development has accelerated. Furthermore, as the body of secular laws, courts, and enforcement agencies has grown, the exchange between law increasingly has involved legal-system protection for the autonomy of religion and religious support for the autonomy of the legal system.

Thus, laws generally specify the rights of religious cult structures to operate, while the beliefs of dominant cults typically become the underlying value premises for at least some of the constitutional principles and higher-order laws in the legal system. At times—for example, in the old Soviet Union—law took little from religion and gave religion very little support; in fact, law often persecuted religious cults. But, more commonly the law is used to provide religion with certain rights and prerequisites, while at the same time limiting the extent to which religion can become involved in the affairs of the state. The state almost always views religion suspiciously as a source of counterpower. Therefore, it uses the legal system to grant religion a certain autonomy that is highly constrained by law. In exchange, religion offers contingent support to polity and the autonomy of the legal system.

Religion and Education

The first practices of formal education were, in all probability, religious in nature, as instructors passed on to their successors the beliefs and ritual practices of religion. Up through the agrarian era, most universities were affiliated with religion in some way; and a considerable portion of the curriculum was religious in nature. At times, religion supported education of the masses, although these efforts did not fully massify the educational system. Still, for the vast majority of the population, education in school structures was confined to perpetuating elites' status-group membership or to providing a few with the secular skills necessary for trade and commerce. Only with industrialization does the massification of education accelerate; and this expansion of education is part of the segregation of religion from ever more spheres of secular life. Even as religion establishes its own school system (such as the Catholic schools), the curriculum is, for the most part, secular and matches the curriculum of state-financed schools. As segregation of religion from schools, or secularization in religious schools, occurs, religion is excluded from much of the socialization of children. Moreover, religion becomes less relevant to social placement in the labor market of the economy. Furthermore, it must adjust beliefs in ways that make them more compatible with the civic culture imposed by the state on the school curriculum.

The exchange between education and religion is thus very imbalanced. The evolving state-financed educational system simply removes much religion from its curriculum or waters it down and incorporates it into civics training. In exchange, religion is allowed to create its own educational system, ranging from "Sunday school" through full educational hierarchies like the Catholic school system. Yet when this religious system becomes involved in mandatory training of children, it generally must meet the same curricular requirements imposed by the state on the public educational system. Thus, religion is given some autonomy to teach dogma and ritual in its own system, but this instruction is constrained by the requirements to teach the state-mandated secular curriculum as well. The expansion of the educational system thereby grants some autonomy to religion as it segregates it from the institutional mainstream.

Religion and Economy

Ultimately, religion provides a sense of meaning to individuals and, in the process, alleviates anxieties and reinforces crucial institutional norms. In contrast, economies organize natural, physical, and human resources for distribution as goods and services to members of a population. The basic exchange between religion and economy thus has revolved around the capacity of religion to alleviate the anxieties associated with economic activity and to reinforce crucial economic norms. Reciprocally, the economy has provided the resources and opportunities for religious mobilization. The way in which this basic exchange has been carried out in the history of human societies has, however, varied enormously as economies have moved from a hunting-gathering to an industrial and post-industrial profile.

Among most hunter-gatherers, the level of uncertainty in securing sufficient resources for survival was generally low; and as a result, religion was not a dominant force in most of these early societies. Yet, where there was danger and uncertainty in economic activity, as was the case with the Eskimos, selection worked to produce clear signs of religion. From hunting and gathering to advanced agrarianism, there was considerable economic uncertainty, aggravated by war, internal conflict, and crushing inequality. Thus, it is no surprise that religion became a prominent institutional system during this phase of human evolution. Moreover, the economic surplus of more-advanced economies provided the resources to build and sustain elaborate cult structures.

Beginning with the commercial revolution of advanced agrarianism and accelerating with industrialization, secularization of social life spread. Secular technologies transformed the process of production, and the emergence and extension of science caused many traditional religious beliefs to be questioned. State-sponsored education increased the salience of secular educational credentials on life chances in competitive labor markets. In the end, market-driven economies tended to commodify and, hence, secularize virtually everything—including services to alleviate anxiety. Thus, as the economy has industrialized, religion has been forced to adjust.

This adjustment represents an accommodation to several changes in the organization of resources and opportunities in the economy. First, a market-driven economy forces all providers of services to compete for market share, thereby forcing religion to become more market-oriented in its provision of services. Second, market economies tend to secularize goods and services, since they must be bought and sold with a neutral medium like money. This requires religion to repackage its message in ways that accommodate or compensate for this secularization. Third, market economies generate new kinds of insecurities—such as unemployment in a competitive job market, obsolescence of skills in a market that constantly upgrades its credential requirements, or marginality for the unskilled in a credentially inflated labor market—thereby creating opportunities for religion to market its message. Fourth, the availability of mass media making it possible to communicate with large numbers of individuals transforms the way goods and services are marketed, thus providing religion with a potentially very effective tool for disseminating its message and securing resources for its survival.

The end result of these changes in the economy is for religion to niche-market itself within the broader market for human services. Traditional religions generally opt for providing a wider range of secular services—such as youth programs, counseling, and recreational facilities—to compete with more-secular economic actors. More-evangelical religions market themselves, often through the mass media, to the chronically insecure, who may feel vulnerable in a highly dynamic post-industrial economy. Through effective marketing, religions have remained viable; and among some evangelical cults, their numbers have expanded. Thus, as industrial and post-industrial economies secularize the orientations of the population, they also create the resources and opportunities for religion to sustain itself in highly competitive markets for human services.

Moreover, though religious dogmas are no longer the direct inspiration for institutional norms in industrial and post-industrial societies, religious values and beliefs are part of these norms. It would be hard to deny that the norms of western capitalist societies (individual hard work and accumulation of wealth, for example) are not reflections of Protestant values and beliefs. And even as nonwestern societies have industrialized, these derivatives of

Protestant values have been imported. Moreover, variations from western norms among these late industrializing societies often follow the premises of their dominant religions, albeit in muted and highly secularized form.

Religion and Kinship

Religion originally emerged within kinship systems, probably in the form of ancestor worship. Therefore, there has always been an important interchange between religion and kinship. Even as the influence of religion has been segregated with institutional differentiation, and as kinship has become nuclearized with agrarianism and industrialism, the basic connection between kinship and religion has remained the same, despite dramatic alterations of these two institutional systems. From the kinship side, this interchange involves socialization of commitments to religious beliefs, the practice of rituals reinforcing these beliefs, and the willingness to commit household surplus to support cult structures. From the religious side, religion provides the means for alleviating tensions in the family, for reinforcing crucial norms, and for marking status transitions (e.g., marriage, dissolution, birth, puberty) in family life.

As kinship has become nucleated and as it has moved from a unit of both production and consumption to primarily one of consumption, this interchange also has been transformed. In the traditional kinship systems of horticulture and early agrarianism, kinship organized considerably more of the institutional activity of the society. As a result, the influence of religion in reinforcing important norms and alleviating sources of tension and anxiety was more consequential. As other institutions differentiated from kinship and with the successive segregation and compartmentalization of religion, socialization by family into religious beliefs has declined, ritual practices have been attenuated or eliminated, and contributions from households have become less certain. Indeed, in post-industrial societies, religion now has to compete with secular organizations in markets offering tension management and recreational diversions. Moreover, law now regulates marriage, dissolution, and support activities within the family.

Thus, only in some families does religion retain its former influence as the principle source of anxiety reduction and normative control; and only some families are willing to socialize intense commitments to religious beliefs and to contribute financially to the maintenance of cult structures. In fact, as family members have begun to move in diverse directions in their daily routines in post-industrial societies, the family unit as the source of collective commitment to religion has diminished, with individual members of the family increasingly making their own personal choices about religious beliefs, rituals, and cults.

Still, a very significant portion of the population in post-industrial and industrializing societies has retained the basic interchange between religion and kinship. In some cases, as in the societies of the former Soviet Union, religion has reasserted its influence on kinship as political and economic insecurities have risen. And in many societies, such as those in the Middle East, this influence has never been lost. Thus, despite the emergence of a secular market economy and the efforts of polity to create a civic culture, religion remains viable and visible because of the commitments generated by kin socialization.

Education and Kinship

For most of human history, education occurred within kinship. When separate educational structures did emerge, they were generally confined to the socialization of religious practitioners and elites, although religious instruction did reach the masses in some societies. Even in this incipient state, however, the basic interchange between education and kinship was evident: Education would assume some of the socialization functions as well as many of the social-placement functions (in occupations, professions, and status groups) of kinship; and kinship would provide the financial and cultural resources for students moving through the educational system.

The establishment of a state-mandated educational system has often posed a threat to the family, since the socialization of children outside the home can reduce parents' control over children. Moreover, the schools can take needed sources of labor or income from the family (in fact, "summer vacation" is a holdover from the agrarian era, in which students were needed to harvest crops). And, in rapidly changing societies, education can create large knowledge gaps between parents and children, which in turn alter balances of power and authority in the family. Only when universal education is mandated by the state and when it is seen to increase economic opportunities is this tension between schools and kinship reduced. As this transition in school-family relationships occurs, families seek to provide the financial and cultural resources that can improve school performance, although vast disparities exist in the capacities of families to do so.

These disparities generated by stratification eventually begin to change the perceptions of lower-class families, who increasingly pressure the state to provide financial and cultural resources that will increase educational opportunities. These pressures become intense as placement in the broader society is determined by educational credentials. Indeed, one of the sources of the credential inflation that has spread among many post-industrial societies like the United States is family pressures to equalize opportunities for less-advantaged students.

Thus, as education becomes a central institution, kinship adjusts to the fact that it must lose socialization and social placement functions. At the same time, kinship becomes ever more willing to provide the resources for students to move up the educational hierarchy; and if the family cannot mobilize the resources, pressure is put on the state to do so. The state generally responds because it seeks to quiet tensions with the lower classes by co-opting their young members into the educational system, which in turn will indoctrinate students into the political culture legitimating the polity.

Table 14.1 BRIEF SUMMARY OF THE DYNAMIC INTERCHANGES AMONG SOCIAL INSTITUTIONS

	Economy	Kinship	Religion	Polity	Law
Kinship	**Kinship** provides human capital for gathering, producing, and distributing. **Economy** provides consumer goods and services necessary to sustain family members.				
Religion	**Religion** provides mechanisms for alleviating economic insecurities, as well as reinforcement of economic norms. **Economy** provides resources and opportunities for religious mobilization.	**Religion** provides resources for alleviating family members' tensions, for reinforcing kin norms, and for marking status transitions of family members. **Kinship** provides commitments to religious beliefs, opportunities to engage in religious rituals, and financial resources to support cult structures.			
Polity	**Polity** regulates the level of physical capital available for gathering, producing, and distributing. **Economy** provides physical capital, especially liquid capital, to support and sustain the polity.	**Polity** allocates power and authority within kinship. **Kinship** provides loyalty to polity, thereby consolidating the symbolic base of power.	**Polity** provides conditional autonomy to religion to organize rituals in cult structures. **Religion** provides contingent support to polity, especially for the consolidation of the symbolic base of power.		

Table 14.1 *Continued*

	Economy	Kinship	Religion	Polity	Law
Law	**Law** provides external entrepreneurial services to coordinate gathering, producing, and distributing. **Economy** generates problems of coordination that stimulate demand for law, while providing (via the polity) resources to sustain the legal system.	**Law** provides external rules, as well as procedures for their adjudication and enforcement, that define and regulate family organization. **Kinship** generates commitments to general tenets of the legal system.	**Law** assures rights of cult structures while specifying their obligations. **Religion** provides moral premises of law while ceding to law regulatory authority.	**Law** provides contingent support for the consolidation of power, especially its symbolic base but other bases as well. **Polity** generates demands for secular basis of legitimation while providing resources to sustain the legal system.	
Education	**Education** provides human capital for gathering, producing, and distributing. **Economy** generates financial resources, directly and indirectly (through polity and kinship), to sustain education, while generating demand in labor markets for credentialed human capital.	**Education** assumes some of the socialization and social-placement functions of kinship, thereby altering kinship norms. **Kinship** provides many of the financial and cultural resources for performance by students in school system.	**Educational** system of polity determines curriculum requirements of religious schools. **Religion** provides financial support of some schools while ceding state-controlled system regulatory authority.	**Education** generates loyalty to the civic cultural legitimating polity, thereby consolidating the symbolic base of power. **Polity** creates and finances mass public education while regulating private education.	**Education** socializes commitments to, while providing training for incumbents in, the legal system. **Law** provides rules for formation and operation of school systems, both public and private.

279

CONCLUSION

As institutions have differentiated from kinship, the institutional order has become complex. Just the cursory review in this chapter of the basic interchanges among six institutions makes clear just how complex this web of interrelations among social institutions can become. And, if more fine-grained and secondary interconnections are added to the analysis, the complexity of the institutional order is even more apparent. This complexity can obscure the fundamental relationships among institutions, but in this chapter we sought to cut through some of the complexity.

To simplify even more in the name of clarity, Table 14.1 summarizes the basic two-way relations among six institutions. In each box of Table 14.1, the effects of institutions listed on the left side on those listed across the top of the table appear first in the box. Below the segment first is the reciprocal effect of the institutions listed across the top on those running down on the left side of the table. Thus, each box summarizes the basic interchange between two institutions.

Although the precise empirical form of these interchanges has varied historically, the more-fundamental relationships among institutions, it is argued, have remained much the same. These connections among institutions are *the institutional order.* This order is fundamental to the survival of humans as a species. Indeed, it is the result of natural-selection forces, both those in the bio-ecology of nature and, increasingly, those contained in the ever more complex nature of sociocultural systems.

Most macro-level sociological analysis examines a piece or portion of the institutional order (for example, "political" and "economic" sociology; or sociology of "family," "religion," "education," or "law"). But rarely does this analysis step back and view the larger complex of institutions as a whole. By taking this step, we bring the institutional order into focus, revealing a distinct and important level of sociological analysis.

Our goal in this book has been to take not only a panoramic view of the institutional basis of human societies, but also to zoom in on the key elements of each institution, the variations in the organization of these elements in long-range societal evolutionary history, and the dynamic interchanges among these elements. Other units of sociological inquiry—from groups and organizations, through communities and stratification systems, to societies and world systems—are constrained by these institutional elements and the order that they create. Indeed, the institutional order imposes parameters on all social processes and structures. To be sure, in some ultimate sense, institutional systems are composed of individual interactions. However, one cannot understand fully the substance of these interactions without viewing them in their institutional context. More importantly, a micro-level focus on interactions among individuals cannot reveal the properties and dynamics of social institutions. Only by moving away from micro-level processes are some of the most important forces structuring the social universe exposed.

In these pages, we have sought to emphasize the regularities, along with historical variations of the regularities, in the institutions that organize the social universe. These pages are, of course, only a partial and incomplete look at the institutional order, but they reveal the potential of a purely institutional-level of inquiry for expanding our knowledge about human societies.

References

Aberle, David F., A. K. Cohen, A. K. Davis, M. J. Levy, and F. Y. Sutton. 1950. "The Functional Requisites of Society." *Ethics* 60 (January):100-11

Abu-Lughod, Janet. 1989. *Before European Hegemony: The World System A.D. 1250–1350*. New York: Oxford University Press.

Almond, Gabriel, and Sidney Verba. 1963. *The Civic Culture*. Princeton: Princeton University Press.

Amin, Samir. [1973] 1976. *Unequal Development: An Essay on the Social Formations of Peripheral Capitalism*. New York: Monthly Review Press.

———. [1970] 1974. *Accumulation on a World Scale*. New York: Monthly Review Press.

Anderson, Perry. 1974. *Passages from Antiquity to Feudalism*. London: New Left Books.

Anyon, J. 1981. "Schools as Agencies of Social Legitimation." *International Journal of Political Education* 4 (2):42–61.

———. 1980. "Social Class & the Hidden Curriculum of Work." *Journal of Education* 161 (1):67–92.

Apple, Michael W. 1988. *Teachers and Texts*. London: Routledge & Kegan Paul.

———, ed. 1982a. *Cultural and Economic Reproduction in Education*. Boston: Routledge & Kegan Paul.

———. 1982b. *Education & Power*. Boston: Routledge & Kegan Paul.

———. 1979. *Ideology & Curriculum*. Boston: Routledge & Kegan Paul.

———. 1978. "The New Sociology of Education." *Harvard Educational Review* 22 (6):10–32.

Applebaum, Richard. 1978. "Marx's Theory of the Falling Rate of Profit: Towards a Dialectical Analysis of Structural Social Change." *American Sociological Review* 43:64–73.

Arjomand, Said. 1988. *The Turban for the Crown: The Islamic Revolution in Iran*. New York: Oxford University Press.

Aung, Maung Htin. 1962. *Burmese Law Tales: The Legal Element in Burmese Folklore*. London: Oxford University Press.

Bainbridge, William Sims, and Rodney Stark. 1979. "Cult Formation: Three Compatible Models." *Sociological Analysis* 40:283–95.

Baran, Paul, and Paul M. Sweezy. 1966. *Monopoly Capital: An Essay on the American Economic & Social Order*. New York: Monthly Review Press.

Barton, Roy. 1969. *Ifugao Law.* Berkeley: University of California Publications in Archaeology and Ethnology, vol. 15 Berkeley: University of California Press.

Bates, Daniel, and Fred Plog. 1991. *Human Adaptive Strategies.* New York: McGraw-Hill.

Beaud, Michel. 1983. *A History of Capitalism, 1500–1980.* New York: Monthly Review Press.

Becker, Howard. 1950. *Through Values to Social Interpretation.* Durham, NC: Duke University Press.

Bell, Daniel. 1973. *The Coming of Post-Industrial Society.* New York: Basic Books.

Bellah, Robert N. 1970. *Beyond Belief: Essays on Religion in a Post-Traditional World.* New York: Harper & Row.

———. 1967. "Civil Religion in America." *Daedalus* 96:1–21.

———. 1964. "Religious Evolution." *American Sociological Review* 29:358–74.

Ben-David, Joseph. 1971. *The Scientist's Role in Society: A Comparative Study.* Englewood Cliffs, N.J.: Prentice-Hall.

Bender, Barbara. 1975. *Farming in Prehistory.* London: Baker.

Berger, Peter L. 1969. *The Sacred Canopy: Elements of a Sociological Theory of Religion.* Garden City, NY: Anchor Books.

———. 1963. "A Market Model for the Analysis of Ecumenicity." *Social Research* 5:21–34.

Berk, Sara Fenstermaker. 1985. *The Gender Factory: The Appointment of Work in American Households.* New York: Plenum.

———. 1980. *Women and Household Labor.* Newbury Park, Calif.: Sage.

Bicchieri, M. G., ed. 1972. *Hunters and Gatherers Today.* New York: Holt, Rinehart & Winston.

Binford, Lewis R. 1968. "Post-Pleistocene Adaptations." In *New Perspectives in Archaeology*, ed. S. R. Binford and L. R. Binford. Chicago: Aldine.

Black, Donald. 1993. *The Social Structure of Right and Wrong.* San Diego: Academic Press.

———. 1976. *The Behavior of Law.* New York: Academic Press.

Black, Donald, and Maureen Mileski, eds. 1973. *The Social Organization of Law.* New York: Academic Press.

Blalock, Hubert M. 1989. *Power and Conflict: Toward a General Theory.* Newbury Park, Calif.: Sage.

Bloch, H. 1973. "The Problem Defined." *Introduction to Civilization and Science: In Conflict or Collaboration.* Amsterdam: Elsevier.

Bloch, Marc. 1962. *Feudal Society*, trans. L. A. Manyon. Chicago: University of Chicago Press.

Block, Fred. 1994. "The State and the Economy." In *The Handbook of Economic Sociology*, ed. N. J. Smelser and R. Swedberg. New York: Russell Sage.

———. 1990. *Postindustrial Possibilities: A Critique of Economic Discourse.* Berkeley: University of California Press.

———. 1980. "Beyond Relative Autonomy: State Managers as Historical Subjects." *Socialist Register:* 227–42.

Blum, Jerome. 1961. *Lord and Peasant in Russia from the Ninth to the Nineteenth Century*. Princeton: Princeton University Press.

Blumberg, Rae Lesser. 1984. "A General Theory of Gender Stratification." *Sociological Theory* 2:23–101.

Blumberg, Rae Lesser, and Robert F. Winch. 1977. "The Curvilinear Relation between Societal Complexity of Familial Complexity." In *Familial Organization*, ed. R. F. Winch. New York: Free Press.

Boas, Franz. 1921. *Ethnology of the Kwakiutl*. Washington, D.C.: Smithsonian Institution Press.

Bohannan, Paul. 1968. "Law and Legal Institutions." In *International Encyclopedia of the Social Sciences*. New York: Free Press.

———. 1964. *Africa and Africans*. Garden City, N.Y.: American Museum Science Books.

———. 1957. *Justice and Judgement among the Tir*. London: Oxford University Press.

Bohannan, Paul T., and K. Hickleberry. 1967. "Institutions of Divorce, Family and Law." *Law and Society Review* 2:81–102.

Boli, John. 1989. *New Citizens for a New Society: The Institutional Origins of Mass Schooling in Sweden*. Oxford: Peragamon Press.

Boli, John, Francisco Ramirez, and John W. Meyer. 1985. "Explaining the Origins and Expansion of Mass Education." *Comparative Education Review* 29:145–70.

Boserup, Ester. 1981. *Population and Technological Change: A Study of Long-Term Trends*. Chicago: University of Chicago Press.

———. 1965. *The Conditions of Agricultural Growth*. Chicago: Aldine.

Bourdieu, Pierre. 1984. *Distinction: A Social Critique of the Judgement of Taste*. Cambridge, Mass.: Harvard University Press.

Bourdieu, Pierre, and Jean-Claude Passeron. 1977. *Reproduction: in Education, Society and Culture*. Newbury Park, Calif.: Sage.

Bowles, Samuel, and H. Gintis. 1976. *Schooling in Capitalist America: Educational Reform and the Contradictions of Economic Life*. New York: Basic Books.

Braudel, Fernand. [1979] 1985. *The Wheels of Commerce*. Volume 2 of *Civilization and Capitalism, 15th–18th Century*. Trans. Sian Reynolds. London: Fontana Press.

———. 1982. *The Wheels of Commerce*. Volume 2 of *Civilization and Capitalism, 15th–18th Century*. New York: Harper & Row.

———. 1977. *Afterthoughts on Material Civilization and Capitalism*. Baltimore: Johns Hopkins University Press.

Braungart, R. G., and M. M. Braungart. 1994. "Political Socialization." *The International Encyclopedia of Education*, 2nd ed., ed. T. Husén and T. N. Postlethwaite. London: Pergamon Press.

Braverman, Harry. 1974. *Labor and Monopoly Capital*. New York: Monthly Review Press.

Bredemeier, Harry C. 1962. "Law as an Integrative Mechanism." In *Law and Sociology Exploratory Essays*, ed. W. J. Evan. New York: Free Press.

Brint, Steven. 1996. *Schools and Society.* Newbury Park, Calif.: Pine Forge Press.

Bronfenbrenner, Urie. 1968. "Soviet Methods of Character Education." In *Comparative Perspectives on Education,* ed. R. J. Havighurst. Boston: Little, Brown.

Burt, Ronald S. 1992. *Structural Holes.* Cambridge, Mass.: Harvard University Press.

Cain, Maureen, and Alan Hunt. 1969. *Marx and Engels on Law.* London: Academic Press.

Cambridge. 1963. *The Cambridge Economic History of Europe.* London: Cambridge University Press.

Carneiro, Robert L. 1987. "Further Reflections on Resource Concentration and Its Role in the Rise of the State." In *Studies in the Neolithic and Urban Revolutions,* ed. L. Manzanilla. International Series, no. 3. Oxford: British Archaeological Reports.

———. 1981. "The Chiefdom: Precursor of the State." In *The Transition to Statehood in The New World,* ed. R. R. Kantz. New York: Cambridge University Press.

———. 1973. "Structure, Function, and Equilibrium in the Evolutionism of Herbert Spencer." *Journal of Anthropological Research* 29 (2):77–95.

———. 1970. "A Theory of the Origin of the State." *Science* 169:733–38.

———. 1967. "On the Relationship of Size of Population and Complexity of Social Organization." *Southwestern Journal of Anthropology* 23:234–43.

Carnoy, M. 1989. "Education, State, and Culture in American Society." In *Critical Pedagogy. The State and Cultural Struggle,* ed. H. Giroux and P. McLaren. Albany: SUNY Press.

Carnoy, M., and H. Levin. 1985. *Schooling and Work in the Democratic State.* Stanford, Calif.: Stanford University Press.

———, eds. 1976. *The Limits of Educational Reform.* New York: Longmans.

Chafetz, Janet. 1990. *Gender Equity: An Integrated Theory of Stability and Change.* Newbury Park, Calif.: Sage Publications.

Chagnon, Napoleon A. 1968. *The Fierce People.* New York: Holt, Rinehart & Winston.

Chambliss, William. 1976. "Functional and Conflict Theories of Crime: The Heritage of Emile Durkheim and Karl Marx." In *Whose Law? What Order? A Conflict Approach to Criminology.* New York: John Wiley & Sons.

Chambliss, William, and Robert Seidman. 1982. *Law, Order, and Power,* 2nd ed. Reading, Mass.: Addison-Wesley.

Chang, Kwang-chih. 1963. *The Archeology of Ancient China.* New Haven: Yale University Press.

Childe, V. Gordon. 1964. *What Happened in History.* Baltimore: Penguin.

———. 1960. "The New Stone Age." In *Man, Culture and Society,* ed. H. Shapiro. New York: Oxford Galaxy.

———. 1953. *Man Makes Himself.* New York: Mentor Books.

———. 1952. *New Light on the Most Ancient East.* London: Routledge & Kegan Paul.

———. 1951. *Man Makes His Way.* New York: Mentor Books.

———. 1930. *The Bronze Age.* London: Cambridge University Press.

Chirot, Daniel. 1986. *Social Change in the Modern Era*. San Diego: Harcourt, Brace, Jovanovich.

Claessen, H., and P. Skalnick, eds. 1978. *The Early State*. The Hague: Mouton.

Clark, Burton R. 1962. *Educating The Expert Society. San Francisco: Chandler.*

Clark, Grahame, and Stuart Piggott. 1965. *Prehistoric Societies*. New York: Knopf.

Clark, J. G. D. 1952. *Prehistoric Europe: The Economic Basis*. London: Methuen.

Clough, S. B., and C. W. Cole. 1941. *Economic History of Europe*. Boston: D. C. Heath.

Cohen, Mark N. 1977. *The Food Crisis in Prehistory*. New Haven: Yale University Press.

Cohen, Ronald, and Elman Service, eds. 1977. *Origins of the State*. Philadelphia: Institute for the Study of Human Issues.

Cohn, Norman Rufus Colin. 1957. *The Pursuit of the Millennium*. Fairlawn, N.J.: Essential Books. (Revised and expanded in 1970 by Oxford University Press.)

Coleman, James S., ed. 1965. *Education and Political Development*. Princeton: Princeton University Press.

Collins, Randall. 1990. "Market Dynamics as the Engine of Historical Change." *Sociological Theory* 8:111–35.

———. 1988. *Theoretical Sociology*. San Diego: Harcourt, Brace, Jovanovich.

———. 1986. *Weberian Sociological Theory*. New York: Cambridge University Press.

———. 1979. *The Credential Society*. New York: Academic Press.

———. 1977. "Some Comparative Principles of Educational Stratification." *Harvard Educational Review* 47:1–27.

———. 1975. *Conflict Sociology: Toward an Explanatory Science*. New York: Academic Press.

———. 1971. "Functional and Conflict Theories of Educational Stratification." *American Sociological Review* 36:1002–19.

Coon, Carleton S. 1971. *The Hunting Peoples*. Boston: Little, Brown.

Cotgrove, S., and S. Box. 1970. *Science Industry and Society*. London: Allen & Unwin.

Cottrell, William Frederick. 1955. *Energy and Society: The Relation between Energy, Social Change and Economic Development*. New York: McGraw-Hill.

Crook, Stephan, Jan Pakulski, and Malcolm Waters. 1992. *Postmodernization: Change in Advanced Society*. London: Sage.

Curwen, Cecil, and Gudmund Hatt. 1961. *Plough and Pasture: The Early History of Farming*. New York: Collier.

David, Rene, and John E. Brierley. 1985. *Major Legal Systems in the World Today*, 3rd ed. London: Stevens & Sons.

Davies, James C. 1962. "Toward a Theory of Revolution." *American Sociological Review* 27:5–19.

Davis, Howard, and Richard Scase. 1985. *Western Capitalism and State Socialism: An Introduction*. Oxford: Basil Blackwell.

Davis, James F. 1962. "Law as a Type of Social Control." In *Society and Law: New Meanings for an Old Profession.* New York: Free Press.

Davis, Kingsley. 1949. *Human Society.* New York: Macmillan.

Davis, L. B., and O. K. Reeves. 1990. *Hunters of the Recent Past.* London: Unwin Hyman.

Dawson, R. E., and K. Prewitt. 1969. *Political Socialization.* Boston: Little, Brown.

Diamond, Arthur S. 1971. *Primitive Law, Past and Present.* London: Methuen & Co.

———. 1951. *The Evolution of Law and Order.* London: Watts & Co.

Duke, James E. 1976. *Conflict and Power in Social Life.* Provo, Utah: Brigham Young University Press.

Durkheim, Émile. [1912] 1965. *The Elementary Forms of the Religious Life.* New York: Free Press.

Earle, Timothy, ed. 1984. *On the Evolution of Complex Societies.* Malibu, Calif.: Undena.

Earle, Timothy, and J. Ericson, eds. 1977. *Exchange Systems in Prehistory.* New York: Academic Press.

Easton, David. 1965. *A Systems Analysis of Political Life.* New York: John Wiley & Sons.

Eberhard, Wolfram. 1960. *A History of China,* 2nd ed. Berkeley: University of California Press.

Eibl-Eibesfeldt, Irenöus. 1991. "On Subsistence and Social Relations in the Kalahaic." *Current Anthropology* 32:55–57.

Eisenstadt, S. N., and A. Shachar. 1987. *Society, Culture and Urbanization.* Newbury Park, Calif.: Sage.

Ekholm, Kajsa, and Jonathan Friedman. 1982. "'Capital' Imperialism and Exploitation in Ancient World-Systems." *Review* 4:87–109.

Eliade, Mircea. 1987. *The Encyclopedia of Religion,* 15 vols. New York: Macmillan.

Elkin, A. P. 1954. *The Australian Aborigines,* 3rd ed. Sydney: Angus and Robertson.

Ember, Carol, Melvin Ember, and Burton Pasternak. 1974. "On the Development of Unilineal Descent." *Journal of Anthropological Research* 30:69–94.

Ember, Melvin, and Carol R. Ember. 1983. *Marriage, Family and Kinship: Comparative Studies of Social Organization.* Princeton: HRAF Press.

———. 1971. "The Conditions Favoring Matrilocal vs. Patrilocal Residence." *American Anthropologist* 73:571–94.

Esping-Andersen, Cösta. 1994. "Welfare States and the Economy." In *The Handbook of Economic Sociology,* ed. N. J. Smelser and R. Swedberg. New York: Russell Sage.

Etzioni, Amati. 1961. *A Comparative Analysis of Complex Organizations.* New York: Free Press.

Evan, William M. 1990. *Social Structure and Law: Theoretical and Empirical Perspectives.* Newbury Park, Calif.: Sage Publications.

———. 1980. *The Sociology of Law.* New York: Free Press.

———, ed. 1962. *Law and Society: Exploratory Essays.* New York: Free Press.

Evans, Peter, Dietrich Rueschemeyer, and Theda Skocpol, eds. 1985. *Bringing the State Back In.* New York: Cambridge University Press.

Evans-Pritchard, E. 1940. *The Nuer.* Oxford: Oxford University Press.

Faia, Michael A. 1986. *Dynamic Functionalism: Strategy and Tactics.* New York: Cambridge University Press.

Firth, Raymond. 1970. *Preface to Ancient Law.* Boston: Beacon Press.

———. 1939. *Primitive Polynesian Economy.* London: Routledge & Kegan Paul.

———. 1936. *We the Tikopia.* New York: American Book Company.

Flandrin, Jean-Louis. 1979. *Families in Former Times: Kinship, Household and Sexuality.* Cambridge: Cambridge University Press.

Flannery, Kent V. 1973. "The Origins of Agriculture." *Annual Review of Anthropology* 2:271–310.

Fock, Niel. 1974. "Mataco Law." In *Native South Americans: Ethnology of the Least Known Continent,* ed. P. Lyons. Boston: Little, Brown.

Fortes, Meyer. 1953. "The Structure of Unilineal Descent Groups." *American Anthropologist* 73:571–94.

Fox, Robin. 1967. *Kinship and Marriage.* Baltimore: Penguin.

Frank, Andre Gunder. 1980. *Crisis: In World Economy.* New York: Holmes and Meier.

———. 1975. *On Capitalist Underdevelopment.* Oxford: Oxford University Press.

———. 1969. *Capitalism and Underdevelopment in Latin America.* New York: Monthly Review Press.

Fried, Morton H. 1978. "The State, the Chicken, and the Egg: Or, What Came First?" In *Origins of the State,* ed. R. Cohen. Philadelphia: Institute for the Study of Human Issues.

———. 1967. *The Evolution of Political Society.* New York: Random House.

———. 1957. "The Classification of Corporate Unilineal Descent Groups." *Journal of the Royal Anthropological Institute* 87:1–29.

Friedman, Lawrence M. 1977. *Law and Society: An Introduction.* Englewood Cliffs, N.J.: Prentice-Hall.

———. 1975. *The Legal System: A Social Science Perspective.* New York: Russell Sage.

———. 1969a. "Legal Culture and Societal Development." *Law and Society Review* 4:29–44.

———. 1969b. "On Legal Development." *Rutgers Law Review* 24:11–64.

Friedman, William. 1959. *Law in a Changing Society.* Berkeley: University of California Press.

Fuchs, Stephan, and Jonathan H. Turner. 1991. "Legal Sociology as General Theory." *Virginia Review of Sociology* 1:165–72.

Fuller, Bruce. 1991. *Growing-Up Modern: The Western State Builds Third-World Schools.* New York: Routledge.

Fuller, Bruce, and Richard Rubinson. 1992. "Does the State Expand Schooling? Review of Evidence." In *The Political Construction of Education,* ed. B. Fuller and R. Rubinson. New York: Praeger.

Garnier, Maurice, and Jerald Hage. 1990. "Education and Economic Growth in Germany." *Research in Sociology of Education and Socialization* 9:25–53.

Gereffi, Gary. 1994. "The International Economy and Economic Development." In *The Handbook of Economic Sociology*, ed. N. J. Smelser and R. Swedberg. New York: Russell Sage.

Gereffi, Gary, and Donald Wyman, eds. 1990. *Manufacturing Miracles: Paths of Industrialization in Latin America and East Asia.* Princeton: Princeton University Press.

Gibbs, James, ed. 1965. *Peoples of Africa.* New York: Holt.

Giddens, Anthony. 1985. *The Nation State and Violence.* Cambridge: Polity Press.

Gills, Barry K., and Andre Gunder Frank. 1992. "World System Cycles, Crises, and Hegemonial Shifts, 1700 B.C. to 1700 A.D." *Review* 15:621–87.

Gintis, H. 1972. "Toward a Political Economy of Education." *Harvard Educational Review* 42:100–15.

Giroux, H. A. 1990a. *Schooling and the Struggle for Public Life.* Minneapolis: University of Minnesota Press.

———. 1990b. *Teachers as Intellectuals: A Critical Pedagogy for Practical Learning.* South Hadley, Mass.: Bergin and Garvey.

———. 1981. *Ideology, Culture, and the Process of Schooling.* Philadelphia: Temple University Press.

Glock, Charles Y. 1973. "On the Origins and Evolution of Religious Groups." In *Religion in Sociological Perspective*, ed. C. Y. Glock. Belmont, Calif.: Wadsworth.

———. 1964. "The Role of Deprivation in the Origin and Evolution of Religious Groups." In *Religion and Social Conflict*, ed. R. Lee and M. Marty. New York: Oxford University Press.

Glock, Charles Y., and Rodney Stark. 1965. *Religion and Society in Tension.* Chicago: Rand McNally.

Gluckmman, Max. 1965. *Politics, Law and Ritual in Tribal Society.* Chicago: Aldine.

———. 1955. *The Judicial Process among the Barotse of Northern Rhodesia.* Manchester: Manchester University Press.

Goffman, Irving. 1967. *Interaction Ritual.* New York: Anchor Books.

Goldschmidt, Walter. 1959. *Man Makes His Way: A Preface to Understanding Human Society.* New York: Holt, Rinehart & Winston.

Goldstone, Jack. 1990. *Revolution and Rebellion in the Early Modern World, 1640–1848.* Berkeley: University of California Press.

Goode, William J. 1951. *Religion among the Primitives.* New York: Free Press.

Goodhale, Jane. 1959. "The Tiwi Women of Melville Island." Ph.D. dissertation, University of Pennsylvania.

Gordon, R. T. 1914. *The Khasis.* London: Macmillan.

Graburn, Nelson, ed. 1971. *Readings in Kinship and Social Structure.* New York: Harper & Row.

Gramsci, A. 1972. *Selections from Prison Notebooks.* New York: International Publishers.

Granovetter, Mark. 1985. "Economic Action and Social Structure: The Problem of Embeddedness." *American Sociological Review* 91:481–510.

Gurvitch, George. 1953. *Sociology of Law*. London: Routledge & Kegan Paul.

Haas, Jonathan. 1982. *The Evolution of the Prehistoric State*. New York: Columbia University Press.

Habermas, Jurgen. 1979. *Communication and the Evolution of Society*. Boston: Beacon Press.

———. [1973] 1976. *Legitimation Crisis*. Trans. T. McCarthy. London: Heineman.

Hadden, Jeffrey K., and Charles E. Swann. 1981. *Prime Time Preachers: The Rising Power of Televangelism*. Reading, Mass.: Addison-Wesley.

Hall, John A. 1985. *Powers and Liberties: The Causes and Consequences of the Rise of the West*. Berkeley: University of California Press.

Halsey, A. H. 1967. "The Sociology of Education" in *Sociology*, ed. N. J. Smelser. New York: Wiley.

Hammond, Mason. 1972. *The City in the Ancient World*. Cambridge, Mass.: Harvard University Press.

Hanson, Mark E. 1995. "Educational Change under Autocratic and Democratic Governments: The Case of Argentina." Masters thesis, University of California, Riverside, School of Education.

Harner, M. 1970. "Population Pressure and the Social Evolution of Agriculturalists." *Southwest Journal of Anthropology* 26:67–86.

Harris, Marvin. 1971. *Culture, Man and Nature: An Introduction to General Anthropology*. New York: Crowell.

Hart, C. W. M., Arnold Pilling, and Jane Goodhale. 1988. *The Tiwi of North Australia*. Chicago: Holt, Rinehart & Winston.

Hart, H. L. A. 1961. *The Concept of Law*. London: Oxford University Press.

Harvey, David. 1989. *The Condition of Postmodernity: An Enquiry into the Origins of Cultural Change*. Oxford: Basil Blackwell.

Hawkes, Jacquetta. 1965. *Prehistory: UNESCO History of Mankind*, vol. 1, pt. 1. New York: Mentor.

Hawley, Amos. 1986. *Human Ecology: A Theoretical Essay*. Chicago: University of Chicago Press.

Hayden, B. 1981. "Subsistence and Ecological Adaptations of Modern Hunter/Gatherers." In *Omnivorous Primates*, ed. R. Harding and G. Teleki. New York: Columbia University Press.

Haydon, E. S. 1960. *Law and Justice in Buganda*. London: Butterworths.

Hays, H. R. 1958. *From Ape to Angel: An Informal History of Social Anthropology*. New York: Capricorn Books.

Heilbroner, Robert L. 1985. *The Making of Economic Society*, 7th ed. Englewood Cliffs, N.J.: Prentice-Hall.

Herskovits, M. J. 1938. *Dahomey*. Locust Valley, N.Y.: J. J. Augustin.

Herskovits, M. J., and F. S. Herskovits. 1933. "An Outline of Dahomean Religious Belief." *Memoirs of the American Anthropological Association* 41:10–25.

Hertz, Rosanna. 1986. *More Equal than Others: Women and Men in Dual-Career Marriages*. Berkeley: University of California Press.

Hess, R. D., and J. V. Torney. 1967. *The Development of Political Attitudes in Children*. Chicago: Aldine.

Hilton, Rodney, ed. 1976. *The Transition from Feudalism to Capitalism*. London: New Left Books.

Hiro, Dilip. 1989. *Holy Wars: The Rise of Islamic Fundamentalism*. New York: Routledge & Kegan Paul.

Hochschild, Arlie R. 1989. *The Second Shift: Working Parents and the Revolution at Home*. New York: Viking Press.

———. 1954. *The Law of Primitive Man: A Study in Comparative Legal Dynamics*. Cambridge, Mass.: Harvard University Press.

Hoebel, E. A., 1954 *The Law of Primitive Man*. New York: Atheneum

Holmberg, Allan. 1950. *Nomads of the Long Bow: The Siriono of Eastern Bolivia*. Institute for Anthropology, no. 10. Washington, D.C.: Smithsonian Institution.

Hose, Charles, and William McDougall. 1912. *The Pagan Tribes of Borneo*. London: Macmillan.

Howell, Nancy. 1988. "Understanding Simple Social Structures: Kinship Units and Ties." In *Social Structures: A Network Approach*, ed. B. Wellman and S. D. Berkowitz. Cambridge: Cambridge University Press.

Huff, Toby E. 1993. *The Rise of Early Modern Science: Islam, China, and the West*. Cambridge: Cambridge University Press.

Hultkrantz, Ake, and Ornulf Vorren. 1982. *The Hunters*. Oslo: Universitets-Forlaget.

Iannaccone, Laurence R. 1992. "The Consequences of a Religious Market Structure: Adam Smith and the Economics of Religion." *Rationality and Society* 3:156–77.

Ichilov, O., ed. 1990. *Political Socialization, Citizenship Education, and Democracy*. New York: Teachers College Press of Columbia University.

Johnson, Allen W., and Timothy Earle. 1987. *The Evolution of Human Societies: From Foraging Group to Agrarian State*. Stanford, Calif.: Stanford University Press.

Johnson, Harry M. 1960. *Sociology: A Systematic Introduction*. New York: Harcourt, Brace, Jovanovich.

Juegensmeyer, Mark. 1993. *The New Cold War: Religious Nationalism Confronts the State*. Berkeley: University of California Press.

Kanter, Rosabeth Moss. 1989. *When Giants Learn to Dance: Mastering the Challenges of Strategy, Management and Careers in the 1990s*. New York: Simon & Schuster.

Kautsky, John H. 1982. *The Politics of Aristocratic Empires*. Chapel Hill: University of North Carolina Press.

Keesing, Robert. 1975. *Kin Groups and Social Structure*. New York: Holt, Rinehart & Winston.

Kirch, P. 1984. *The Evolution of Polynesian Chiefdoms*. Cambridge: Cambridge University Press.

———. 1980. "Polynesian Prehistory: Cultural Adaptation in Island Ecosystems." *American Scientist* 68:39–48.

Kohl, Philip. 1989. "The Use and Abuse of World Systems Theory: The Case of the 'Pristine' West Asian State." In *Archaeological Thought in America*, ed. C. C. Lamberg-Kavlovsky. Cambridge: Cambridge University Press.

Kolata, Gina. 1974. "!Kung Hunter-Gatherers: Feminism, Diet, and Birth." *Science* 185:932–34.

Kramer, Samuel Noah. 1959. *It Happened at Sumer.* Garden City, N.Y.: Doubleday.

Kroeber, Alfred. 1926. *Law of the Yurok Indians.* International Congress of Americanists, Proceedings 22, vol. 2.

———. 1925. *Handbook of the Indians of California.* Washington, D.C.: Bureau of American Ethology.

Kumar, Krishan. 1992. "The Revolutions of 1989: Socialism, Capitalism, and Democracy." *Theory and Society* 21:309–56.

Kuper, Adam. 1971. "Council Structure and Decision-Making." In *Councils in Action*, ed. A. Richards and A. Kuper. Cambridge: Cambridge University Press.

Kuper, Hilda, and Leo Kuper, eds. 1965. *African Law: Adaptation and Development.* Berkeley: University of California Press.

Kurtz, Lester. 1995. *Gods in the Global Village: The World's Religions in Sociological Perspective.* Thousand Oaks, Calif.: Pine Forge Press.

Lambert, A. E. 1956. *Kibuyu Social and Political Institutions.* London: Oxford University Press.

Landtman, Gunnar. 1927. *The Kiwi Papuans of British Guinea.* London: Macmillan.

Lash, Scott. 1990. *Sociology of Postmodernism.* London: Routledge.

Lash, Scott, and John Urry. 1987. *The End of Organized Capitalism.* Cambridge: Polity Press.

Laslett, Peter, and Richard Wall. 1972. *Household and Family in Past Time.* Cambridge: Cambridge University Press.

Leach, E. R. 1954. *Political Systems of Highland Burma.* Boston: Beacon Press.

Lee, Richard. 1979. *The !Kung San.* Cambridge: Cambridge University Press.

Lee, Richard, and Irven DeVore, eds. 1976. *Kalahari Hunter-Gatherers.* Cambridge: Cambridge University Press.

———, eds. 1968. *Man the Hunter.* Chicago: Aldine.

Lenski, Gerhard. 1966. *Power and Privilege.* New York: McGraw-Hill. Reprinted by the University of North Carolina Press.

———. 1963. *The Religious Factor: A Sociologist's Inquiry.* Garden City, N.Y.: Anchor Books.

Lenski, Gerhard, Patrick Nolan, and Jean Lenski. 1995. *Human Societies: An Introduction to Macrosociology.* New York: McGraw-Hill.

Levy, Daniel C. 1986. *Higher Education and the State in Latin America.* Chicago: University of Chicago Press.

Linton, Ralph. 1936. *The Study of Man.* New York: Appleton-Century Crofts.

Lipset, Seymour Martin. 1960. *Political Man.* New York: Doubleday.

Llewellyn, K. N., and E. A. Hoebel. 1941. *The Cheyenne Way.* Norman: University of Oklahoma Press.

Lloyd, D. 1964. *The Idea of Law.* Baltimore: Penguin Books.

Loftland, John, and Rodney Stark. 1965. "Becoming a World-Saver: A Theory of Conversion to a Deviant Perspective." *American Sociological Review* 30:862–74.

Lowie, Richard H. 1966. *Social Organization.* New York: Holt, Rinehart & Winston.

Lowie, Robert H. 1948. *Primitive Religion.* New York: Boni & Liveright.

———. 1937. *The History of Ethnological Theory.* New York: Holt, Rinehart & Winston.

Luckmann, Thomas. 1967. *The Invisible Religion: The Transformation of Symbols in Industrial Society.* New York: Macmillan.

Luhmann, Niklas. 1985. *A Sociological Theory of Law.* Boston: Routledge & Kegan Paul.

———. 1984. *Religious Dogmatics and the Evolution of Societies.* New York: Edwin Mellen.

———. 1982. *The Differentiation of Society.* New York: Columbia University Press.

MacNeish, R. 1964. "Ancient Mesoamerican Civilization." *Science* 143:531–37.

Mair, Lucy. 1962. *Primitive Government.* Baltimore: Penguin Books.

Malinowski, Bronislaw. [1925] 1955. *Magic, Science, and Religion.* Garden City, N.Y.: Doubleday.

———. 1926. *Crime and Custom in Savage Society.* London: George Routledge & Sons.

———. 1922. *Argonauts of the Western Pacific.* London: George Routledge & Sons.

———. 1913. *The Family among the Australian Aborigines.* New York: Schocken.

Malthus, Thomas. [1798] 1926. *First Essay on Population.* New York: Kelley.

Mann, Michael. 1986. *The Social Sources of Power,* vol. 1. Cambridge: Cambridge University Press.

Marty, Martin E., and R. Scott Appleby, eds. 1993. *Fundamentalism and Society: Reclaiming the Sciences, the Family, and Education.* Chicago: University of Chicago Press.

Marx, Karl. [1867] 1967. *Capital: A Critical Analysis of Capitalist Production.* New York: International Publishers.

———. 1965. *Pre-capitalist Economic Formations.* New York: International Publishers.

———. [1843] 1963. *Karl Marx: Early Writings,* ed. T. Bottomore. New York: McGraw-Hill.

Maryanski, Alexandra, and Jonathan H. Turner. 1992. *The Social Cage: Human Nature and the Evolution of Society.* Stanford, Calif.: Stanford University Press.

Massell, G. J. 1968. "Law as an Instrument of Revolutionary Change in a Traditional Milieu: The Case of Soviet Central Asia. *Law and Society Review* 2:179–228.

Mathews, Warren. 1991. *World Religions.* St. Paul, Minn.: West.

McCarthy, John D. and Mayer Zald. 1977. "Resource Mobilization of Social Movements." *American Journal of Sociology* 82 (6):1212–41.

McNeill, William. 1963. *The Rise of the West.* Chicago: University of Chicago Press.

Mellaart, James. 1965. *Earliest Civilizations of the Near East.* London: Thames & Hudson.

Mensching, Gustav. 1959. *Die Religion.* Stuttgart: Curt E. Schwab.

———. 1947. *Soziologie der Religion.* Bonn: Ludwig Röhrscheid.

Merton, Robert K. 1957. *Social Theory and Social Structure.* New York: Free Press.

Meyer, John. 1992. "The Social Construction of Motives for Educational Expansion." In *The Political Construction of Education,* ed. B. Fuller and R. Rubinson. New York: Praeger.

———. 1977. "The Effects of Education as an Institution." *American Journal of Sociology* 83:340–63.

Meyer, John W., Francisco O. Ramirez, and Y. N. Soysal. 1992. "World Expansion of Mass Education, 1870–1980." *Sociology of Education* 65:128–49.

Mizruchi, Marks, and Linda Brewster Stearns. 1994. "Money, Banking, and Financial Markets." In *The Handbook of Economic Sociology,* ed. N. J. Smelser and R. Swedberg. New York: Russell Sage.

Moberg, D. O. 1962. *The Church as a Social Institution.* Englewood Cliffs, N.J.: Prentice-Hall.

Moore, Barrington, Jr. 1966. *Social Origins of Dictatorship and Democracy.* Boston: Beacon Press.

Moore, John H. 1977. "The Evolution of Exploitation." *Critique of Anthropology* 8:33–58.

Moore, Sally Falk. 1978. *Law as Process: An Anthropological Approach.* London: Routledge & Kegan Paul.

Moseley, K. P., and Immanuel Wallerstein. 1978. "Precapitalist Social Structures." *Annual Review of Sociology* 4:259–90.

Murdock, George Peter. 1965. *Culture and Society.* Pittsburgh: University of Pittsburgh Press.

———. 1959. *Africa: Its Peoples and Their Culture History.* New York: McGraw-Hill.

———. 1953. "Social Structure." In *An Appraisal of Anthropology Today,* ed. S. Tax, L. Eiseley, I. Rouse, and C. Voegelin. Chicago: University of Chicago Press.

———. 1949. *Social Structure.* New York: MacMillan.

Murphy, W., and J. Tannenhaus. 1968. "Public Opinion and the United States Supreme Courts." *Law and Society* 2:357–84.

Murra, J. 1980. *The Economic Organization of the Inka State.* Greenwich, Conn.: JAI Press.

Nee, Victor. 1989. "A Theory of Market Transition: From Redistribution to Markets in State Socialism." *American Sociological Review* 81:1408–18.

Newman, Katherine. 1983. *Law and Economic Organization: A Comparative Study of Preindustrial Societies.* Cambridge: Cambridge University Press.

Nohria, Nitin, and Ranjay Gulati. 1994. "Firms and Their Environments." In *The Handbook of Economic Sociology,* ed. N. J. Smelser and R. Swedberg. New York: Russell Sage.

Norbeck, E. 1961. *Religion in Primitive Society.* New York: Harper & Row.

Oates, Joan. 1978. "Comment on 'The Balance of Trade in Southwest Asia in the Mid-Third Millennium.'" *Current Anthropology* 19:480–81.

O'Dea, Thomas F. 1970. *Sociology and the Study of Religion.* New York: Basic Books.

———. 1966. *The Sociology of Religion.* Englewood Cliffs, N.J.: Prentice-Hall.

O'Dea, Thomas F., and Janet O'Dea Aviad. 1983. *The Sociology of Religion*, 2nd ed. Englewood Cliffs, N.J.: Prentice-Hall.

Parsons, Talcott. [1935] 1990. "Prolegomera to a Theory of Social Institutions." *American Sociology Review* 55 (June):319–33.

———. 1971. *The System of Modern Societies.* Englewood Cliffs, N.J.: Prentice-Hall.

———. 1966. *Societies: Evolutionary and Comparative Perspectives.* Englewood Cliffs, N.J.: Prentice-Hall.

———. 1962. "The Law and Social Control." In *Law and Sociology: Exploratory Essays.* New York: Free Press.

———. 1951. *The Social System.* New York: Free Press.

Parsons, Talcott, and Neil J. Smelser. 1956. *Economy and Society.* New York: Free Press.

Pashukanis, Eugenic. 1978. *Law and Marxism: A General Theory.* London: Ink Links.

Pasternak, Burton. 1976. *Introduction to Kinship and Social Organization.* Englewood Cliffs, N.J.: Prentice-Hall.

Pfautz, H. W. 1955. "The Sociology of Secularization: Religious Groups." *American Journal of Sociology* 61:121–28.

Pospisil, Leopold J. 1978. *The Ethnology of Law*, 2nd ed. Menlo Park, Calif.: Cummings.

———. 1974. *Anthropology of Law: A Comparative Theory.* New Haven: Yale University Press.

———. 1958. *Kapauku Papuans and Their Law.* New Haven: Yale University Press.

Postan, Michael. 1972. *The Medieval Economy and Society.* Berkeley: University of California Press.

Price, Derek J. de Solla. 1986. *Little Science, Big Science . . . and Beyond.* New York: Columbia University Press (expanded of Price, 1963, below).

———. 1982. "The Parallel Structures of Science and Technology." In *Science in Context: Readings in the Sociology of Science*, ed. B. Barnes and D. Edge. Milton Keynes England: Open University Press.

———. 1963. *Little Science, Big Science.* New York: Columbia University Press.

Quinney, Richard. 1974. *Critique of Legal Order: Crime Control in Capitalist Society.* Boston: Little, Brown.

Radcliffe-Brown, A. R. 1952. *Structure and Function in Primitive Society.* Glencoe, Ill.: Free Press.

———. 1938. *Taboo.* Cambridge: Cambridge University Press.

———. 1935. "On the Concept of Function in Social Science" (reply to Lesser 1935). *American Anthropologist* 37:394-402.

———. 1930. "The Social Organization of Australian Tribes." *Oceana* 1:44–46.

———. 1914. *The Andaman Islanders.* New York: Free Press.

Ramirez, Francisco O., and John Boli. 1987. "Global Patterns of Educational Institutionalization." In *Institutional Structure: Constituting State, Society, and the*

Individual, ed. George M. Thomas, John W. Meyer, Francisco O. Ramirez, and John Boli. Newbury Park, Calif.: Sage.

Rattray, R. S. 1929. *Ashanti Law and Constitution.* London: Oxford University Press.

Reasons, Charles E., and Robert M. Rich, eds. 1978. *The Sociology of Law: A Conflict Perspective.* Toronto: Butterworths.

Rich, Robert M. 1977. *The Sociology of Law: An Introduction to Its Theorists and Theories.* Washington, D.C.: University Press of America.

Riches, David. 1982. *Northern Nomadic Hunter-Gatherers.* London: Academic Press.

Rick, J. 1978. *Prehistoric Hunters of the High Andes.* New York: Academic Press.

Ritzer, George. 1993. *The McDonaldization of Society.* Thousand Oaks, Calif.: Pine Forge Press.

Robbins, Thomas, and Dick Anthony, eds. 1990. *In Gods We Trust: New Patterns of Religious Pluralism in America,* 2nd ed. New Brunswick, N.J.: Transaction Books.

Robinson, John. 1988. "Who's Doing the Housework?" *American Demographics* 10:24–28.

Roth, H. Ling. 1890. *The Aborigines of Tasmania.* London: Kegan, Paul, Trench & Trubner.

Rubinson, Richard, and Irene Browne. 1994. "Education and the Economy." In *The Handbook of Economic Sociology,* ed. N. J. Smelser and R. Swedberg. New York: Russell Sage.

Rueschemeyer, Dietrich, Evelyne Huber Stephens, and John D. Stephens. 1992. *Capitalist Development and Democracy.* Chicago: University of Chicago Press.

Sahlins, Marshall. 1972. *Stone Age Economics.* Chicago: Aldine.

———. 1968a. "Notes on the Original Affluent Society." In *Man the Hunter,* ed. R. Lee and I. DeVore. Chicago: Aldine.

———. 1968b. *Tribesmen.* Englewood Cliffs, N.J.: Prentice-Hall.

———. 1963. "Poor Man, Rich Man, Big Man, Chief: Political Types in Melanesia and Polynesia." *Comparative Studies in Society and History,* vol. 5. Cambridge: Cambridge University Press.

———. 1958. *Social Stratification in Polynesia.* Seattle: University of Washington Press.

Salisbury, W. S. 1964. *Religion in American Culture.* Homewood, Ill.: Dorsey Press.

Sanders, J. 1992. "Short- and Long-Term Macroeconomic Returns to Higher Education." *Sociology of Education* 65:21–36.

Sanders, William T. 1972. "Population, Agricultural History, and Societal Evolution in Mesoamerica." In *Population Growth: Anthropological Implications,* ed. B. Spooner. Cambridge, Mass.: MIT Press.

Sanderson, Stephen K. 1995. *Macrosociology: An Introduction to Human Societies,* 3rd ed. New York: HarperCollins.

Sawer, G. 1965. *Law in Society.* Oxford: Clarendon Press.

Schapera, Isaac. 1956. *Government and Politics in Tribal Societies.* London: C. A. Watts & Co.

———. 1930. *The Khoisan Peoples of South AfriCalif.: Bushmen and Hottentots.* London: Routledge & Kegan Paul.

Schneider, David, and Kathleen Gough, eds. 1961. *Matrilineal Kinship*. Berkeley: University of California Press.

Schrire, Carmel, ed. 1984. *Past and Present in Hunter Gatherer Studies*. Orlando, Fla.: Academic Press.

Schwartz, Richard D., and James C. Miller. 1964. "Legal Evolution and Societal Complexity." *American Journal of Sociology* 70:159–69.

Seidman, Steven, and David G. Wagner. 1992. *Postmodernism and Social Theory*. Oxford: Blackwell.

Selznick, Philip. 1968. "Law: The Sociology of Law." *International Encyclopedia of the Social Sciences*, no. 9:50–59.

Service, Elman, 1975. *Origins of the State and Civilizations: The Process of Cultural Evolution*. New York: W. W. Norton.

———. 1966. *The Hunters*. Englewood Cliffs, N.J.: Prentice-Hall.

———. 1962. *Primitive Social Organization: An Evolutionary Perspective*. New York: Random House.

Silver, Morris. 1985. *Economic Structures of the Ancient Near East*. London: Croom Helm.

Simmel, Georg. [1907] 1978. *The Philosophy of Money*. Trans. T. Bottomore and D. Frisby. Boston: Routledge & Kegan Paul.

———. 1903. "The Sociology of Conflict." *American Journal of Sociology* 9:490–525.

Singer, Charles. 1954–56. *A History of Technology*, 2 vols. Oxford: Clarendon Press.

Sjoberg, Gideon. 1960. *The Preindustrial City*. New York: Free Press.

Skocpol, Theda. 1979. *States and Social Revolutions*. Cambridge: Cambridge University Press.

Smelser, Neil J. 1959. *Social Change in the Industrial Revolution: An Application of Theory to the British Cotton Industry*. Chicago: University of Chicago Press.

Smith, Adam. [1776] 1937. *An Inquiry into the Nature and Causes of the Wealth of Nations*. New York: Modern Library.

Smith, W., and J. Roberts. 1954. *Zuni Law: A Field of Values*. Cambridge, Mass.: Harvard University Press.

Spencer, Baldwin, and F. J. Gillen. 1927. *The Arunta: A Study of a Stone Age People*. London: Macmillan.

Spencer, Herbert. [1874–1896] 1898. *The Principles of Sociology*, 3 vols. New York: D. Appleton.

Spiro, M. E. 1956. *Kibbutz, Venture in Utopia*. Cambridge, Mass.: Harvard University Press.

Stark, Rodney, and William Sims Bainbridge. 1985. *The Future of Religion: Secularization, Revival and Cult Formation*. Berkeley: University of California Press.

———. 1980. "Towards a Theory of Religious Commitment." *Journal for the Scientific Study of Religion* 19:114–28.

Stearns, Linda Brewster. 1990. "Capital Markets Effects on External Control of Corporations." In *Structures of Capital: The Social Organization of the Economy*, ed. S. Zukin and P. DiMaggio. Cambridge: Cambridge University Press.

Stephens, W. N. 1967. "Family and Kinship." In *Sociology*, ed. N. J. Smelser. New York: John Wiley & Sons.

————. 1963. *The Family in Cross-Cultural Perspective.* New York: Holt, Rinehart & Winston.

Steward, Julian. 1930. "The Economic and Social Basis of Primitive Bands." In *Essays on Anthropology in Honor of Alfred Louis Kroeber,* ed. R. Lowie. Berkeley: University of California Press.

Swanson, Guy E. 1967. *Religion and Regime: A Sociological Account of the Reformation.* Ann Arbor: University of Michigan Press.

————. 1960. *The Birth of the Gods: The Origin of Primitive Beliefs.* Ann Arbor: University of Michigan Press.

Swedberg, Richard. 1994. "Markets as Social Structures." In *The Handbook of Economic Sociology,* ed. N. J. Smelser and R. Swedberg. New York: Russell Sage.

Szelenyi, Ivan, Katherine Beckett, and Lawrence P. King. 1994. "The Socialistic Economic System." In *The Handbook of Economic Sociology,* ed. N. J. Smelser and R. Swedberg. New York: Russell Sage.

Szymanski, Albert. 1978. *The Capitalist State and the Politics of Class.* Cambridge, Mass.: Winthrop.

Thompson, E. P. 1966. *The Making of the English Working Class.* New York: Random House.

Tilly, Charles. 1990. *Coercion, Capital and European States,* A.D. 990–1900. Oxford: Blackwell.

————. 1978. *From Mobilization to Revolution.* Reading, Mass: Addison-Wesley.

————, ed. 1975. *The Formation of Nation States in Western Europe.* Princeton: Princeton University Press.

Tonkinson, Robert. 1978. *The Marduojara Aborigines.* New York: Holt, Rinehart & Winston.

Touraine, Alan. 1988. *Return of the Actor; Social Theory in Postindustrial Society.* Minneapolis: University of Minnesota Press.

Troeltsch, Ernst. [1911] 1960. *The Social Teachings of Christian Churches,* 2 vols. Trans. O. Wyon. New York: Harper & Row.

Turnbull, Colin. 1961. *The Forest People.* New York: Simon & Schuster.

Turner, Bryan S., ed. 1990. *Theories of Modernity and Postmodernity.* London: Sage Publications.

Turner, Jonathan H. 1995. *Macrodynamics: Toward a Theory on the Organization of Human Populations.* Rose Monographs. New Brunswick, N.J.: Rutgers University Press.

————. 1991. *The Structure of Sociological Theory,* 5th ed. Belmont, Calif.: Wadsworth.

————. 1984. *Societal Stratification: A Theoretical Analysis.* New York: Columbia University Press.

————. 1980. "Legal System Evolution: An Analytical Model." In *The Sociology of Law.* New York: Free Press.

————. 1974. "A Cybernetic Model of Legal Development." *Western Sociological Review* 5:3–16.

———— 1972. *Patterns of Social Organization: A Survey of Social Institutions.* New York: McGraw-Hill.

Turner, Jonathan H., and Alexandra Maryanski. 1979. *Functionalism*. Menlo Park, Calif.: Benjamin-Cummings.

Turner, Ralph H. 1960. "Sponsored and Contest Mobility and the School System." *American Sociological Review* 25:855–67.

Underhill, Ralph. 1975. "Economic and Political Antecedents of Monotheism: A Cross-Cultural Study." *American Journal of Sociology* 80:841–61.

UNESCO. 1994. *Statistical Yearbook*. Paris: UNESCO.

Vago, Steven. 1994. *Law and Society*, 4th ed. Englewood Cliffs, N.J.: Prentice-Hall.

Verlinden, O. 1963. "Markets and Fairs." In *The Cambridge Economic History of Europe*, vol. 3, ed. M. M. Postan and E. E. Rich. Cambridge: Cambridge University Press.

Vernon, G. M. 1962. *Sociology of Religion*. New York: McGraw-Hill.

von Hagen, Victor. 1961. *The Ancient Sun Kingdoms of the Americas*. Cleveland: World Publishing.

Wallace, Anthony F. C. 1966. *Religion: An Anthropological View*. New York: Random House.

Wallerstein, Immanuel M. 1974. *The Modern World System: Capitalist Agriculture and the Origins of the European World Economy in the Sixteenth Century*. New York: Academic Press.

Washburn, Sherwood, ed. 1961. *Social Life of Early Man*. Chicago: Aldine.

Weber, Max. [1922] 1978. *Economy and Society: An Outline of Interpretive Sociology*, ed. G. Roth and C. Wittich. Berkeley: University of California Press.

———. [1916–17] 1958. *The Religion of India: The Sociology of Hinduism and Buddhism*. Trans. Hans H. Gerth and Don Martindale. New York: Free Press.

———. [1904–5] 1958. *The Protestant Ethic and the Spirit of Capitalism*. Trans. Talcott Parsons. New York: Charles Scribner's.

———. [1922] 1954. *Law in Economy and Society*. Trans. E. Shils and M. Rheinstein. Cambridge, Mass.: Harvard University Press.

———. [1917–20] 1952. *Ancient Judaism*. Trans. Hans H. Gerth and Don Martindale. New York: Free Press.

———. [1915] 1951. *The Religion of China: Confucianism and Taoism*. Trans. Hans H. Gerth. New York: Free Press.

Webster, D. 1975. "Warfare and the Evolution of the State." *American Antiquity* 40:467–70.

Weil, Frederick D. 1989. "The Sources and Structure of Legitimation in Democracies: A Consolidated Model Tested with Time-Series Data in Six Countries since World War II." *American Sociological Review* 54:682–706.

Wells, Alan. 1970. *Social Institutions*. London: Heineman.

White, Andrew Dickson. 1896. *A History of the Warfare of Science with Theology in Christendom*. New York: D. Appleton & Co.

White, Harrison C. 1988. "Varieties of Markets." In *Structural Sociology*, ed. B. Wellman and S. D. Berkowitz. New York: Cambridge University Press.

———. 1981. "Where Do Markets Come From?" *American Journal of Sociology* 87:517–47.

Whiting, Beatrice. 1950. *Paiute Sorcery*. New York: Viking Press.

Williams, Peter W. 1980. *Popular Religion in Ameri: Symbolic Change and the Modernization Process in Historical Perspective*. Englewood Cliffs, N.J.: Prentice-Hall.

Williams, Robin M., Jr. 1970. *American Society: A Sociological Interpretation*. New York: Alfred Knopf.

Wilson, Bryan. 1969. *Religion in Secular Society*. Baltimore: Penguin Books.

Winterhalder, Bruce, and Eric Alden Smith, eds. 1981. *Hunter-Gatherer Foraging Strategies*. Chicago: University of Chicago Press.

Wolf, Eric. 1982. *Europe and the People without History*. Berkeley: University of California Press.

Wolley, Leonard. 1965. *The Beginnings of Civilization, UNESCO History of Mankind*. New York: Mentor Books.

Woodburn, J. 1968. "An Introduction to Hadza Ecology." In *Man the Hunter*, ed. R. Lee and I. DeVore. Chicago: Aldine.

Wuthnow, Robert. 1994. "Religion and Economic Life." In *The Handbook of Economic Sociology*, ed. N. J. Smelser and R. Swedberg. New York: Russell Sage.

———. 1989. *Communities of Discourse: Ideology and Social Structure in the Reformation, the Enlightenment, and European Socialism*. Cambridge, Mass.: Harvard University Press.

———. 1988. "Sociology of Religion." In *Handbook of Sociology*, ed. N. J. Smelser. Newbury Park, Calif.: Sage Publications.

———. 1987. *Meaning and Moral Order: Explorations in Cultural Analysis*. Berkeley: University of California Press.

———. 1980. "World Order and Religious Movements." In *Studies of the Modern World System*, ed. A. Bergesen. New York: Academic Press.

Yates, Kyle M., ed. 1988. *The Religious World: Communities of Faith*, 2nd ed. New York: Macmillan.

Yinger, Milton J. 1970. *The Scientific Study of Religion*. New York: Macmillan.

Name Index

Subject Index